DEMOCRACY, GOVERNANCE AND TRIBES IN THE AGE OF GLOBALISED INDIA

Democracy, Governance and Tribes in the Age of Globalised India

(In Two Volumes)
Volume-II

Ramdas Rupavath

GYAN

ISBN : 978-81-212-1248-9 (Set)

ISBN : 978-81-212-1299-1 (Vol. II)

Price : Set (₹ 2000) Price : Volume II (₹ 1000)

First Published, 2015

Published by

Gyan Publishing House
23, Main Ansari Road, Darya Ganj
New Delhi-110002
Ph. : 23242060, 23261060
Fax : 011-23285914
E-mail: books@gyanbooks.com
Website : www.gyanbooks.com

Laser Typesetting: Abhishek Mandal, Delhi
Printed at : G. Print Process, Delhi

Cataloging in Publication Data—DK
Courtesy: D.K. Agencies (P) Ltd. <docinfo@dkagencies.com>

Democracy, governance and tribes in the age of globalised India / Ramdas Rupavath.
pages cm
Includes bibliographical references and index.
ISBN 9788121212489

1. India—Scheduled tribes—Economic conditions—Congresses. 2. India—Scheduled tribes—Social conditions—Congresses. 3. India—Scheduled tribes—Education—Congresses. 4. India—Scheduled tribes—Government policy—Congresses. 5. Rural development—India—Congresses. I. Rupavath, Ramdas, editor. II. University of Hyderabad. Department of Political Science.organizer.

DDC 305.800954 23

In Loving Memory of My Parents

Smt Sony and Shri Jayaram Naik Rupavath

Contents

Acknowledgements

I would express my gratitude to ICSSR, New Delhi and University of Hyderabad for their co-operation in particular for their whole-hearted and continued support to endeavour. I would thank the Dean, and Faculty of School of Social Sciences. I want to offer special thanks to the Faculty and Head, Department of Political Science and non-teaching staff of the Departments for co-operation during the seminar. This book is a product of a two-day national seminar. This was organised by the Department of Political Science, University of Hyderabad.

I would express my gratitude to the participants of the seminar for their co-operation and submission of the full paper within the stipulated time without which this book should not have taken a shape. The presence of key participants like Prof Ramakrishana Ramaswamy, Vice-Chancellor, University of Hyderabad, Prof G. Hargopal, Gaddar (Prajayuddanouka), Prof. Kunhamam, Prof E. Haribabu and Prof Sudhir Jacob George, Prof I. Ramabrahmman, Prof G. Sudharshnam, Prof Shantha Sinha, Prof Virginius Xaxa, Prof Prithviram Mudiam, Prof Manjari Katju, Prof Sudhakar Rao, Dr Nehginpao Kipgen, Dr George Tharakan, Prof Sudhakar Reddy, Dr B. Nagarjuna and their academic deliberations has provoked a new academic thrust in the area of Tribal Development in the globalised world.

I want to give special thanks to my wife R. Jayasri and daughters Sai Srinidhi and Gayathree Ram, brothers and sisters for their moral encouragement.

I want to give special thanks to the research scholars of the Department of Political Science namely, Tapan Kumar Bihari, M. Ramulu and K. John Bosco Sote for their managerial skill in organising this seminar. Also, I express my sincere thanks to the students and research scholars, school of social sciences for their co-operation during the seminar.

Finally, I put my gratitude to the team at Gyan Publishing House, New Delhi for the valuable suggestions on the structure of the book and help in its production.

I hope this book would be a substantial contribution to Tribal Studies in India, even more, help chart a more meaningful developmental path for Tribals in India.

Ramdas Rupavath

Foreword

Indigenous peoples are on the cusp of the crisis in sustainable development. Their communities are concrete examples of sustainable societies, historically evolved in diverse ecosystems. Today, they face the challenges of extinction or survival and renewal in a globalised world. The impact of globalisation is strongest on these populations perhaps more than any other because these communities have no voice and are therefore easily swept aside by the invisible hand of the market and its proponents. Globalisation is not merely a question of marginalisation for indigenous peoples it is a multi-pronged attack on the very foundation of their existence and livelihoods.

The volume 'is a collection of papers presented at national seminar in Department of Political Science of University of Hyderabad. The issues which are dealt in the book are both relevance in theoretically and policy level. This book specially focused on how the marginalised community can be included in the mainstream of society not only sharing the benefits of the globalisation but also in the decision making process. This theme has been a subject of serious deliberation and discussion both at academic and non-academic forum and at regular intervals. However, more often than not they are deliberated at the macro level, that is, national and state context and that too without any reference to diversity that marks India.

Broadly speaking, the contributors of the book has highlighted how the marginalised section of the society, i.e. Adivasis can be achieved their share in the context of globalisation. The book not only evaluated various welfare programmes but also dealt theoretically in the context of tribal's

Ramdas Rupavath the coordinator of the seminar and editor of this volume, worked to make the seminar a success following which he put together this volume and saw it through to press.

The contributors to this book analyse many shortcomings and problems of Indian democracy in the context of globalisation but by and large they conclude both that it is robust and that it can be deepened and extended. It is the right conclusion to each.

Prof.Shantha Sinha
Department of Political Science
University of Hyderabad

Introduction and Overview

Indian democracy has been intensively analysesd, debated and criticised for long time. However democracy is not only just a elections and government formation, it is more about values, habits of thoughts and practices, democracy need not electoral but replacement with social justice. Through democratic method existing unequal social, economic and political justice situation can be removed. The tribals are most affected people in such democratic set up with developmental approach. The new tribal politics will be based on two things the resource politics of the Adivasis and survival politics of the informal sector.

Though Indian Constitution takes an unambiguous position against *adivasis* resources, these continue in a different forms. That over the years the centre of gravity of the Indian polity and economy has shifted to the intermediate class groups has been widely recognised. With in the class hierarchy, the economic high point is the polarisation between rich non-triblas and the triblas who are largely land alienated and displaced. The political parties at the Centre and the State drastically changed emergence of powerful non-tribal leaders who have changed the very mosaic of Indian federal polity. In this process we have today strong states and weak centre. Regional parties are playing important role in the Indian political process.

The State has shifted its orientation from welfare state to market-oriented due to the liberalisation. However, the process of liberalisation has created inequality in the society with the concentration of fruits of growth in little rich class. The opportunity is becoming unequal. while poverty has seldom posed a threat to the system any where, inequality in a milieu of rising democratic and human rights consciousness can potentially become a grave danger.

After India became independence our political leader's recognition of the fact of the participation of the entire people. The leader of the rich ad western educated, feudal back ground was the rulers of the Indian state. This scenario began to change only with the political mobilisation of the *dalits*, of course, within the parliamentary framework. This did not heralds true democracy. Democracy to be people rule, rather than the rule of the rich and powerful;

there must be equality, economic, social and political. In other words, only an egalitarian society can be truly democratic. for that the precondition is equal access to the means of production, not only for expansion of the productive forces, but also for enabling and ensuring the fruiton of the creative potential of every individual. The growth brought about by a few dynamic and enterprising individuals must be expanded into one brought about by all persons in society. If high growth is the creation of a few, growth will be higher if all realise their creative potential. This calls for a new vision as well as a new strategy of development which can herald democracy from below organically evolving as a natural and spontaneous process. Political inclusion and economic exclusion are the order of the day. The panchyat raj or pesa Right Act of Forest Rights act are not reassuring in this regard the resources viz., land, water, forest, cattle, credit and market controlled by the few rich non-tribal families. this has created new kind of development according to Foucault disbursed poer is difficult to tackle. Wthout economic democracy, social, political democracy cannot be realised this was the remark by BR Amedkar and also warned that unless the latter two democracies brought about soon, the victims of the system would throw the Constitution which the constituent Assembly laboriously built. Ofcorse, the system permits individual inclusion even as its functioning is resulting in group exclusion, a phenomenon conspicuously happening particularly in case of the social constituency he was representing parliamentry democracy is bursting at the seams competitive politics uneasily co-exist with a competitive economy prdected on an unbroken scaffolding of a caste-based, hierarchcal social and economic order.the transiton from state capitalism of the planning era to the market capitalism of the liberalisation era has only has rendered the opportunities matrix skewed and reinforced the old prejudices.

The knowledge production, media are controlled by the non-tribal rich upper class elites, who sit in judgment of the quality and efficiency of the *adivasis* and other subalterens. Of course, there is nominal presence of a few persons belonging to these social groupsin the academics, but they lack lack the power to influence policy and structure of knowledge. They remain silent un less until they are safe so long as they they dono raise and debate social issues the corruption which is part of our strutre. The tribal society and sub-plans budgets taken away by the non –tribal bureaucrats. with out tackling inequality corruption and corruption thrives in an unequal system though the the question of equalty accepted at the launch of planning commission with the declaration attaining growth with social justice and to egalitarian society.in fact, the present scenario is characterised by the verbal fetishism created through the globalised use of words such tribal empowerment, sustainable development what not the word equlity, liberty, and justice finds a place in the academies and media discourse.behind verbal usage very harmfull policies and programmes are introduced.any resistnace against these policies the state use the forces to suppress the movements. the NGOs and and Acts primarly playing depolitising the tribals, are abetting the policy makers. what is beneficial to a few is presented as beneficial to all.the poor tribes, ignorant and illiterate, whose immediate concern is the next meal,are seldom concerned about policies and perspectives are no where concerned to them.rather than competition, more profit and capital accumulation,state support primitive accumulation and private appropriation of public resources.In andhrapradesh or Telangana state the land alienated tribals agitating for *Jungle* (Forest) *Jamin* (land) *Jaal* (Water) was put in jail. The land alienated tribes are the traditional indigeneous people who were denied land rights and displaced and do not have even the right to agitate.the land struggle in frontieir agency and non-frontieir agency hostility over the displacement issue when brutal state force beating, killing including children, women. the state using in human attitudes towards tribs in India and violating human rights. it seems, in the extant bourgeois democratic milieu and it is deficient in envisioning, upper caste and its top leadership structure and involute in its understanding of the socio economic reality of India.

The most paradoxical thing is that every body talk about the equality, liberty and fraternity but in practice most are afraid of democracy. what is available to people is the freedom to agree not to disagree. This is the in human condition is decision taken by a few who are rich and powerfull for the people. Infact, the legislators are elected by the people funded by the rich.since inequality that lead to corruption basic bane and gravest threat to tribal sustainable security a no threatening order needs to put in place.

This book aims to place India's democracy, development in the tribal context. This volume is basically to focussing to understand contemporary tribal societies which requires a basic appreciation of the historical processes which have been determined the course of successive changes in economic, socio-cultural, ideological and political life of the tribes. Indian state and governments are talked about as models of federalism in a large and multinational society, ensuring rights of ethnic and religious groups in a truly pluralistic society, and striving for social justice in a society marked by social hierarchies for a long time. However, the democratic experiment has not been without significant challenges, namely that of ensuring inclusive development. Economic equality, social justice, cultural pluralism, human rights, dignity and security are all important aspects of development which have been consolidated and expanded through the existing structure of participatory democracy. But this has not always been an easy task.

During the last couple of decades, Indian tribes have also witnessed transformation in their culture, with the proliferation of special plan and policies for the welfare of the tribal people. Despite the development, crisis in the governance, migration, displacement, and exploitation are rampant. The impact of globalisation of Indian economy is percolating down and their effects are being felt by the tribal people who displaced from their habitation, which ultimately resulting upon resistance and ethnic conflict. Introduction of tribal communities to development through state policies needs to be considered from different angles. It is in this context that a state policy is required to be inclusive and comprehensive enough to safeguard tribal interests. To address the issue of situating tribal communities to developmental perspective in a democratic atmosphere doubted provides both opportunities and challenges

The majority of the articles are a set of mainly empirical essays which seeks to answer this linked question at ground level. The majority process of development in the tribal context with democratic process has been highlighted. Some theoretical work like threat to secularism, politics of development, voice of tribal in contemporary democracy has included.

The first aspect which is most sensitive and thought-provoking was **Democracy, development and Resistance.** On this aspect, it has highlighted concerns, concepts and issues related to democracy, development and resistance in regard to the tribals and with relevant case studies. The session talked about how development has come to be a bad omen for displaced tribals. With displacement, several tribes were uprooted with the onslaught of development. We talked about the case study of Indira Sagar Project in Andhra Pradesh with special emphasis on development projects, displacement and tribal livelihood issues. Livelihoods of tribals were severely affected as argued by projects of development and the resultant displacement overdrive. There was a valuable insight into risks, rights, alternatives, policy and practices followed by Development-Induced Displacement and Rehabilitation and Resettlement of Indigenous Communities in India. There was another paper that drew a perspective from census survey in studying mining and displacement in South Odisha. This session has touched various tribal state of Indian and focussed how in the name of the development trilbal land allenation has been done and who are getting benefit out of this.

The second aspect was **Issues of Governance**. This session talked about issues, concerns and themes related to governance. PESA, Tribal development and idea of commons and related issues were discussed. The struggles and politics of the exclusion in understanding denotified tribes in India were examined. Democracy and Development as in Fifth Scheduled areas was debated.

The issues of **Tribal voice in Contemporary Democracy** have been highlighted in the third aspect. In the era of globalisation, seldom the voice of the tribes are suppressed and marginalised. So in this regard, we started with looking at the case of Scheduled tribes in North Coastal Andhra Pradesh whose voices and struggles have been excluded and marginalised. The paper contests the inclusive development. Next paper attempts to question where democracy in India lies and look at its withering away and its effect on tribal resistance.

This theme, **Livelihood issues and concerns** contains many primary work and highlights various lacunaes in the institutions, policies and etc.. An empirical study on chenchus of Andhra Pradesh was looked to draw our attention to their livelihood security through land distribution. Next paper talked about migration from village to city in Bangalore and how it affects livelihood, creates displacement and calls for rehabilitation. Another paper dealt incisively with the trends in cropping pattern and its impact on the tribal households in the scheduled areas taking the case study of three scheduled areas villages in the West Godavari district of Andhra Pradesh.

The next theme of the seminar was **socio cultural issues of tribals**. There was first a paper that looked at the struggles of *adivasi* towards habitation and how it has been affected by the forces of globalisation and accumulation. Another paper examined at the storage practices of tribal community of Warangal district Andhra Pradesh. There was also a paper that drew a critique on Yerukula reformation in Andhra Pradesh.

In **Public Policy and tribal Development** theme, it has been discussed arena of tribal development and public policy interventions. The first paper talked in general sense the *adivasis* from the public policy perspective in India. The next paper evaluated the implementation of MGNREGA and its effect on tribes taking the case study of Nupada district in Odisha. There was a presentation on the embedded identity and politics that is played out in ST reservation in Asssam. In the last paper of this session, ST as the beneficiaries of BPL in Mayurbhanj district Odisha was examined.

The Session **Social Movement, Ethnic issues and Conflict** discussed the role of social movements, ethnic issues and conflict resulted thereof was discussed. There is a deep-seated conflict between tribes and forest department in scheduled areas. This was bought out by a case study of recently declared kawal tiger reserve in adilalabad district, Andhra Pradesh. Similarly, tribal-caste conflict was bought out in another paper taking the case study of kandhamal district, Odisha. Another vital paper was the analysis of Gujjar agitation for tribal status in Rajasthan that examined contentions, agitations, resistance and state interventions therewith. There was another case study paper of Niyamgiri Movement in Odisha that examined tribal development and resistance that followed. Another paper takes the cast studies of Manipur that discussed Meitiei resistance and response of the State. The failure of Indian Secularism was brought out through the politics of SC and ST conflict in Kandhamal. The Contemporary issues of democracy, development and tribal resistance were widely discussed in another paper. The role of tribal women in MGNRGEA was also discussed in the study of Barwani block of Madhya Pradesh. The policies and challenges of Scheduled Tribes in Jammu and Kashmir at literacy and educational levels were also presented. Then, the tribal education policy of Karnataka was up for review by looking at its attainment and challenges ahead.

In this session, **Tribal ecology and Environmental issues**, a paper was presented on environmental approaches to tribal development. The environmental aspect is significant given the harmony that exists between tribal and nature.

In the session **issues of the tribal women and children** various issues like gender inequalities and development issues was examined with the study of Toda, Niligiri Hills from an anthropological perspective. The Lamabada community was next case study that examined the status of girl child in south Telangana region in Andhra Pradesh.

The session, **Politics of Development** discussed on the concept of Development and its effect on tribes on AP was examined and discussed. The role of NYKS on tribal youth development was discussed through the case study of koraput district, odisha. Approaches to development were examined and the role of civil society organisation in tribal development was discussed. The myth of development and tribals in odisha was examined in a macro-view.

In **Development, Displacement and resistance** session the question of human rights was raised through the study of posco project in odisha in the context of development and displacement. The land alienation of tribals in Andhra Pradesh and tribal land alienation in general sense was examined and debated. The case study of Gadchiroliapotential zone of development induced displacement was looked into.

The last session on **education status of scheduled tribes** talked the need for empowerment of tribals. The paper on the impact of multilingual education in the education of tribal children stressed the nature of multilingual character and its usage for tribals. A case study of Lanbadi tribe in AP was examined to understand the educational status of Scheduled Tribes. Another paper talked about need to bring about awareness of human rights among the tribals and non-tribals secondary students. This comparative study calls for empowering and enhancing the rights of tribals. Lastly, the achievement and challenges of secondary education of Scheduled Tribes in Manipur was discussed.

All the above articles will present an overview of a range real problem that not only touch the lives of Indian people but also raise significant issues for thinking about democracy and development in the tribal context in India. The world has been changing a great deal since 1950, so as India. The country is now carving out a niche in a global market-place dominates thus far by the developing countries. Major questions remains however about the accommodating the tribals in the democracy and distributing the share of growth among them. Thus, basic objective of the book is to contribute in some small way to these continuing debates.

List of Contributors

KM Metry is Professor and Head, Dept of Tribal Studies, Kannada University, Hampi.

Malli. Gandhi is Professor, Regional Institute of Education, NCERT, Mysore.

Ramdas Rupavath is Associate Professor, Department of Political Science, School of Social Sciences, University of Hyderabad, Telengana State.

Jakka Parthasarathy is visiting professor (ICSSR), Dept of Tribal Studies, Kannada University, Hampi-Vidyaranya.

Harsha S is Assistant Professor, Department of Political Science, Assam University, Silchar.

Antibum Ranglong is research Scholar, Department of Political Science, Assam University, Silchar.

Akhaya Kumar Nayak is Lecturer in Pol. Sc. Ragunath Jew College, Cuttack, Odisha.

Bharat Chandra Rout is Research Associate, ICSSR, New Delhi.

Bikku is research scholar, Department of Anthropology, School of Social Sciences, University of Hyderabad.

Chitta Ranjan Mishra is research Scholar, Central University, Gujarat.

Dasarathi Bhuiyan is Lecturer, P.G. Department of Political Science, Berhampur University, Odisha.

Dattatary Bhandalkar is research Scholar, Tata Institute of Social Sciences, Mumbai.

Niharranjan Mishra, Assistant Professor, Department of Humanities and Social Sciences, NIT, Rourkela, Odisha.

Dinabandhu Sahoo, Research Scholar, Department of Humanities and Social Sciences, NIT, Rourkela, Odisha.

C. Rama Mohan Reddy is Lecturer in Political Science, Govt. Degree College, Jammalamadugu Town, YSR, Kadapa.

T. Sasikanth Reddy is Lecturer in English, S.C.N.R Govt. Degree College, Proddatur Town, YSR Dist, A.P.

Johani Xaxa is Reader, PG Department of Political Science, Public Administration, Sambalpur University, Odisha.

Palla Trinadha Rao is Advocate and Researcher, Rajmundry, A.P.

Pradip Kumar Parida is Asst Prof., IIPA, New Delhi.

Satchidananda Misra is Reader in Political Science, Revenshaw University, Odisha.

Satyam Sunkari is Assistant Professor, Council for Social Development (CSD), Hyderabad.

KV Sridevi is Principal, School of Education, Amrita Vishwa Vidyapeetham University, Mysore.

Asha BN is Principal, Somani College of Education, Mysore.

BK Mahakul is Faculty, Department of Political Science, Hidayatulla National Law University, Uparwara, Raipur, Chhattishgarh.

Girija Brahma is research Scholar, Department of Political Science, School of Social Sciences, University of Hyderabad.

Himanshu Sekhar Mishra is research Scholar, JNU, New Delhi.

Janmejay Sahu is research Scholar, Department of Political Science, School of Social Sciences, University of Hyderabad.

Ashok Behera is working in NYKS, Zonal Office, Odisha.

Janmejaya Mishra is with Aga Khan Rural Support Programme (India), Gujarat.

Justin Jos is student in National Law University, Cuttack, Odisha.

KR Rama Mohan is Assistant Director, Centre for Study of Social Exclusion and Inclusive Policy, Andhra University, Visakhapatnam, A.P.

B. Nageswara Rao is Assistant Professor, School of Economics, UOH.

Kapil Sikka is Research Scholar, Dept of Political Science, Jamia Millia Islamia, New Delhi.

Vijender Singh Beniwal is Research Scholar, Dept of Political Science, Jamia Millia Islamia University, New Delhi.

L. Reddeppa is Associate Professor, Council for Social Development (CSD), Hyderabad.

1

Tribal Education of Karnataka: Attainments and Challenges

KM Metry

Introduction

The term tribe has been widely used in sociology and anthropology. The term tribe originates from the Roman word *'tribua'*, meant a political unit and was used to refer to social groups defined by the territory they occupied. Morgan (1877) defined the tribe as a group which possessed social institutions but not political ones. Maine (1861) characterised it as a group in which legal relations were based on the principle of status rather than that of contract. In this sense of a pre-political or pre-contract society, the term passed into general usage as a synonym for a primitive social group. There is another use of the term tribe, linked especially to the history of Indian which has different implications from those other advanced communities. Tribe in the context of post–colonial India has been the subject of considerable debate particularly on their ability to understand the knowledge of literacy or education.

Education, means with a broad range of meaning, embracing both the notion of socialisation or enculturation in general and the specific process of formal education which may also be called 'schooling'. The growth of formal educational institutions is generally linked to specialisation in society and to the development of literacy. Formal education is generally designed predominantly with technical and occupational needs in mind and its purpose is to prepare students to fill available occupational roles, as well as to encourage certain values and attitudes.

In a democratic India, education is a key to the development of disadvantaged and constitutionally not identified social groups.

Education system of the country encompasses formal education which is imparted in and through institutions and follows prescribed and/or recognised curriculum as well as pedagogy under the framework of the policy and rules formulated by the state.

We focus on educational institutions—their role in providing equal educational opportunities, develop skills, questioning mind and lead to improving life chances.

In other words, value addition of educational institutions in developing capabilities of students in general and of the SCs and STs students in particular.

This paper seeks to examine the tribal education and its attainments and challenges in Karnataka state.

Tribal Education in Karnataka

In India, the total number of tribal groups, identified by Government of India, are 461, of which 172 are sub-segments (KS Singh: KM Metry: 2006: 133) many of these groups are as good as discrete categories. The total population of Scheduled Tribes in India stood at 5,16,28,638 (1981 census), 6,77,58,000 (1991 census) and 8,43,26,240 according to 2001 census. Their population constitutes 8.14 per cent of the total general population.

In Karnataka as on 15th August, 2010, fifty tribes have been constitutionally recognised as Scheduled Tribes. The total population of the Scheduled Tribes in Karnataka, as per 2001 census are mentioned in the Table 1.1.

Table 1.1: Scheduled Tribe Population in Karnataka (2001)

Total	*Population*	*Male*	*Female*	*Percentage of literacy rate*
Total	3463986	1756238	1707748	48.27
Rural	2934530	1486073	1448457	45.26
Urban	529456	270165	259291	64.26

The Directorate of Tribal Welfare is implementing several schemes for the progress and development of the STs in the state. The extent of infrastructure facilities like physical space, equipment, teaching aids and teacher-pupil ratio available in the schools are some of the indicators for the quality of education provided in Ashram schools.

Though the Ashram schools are the best means of educating the tribals, the outcome of these in some of the areas is not upto the mark due to various factors.

Further socio-cultural and economic conditions of the tribals may not permit them to succeed even at primary level of education. It is commonly accepted that socio-cultural and economic aspects of the family greatly influence the educability of the children in all societies.

The literacy rate among the STs which was 36.0 per cent in 1991 increased to 46.3 per cent in 2001. The female literacy rate among the STs in 1991 was 23.6 per cent and it increased to 36.6 per cent in 2001.

The literacy rate for rural ST women is 33.3 per cent compared with 56.9 per cent for men. Overall the STs in the state have markedly lower literacy rates than other groups. The fact that they are above the all India average in respect of men and women is of course an indicator that Karnataka has performed better than many other states.

Many schools in tribal areas suffer from high drop out rates. Children either never enroll or attend for the first three to four years of primary school.

For instance the Gross Enrollment Ratio (GER) in 2001 for STs for Classes I-VIII (90.12) was significantly lower than the gross enrollment ratio for all students (98.81) and SCs (104.57). This inequality is heightened even more by the gap between the gross enrollment ratio for South Karnataka (110.62) and North Karnataka (74.21). Gross enrollment ratio for girls (103.64) is also much better in the southern districts than in North Karnataka (70.22).

Scheduled Tribes in South Karnataka more closely approximates the overall GER of other social groups. The northern districts are caught up in a cycle of deprivation. They have the higher levels of ST population and also have poor human development indicators.

Girls are the first to be pulled out of school to work at home and take care of siblings to enable their parents to work. In such cases, families do not find the many incentives offered by the government such as free uniforms, textbooks and even scholarships, an adequate compensation for lost wages. For boys agricultural labour, coolie work and family work is the main reason for dropping out. '*Akshara Dasoha*', the recently introduced mid-day meals programme (*Bissivuta*) for school children showed a more sustained impact on ensuring the enrollment and retention of the tribal children in the schools.

There is a marked disparity in the enrollment of boys (3,209) and girls (1,652) in Tribal Ashram schools in Karnataka. The 2001 Census data reveals that around half of the ST population is in the workforce. Women constitute about 41.7 per cent of the workforce. More than 85 per cent of the working population is in rural areas.

This clearly indicates the highly precarious livelihood conditions of STs in Karnataka bearing the serious consequences on the education of the tribal children. The children joined in the Ashram schools also had serious impact on them with these conditions.

Government Programmes for Ashram School Education in Karnataka

Direction and Administration of Tribal Areas

The Government of Karnataka established the Directorate of Tribal Welfare on 30.8.1994 for the welfare of the STs. The Directorate is implementing several schemes for the progress and development of the STs in the State.

There are 122 Ashram schools benefiting 9,125 ST children run by the Directorate. Primary education from I to IV standard is being given to these students. Besides during 2006-07 the Government set up five new Morarji Desai Residential Schools for the educational benefit of Scheduled Tribe children.

Educational Policy in Tribal Areas of Karnataka

Apart from the general policy relating to the development of the Scheduled Tribes, the Government of Karnataka has not come up with any specific policy decisions relating to the use of Tribal Language in tribal education in the Ashram schools. However, under the *Sarva Shiksha Abhiyan* (District Primary Education Programme) '*Soliga Siddhi*'—a special book for Soliga children of Standard First was published in 1999 and distributed for use in Ashram Shalas with a high concentration of Soliga children. '*Soliga Siddhi*' (SS) was the first and only such specialised textbook for tribals developed at the initiative of Dr H. Sudarshan whose NGO, Vivekananda Girijana Kalyana Kendra (VGKK) has been working for several decades with the Soliga tribe in Chamarajanagar district. The project did not progress as envisaged to cover the other tribal languages as the SS experiment did not generate the expected results.

In Karnataka the general policy of using regional medium at the primary stage of education, which is applicable to the entire State, is also being used in the case of the Ashram Schools. On the other hand, the Government of Karnataka in the field of primary education is implementing or number of schemes and programmes for the tribes. They include the following:

1. Free textbooks, uniforms, school bags and note books are supplied to Scheduled Tribe children from Classes I to IV.

2. Children studying in Government Schools upto V standard with 80 per cent attendance are provided with three kgs of rice per child every month under mid-day meals.

3. 'Keli Kali' (hear and learn) programme especially for the children of Classes I to IV through Akashavani broadcasting.

4. Under the Samudayadatta Shale Programme people themselves are made to involve actively bringing back the dropout children back to school.

5. School Adoption Programme is another novel exercise where in Government Schools, which are in slums or backward areas and not so developed are entrusted to the care benefactors who voluntarily come forward to improve school education.

6. Chinnaraangala a bridge course programme was started during 2001-02 to bring back the drop out and non-enrolled school age children into the mainstream and to have access, retention and achievement.

7. '*Shaishika Samkrina*' is initiated by the Government of Karnataka to provide education for the poor among tribal girls only.

8. '*Nali Kali*' (a process of joyful learning) was launched in October 1995. The curriculum is learnable by the child in a manner with minimum levels

of learning expected to be achieved. The teacher encourages responsibility among children and the learner learns at his/her own pace.

9. '*Chaitanya*', the content-based training programme was launched in 2001 to bring about a gradual transformation of newly-recruited teachers in developing professional competencies and commitments.

10. In order to achieve Universal Elementary Education the *Sarva Shiksha Abhiyan* (SSA) was launched in 2001 covering the whole country. The SSA programme is an attempt to provide an opportunity for improving human capabilities to all children through provision of community owned quality education on a mission mode.

Current Situation of Tribal Education in Karnataka

The tribal education in Karnataka even though is in progress through Ashram schools, it is blistering with a number of problems. They can be identified under five areas namely, economic factors, social factors, administrative factors, cultural factors and school factors. Poverty of parents, lack of parental demand, child labour, lack of Early Childcare Education (ECE) facilities are some of the economic factors which stand in the way of education of the tribal children. Illiteracy of the parents, early marriages, community loyalties and lack of awareness are some of the problems which retard the educational development of the tribal children. Tribal festivals, tribal traditions, value system and problem of language are some of the cultural factors which stand as a hurdle with tribal children's education. There are a large number of school factors and administrative factors which hamper the educational development of the tribal children. To quote some of them are lack of access, incomplete schools, teacher absenteeism, poor quality of teaching, unserviceable curriculum, unsuitable working hours, etc., and lack of co-ordination among different managements, delays in supplies and incentives, weak inspectorate, lack of enrollment campaigns, lack of community control, lack of incentives for better performance are some of the school and administrative factors which are standing in the way of the education of tribal children. The following diagrammatic representation provides the specific problems of ST children in their education.

Factors Affecting the Education of Tribal Child in Ashram Schools

Economic Factors

- Poverty
- Agriculture labour
- Caring cattle
- Lack of parental demand
- Opportunity cost
- Child labour
- Domestic work
- Seasonal work participation

- Migration
- Lack of ECE Facilities

Social Factors

- Lack of awareness
- Community loyalties
- Early marriages
- Lack of community
- Involvement
- Illiteracy of parents
- Sibling care

Administrative Factors

- Lack of co-ordination among different managements
- Delay in supplies incentives
- Weak inspectorate
- Deputation of teachers to other places
- Non-involvement of NGOs
- Lack of enrollment campaigns
- Lack of community control
- Non-residence of teacher
- Lack of teacher quarters
- Lack of incentives for better performance

Cultural Factors

- Value system
- Tribal traditions
- Tribal festivals
- Unattractive textbooks
- Language problem

School Factors

- Lack of access
- Incomplete schools
- Lack of physical facilities
- Disinterested teachers
- Teacher absenteeism
- Poor quality of teaching
- None teaching
- Unattractive classrooms
- Unserviceable curriculum
- Unqualified teachers
- Vacancies of teachers posts
- Punishment by teacher
- Continuous sickness due to malnutrition
- Non-suitability of working hours and holidays
- Absenteeism due to ill-health

- Literacy rate among the ST children
- Enrollment
- Retention
- Dropouts
- Low Attendance of Tribal Children in Schools
- Problem of Absenteeism
- Disparities in the Existing Ashram Schools in Karnataka
- School Education: Access and Participation
- Socio-economic and Cultural Constraints
- Content and Curriculum
- Language and Medium of Instruction in Ashram Schools
- Shortage of Teachers
- Lack of Suitable Teachers
- Attitude of Non-Tribal Teachers Towards Tribal Children
- Lack of Basic Facilities
- Inefficiency in Ashram Schools
- Mismanagement, Nepotism and Corruption in Ashram Schools
- Absence of Central Monitoring Unit

Notes and References

1. Karnataka, *Human Development Report, 2005.*

2. Karnataka, *State Gazetteers.*

3. Midatala Rani, *Problems of Tribal Education in India*, New Delhi, Kanishka Publishers, 2009.

4. Government of Karnataka, Bangalore, Social Welfare Department, *Annual Report 2006-07.*

5. Padma S. Sarangapani, Indira Vijay Simha, Assessment of Utility and Usage of Soliga Siddhi Textbooks Developed for Soliga Tribal Ashram Shalas of Chamarajanagar District, *Project Report*, National Institute of Advanced Studies, Indian Institute of Science Campus, Bangalore, December, 2005.

6. Bibuthi Mishra, "*Re-orienting Tribal Education*", The Hindu, dated 3/8/2004.

7. Newspaper Clippings, *The Hindu, Deccan Herald, Star of Mysore, Kannada Prabha, Prajavani, Mysore Mail, Vijaya Karnataka.*

8. *Annual Report, 2000-2001*, Social Welfare Directorate, Government of Karnataka, Bangalore (Kannada).

9. *Abyudya – Manual of Welfare Programme for the Development of Scheduled Castes and Scheduled Tribes*, Government of Karnataka, Bangalore, 1996 (Kannada).

10. Biligiri, H.S, "*Problems of Tribal Languages in India*", in *Language and Society in India*. Indian Institute of Advanced Study, Simla, Vol. 8, 1969, pp. 245-250.

11. Edgar Turston, *Castes and Tribes of Southern India*, Cosmo Publications, Madras, 1909, Vol. 1 to 7.

12. Gnanasundaram, V, Use of Tribal Languages in Education – Some Issues and Problems (*Seminar Paper*).

13. *Nali-Kali*, District Primary Education Programme, Mysore, ND.

14. *National Policy on Education*, Government of India, New Delhi, 1986.

15. *Neravu-Nirdeeshana*, Information and Publicity Department, Government of Karnataka. 1995 (Kannada).

16. *Perspectives for Education Sector - Policy Paper for VIII Five Year Plan.* Department of Education, Government of Karnataka, 1989.

17. *Report of the Directorate of Tribal Welfare*, Government of Karnataka, Bangalore, ND.

18. *25th Report of the Commission for Linguistic Minorities*, Government of India, New Delhi, 1985.

19. Roy Burman, B.K., "Languages of the Tribal Communities of India and their use in Primary Education" in *Language and Society in India*, Indian Institute of Advanced Study, Simla, Vol. 8, 1969, pp. 251-259.

20. Sudhir Shukla, "*Aliens in Their Own Home*", The Hindu, dated 14th March, 1993.

21. *Social Welfare Department Programmes 1991-92*, Government of Karnataka. Bangalore (Kannada), ND.

22. *Sarvashiksha Abhiyan – Perspective Plan 2002-2010*, Office of the District Project Co-ordinator, DPEP, Mysore, ND.

23. *Tribal Education in India, Publication No. 20*, Tribal Education Unit. Department of Adult Education, NCERT, 1967.

24. *Welfare Programmes for Scheduled Tribes*, Directorate of Social Welfare, Government of Karnataka (Kannada), ND.

25. Midatala Rani, Functioning of Ashram Schools in Karnataka in Budakattu Adhyayana Journal (Hampi: Kannada University, 2012).

26. Census of India 2001in SC Bhatt and Gopal K Bhargava (Editors), *Land and People of Indian States and Union Territories,* Vol. 7, Kalpaz Publications, Delhi, 2006.

2

Salvation Army Boon or Bane? A Critique of Yerukula Reformation in Andhra Pradesh

Malli Gandhi

"As white man's rat has driven away the native rat so the European fly drives away our own, and the clover kills our fern, so will the Maoris disappear before the white man himself".

—A Maori Proverb

Numerous tribes in India were proclaimed "criminal" by the British government were declared as ex-criminal, denotified communities during the year 1952. Even after 63 years of Independence they are living in miserable conditions. They are placed at a disadvantaged position in the present caste-based system. The Government has to consider the anomalies in identifying and characterising the various denotified communities in the country. Their condition is worsening day by day. The present reservation provided by the government is not sufficient to meet the developmental demands of these communities. The aims and objectives of the paper is to discuss the impact of the CT Act on the DNT communities in general and Yerukulas in particular, modernisation of the criminal tribes and the role of the Salvation Army, and the impact of the Indian leaf tobacco company in transforming the Yerukulas as industrial wage workers from itinerant trading communities.

The British imperial government launched many projects to declare certain wandering communities as criminal tribes. The most important project that was launched was introducing the Criminal Tribes Act of 1871, and preparing a detailed demographic profile of Indian population as their subjects.[1]

The forest tribes led a nomadic life. These tribes were engaged in barter trade with the surrounding agricultural communities, exchanging forest produce such as herbs and honey, salt, clothes and grain. Nineteenth century colonial economic policies destroyed the occupations of a number of such communities. The salt policy of the government destroyed the trade of Koravars, Yerukulas, Korchars, Brinjaries and Lambadis.[2] Like Yerukulas and Banjaras many groups were badly affected by the forest policies. Lieutenant Balmer wrote: "The crimes they are addicted to are dacoity and highway robbery. They are the most troublesome of our wanderers".[3]

In the last quarter of the 19th century the British Government launched census operations throughout the country. The colonial administrators did not understand the cultural pluralism of the Indian people and their sense of accommodation and adjustment with different religions and communities. The colonial masters started looking at these communities with the glasses of modernity. Michel Foucault said: The episteme of difference has taken precedence over the episteme of resemblance".[4] The imperial rulers could not understand the meaning of nomadism. They could not understand that nomadism as a way of life for a large number of communities in India and outside. Nomadism was the way of their life. It is their philosophy of their life. They did not like to stick on to one place. They do not want to change the nature and intervene in its practices.[5] Thus many classes of people and communities lived with nature and practised nomadism. Their nomadic way of life was misunderstood by the imperial rulers and administrators. They considered them as uncivilised, uncultured, savage and barbarous. They thought that these nomadic people will pose a threat to the law and order to the society. They were very poor, they lack definite means of production to earn their living. Therefore, the colonial government assumed these communities as thieves and dacoits. Thus, they are dubbed as criminal tribes. David Arnold wrote: "The Criminal Tribes Act of 1871 was used against the wandering groups, nomadic petty traders and pastoralists, gypsy types, hill- and forest-dwelling tribals, in short, against a wide variety of marginals who did not conform to the colonial pattern of settled agricultural and wage labour".[6]

The different laws on the so-called criminal tribes have been influenced by the colonial considerations of political mechanism and economic needs. The colonial administrators believed that maintenance of law and order would be a mere exercise in vacuum unless a better control could be achieved over the indigenous population. It was then imperative that a strong and shifting population could not be conducive to the so-called 'good' government and the colonial notion of 'Pax Britanica'. In order to achieve this, unlike in the West where legislation regulated incidences of crime, in India, interception of crime was attempted. The colonial government here tried to confine would-be-male factors to settlements.[7] Some wandering tribes without any fixed habitat became, dubbed as 'criminal' and were setup in settlements. Mackenzire writes, "these tribes led a vagrant life in jungles, hills and deserts with no fixed abodes. They wandered about with their bag and baggage and pitch their tents on the outskirts of a village or some secluded place".[8] A gypsy way of life necessitated by early trading activities, came to be described as vagrancy or lust for wandering. It was stated that, "if the local government has reason to believe that any tribe, gang or class of persons or any part of a tribe gang or class is addicted to the systematic commission of offences it may declare that such tribe, gang or class or part of the tribe, gang or class as a criminal tribe".[9]

Yerukulas were declared a criminal community under the Criminal Tribes Act, 1991. The salient features of the Criminal Tribes Act were as follows:

1. Before a community was declared a criminal tribe, 'respectable members' of a village were consulted, who were invariably either headman, or high caste sections or landlords; often these categories overlapped. The notified criminal tribe members had to take the permission of the headman before they could enter or leave a village. There is evidence that these headmen-cum-landlords used the act to extract free labour from the criminal tribe members before they allowed an itinerant community to pass through the village.

2. One of the provisions required the notified criminal tribe members to report to the nearest police station to register their attendance twice a night. These powers were used by the subordinate police for extortions and harassment so widely that it caused some administrative concern.

3. The criminal tribe members were forced to work in mills, factories, mines, quarries and plantations by the police administration as a part of relieving their own vigilance duties, and handing over to the employers extraordinary powers of control under the Criminal Tribe Act. Under this, even ordinary workers could be declared criminal tribes in case their work performance was not satisfactory and in fact in crucial ways this act also effectively replaced the Workmen's Breach of Contract Act, especially on the plantations. As far as this particular use of the Criminal Tribes Act was concerned, any low caste, vulnerable section of the people could be declared a criminal tribe and forced to work in an enterprise; any persons including a manager of an enterprise could be made responsible for their control and any site, including an enterprise could be declared a criminal tribe settlement.

4. A section of those declared criminal could be interned into special settlements set up under one of the provisions of the Criminal Tribes Act.[10]

The Criminal Tribe settlements were managed by several Christian missionaries and philanthropic societies who worked for their moral upliftment and modernisation of the criminal tribes.

The following missionaries may be cited:

1. The Canadian Mission,
2. Arya Samaj,
3. The Servants of India Society,
4. The Salvation Army,
5. The American Baptist Telugu Mission,
6. The Ramakrishna Mission, etc.

The Government found the successful work done by the Missionaries such as Salvation Army.[11] The Salvation Army was the first organisation that stepped into the activities among the Criminal Tribes. Dadabhai Naoroji said, "The Salvation Army's help has been requisitioned from time to time. Whether it is Salvation Army or whether it is any other reforming body. The religious zeal is very often a necessary element in pursuing difficult task of people of this kind and winning them from evil ways".[12]

Criminal Tribe settlements were established in such districts where grave crime was prevalent. In order to provide a settled and modern life the government opened agricultural, industrial, reformative, and voluntary settlements. The earliest nomadic settlement was established by the American Baptist Telugu Mission in 1912 at Kavali (Bitragunta). Sitanagaram settlement was established in 1913. Vedullapalli or Betapudi settlement was established in 1914 by the Salvation Army. The Lingala settlement was established during the year 1917 by the Nizam's government for the welfare and development of the Yerukulas in the erstwhile Madras Presidency-Andhra State.[13]

Stuartpuram or Betapudi settlement was one of the biggest settlements in Madras Presidency. There were about 10,000 Yerukulas lived for several decades from 1911 onwards. The settlement was named after Stuart, the moving force behind settlements in general. He was a senior government official and incharge of the police establishment. The spirit behind these settlements was punitive rather than reformative.[14]

By 1910, several CT settlements were established in Madras Presidency. Many itinerant communities were singled out for settling by the policy. The official directive of the government was "worst characters, especially wandering gangs" must be settled.[15] The Salvation Army was entrusted with the reformatory work of the itinerant communities. The responsibility of the sedentary criminals was taken up by the police. Stuartpuram settlement became the literal 'site' for the British Administration and the Salvation Army to 'experiment in crimino curology'. The Salvation Army was responsible for a number of settlements. It is the main organisation working with the criminal communities in India.[16]

The Salvation Army was identified itself with the imperial aims of England. It was born in 1870s when the British imperialism was in the peak point. It was called itself as the Salvation Army. The Salvation Army encashed on the popular image of romanticised imperialism. It had adopted marches, flags, brass bands and uniforms for its employees. 'General' Booth was their head. Their officers had signed on the 'articles of war'. Their newspaper was called *The War Cry*. They had open air 'bombardments' not prayers or meetings. They do not say that they were going to start work in a new region. First they occupy the new territory and then they declare religious war. In short, the Salvation Army was a shadow imperial body. It had identified with the aims and projects of England. General Booth had envisaged for the English poor what he called the settlements as city colonies and farm colonies. For the Indian 'Criminal' classes he declared them as 'settlements'. The imperial term 'settlement' took a modern meaning. The itinerant communities were to be settled down instead of wandering aimlessly.[17]

Stuartpuram Settlement was meant for the well-behaved people. Those persons who were reformed and non-criminal members were drawn from Sitanagaram were placed in the settlement.[18] When the Government provided land to the Salvation Army in Guntur to set up the settlement there were a number of protests posed in different ways. The local landlords were particularly infuriated. They charged that the CT members escaped at night and committed crime. Thus, this settlement was declared as a 'criminal' settlement. The government increased the police force to watch their movements carefully.[19]

Stuartpuram settlement was initially planned as an agricultural settlement. A total number of 500 acres of sandy land and 1000 acres of swamp land were handed over to the Salvation Army by the government, free of assessment.[20] Due to various reasons the plan of the government was failed. Essentially, the land was of very poor quality, and the implements of the agriculture production were primitive. The Yerukulas were not keen on tilling the land. They were not enthusiastic agriculturists in the beginning. The manager of the settlement once said: The Salvation Army found it very tedious to convert them into good cultivators industrious to work on land they were forced and could not be induced. Through driven like a flock of sheep, the first crop failed . . . No crowbars, no proper spade and no physical strength. So work turned out did not reach the desired length. In the beginning, I had recourse to a stick, I was glad, as it brought the desired result quick.[21]

There was free opposition by the landlords in the area. They objected the very concept of low caste communities being granted land. In addition to their fear, they understood if the paddy land suitably irrigated, was very profitable and valuable for them. It was stated that: "the monied folk of Bapatla had counted . . . on buying the swamp land at cheap rates and rack renting the actual cultivator whenever a crop could be raised".[22] This plan was unwillingly foiled by the administration by parcelling out large tracts of land to the Salvation Army. The protest by the landlords was also in a large measure due to their anxiety about losing the services of Yerukulas as agricultural workers on their own land.[23]

All this opposition took place in the era when landlords were important political allies of the British administration, and on balance, the administration decided not to alienate the landlord/headmen sections any further. Irrigation facilities, plans to make available water from the Krishna river to the settlement – were withheld, and alternative means of supporting the settlement had to be now seriously considered.[24]

The Indian Lead Tobacco Company (ILTD) began its administration with the help of the Salvation Army. The Company invited the Yerukulas as alternative employees. The ILTD had existed in Guntur district since 1908 in order to procure local tobacco. The ILTD started to work as the leaf wing of British American Tobacco Company and Peninsular Company. By 1925, the factory was able to employ half of the total adult population of the settlement. According to government policy, once infrastructure for the settlement had been provided by the government, the settlements were to be self-supporting. But the income from the land was found not enough for the Yerukulas. Therefore, the entire settlement gradually depended on the factory for employment.[25] The Salvation Army had no other means of finding employment for the Yerukulas.

The company's initial contact with the Stuartpuram settlers seems to have been through the mats made by the Yerukula women and children. They made the mats and baskets very fast. The mats and baskets were, infact, an essential part of the manufacturing process at the factory. The Salvation Army was the medium through which the sales took place to the ILTD. Slowly, women came to be employed in the factory as regular wage workers. The men continued to work fruitlessly on the land. The financial situation of the settlement was quite stable for a few years after the women settlers from Stuartpuram began to work in the tobacco factory. The ILTD management, the Salvation Army and the government was very optimistic with regard to the future progress of the Yerukulas.[26]

Stuartpuram became a large settlement in terms of numbers as whole communities – not individuals – were put in at a time. The CT Act was meant to work with the concept of whole communities. Even the Salvation Army said they were embarrassed by what they called "this rain of riches". The Salvation Army officials said: "To others, these criminals may hardly appear in the light of riches, but to us each bears the image and supersubscription of the Divine Mint".[27]

Stuartpuram is the largest settlement. It needed extensive police presence outside to prevent escapes and inside, the Salvation Army took attendance upto five times in a day, including nights.[28] There was strict punctuality and discipline for the adults, males, children and women. The system of fines and corporal punishment to deter disorderly behaviour was imposed. Incidentally, virtually no outsiders were allowed into the settlement for scrutiny, and enquiry committees could enter into the settlements. When the nationalists took up this issue in 1940's seriously this has come down a little bit.[29]

Stuartpuram settlement was primarily an agricultural settlement. The official rationale was that it should become an agricultural colony. Agriculture was the chief profession of the Yerukulas in the settlement. The British Government had the deep anxiety for the reclamation of the waste land, forest and swamp lands. In fact, land reclamation was synonymous with the reclamation of the criminals.[30] Once cultivable, the land could start paying revenue. A large tract of waste land was given to Salvation Army for cultivation by the Yerukulas. This needed some reorganisation of the community's social and cultural priorities.[31]

Drastic modern transformation in the lives of the Yerukulas was followed. Most important modern transformation was the itinerant mode of existence was suddenly replaced by a forced settled life. The Salvation Army divided the community into families, which were now the new operational social and economic unit – each family was given a small piece of land, which it was responsible for cultivating or else punishment was followed.[32] The family was further broken up by removing the children to another part of the settlement. The Salvation Army felt that the 'rising generation' should be kept away from their wicked parents, and brought up in a more wholesome atmosphere. Separate schools and dormitories were established for these children, and they were allowed to meet their parents only on Sundays during Church activities. The two components of the modernisation of the Yerukulas were: (1) moral education and (2) hard work. The Salvation Army concentrated on the Yerukula boys and girls for moral education and on the adult men and women for hard physical work.[33]

The Salvation Army did not normally prepare women for wage work in any of its settlements. Ideally, they were to be trained in feminine virtues and were expected to sew, embroider and cook for their families. In Stuartpuram settlement, a new division of labour within the family was devised and appropriate gender roles were defined. In fact, mat-making, which was a traditional activity of both men and women of the Yerukula community, was now handed over exclusively to women. It was combined with their indoor activities. The Yerukula men now ploughed and tilled the waste land, though it was unsuccessful many times.[34]

There were a number of ways in which the Yerukula women was fashioned and modernised. True women were fashioned out of what the Salvation Army called "thievish raw material".[35] For example, they were taught to pay attention to their appearances. The Salvation Army even held periodic parades of the most neatly dressed women and gave the winners prizes.[36] The women were not allowed to go outside the settlement on a pass if they looked like "so many vagrants".[37] The before and after photographs of the women in the Salvation Army records show the 'after' version with a completely changed Hinduised appearance, complete with neatly tied saris, oiled hair with flowers and vermillion marks on their foreheads.

After more than a decade of such remoulding, something happened. The newly-domesticated women were required to work outside their homes for a wage as the land was found unable to support the families. The government expected the Salvation Army to make the settlements under their care completely self-supporting once the initial infrastructure had been paid for. Due to severe financial crisis the Yerukula women was persuaded or forced in hundreds to go and work in the newly-established tobacco factory near Ramanagaram a few miles away from the settlement.

The Salvation Army systematically inculcated in them an indoor culture of housekeeping and child rearing. The Yerukulas used to walk seven kms everyday and spend 12 hours outside their homes, earning a wage in the ILTD factory. The Salvation Army asked the government to provide crèches for the infants and toddlers in the settlement, so that the young mothers could go as well for the factory work. Thus within a period of 10-12 years, the Yerukula women alone earned as much as 80 per cent of the entire settlement income.

The Yerukula women became the principal earners in their families. The Salvation Army consolidated the new moral code for them. The Salvation Army began to take a more active role in their personal and material life. This was done in order to keep their own control and to make sure that economic independence did not confound gender identities and gender roles.

The Yerukula women used to have the freedom to choose their spouses. The Salvation Army granted permission for marrying the males in the settlement limits only. The Salvation Army officials had always been votaries of proper match-making in the settlements. The Salvation Army became very active on the issue of the marriages of the Yerukula males and females. They wrote to the government wanting "a voice in the choice of spouses" and got it. They were finding to their alarm that bride price, something they had been trying to suppresses as it meant mere selling of females, now rose steeply, sometimes as much as rupees five hundred. The Salvation Army substituted it with dowry, which they gave themselves. It always consisted of saris and vessels for the bride, the true symbols of lost domesticity. Incidentally, in other settlements, the Salvation Army used to insist that the man be able to support his wife before letting them marry. They also forbade completely what they called "desertions" by women of their husbands. Ironically, the women lost their autonomy in material affairs at a time when they were the principal contributors to the family income.

The ILTD company where the women worked supported the Salvation Army on the severe discipline in the settlement, and showed their active role in the affairs of the families of the Yerukula women. In fact, the ILTD management became active on the issue of interfering in the personal issues of the Yerukulas in the settlement. The strict discipline, punctuality, regularity, sincerity, orderly behaviour and a system of harsh punishments – resonated very well with the ILTD factory life. The ILTD management found that these workers were "less trouble some" than others. The Salvation Army insisted on an irrevocable form of marriage worked in the favour of the company. They could not continue to pay a family wage which was much lower than the sum paid to an individual man and woman. By the year 1930, the whole families of the Yerukulas in the Stuartpuram settlement became the employers of the Salvation Army. The men sued to work upto 20 hours a day in different shifts. The Salvation Army had an interest in keeping families together in the settlement. The Yerukula men and women requested the management to intervene and help them in getting their wives to stay with them. The ILDT literally threatened the women with the loss of their jobs in case they divorced their husbands.

Today Stuartpuram of course was officially not called a criminal tribe settlement any more and the Yerukula community was not criminal tribes anymore – after Independence, the CT Act, under which they had been notified by the Colonial administration, had been repealed. Salvation Army now a much depleted organisation both as far as its authority and number of personnel were concerned. However, it is still operating in the settlement with a church, schools, hostels and a few welfare activities.

The entire gamut of modernising the Denotified Communities depends on how best educational facilities are provided to the children of the DNT communities. Education paves a way for them to become a part and parcel of the mainstream of national life. Education helps to channelise their energies into productive purposes. Education is an effective weapon and instrument of social transformation. Education plays a significant role in changing the fortune and life-style of the children of the DNT communities. Their economic plight and environmental influence have direct impact on their education. A detailed study of the schooling facilities presents a grim picture in all DNT colonies today. The children in these schools when examined were highly intelligent, active and alert. Lack of education among them leads to lack of social and political consciousness. Another problem that the Yerukulas are facing today is the inferiority complex that they have suffered since a long time. This is due to their economic backwardness. A stigma is attached to the community. "The stigma of their being 'criminal' strained them more glaringly as people always doubted a person who had spent sometime in a criminal reformatory". In order to modernise the Yerukulas what is urgently required is to remove them from the influence of petty crime, the pernicious influence of the environment of the 'settlement', profitable industrialisation, improvised agricultural facilities, proper and conducive environment, improvised health facilities, banks, free from oppression, stigma, harassment and exploitation.

Notes and References

1. Singh, Birinder Paul, Ex-Criminal Tribes of Punjab, *Economic and Political Weekly,* Vol. XLIII, No. 51, December 20-26, 2008, p. 58.

2. Gandhi, Malli, Development of Denotified Tribes: Policy and Practice, Sarup and Sons, New Delhi, 2006, p. 7.

3. Government of Madras, Madras Criminal Tribes Manual, Criminal Tribes Act VI of 1924, brought upto 31st March 1927, Madras 1928.

4. Singh, Birinder Paul, *op.cit.*, p. 58.

5. *Ibid.*

6. Arnold, David, 'Crime and Crime Control in Madras 1885-1947' in Yang (ed), Crime and Criminality in British India, University of Arizona Press, Tucson.

7. Gandhi, Malli, *op.cit.*, p. 10.

8. Mackenzie, Mildred, E., *The Mud Bank*, Pensilvania, 1894, p. 60.

9. Madras Criminal Tribes Manual, *op.cit.*, p. 18.

10. Radha Krishna, Meena, Colonial Construction of a Criminal Tribe, Yerukulas of Madras Presidency, *Economic and Political Weekly,* July 8-15, 2000, p. 2256.

11. Malli, Gandhi, Denotified Tribes: Dimensions of Change, Kanishka Publishers, New Delhi, 2008.

12. Government of Madras, Home Department, G.O. No. 1675, dt. 2.12.1919.

13. Lalitha, V., The Making of Criminal Tribes, Patterns and Transition, New Era Publications, Madras, 1995.

14. Malli, Gandhi and Lalitha, V., *Tribes Under Stigma: Problem of Identity*, Serials Publishers, New Delhi, 2009.

15. Radha Krishna, Meena, *Dishonoured by History 'Criminal Tribes' and British Colonial Policy*, Orient Longman, Hyderabad, 2001, p. 14.

16. Radha Krishna, Meena, 'The Criminal Tribes Act in Madras Presidency: Implications for Itinerant Communities', *The Indian Economic and Social History Review,* Vol. 26, 3.

17. Radha Krishna, Meena, 'Surveillance and Settlements Under the Criminal Tribes Act in Madras', *The Indian Economic and Social History Review, 29, 2*.

18. Government of Madras, Note showing the progress made in the settlement of Criminal Tribes in the Madras Presidency up to January 1925, Madras, 1927, p. 28.

19. Government of Madras, *Note showing the Progress made in the settlement of Criminal Tribes in the Madras Presidency up to September, 1916*, Madras, 1917, p. 21.

20. Government of Madras, Law (General) Department, G.O. No. 1327, dated 14.2.1925, p. 3.

21. Government of Madras, Law (General) Department, G.O. No. 1714, dated 22.10.1921, p. 4.

22. Government of Madras, Home Judicial Department, G.O. No. 305, dated 7.2.1918, p. 3.

23. Government of Madras, *Note Showing the Progress Made in the Settlement of Criminal Tribes in the Madras Presidency upto September 1916*, Madras 1917, p. 22.

24. Home Judicial Department, G.O. No. 2074, dt. 18.8.1916, p. 5.

25. Government of Madras, Law (General) Department, G.O. No. 3187, dated 14.11.1924, p. 1.

26. Government of Madras, Law (General) Department, G.O. No. 1551, dated 10.7.1927, p. 3.

27. Mackenzie, Mildred, E., The Mud Bank, Pensilvania, 1894, p. 42.

28. Radha Krishna, Meena, 'Surveillance and Settlements under the Criminal Tribes Act in Madras', *The Indian Economic and Social History Review, 29, 2*.

29. Radha Krishna, Meena, Colonial Construction of a 'Criminal' Tribe, Yerukulas of Madras Presidency, Economic and Political Weekly, July 8-15, 2000, p. 2558.

30. Government of Madras, *Judicial Department, G.O. No. 2308, dated September 22, 1916.*

31. Government of Madras, *Note showing the Progress Made in the Settlement of Criminal Tribes in Madras Presidency upto 1925*, Madras 1927.

32. Government of Madras, Home Judicial Department, G.O. No. 1759, dated August 5, 1918.

33. *Ibid.*

34. Government of Madras, *Public Works Labour Department, G.O. No. 1654L, dated July 6, 1928.*

35. Salvation Army, *The War Cry*, London, June 1913.

36. Government of Madras, Judicial Department, G.O. No. 1759, dated August 5, 1918, p. 4.

37. Government of Madras, *Note showing the Progress Made in the Settlement of Criminal Tribes upto 1925*, Madras, 1927, p. 40.

3

Socio-economic Conditions of Tribals and Resulting Social Alienation

Ramdas Rupavath

Since Independence many development schemes and protective measures have been attempted by the Central and State governments for the trial areas of Andhra Pradesh. However, the conditions of majority of the tribals have deteriorated. While exploitation and backwardness are found in many communities and social groups in India, among tribes it has resulted in social alienation. The existence of a distinct culture and life style make the problems of tribals different from those of other deprived groups in India. In this chapter, an attempt has been made to focus upon social alienation in Adilabad district, while specific economic problems such as land alienation have been dealt with in the next chapter.

Tribal Society and Culture

The tribals of this area belong mainly to the Gond tribe. They form a socially dominant section among the rest who belong to the Bhil, Koya, Kolam, etc., tribes and are much fewer in number. Their mother tongue is Gondi, Tribal life among the Gonds exhibits unique symbiosis of man and nature. Their culture being an outcome of living with nature and learning from it. Traditionally Pujaris also called 'Kolams', were a priestly class who performed rituals and were the medicine men and story tellers of the tribe. They enjoyed social prominence together with the tribal chiefs. Tribal spiritual life was rich with creative mythologies and religious stories. Each clan member even today possesses the house deities of the tribe though there is a village priest called the "Devari" and clan priest (Kalotra) and a village seer (Bhaktal). There is no discrimination among the Gonds on the basis of sex. Women traditionally had an important position within the family and society. The Gonds even today have their distinct folk dances and music. However, they celebrate the main "Hindu" festivals of Diwali, Dussehra etc.[1]

Since independence Gond society has been profoundly influenced by the twin process of 'Sanskritisation and modernisation.[2] Due to this the social and economic life of the Gonds has undergone change. For example, change has taken place in the position given to women and the rituals associated with marriage. Gond women traditionally were very independent and took part in both cultivation of land, setting of produce etc. Today, due to cultural contact women are secluded. While earlier marriages were simple affairs, today the custom of dowry has penetrated into tribal life forcing many into the hands of local moneylenders. Non-tribal intrusion has created an unequal social fabrication and mentality.[3] Non-tribals in order to sustain their economic exploitation and hegemony over the tribals have attempted to propagate the Hindu religion as superior to the tribal god who is described as 'evil spirits'. The backwardness of described as an outcome of religious beliefs and practices. This has led to breakdown of the social fabric and adoption of Hindu practices such as pilgrimages to Tirupati. Animist practices such as free worship has been replaced by temple workshop. The establishment of institutionalised religion has made temple surroundings place of commercial activity useful to the non-tribal trading classes. Haimendorf records that the 'Khelaspur Jatara' a tribal festival has been replaced by a temple, which has been used as a platform by politicians during election campaigns. Temple offerings (amounting to Rs 1911 in 1977) have attracted Hindu priests, and have treated disputes within the tribe.[4] A court order however, returned the control of the temple to the tribal population.

The Gonds still practice traditional method of agriculture. They are dependent upon the rains for irrigation. Jowar is the main crop cultivated, but is available for only three months in the year. Rest of the time they survive on forest produce. The dependence of tribals on nature has led to most of them living close to starvation.

Of the 35 lakh tribals population only 6.6 per cent are literate in Adilabad.[5] Table 3.1 shows that very few tribals have managed to even get a few years of schooling. The first attempt to educate the Gonds was made in the 1940's by the Nizam's government.[6] Books were published in the language of the Gonds, however this did not have any impact. In the post-independence period the government of Andhra Pradesh has not taken any keen interest in educating the tribals. The Gonds consider children as a source of income and are reluctant to send them to school.[7] In recent years due to increasing pressure on land and resulting protests the state government has tried to introduce schools and increase literacy and vocational training. In 1989, the Andhra Pradesh government introduced 451 tribal hostels and 12 residential schools.

Table 3.1: Educational Levels of the Scheduled Tribes in Adilabad District, 1981

Total Tribals	*Matriculation*				*Higher Secondary /Intermediate*		*Non-technical Diploma or certification of equal des.*		*Technical Certificates*		*Graduate and above*	
	M	F	M	F	M	F	M	F	M	F	M	F
Gond												
Rajgonds	704	33	422	21	92	3	-	-	19	1	33	1
Naikpod	564	26	152	4	42	-	-	-	11	-	13	1
Sugalis												
Lambardar	10	5	3	-	1	-	-	-	-	-	-	-
Yerukal												
	21	2	3	1	-	-	-	-	-	-	-	-
Kolam												
Manana	1	-	-	-	-	-	-	-	-	-	-	-
Varlu												
Konda doras	-	-	-	-	-	-	-	-	-	-	-	-
Konda	-	-	-	1	-	-	-	-	-	-	-	-
Reddy	84	4	4	16	2	5	-	-	-	-	-	-
Bhil	-	-	-	-	-	-	-	-	-	-	-	-
Koya	1384	70	580	25	134	3	-	-	19	1	46	2
Yenadis												
Total												

However, such facilities have been utilised only by the children of a few rich farmers and according to the Gondwana Sanrakshna Samiti, such schemes do not benefit the tribal population. The first attempt to educate Gonds was made in the 1940s by the Nizam's government.

And are merely to fill the quota of education seats set aside to schedule tribes. Most of the tribal students in the scheme were unable to pass the matriculation examination. Training for provision of skilled or semi skilled jobs would be far more beneficial. For example, after the violent incident in Allampali Taluk where 12 policemen were killed in a land mine explosion the Telugu Desam Government announce that 1000 teachers posts would be reserved for scheduled tribe candidates. However, very few of the trial population had the required certificates and qualifications.[8] Thus lopsided development policies and schemes introduced by the Government policies and schemes introduction by the Government have not been of much use and help only some vested interests.

Changing Local Structures of Powers

In the pre-independence period in Andhra Pradesh there were 37 tribal chiefs some of whom bore the title of Raja '*Mokashi*' or '*Deshmukh*'. They had political power within their jurisdiction and exercised varying degrees of feudal oppression. They were assisted by village headmen in solving tribal problems. In the 1940s these traditional structures of power were removed by the Nizam's government in spite of resistance by the tribals.[9] The Nizam's government succeeded in abolishing the old system and replacing it by a village headman nominated by the Village Panchayat who settled dispute and had judicial authority. Thus before independence itself the old tribal structure had begun to disintegrate.

There was further erosion of local authority after independence with the passage of the Hyderabad Tribal Regulation Act in 1963.[10] Under this the village headman came under the control of the district bureaucracy under the new Panchayat System members are elected each block, who in turn elect the Sarpanch. In some cases it is reported that non-tribals have been able to manipulate the system and become a sarpanch, a position that gives it holder considerable patronage and power. Sarpanch has the power to grant licenses for shops and collect some local taxes.[11] They however have power to settle disputes. Some villages in the blocks have village headman who help the local tribal population to dig wells, plant trees etc.

The erosion of local autonomy has had an impact on the social and economic life of the tribals. Under the traditional tribal structure outsiders had to gain permission from the village headman to reside in the area. Massive demographic increases, after 1951 and the opening up of tribal areas due to the process of modernisation and inclusion of tribal areas in States, propelled non-tribals into tribal territory. In Adilabad this has led to non-tribals from the coastal area establishing factories cement mills, paper factories shops etc. The labour in these factories also consists of non-tribals, hence modernisation has not provided employment to the local tribals. It has led to establishment of liquor shops or increased prostitution. Commercialisation has led to breakdown of the traditional systems of authority within the tribal system.[12]

Table 3.2: Structural of Power at the Gram Taluk and District Levels Established in 1983 by Tribal Leaders

Rai Centres		
Gram Sabha	*Taluk level*	*District level*
1. Napapal: Village headman 2. Sar Pathal: Additional village headman 3. Raipatal : Asst. Village headman 4. Geeta Daralal: Maintaining the records. 5. Gatilal: Accountant 6. Devari: In charge of religious rituals 7. Hawaldar: Messenger.	1. Sri Medial : the President 2. Rai Medial : General Secretary 3. Geeta Medial: Joint Secy. 4. Ghat Medial : Accountant 5. Raipatals: Advisors to Sir medials.	1. Zill mall: President 2. Bpa Mandal: Vi. President 3. Zilla Rai: Gen. Secy. Medial 4. Khaajandhar: Accountant

In 1983 in order to help the tribals and grant them greater autonomy to manage their local affairs the Gondwana Sangrashna Samiti was established by educated tribal leaders.[13] It is a village level council, which solves local problems and helps implement developmental schemes. The various tribal groups in the villages nominate a representative to the Council. It consists of 7 – 14 members. In addition to this tribal leaders have also established developmental or "Rai Centres" patterned on their traditional power structures. These have been set up at the Gram, Taluk, and District levels. These help the tribals settle internal problems. Moreover, any Government schemes to be taken up at village level must obtain the consent of concerned Gram Sabha/village council. Contractors are not allowed, nor the Patel or Patwari, in the village council or Rai Centres. The Village Council can impose fines between Rs 50 to Rs 500. (assault, theft, etc.). They are also managing tribal lands and controlling forest produce.

The Samithi also introduced the grain procurement system. Each tribal agricultural family must donate 60 kgs of grains and Rs 50. Those who are not in a position to donate at one time can give in installments. The Integrated Tribal Development Scheme also contributes an equal quantity of grains and cash as government subsidy. They have set up grain banks, which advance loans for religious ceremonies and marriages at very low interest rates.[14]

Investment by the Government in Tribal Welfare

Table 3.3 gives the per capita and total expenditure by the Government of Andhra Pradesh over the various Plan periods. It is only from the fifth Plan period that there is a sharp rise in the amount invested. Under the Five Year Plan the Government has undertaken Schemes to construct pucca houses and cattle sheds. Integrated Tribal Development Schemes have also been formulated under the Tribal Development Schemes have also been formulated under the Tribal Development Agency.[15] A Girijan Co-operative Corporation was set up under it. It was expected to purchase the timber collected by the tribals and thereby eliminate private timber contractors. Primary Societies affiliated to the co-operative were supposed to supply at proper rates, the daily requirements of the tribals, provide hedit etc. However, the co-operative has been giving very low rates to tribals, for example Rs five-eight per kg. Of gum while private contractors pay Rs 12 per kg. This led to tribals setting their produce to contractors rather than the co-opertive.[16]

Nationalised Banks have entered the area. A study shows that 61 per cent debtors are landless holders. A quarter of the loans advanced by the official and government agencies 67 per cent are used for consumption purposes. The Andhra Pradesh government introduced a drinking water scheme named Jeevandhara" to provide drinking water irrigation facilities.[17] Under it Rs 15000 were given to each selected family in installments to dig wells on their own. According to the government 10,000 wells for agricultural purposes and 11,000 wells for drinking water have been dug. The Integrated Tribal Development agency had also started new loans to tribals for buying bullocks. However, many tribals have alleged that old and useless bullocks were supplied and only after a considerable period of delay.[18] Medical facilities under the ITDA are also very poor.

Table 3.3: Per Capita Expenditure and Total Expenditure during Plan Period in Andhra Pradesh for Schedule Tribes

Plan	*Period*	*Per capita Expenditure in (Rs)*	*Total expenditure Rs in Lakhs*
I	Plan	15.05	118.77
II	Plan	18.89	250.25
III	Plan	13.56	178.77
IV	Plan	59.00	977.77
V	Plan	266.00	4,879.85
VI	Plan	750.47	13,598.00
VII	Plan	1,639.16	30,026.00

Source: Statistical Abstracts of A.P. 1960 and 1983, Bureau of Economics and Statistics. Government of Andhra Pradesh.

Many plans put forward by the government are not relevant to the needs of the tribal areas. Schemes like medium irrigation, small industry, commercial forestry etc. Which often constitute a sizeale portion of the tribal sub-plan are often irrelevant or counter-productive as far as the local tribal economy is concerned.[19]

Control over Forests

There is a symbiotic relationship between tribals and the forest. It has been their home for a long time and provided them with many required resources. The forest conservation and regulation act was passed in 1920.[20] This imposed rules on the tribals, mainly restrictions; on collection of forest produce. This led to conflicts between the tribals and the government. The tribals required wood to build huts and for their ploughshare.

In the post-independence period, forest policy has led to hardship in tribal communities. On the one hand, these communities are not allowed to collect forest produce, but on the other hand large-scale deforestation has occurred because of various developmental projects and extension of cultivation by reclamation of land.[21] Instead of the entire community being consulted about the extraction of forest produce, arrangements are often made between chiefs and contractors bypassing the community, as the forest department was interested mainly in the collection of revenue this alliance was encouraged, leading to destruction of forests. This has also led to increase in wealth of chiefs and their capacity for graft and duplicity.[22]

In the case of Adilabad, notwithstanding various lambadas and regulations to prevent deforestation, a large part of the forests have been, as reported by a fact-finding committee continuously "dereserved" by the Congress Government in 1980 to facilitate private trade. Thus of the 500,000 acres of forest land dereserved in the last years in the state, more than 150,000 acres are from Adilabad. The net result of this policy has been the progressive alienation of the forest from the tribals. Consequently, they have been reduced to the status of daily wage labourers at the mercy of private contractors and forest officials.[23]

Table 3.4 shows the plantation area in Andhra Pradesh in 1983-84.

Table 3.4: Plantation Area up to 1983-84

Species	*Total Areas (in hectares)*	
	Department	*Corporation*
Teak	76,114	---
Eucalyptus	26,271	20.522
Bamboo	28,139	10,138
Cashew	18,949	16,511
Coffee	130	2,438
Red Sander's	1,913	---
Sandal Wood	2,670	---
Silver oak	8,942	---

(Contd.)

(Contd. Table 3.4)

Species	*Total Areas (in hectares)*	
	Department	*Corporation*
Babul	12,415	---
Casurima	13,690	---
Sissoo	1,435	---
Burrara	300	---
Piner	325	---
Other Miscellaneous	55,743	---

Source: A.P. forests at a glance 1983-84 Chief Conservator of Forest A.P. Hyderabad.

Table 3.5: Major Wood-based Industries in Andhra Pradesh

S.No.	*Name of the Company*	*Present installed capacity in T/Yr.*		*Variety*	*Approximate raw material commitment by the forest department in tonnes*
1.	A.P. Paper Mills Rajahmundry East Godavari	Paper	75,000	Bamboo Hardwood	1,10,000 75,000
2.	Sirpur paper mills Kagaz Nagar Adilabad	Do	61,00	Bamboo Hardwood	75,000 45,000
3.	Sree Rayalam Kurnool	Do	42,000	Bamboo Hardwood	45,000 45,000
4.	Badhrachalam Paper Boarder	Do	50,000	Bamboo Hardwood	60,000 74,000
5.	A.P. Rayons Limited Yetura nagaram Warangal	Rayon grade pulp	27,000	Hardwood Eucalyptus	75,000 10,000
6.	Novopars India Limited Patancheru (Ranga Reddy District)	Particle board	20,000	Hardwood	38,000
7.	Hyderabad Plywood Limited	Plywood	0.018 lakhs sq.mts.	Teak teaknon-teak	700 cm. Mts 1,700

Source: A.P. forests at a glance 1983-84, Chief Conservator of Forests A.P. Hyderabad.

It shows that the government of Andhra Pradesh has been concentrated on growing mostly teak, eucalyptus and bamboo, which are needed by the paper industry, and the big timer markets in urban areas. This shows growing commercialisation of forest areas in the state. Table 3.5 gives the major wood industries in the state and the raw material supplied to them by the forest department. Hence, it is not the tribals the industrial class which is benefiting from the forests. The wood from the forests is largely deployed in urban areas and it is the contractors who are profiting from the same. Left activists have claimed that highly placed politician and bureaucrats are also involved in elicit timber trade.

The process of industrialisation in tribal areas has also resulted in the pauperisation of tribals. Many tribals have become property fewer workers after industries were set up and land were acquired from them with minimal compensation. The construction of roads into the tribal areas has hastened this process. The forest guards also exploit the tribals in Adilabad demanding illegal taxes. Data collected during fieldwork shows that in Adilabad they demand Rs 17 to 40 per plough in additional contribution in grain from each household. Atrocities against the tribal population in general have also increased in recent years. Table 3.6 below gives the atrocities reported against Scheduled Tribes between 1979 and 1983. Many more go unreported.

Table 3.6: Atrocities Reported on Schedule Tribes in 1979-1983

State	*No. of Cases Reported During Years*					
	1979	*1980*	*1981*	*1983*	*1983*	
Andhra Pradesh	13	14	29	31	33	
	Atrocities in 1983					
	Murder	Violence	Rape	Arson	Others	Total
Andhra Pradesh	1	8	9	1	14	33

Source: Report of the Commission for Scheduled Castes and Tribes, Sixth Report, April 1983, Chap V: Government of India, New Delhi, 1984.

Thus, we find that in spite of several protective measures, the economic conditions of the tribals has deteriorated and they are also experiencing social alienation, both of which constitute important causal factors in recent tribal movements. This has been due to extensive exploitation of the rich natural resources of their habitat decline of traditional activities without any viable alternative, and consequent marginalisation and exploitation of cheap labour. This has been accompanied by alienation of agricultural land, which is the subject of the next chapter.

References

1. Von furer-Haimendorf. (1977). *The struggle for survival*, Oxford University Press, Delhi, 1982.
2. M.N. Srinivas, *Social change in Modern India*.
3. Von Furer-Haimendorf. N.I. *Ibid*.

4. *Ibid.,* pp. 117-178.

5. B.D. Sharma: *Tribal Development Concept and Frame*, Prachi Prakashan, New Delhi, 1978.

6. Von Furer-Haimendof N.1.p. 175.

7. Andhra Prabha (Telugu Daily Newspaper) 21st July, 1990.

8. The President of the bond wave. Savrakshan Samiti (GSS) – a local organisation – supplied this information in an interview in Adilabad.

9. Von-Furer Haimendorf m. p. 153.

10. Hyderabad Regulation Act 1963, pp. 159, 163.

11. *Ibid.*

12. Fieldwork in the area was done and member of the GSS were interceived. See chapters IV part II.

13. K. Balagopal, "Adilabad Girijan Portaloo" (Telugu) Srujana, 1981, p. 7.

14. Report of the Commission for Schedule Castes and Schedule Tribes Sixth Report April 1983-March 1984. Government of India, New Delhi, 1984.

15. President of G.S.S.

16. E.P.W. September 24, 1983 p.VII, a report.

17. President of G.S.S.

18. Balagopal, Agrarian Classes and Conflicts pp. 71, 74.

19. "A.P. Forest at a Glance" Adilabad Birijan Porataloo" (Telugu) Srujana, 1981, p. 7.

20. This has been reported by among other (i) J. Breman, of Peasants, Migrants and Pampers: rural Labour Circulation in West Asia, Delhi, O.U.P. 1985. (ii) G. Shah, "Ethnicity and Politics: A Study of Scheduled Tribes in Gujarat" (Mins) Surat: Centre for Social Studies, 1978.

21. Ashok Mitra, "Tribal Habitat", Frontier 9, 1977 pp. 24-26.

22. Frontier, Vol. 13, 42, 1981, pp. 6-11.

23. In an interview with Varavara Rao, noted left-leader and Intellectual on 10-11-1991.

4

Gender Inequality and Development: A Study on the Toda of Nilgiri Hills in Anthropological Perspective

Jakka Parthasarathy

Introduction

In modern anthropology, the term 'gender' has increasingly replaced the term 'sex' in discussions of socially and culturally determined differences in the behaviour, role and status of men and women. Charlotte Seymour Smith (1986:129) has aptly remarked that "more recently gender has been used to refer to the social, cultural and psychological patterning of differences between males and females. The distinction between sex, which is biological phenomenon, and gender, which is a cultural classification, allows for the separation of the biological and cultural aspects of differences between males and females, thus avoiding a biological determinist position". Social inequality is a concomitant of human classification according to differential status, power and prestige. Some authors would reserve the term 'stratification' for inequality or ranking in tribal societies. In the so-called patrilineal societies, the gender inequality is based on criteria such as man and woman, division of labour, distribution of status and personal attributes.

The notion of development, in its broadest sense, includes both economic development and the social and cultural changes which accompany it. Thus economic development is the process of transition from one type of economic system to another, implying both economic growth and socio-cultural change. Recent anthropological studies have presented an increasingly critical attitude towards the concept of development.

This paper seeks to examine the gender inequality and its close bearing on the concept of development among the Toda, a primitive tribal group, inhabiting Nilgiri district of Tamil Nadu.

Method of Study

The study was conducted among the Todas, inhabiting in selected nine Toda settlements, among which three settlements are exposed to town, three are located in inaccessible region and other three are identified amidst or nearby non-tribal neighbourhood community in the respected taluks of Udhagamandalam, Kotagiri and Coonoor in the Nilgiri district of Tamil Nadu state. The author of this article is living on the upper plateau of the Nilgiri district, nearby tribal entitlements, since 1984. The events and occurrences among the Todas were observed and considered now while collecting the data and interpretations for this study. Participant observation and case study techniques were used as tools of methodology. The recent data is cross-checked with the adult Todas and their neighbourers. The secondary data was collected based on the indigenous literature on the Todas and the process of hill development. The gender inequality among the Todas was considered on the basis of a few cultural traits found among them.

Area of Study

On the earth, in this world, Todas are found only on the upper plateau of the Nilgiri hills in Tamil Nadu state of India. The present paper is based on the data collected from nine Toda munds (settlements) located in the Nilgiri district. The Nilgiri district, also called as 'The Nilgiri hills', is one of the smallest districts in Tamil Nadu. The district is a hilly area of 2549.0 sq kms located at the junction on the eastern and western ghats. With an average elevation of 6,500 ft, the Nilgiri district is bounded on the west by Kerala, on the north by Karnataka and on the south-east by Coimbatore district. The Nilgiris are characterised by cool climate and upper plateau is covered with unique 'shola' (montane forests) vegetation. Throughout three principal periods-aboriginal, colonial, national independence, the Nilgiri region has constituted a singularly instructive enclave. The district is divided into six taluks and Ooty (Udhagamandalam) town is the headquarters for the district administration. According to 2001 census, the total population of the Nilgiri district is 7,64 lakh out of which the total Scheduled Tribes population is 28373, constituting 4.32 per cent of the total general population. The tribal communities living in the district, namely, Todas, Kotas, lrulas, Kurumbas, Paniyans and Kattunayakans. These tribes are considered as indigenous groups, whereas, non-tribal Badagas, an agricultural dominant community along with other non-tribal groups are considered as migrant groups. On the Nilgiri plateau, Todas, Kotas and Kurumbas are living on the upper plateau; Irulas are living in the middle zone of the hills; Paniyans and Kattunayakans are living at the foothills of the Nilgiris. The details of the studied sample Toda settlements and their population are mentioned in the Table 4.1.

Table 4.1: Details of the Studied Sample Toda Settlements and their Population

Sl.No.	*Name of the Taluk*	*Name of the Toda mund*	*No.of House holds*	*Total Population*		
				Male	*Female*	*Total*
1.	Udhagamandalam	1. Manjakal mund	27	89	73	162
		2. School mund	16	47	41	88
		3. Tarnad mund	19	49	46	95
2.	Kotagiri	4. Bedukkal mund	12	34	31	65
		5. Nerin mund	9	28	24	52
		6. Pankod mund	11	31	29	60
3.	Coonoor	7. Nirkas mund	16	42	46	88
		8. Timod mund	9	31	26	57
		9. Kabirmund	7	16	18	34

The Toda

Todas are known by several names like Tudas, Tudavans, Toras and Todar. The Government of India identified the Toda people as one of the Primitive Tribal Groups of India. The first government census in 1871 revealed the total Toda population in Nilgiri region as 693 persons. In 1971 census their population was 930 persons, now according to 2001 census, the total population of the Toda was 1560 persons. According to Toda Youth Forum census in 2012, the Toda population is 1648 persons. As compared to the sex ratio for overall population (933 females per 1000 males), the sex ratio among the Toda is 908 females per thousand males. Anthony R Walker (1986: 58-59) adds that, "it is not difficult to discover why the Toda community has never been large and why, until recently, it singularly failed to conform to the general pattern of population increase in India. Traditionally, these people practised female infanticide. After a woman had borne one or two daughters, it seems, subsequent females were suffocated at birth by an older woman. The custom was officially prohibited by Sullivan, Collector of Coimbatore, towards the end of 1819, but the disproportionate sex ratio recorded in every census until 1951 suggests that the practice must have continued with some regularity until at least the turn of the century."

The Toda village or hamlet is called a mund, means a herd or a cattle-pen. It is usually a collection of seven to fifteen half barrel shaped huts with a smaller doorway. A typical Toda mund comprises five to ten dwelling huts, one dairy (temple) hut and one buffalo-pen (shelter) along with one calf shed. Toda people are white (fair) in colour, being tall, strong built and well-shaped. The striking feature of the women is the arrangement of their hair which is dressed in ringlets and flows waving down to the shoulders. The traditional garment of a Toda is known as put-kuli, is of thick white cotton cloth with red and blue strips which is embellished further embroidery by the Toda women, is thrown around the body by men and women, worn in a slightly different manner like ancient Greek toga. Jewellery is worn by both men and women. They are lacto-vegetarians.

The Toda community is divided into two endogamous divisions known as Tarthar and Teivali, which are further divided into fourteen exogamous clans. In the past, the Toda followed the fraternal polyandrous form of marriage, a plural marriage, warrants that the husbands who marry a woman are brothers in relationship among themselves. The life cycle rituals are markedly different from other tribes. During the dead body cremation, they sacrifice buffaloes.

The Toda were purely a pastoral people. The Toda women are experts in embroidery work. The Toda tribal council is not a permanent body but only a group of elderly Toda men selected by common consent for a particular dispute. Their concept of religion is associated with the dairy and sacred buffaloes. Toda divinities are called as 'gods of the mountains'. Anthony Walker (1986: 120) found that, "of all deities, the goddess 'Tokisya' is the most important to the Todas. To her is attributed the division of the sacred buffaloes and dairies between the subcastes and clans. Indeed she is believed to be the creator and supporter of the greater part of the social and ritual institutions of the Toda people". A few Todas have embraced to Christianity. Todas speak their own dialect.

Gender Inequality among the Toda

As mentioned earlier, the major social division of Toda society is into two endogamous groups called Tarthar and Teivali. After birth, Toda male or female belongs to one of the two endogamous groups and also a member of an exogamous patriclan and also an exogamous matrilineal clan.

The most striking feature common to two Toda endogamous divisions is the gender relationships to the sacred dairy temple complex, where, the Toda women are not allowed even to go near by the sacred dairy temple and they allowed only to see the rituals conducted by men only from long distance, at least 200 meters. A woman is incorporated by marriage into her husband's patriclan, while retaining some ties with the clan into which she was born. Since infant marriage is a ritual requirement in this society, this incorporation takes place at a very early age. Socialisation of female girls towards gender inequality took place after infant marriage. Traditionally, three tasks everyday are particularly associated with the Toda women: sweeping the hut, pounding the grain and then winnowing, besides rearing children, cooking and doing embroidery work on the cotton shawl. Women must also fetch water from the domestic water supply, cleanse their household utensils and wash clothes when necessary.

Among the Toda the care of buffaloes falls exclusively in the male domain. Culturally the separation of women from the tasks of the herdsman is absolute. The women are not allowed to milk certain of the buffaloes and not allowed even churning the milk to get butter. The ownership of buffaloes is only by men. The religion of the Todas is a highly ritualised buffalo-cult. They have sacred (temple) and ordinary (domestic) buffaloes. Toda ritual life revolves around the operations of their sacred dairies, which are worshipped by Toda men and dairy male priests by offering buffalo milk. Their women are totally kept away from there rituals. Their women are not, even by mistake, should cross or touch the boundary of the dairy temple. The gender inequality are found among the Todas in their traditional practices like polyandry, social paternity, kinship terms, and marital uncertainties like wife-capture, defloration rites etc.

Development of the Nilgiri Hills and the Changing Toda Society

The Nilgiri district has a little history. Its inhospitable climate and highest mountains never attracted the territory invaders, except the bold Toda people who were pastorals. The marginal invasion of the hills by Hindu kings and Muslim rulers led gradually towards British East India Company. In 1822, the British rulers made the upper plateau of the Nilgiri hills, where Todas live, as India's first hill-station. A military cantonment was established and the British soon built a network of roads linking the hills with the plains of Coimbatore, Mysore and Malabar, thus making the high plateau more accessible to lowlanders. A narrow-gauge mountain rack-railway running from plains Mettupalyam to high hill, Ooty was erected. From 1870 to 1937 the old Madras Presidency administration was migrated to the Nilgiris. The settled British administrators discovered the Nilgiri soils and climate for commercial crops. European fruits, vegetables, tea, eucalyptus etc., were introduced. Most of the local inhabitants took up wage-labour on the plantations and labourers from the lowland plains flocked to the hills. The post Independence Tribal Development Programmes by the Government, the centrally sponsored 'Hill Area Development Programme (HADP) and the quick income generative schemes for tribal communities have changed the scenario of tribal areas. Now let us know briefly about Toda community development during British period and after Indian Independence.

British Period

The British dominated Government and an English Missionary Society have promoted welfare programmes for Toda people. The British administration promoted the Toda in the following areas:

1. *Toda Lands*

Toda patta lands were preserved with legal conditions that Toda grazing lands were to be kept within the community for the sake of the Toda themselves and no Toda shall permit any other person except Toda to cultivate or assist in the cultivation of such lands. The concern of the Government was to prevent the alienation of Toda lands and to preserve the shola forest.

2. *Community Leadership*

British ruler appointed a Toda 'headman' to whom he gave the title of monegar, with a reason that lack of a leader among the tradition-conscious Toda society.

3. *Education*

The notion of educating Toda children was moved fairly early in the British period. A school was set up for Toda children near Pykara region.

4. *Social Welfare*

British Government had demanded the cessation of female infanticide and interfered with traditional Toda social institutions. It constituted a Toda welfare committee in the year 1926 with a Toda Amelioration Scheme with four main objectives:

1. To obtain financial assistance for the Toda so that they might be freed from the clutches of money lenders.
2. To provide for the healthcare of the community.
3. To encourage the Toda to abandon such 'detrimental' Social customs on were believed to be abetting their decline in numbers, namely polyandry, the defloration of prepubescent females and the tolerance of sexual promiscuity, and
4. To encourage the Toda to broaden their economic base from pastorals to one of herding and horticulture (Anthony Walker: 1986: 257).

5. *Health*

The Government ordered a special medical survey of the Todas and survey was conducted in 1927, and found that wide spread incidence of venereal disease. It was also found that nearly 20 per cent of the Toda women are sterile and community is suffering with the low state of bestiality.

6. *Agriculture*

Potato cultivation was encouraged on Toda patta lands.

7. *Christian Convection*

The Basel Mission Society had succeeded to convert a few Todas to Christianity.

Post Indian Independence Period

1. *Toda Land Issues*

Todas demanded the Government to assign permanent and unrestricted rights over all their patta lands. In 1956 the Toda registered, The Nilgiri Thothuvar Munnetram Sangam and med this noniety to demand their land rights. Till today their demand of legal rights on their lands is continuing.

2. *Agriculture*

Todas established themselves as potato farmers and vegetables cultivators, besides grower of fodder crops. They realised the economic advantage to be had from farming their land for themselves.

3. *Animal Husbandry*

Being a traditional breeders of buffaloes, Todas are well-adapted to rear more buffaloes and started selling milk to milk collection centres.

4. *Health, Education and Social Welfare*

Government introduced mobile medical unit in Toda habitat. A special 'Toda ward' was established in Government Hospital. The Servants of India Society started a school and government schools are started admitting Toda children. First time in the year 1985, government officials attention was received on Toda women's welfare and housing. All India Handicrafts Board had encourages Toda women to Traditional Toda embroidery work.

5. *Toda Women Self-help Groups*

Women self-help groups are formed among the Todas and began to work since 2006 with the help of loans provided only to women members. This helped Toda women empowerment in the Nilgiri hills.

Impact of Development on Gender Inequality

The development of the Nilgiri hills and tribal development programmes made dent in creating awareness among the Toda men and women towards modern life and the taste of mainstream life styles. Though men are concentrated on the buffalo economy and agriculture, but women totally accepted the value of education. A Toda woman in 1994 has become a first graduate among the Todas. The women, being expects in embroidery, nowadays they also started embroider other items for sale, such as table cloths, placemats, bedcovers and also cell phone cover, mini bags with their traditional designs of embroidery. Some women also visit neighbouring hamlets and others accompany their husbands to market. Some anthropologists even remarked that 'the tender fingers of women engaged in embroidery work and the strong hands of men that milked the buffaloes have now turned rough due to the handling of digging forks and agricultural implements for cultivation. As mentioned elsewhere (Rivers: 1906; Parthasarathy: 2008) the traditional outlook of the Toda men and rigid following of cultural inequality of gender issues, led the modern Toda women feel social pinch when they were excluded during the rituals of life-cycle ceremonies and the religious practices at sacred dairy temples. Even today most of the Toda women hate the age old practice of wife-capture and other cultural practices. The Toda women today still remember, often, their great grandmother's petition, during the year 1910, to the government to give them means to legalise their marriages and their petition concluded, you have protected our buffaloes, will you not protect us women? (Ling: 1910: 14-15). In the year 2011, a few women tried to give the petition on the same lines to the collector of Nilgiris, who was a woman of IAS cadre. The study concludes that primitive belief system, division of work, Indigenous ethnography, kinship terms, existence of sacred buffaloes, bow and arrow ceremony, social paternity etc., are the major causes for the existence of gender inequality in Toda modern society.

Acknowledgement

The author is thankful to Dr KM Metry, Professor and Head, Department of Tribal Studies, Kannada University, Hampi (Karnataka) for his encouragement to write this paper.

References

1. Ling, Catherine F., 1910, Dawn in Toda Land: A Narrative of Missionary effort on the Nilgiri hills, South India, London, Morgan and Scott.
2. Parthasarathy, Jakka, 2008, The Toda of the Nilgiri District, Tamil Nadu: A Study of a Pastoral Tribe and Development, TRC-HADP, Govt of India, Ooty.
3. Rivers, W.H.R, 1906, The Todas, Macmillan and Co. London.
4. Seymour-Smith Charlotte, 1986, Macmillan Dictionary of Anthropology, Macmillan Reference Books, London.
5. Walker, Anthony 1986, The Toda of South India: A new look, Hindustan Publishing Corporation, Delhi.

5

Tribal Development and Insurgency Movement in Tripura

Harsha S and *Antibum Ranglong*

Abstract

Tribal Development in Tripura could not be studied without insurgency movement. Since partition of India badly affected the tiny state, there was uprising from the tribal section. Insurgency movement started with the objective of liberation and sending back the immigrant. On one side, tribal were represented as having link with Christian missionaries. However, the government, both center and state, takes various measures to counter-balance the political situation. But, tribals in Tripura are still the most backward (socially, culturally and economically), as compared to other north-east tribals. The paper discusses the practical situation.

Key words: Development, Insurgency, Autonomy, Decentralisation.

Introduction

After the merger in the Indian Union on 15th October, 1949, the demographic setting of Tripura was totally changed. Tribal becomes a minority in their own land due to huge influx of Bengalis from neighbouring Bangladesh (former East Pakistan). 'Tripura is the only state in the north-east which has been transformed in the recent past from a predominantly tribal to a predominantly non-tribal state due to the massive influx of Hindu-Bengali migrants from Bangladesh.'[1] Tribals who once live a happy life with forest base resources were alienated in their home land. In fact, much has been discussed by various social scientists on the socio-economic and political history of Tripura.

Tribal development in Tripura has a long history like many other states in North-East India. In the name of tribal development and tribal liberation, different groups of insurgency outfits crop up. There were continuous demands for more power and responsibility to tribals. So, for looking after the interests of the tribal communities of Tripura, the Government of Tripura decided to set up an Autonomous District Council to introduce internal autonomy in tribal compact areas and thereby protecting the socio-economic and cultural interests of the Tribal population in Tripura. Accordingly, the Tripura Tribal Autonomous District Council Bill was unanimously passed by the Tripura Legislative Assembly on March 23, 1979.

Autonomous District Council and Tribal Development

As stated earlier, the Tripura Tribal Areas Autonomous District Council (TTAADC) was established as an independent district council, administering the tribal areas within the State after a series of democratic movements launched by the tribal people of Tripura. Following the 49th amendment of the Constitution of India, TTAADC was brought under the provisions of the Sixth Schedule of the Constitution with effect from 1st April, 1985.

Despite the Council's impressive principles to uplift the indigenous tribals in Tripura, it still remains a topic of criticism. 'Though under the Sixth Schedule, the TTAADC is also the custodian of and entrusted the task of preservation of the society and culture of indigenous people within its territorial jurisdiction, customary laws have not been codified. There is a large gap between the approved budget and the flow of funds from the state government to the Council, which undermines both planning and execution.'[2]

Unlike, District Council in other part of North-East India, TTAADC is unique, as its jurisdiction is not contiguous with revenue district boundaries. It straddles four revenue districts (recently, another four new districts were formed). It is a large body and covers an area of 7132.56 sq. km (67.98 per cent of the geographical area of the state), extending to all four Revenue Districts of the State.[3] Thus, there is constant criticism that no clear role is assigned to the TTAADC, which is a multi-district body, in the decentralised planning process. Moreover, 'the state government releases share of taxes and Plan Grant in installments. Most of the resources of the council are incurred for the payment of salary and allowances of the staff. Little fund is left for utilisation in development programmes.'[4]

As a consequent, demands for more power to the Council are raised from different angle. A delegation of the Congress and Indigenous Nationalist Party of Tripura (INPT) met Union Home Secretary Sambhu Singh on 31st January, 2014.[5] The delegation pressed to table a bill providing for allowing more power to TTAADC. To express their dissatisfaction, the INPT held a five hours long sit-in-demonstration at the Vivekananda Maidan, Agartala, on 15th February, 2014, to seek more power for TTAADC.[6] So, it is suggested that TTADC should be more empowered because development is not possible without more autonomy and financial empowerment.

Education and Tribal Development

Ignorance and illiteracy among the tribals are the basic problems to development in any part of our country. The case is same to Tripura. However, the '*Times of India*' (a reputed national dailies), published on 8th Sept., 2013, sketch out that, 'India's northeastern state of Tripura achieved the first position in literacy with 94.65 per cent, beating Kerala (93.91 per cent), Tripura Chief Minister Manik Sarkar, announced here on Sunday. Sarkar said at a function on the occasion of International Literacy Day that Tripura jumped to first position among the states of the country in literacy from the 12th position in the 2001 census and the fourth position in the 2011 census. Sarkar further said that after Tripura attained 87.75 per cent literacy in the 2011 census, a government survey was conducted by the eight district magistrates in August 2012, which found that only 131,634 people of the state's 3.7 million people, including those aged 50 and above were illiterate.'[7]

It is a matter of pride for the people of Tripura to be on top of the country in literacy. But practical experience shows that tribals in Tripura are still far behind in gaining access to proper education. As per the provision of the Sixth Schedule to the Constitution of India, primary schools were handed to TTAADC. Maximum of the primary schools administered by TTAADC are functioning with staff recruited through Sarva Siksha Abhiyan (SSA). They have little interest in the job with meagre salary. Classes end up within one hour or two.

Besides, the tribal in general preferred English Medium of instruction than Bengali. Thus, maximum of the rural tribals go to expensive private English Medium School for their education. Those parents who could not effort their children to send to such schools ultimately become the victims. It can be said that majority of the educated rural tribals in Tripura, are the product of Private English Medium Schools run by various Christian congregation.

So, it is suggested that the task should not end up in establishing maximum schools in tribal belt. Does it practically function is the point to be noted. If the rural tribals are more in favour of English Medium, the government should take necessary steps, as it has already started. The literacy may reach the climax, but if quality education does not reach the tribals, it will have little impact on tribal development.

Insurgency and Tribal Development

Tripura used to be one of the worst insurgency affected state in North-East India. Unprecedented influx of Bengali refugees created a sense of insecurity among the tribals. Tribals feel that development process among them retarded severely. Feeling of insecurity led to aggressive reaction from the tribals which ultimately create insurgency movement. First organised-armed tribal movement was known as *Sengkrak* (clenched fist) which manifested itself in mid-sixties. This movement was started as a reaction against settling down of non-tribal refugees in the Tribal Reserve Forest Areas. A Sengkrak activist launched a large number of violent attacks but was however, controlled in 1968.

Again, B.K. Hrangkhawl, a young tribal leader of Tripura Upajati Juba Samity (TUJS), a regional party for the tribal, formed an underground organisation styled as Tripura National Volunteers (TNV) on 10th November, 1978 with a design to conduct insurgent activities in collaboration with the Mizo National Front (MNF) of Mizoram. He was arrested in June, 1980 and was imprisoned. On his released from jail, in Dec. 1980, he announced dissolution of TNV. However, on 10th Nov. 1982, TNV was revived again with B.K. Hrangkhawl as its President. But on 12th December 1988 a Tripartite Accord was signed by the Government of India, Government of Tripura and the TNV. B.K. Hrangkhawl and his party surrendered before the government with arms and ammunitions.[8]

After the formal end of TNV insurgency movement, a series of groups came into existence. There were several split and reunion among them. Mention may be made, like Army of Tripura People Liberation Organisation (ATPLO) Tripura Resurrection Army (TRA), Tripura National Liberation Front (TNLF), Tripura Tribal Volunteer Force (TTVF), All Tripura Volunteer Force (ATVF), Tripura Tribal Democratic Force (TTDF), All Tripura Volunteer Association (ATVA), Tripura Tribal Action Committee Force (TTACF), Liberation of Tripura Tribal Force (LTTF), Tripura National Sengkrak Force (TNSF) etc. Most of these groups have ceased to operate and were non-active during their existence.[9]

The last phase of insurgency in Tripura started from1989. It is dominated mainly by two groups, namely, National Liberation Front of Tripura (NLFT) and All Tripura Tiger Force (ATTF). Both the groups are armed with sophisticated weapons, well trained and have links with other North-Eastern insurgent groups. The Government of India has declared both these groups as unlawful, under the Unlawful Activities (Prevention) Act, 1967, on the proposal of the State Government. Whereas, the main objective of the NLFT is to establish an Independent Tripura through an armed struggle, ATTF on the other hand, were expulsion of all foreigners who entered Tripura after 1956, restoration of land to tribal under Tripura Land Revenue and Land Reforms Act, 1960, and removal of names of migrants who entered Tripura after 1956 from electoral roll.

Now, the question is whether insurgency movement in reality helps the tribals in fulfilling their demands and objectives. Ideally speaking, in case of Tripura, establishing and Independent Tripura is a utopia. Besides, removal of all foreigners who entered Tripura after 1956 is simply a vision that cannot be achieved. But, to a certain extent tribal insurgency in Tripura have succeeded in making the government focus its attention on the development of tribal areas and in improving the conditions of the tribals.

Thus, 'in pursuance of looking after the communities of Tripura, the Parliament in 1960 passed, *'The Tripura Land Revenue and Land Reforms Act,'* under Articles 186 of the said Act. It was further amended in 1974 by laying more rigorous conditions in respect of transference of holdings. It laid down that if any tribal community desire to sell his land, the first offer shall have to be made to his co-sharer and failing that, the offer may be made to the adjoining tribal land-holders. In the absence of any such tribal, the offer shall have to be made to any landless Scheduled Tribes living in that area.' Besides, the establishment of TTAADC can also be regarded as a government mechanism to fulfill the aspiration of the tribals. It was in fact, created as a result of continuous demands from all sections of the Tripura tribals. Insurgency movement in this sense has been very beneficial to tribals and gave relief to some of their problems. However, it is not desirable to encourage this sort of movement for any types of demands, since political disorder can be resolve through negotiation and compromise.

Often, causes of existence of insurgency in North-East India are usually made associated with unemployment and lack of exposure among the tribal youth. But, causes can be different with places. Tripura is relatively different with rest of the north-east region. Exploitation and assimilation is so extreme, that the well aware tribal youth would not find alternative, at one point of time, than going for armed struggle. But, the government of Tripura under the rule of Communist Party of India Marxist CPI (M) has considerably counterbalanced the insurgency activities. Jobs, employment and assistance were given to the surrendered insurgent based on their skill and talent. Nevertheless, this might not be the end of insurgency in Tripura. There is a rumour about fresh reorganisation of tribal youth. The government should be aware of all the cause and effect relationship.

Linkages between Insurgency and Christianity

In this connection, it is unfortunate to mention that some writings were available on tribal insurgency in Tripura, which make direct link between religion and insurgency. They claim that the 'Christian Missionaries with the help of underground Mizo evangelical teachers of Baptist Missions exploited this growing unrest and converted some of the boys and girls with a move to politicise their culture and make them indifferent from the mainstream of national life.'[10] 'All the top leaders of insurgency initiated either by Army of Tripura People Liberation Organisation (ATPLO) or Tripura National Volunteers (TNV), in Tripura is committed to Christianity.'[11] They further claim that the 'insurgents ranks included a large number of young boys and girls who had been converted to Christianity, although, they were of Hindu parenthood, by underground Mizo rebels working in Baptist missions as evangelical teachers.'

To disagree with, the fact is that, tribal Hindu tradition is not alike with that of Bengali system, at least in Tripura. The Hindu tradition among the tribals in Tripura is so primitive that, once a person converts to Christianity, he/she got enlightenment (to have knowledge of the surrounding), and becomes aware of the entire practical scenario. Being assimilated, exploited and alienated, one cannot remain a spectator and overlook the ground political situation. So, many young Christian boys used to join the insurgency outfits. But, in case of Tripura, religion is not the criteria for recruitment and in fact, the outfits comprised both the tribal Hindu and Christians. Besides, the Christian Missionary never and ever politicised the situation but rather give sermons to discontinue insurgency movement and go suit with the law of the land.

Conclusion

Tribal development in Tripura has yet to take its shape. Majority of the tribals lived in rural areas. The benefits of development have remained concentrated in the western segment of the State, thus, leaving out huge areas in eastern parts largely inhabited by Scheduled Tribes far behind, in respect of various amenities.

The ignorance of tribals has given advantage to flourish trade and business by non-tribals who hold the reins of economic and political powers in the tribal areas and functioning of the government machinery. Directly or indirectly, they have huge control over the lands and resources of the tribals. Tribals being inseparably bonded to land and forest, face serious problems with non-tribals in regaining their control over their lands.

Non-tribals dominate the government machinery in the tribal areas. They often feel envious about the various welfare programmes designed for tribals, and try to get into an exploitative relationship with the local traders, contractors. This results in few benefits actually reaching the tribals. While tribals revere the natural resources as life sustaining forces, the non-tribal's outlook is of short term commercial exploitation. This disregard for tribal-nature symbiosis is causing not only a threat to tribal survival but is also leading to depletion of resources in the tribal areas.

The government has to recognise that the tribal people have a distinct socio-cultural life and the administration has to understand and respect these systems while designing and implementing development programmes. Programmes should be sympathetic to tribal needs, addressing the real issues and conflicts. It should be emphasised, that the machinery should work without social and political bias toward tribal communities. The state government should also follow a people-friendly and sympathetic development policy with programmes and projects planned in the tribal areas. It should first consider the social and economic progress of the local communities.

In conclusion, it is a fact that, unless decentralisation and empowerment to tribals are engendered, development activities could not be speedy. To address this problem, government of India has enacted Sixth Schedule (establishment of Autonomous District Council) for the tribals in north-east India. Autonomous Council is an important mechanism for empowering the tribals to administer themselves and to preserve their culture and tradition.

So, instead of charging the tribals as troublemaker, lawbreaker and with all sort of insurgency activities, they should be rather empowered with a democratic norm of decentralisation and self-rule.

References

1. Subramaniam, K.S. (2000). Tribal Insurgency and Rural Development in Tripura. *Economic and Political Weekly,* Vol. 35, No. (8/9), pp. 601-602.
2. Report of the Expert Committees, on *'Planning for the Sixth Schedule Areas,'* Sept. 2006, New Delhi: Ministry of Panchayat Raj, Govt. of India, p. 63.
3. An Official Website of TTAADC contains basic link of Council's related information, (http://www.ttaadc.nic.in).
4. Report of the Expert Committees, *ibid.* p. 63.
5. A Statement Published in the Website, http: // www.*tripurainfo.com* , dated: 1st February, 2014.
6. *Ibid.*, Dated: 15th February, 2014.
7. A Statement Published in the *'Times of India,'* Dated: 8th Sept. 2013.
8. Upadhya, R. (2005). Tripura Bleeds: In the Crossfire of Mainstream Political Parties and Virulent Ethnic Conflict. *South Asia Analysis Groups,* 15th Nov. No. 1613.
9. Information obtained from the insurgency section of the website http://www.tripurapolice.nic.in.
10. Tripura Land Revenue and Land Reforms Act, 1960. No. 43, Government of Tripura.
11. Upadhya, R. (2005). *Ibid.* 15th Nov. No. 1613.
12. Bhattacharjee, S.R. (1989). *Tribal Insurgency in Tripura*, New Delhi: Inter India Publication, p. 151.
13. *Ibid.*, p. 152.

6

Voice of Tribals through RTI Act, in Contemporary Democracy: A Case Study of Odisha

Akshaya Kumar Nayak

India is having a largest democracy with a model federal structure and a truly pluralistic society, which promises to provide social justice to the common men since independence. In this era of liberalisation, privatisation and globalisation, India has emphasised on participatory, decentralised and sustainable development for all. At the same time the greatest challenge before India is to provide social justice to the Scheduled Castes and Scheduled Tribes people by ameliorating their socio-economic and educational conditions. Not only the scheduled tribal, scheduled castes and denotified tribes constitute the weakest section of India's population, from the ecological, economic and educational angles. But also, they constitute the matrix of India's poverty. Though the tribals are the sons of the same soil, and the citizens of the same country, but they have been subjected to the worst type of socio-economic and political exploitation, and living away from the modern and civilised society. There are about two hundred million tribal people in the entire globe. According to 1981 census, the scheduled tribe population in the country was 5.16 crore, consisting of 7.76 per cent of total Indian population which means one tribesman for every 13 Indians. There are about 428 scheduled tribe communities in India speaking 106 languages in 19 states and six union territories. About 50 per cent of the tribal population of the country is concentrated in Madhya Pradesh Chhatisgarh, Jharkhand, Bihar and Odisha.

Odisha is regarded as the homeland of Tribals. It has a Tribal population of 81,45,081 (as per 2011 census) accounting 22 per cent of the total population of the state and 9.7 per cent of the total population of the country. Malkanagiri is having highest number of STs—57.4 per cent. Followed by Mayurbhanj—56.6 per cent, Rayagada—55.8 per cent and Nabarangpur—55 per cent. Out of 62 STs in Odisha, '*Khond*' is the most populous followed by *Gond, Santal, Kolha, Munda, Saora, Shabar, Bhottada, Bhumij, Bhuiya, Oraon, Paraja* and *Kissan*.

The tribal people of Odisha live in cloistered, exclusive, remote and inhospitable areas such as hills and forests. Their livelihood is based on primitive agriculture, a low value closed economy with a low level of technology that leads to their poverty. They have low level of literacy and health. But, they developed their own distinctive culture, language and religion, who have a marginal degree of contact with other cultures and people. Most of the STs of Odisha have adopted either Hinduism or Christianity.

But, the Tribals of Odisha are confronted with a number of problems like:

- Food insecurity,
- Low level literacy (poor education),
- Poor health-care facilities and prone to fatal diseases,
- Poor communication facilities,
- Language a stumbling barrier,
- Loss of habitation (Loss of land rights)
- Poor employment opportunities and low-level income
- Displacement and migration due to mines and development projects,
- Growing extremism,
- Lack of awareness,
- Huge distance from modern urban life,
- Poor agricultural and irrigation facility,
- Increasing Ethnic Tension in tribal areas,
- Forcible conversion of religion,
- Exploitation by the rich Non-Tribals,
- Land grabbing by the Non-Tribals,
- Replication of tribal traditional/Indigenous arts and craft design by non-tribal multi-nationals,
- Administrative apathy and carelessness of the administration,
- Corruption among the politician and officials,

Since independence both the Government of India and Government of Odisha have formulated many plans programmes, projects and set up many commissions to uplift the tribals from the bottom of our social fabric.

They are:

1. The Social Welfare Team of the Committee on Plan Projects 1959.
2. The Verrier Elwin Committee on Tribal Development.
3. The Committee on Tribal Economy in Forest Arear–1967.
4. The Scheduled Areas and Scheduled Tribal Commission (Dhebar Committee 1961).
5. The Special Working Group on Co-operative and for Backward Classes 1961.

6. The Task Force on Development of Tribal Areas 1972.

7. The Dube Committee 1972.

8. The Study Team on Co-operative Structure in Tribal Development Project Areas1976.

9. The Study Group on Relief of Indebtedness Land Alienation and Restoration in Development Agency Area 1973.

10. The Team of Marketing, Credit and Co-operation in Tribal Areas 1978.

11. The Working Group on Development of Scheduled Tribes during the 7th Five Year Plan (1985-1990).

On the other hand, the Government of Odisha has created 21 Integrated Tribal Development Agencies (ITDAS), covering 118 Tribal Development Blocks; 46 Modified Area Development Agencies (MADA) in 47 Blocks; Disbursed Tribal Development Agencies (DTDA). Apart from this, there is Departments of ST and SC to monitor the Tribal Development works. The Government of Odisha become the best state in India in distributing Patta both for the individual and community claims in settling land rights of the Tribals under the Forest Rights Act. It has decided to open 1000 hostels for ST boys and girls; to provide pre-matric scholarship; to provide two pairs of school uniforms from class-1 to VIII; Free bi-cycle to ST boys and girls; Free Coaching for ST students of Higher Secondary Level; to provide capacity building training; to set up project management unit (PMU).

But, there is huge gape between the theory and practice. Still the tribals are considered as Tribabls of the remote dark world. In most of the cases the clouds of development passes over them without a little drop of rain. Because the tribals are the illiterate and what they need is 'Awareness' through proper education.

At this juncture the best weapon to protect the Tribal Rights is——'The Right to Information Act (RTI Act) of 2005', which is a milestone in the history of India. By using this Act the poor, and the vulnerable Tribals will understand their rights, and every unit of National and state level developmental plans and projects. They can ask the officials from the Panchayat to the state and the National Government, about the developmental programmes and check exploitation from top to bottom. The voice of Tribals can be raised in Indian democracy by using RTI Act. The best example is the RTI clinics set up in the Kalahandi district of Odisha, which have enabled the poor and the marginalised communities to demand and protect their entitlements. It was possible under the joint venture of UNDP and the ministry of Law and Justice, Government of India.

So, the RTI Act can protect the tribals from the nasty politicians, corrupt officials and the fraud NGOs. It can bring them to the mainstream of modern civilisation with participatory and contemporary democracy.

7

Determinants of Students Dropout in Indian Higher Education

Bharat Chandra Rout

Background

Students in higher education undergo various processes of institutional/ societal and personal interactions when they progress through education. Student behaviour that is related to their retention therefore requires theoretical constructs that encapsulate the multiplicity of institutional, personal/familial and interactional factors emerging from the environment of student participation in higher education. Many national and international studies on student retention are based on the empirical enquiry of problems of student drop-out and attrition—very often looking various possible factors that impact student retention. On the basis of findings they come out with their own theoretical constructs. For instance, Tinto's theory of individual departure [Tinto, 1975, 1987, 1993] in which Tinto has developed a longitudinal interactionist model of student departure which has been widely accepted by the research community on the basis from which to work. Similarly, Rong C. [2008] studies the impact of financial aid on students' decision to dropout from higher education and on the basis of which the author provides an analytical and theoretical framework to study student retention. Probably one of the benchmark work on student departure is done by Durkheim [1951] in his theory of suicide and student departure, in which he argues, the individual persistence in, and drop out from institution of higher education can be viewed as arising out of a longitudinal process of interactions between an individual and with the given attributes, skills, prior educational experiences, dispositions and academic and social systems of the institution [Durkheim, 1951, cited in Tinto, 1987].

Thomas [2002] makes a clear distinction among various conditions that enable students to continue in higher education and absence of which presumably hurdle students to continue and complete a higher education degree. They are academic preparedness [i.e., the extent to which students feel they are ready to study for higher education], academic experiences [i.e. curricula, teaching-learning issues, relationships with staffs and students etc.], institutional expectation and commitment [i.e., the expectation that student had about higher education and the extent to which they thought the institution they were attending would realise their goals], academic and social match [i.e., the extent to which students felt they fitted in at their institution and this included both academic, social and cultural inclusiveness], finance and employment [i.e., this is the way financial issues influence student decision to continue or leave higher education], family support and commitment, university support services etc.

Existing Literature on Student Dropout

Most of the research studies conducted in India on student retention/ dropout have focussed on the contribution/influence of socio-economic factors and institutional/academic factors on student persistent in higher education. Some notable studies are reviewed below.

Socio-economic Characteristics

Several studies have reported a low rate of completion and a high rate of failure in examinations and low standards of achievement have marred the efficiency of the Indian education system. Further studies found that just about 50 per cent out of the total enrolled in a given year get their degree [Singh, 1981; Rawat 1970; UNESCO, 1965]. Singh and Sharma [1981] observed that for every ten students joining in the colleges, not more than five are likely to get their degree. They emphasised that the stagnation and wastage is so prevalent that everyone comes to accept it as a fact of life. In a similar account Rawat [1970] found that any hundred college freshmen entering the first year of college, the likelihood of completing the degree is 41 per cent. Phadke [1980] and Ahuja [1980] study the drop out behaviour of ST college students in rural regional/local colleges. They found the college wastage is strongly associated with tribal culture and life style, the way they have been told about education and more significantly the factors that barrier their mainstreaming.

Kamat and Deshmukh (1963), studied the students of Fergusson College of Poona University and found that more female than male students' dropout and that the number of married students in both the sexes is very small. Studying the socio-economic background of the regular students he found that more than 50 per cent of male students and more than 70 per cent of women students belong to high socio-economic status. In relation to the previous level of education and merit, 66 per cent drop out was among the students who scored less than 50 per cent marks, 42 per cent drop out was among the students who scored between 50 and 55 per cent and 28 per cent dropout among those who scored more than 55 per cent in S.S.C. This study also shows that dropout increases with the advance in age in entry, the type of school from which the student comes. Bean (1979) in his study found that male and female students leave HE for different reasons. One of the important reasons for droppingout was dissatisfaction with the course. Educational quality, as well as usefulness of education for getting a job, was also related to be significant variables. He also found that the opportunity available for transferring to another course college was another important reason.

The findings from the studies by Sewell and Shah [1967], Sharma [1972], Khan and Singh [1978], Reddy [1971], Jackson [1978] and Astin [1964] more or less in a similar account suggest that socio-economic background has tremendous influence on intelligence level, planning for and completion of Higher Education. Reddy (1971) found that children whose fathers were engaged in manual work or had blue collar job were less adjusted than children whose parents were in good business or professions like teaching, medicine and engineering.

Institutional [Academic] and Attitudinal Aspect

First, there are several studies who have revealed that dropout is a phenomenon of and resulting from student institution interactions. They argued that students who dropout from HE are students who have a negative attitude towards their institution, poor attendance and low achievement and faces non-congenial atmosphere in institution [Turkel and Abramson, 1986, Chitnis, 1972]. For instance, Chitnis (1981) studied the dropouts and situation of the SC students in Bombay and found that the negative attitude of the other students towards them and non-conjugal atmosphere at college were the main reasons for them to dropout of HE. Malik (1984) studied the university students attitude towards HE and found that age, sex, rural urban area, parental level of education play important role in influencing the attitude. She found that there is a positive correlation between age and attitude. The first generation learner had a more positive attitude towards HE then the second generation learner. Yet, other researches reveal that lack of personality adjustment, lack of motivation, emotional problem, inconsistencies etc., are reasons for student dropout from HE [Malik 1984; Grace 1957; Edelbrock 1975; Maxwell 1960; Astin 1964; Bayer 1968; McCloy 1980]. Kumar (1980) demonstrated that the students having lower academic performance appear to have more personal problems.

Moreover, social and academic integration of student, prior academic preparedness, minimising social distance, collaborative and inclusive teaching-learning strategies etc., have significant direct effects on classroom participation, meaningful interaction and eventually on the examination grade of students [Smith and Naylor 2001; Donovan 1984; Thomas 2002]. Mathews (1957) and others found that the greatest cause of academic failure was lack of interest including meaninglessness of course of studies. Moreover, Forster [1959], Schonell [1962, 1965] found that students' performance was influenced by their adaptability, maturity, self-discipline, intrinsic motivation, pupil-teacher relationship, motivation by parents, and personal qualities of persistence and toughness. Blanchfield (1971), Bragg (1956) and Yoshino (1964) studied the educational background of dropout and non-dropouts and found that the dropout had relatively low of educational background as compared to the non-dropouts. Maxwell (1960), Astin (1964), Bayer (1968) and Edelbrock (1975) studied the personality characteristics of the dropouts and they were of the view that dropouts were low adjusted, had more personal and emotional problems than the non-dropouts.

Research studies on student dropout that are briefly reviewed above clearly brought out two significant dimensions. First, a good number of studies and their findings agreed upon the fact that socio-economic characteristics of students significantly influence their prospects of continuing/droppingout from higher education. Student age, gender, nativity, socio-religious background, parental education and occupation and family income, etc., have tremendous influence on students' decision to continue/withdraw from studies. Second, several other research studies explored various academic/institutional and attitudinal factors which are strongly associated with student decision to complete higher education.

Our results on student dropout in higher education in India are based on data from one important sources. First, by using 64th round of NSS data [2007-08], we provide an estimate of the factors that are significantly affecting student continuation in higher education at all India level. These data give results for five to 29 years who had enrolled sometime but currently not attending [completed] higher education, and is done for both rural and urban samples separately.

The paper is divided into three sections. Section A specifies the logistic regression models by defining the data sources, variables and their definitions. Section B deals with the estimates and results of the determinants of students who could not complete higher education [estimates from 64th round of NSSO]. The final section of the paper discusses the findings and concludes the paper.

SECTION—A

Specification of the Models: Data, Variable and their Definitions

Studies on student dropout have used various methods of analysis. For example, many studies have done discriminate analysis (Chapman and Hutcheson 1982; Stork and Berger 1978; Terenzini and Pascarella 1977), multiple regression (Aitken 1982; Bean 1980; Kohen Nestel and Karmas 1978; Lunneborg and Lunneborg 1973; Munro 1981; Peng and Fetters 1978; Terenzini and Pascarella, 1978), probit analysis (Rumberger 1983), chi-square analysis (Leob and Duff 1974) and simple tabulations (Naylor and Sanford 1982). However, when the dependent variable is qualitative and dichotomous, for instance in a 'yes' or 'no' format logistic regression is an ideal choice of analysis.

One of the significant objectives of this research is to identify the factors responsible for student dropout in higher education. In this paper, logistic regression models for qualitative dependent variables are run to know the determinants of students' dropout from higher education. Logit analysis can be used to determine which independent variables and interactions are required to describe student dropout behaviour. Logit analysis also enables one to develop predicted probabilities of dropping out for each combination of the independent variables (Ott Mary *et al.* 1984). Qualitative response regression model refers to models in which the response or regress and variable is not quantitative or an interval scale. A logistic model provides the probability or likelihood of happenings (changes) in dependent variable by the influence of independent/explanatory variables. The model gives odds ratio which is explained as the ratio of the probability of success to the probably of failure. In addition to the odds ratio, I shall present the corresponding 'Marginal Effects' in order to assess the magnitude of impact of explanatory variable.

For example,

If, Pi = the probability of a student securing sixty per cent marks in 12th, (probability of success), and 1 – Pi = the probability of not securing sixty per cent in 12th (probability of failure).

Thus, odds ratio in the logit model = (Pi/1–Pi)

A ratio of the probability in favour of securing 60 per cent in grade 12 to the ratio of not securing 60 per cent in grade 12.

Model 1: Determinants of Students who could not Complete Higher Education [NSS 64th Round]

Data Sources, Variables and their Definitions

The data source for logistic model 1 is National Sample Survey's 64th Round 'Participation and Expenditure in Education' survey (July 2007 to June 2008). The survey covers the whole of Indian Union except Ladakh, Kargil, interior villages of Nagaland and villages in Andaman and Nicobar Islands which remain inaccessible throughout the year. By adopting a stratified multi-stage sampling technique the survey covers 12688 First Stage Units (FSUs) for central sample and 13624 FSUs for state sample. FSUs are census villages/ wards in the rural sector and blocks in the urban sector as per the 2001 census.

For the purpose of present analysis sample students were identified who have had enrolled sometimes in a degree in higher education but did not complete (some have completed) their degree. For this purpose enrollment in grade 13 and above years of education (enrolment in graduate, post-graduate and above degree) are considered as by that year of education it is ideally considered to be higher education.

Dependent Variable: Whether Completed Higher Education [Yes= 0, No= 1]

Independent Variables: Sex, types of institution last attended, marital status, religious background, social background, hectares of land possessed by household, types of education, reasons for droppingout/discontinuing studies, monthly per capita household consumption expenditure (MPCE), Household type etc. Appendix 1 reports detailed percentage tables of independent variables in relation to the dependent variable.

Table 7.1: Definition of Key Variables used in the Model

Variables	*Definitions*
Sex	Dummy variable that takes the value of one in case of male and zero for female
Types of Institution last attended	A dummy variable that takes the value of one if the students' last attended institution is government and zero
Marital Status: Never married, currently married and widowed/ separated/divorced	Each is a dummy variable that takes the value of one for each marital status and zero otherwise.
Religion: Hinduism, Islam and non-Hindu/Islam-'Others'	Each is a dummy variable that takes the value of one for each category of religion and zero otherwise.
Social Category: SC, ST, OBC and non-SC/ST/OBC Others	Each is a dummy variable that takes the value of one for each social category and zero otherwise.
Land possessed by Household (in hectares): < 0.005, 0.005 to 0.01, 0.02 to 0.40, 0.41 to 1.00, 1.01 to 8.00	Each is a dummy variable that takes the value of one for each interval of land possessed and zero otherwise.
Types of Education: General, Professional/technical and Vocational	Each is a dummy variable that takes the value of one for each types of education and zero otherwise.
Reasons for droppingout/ discontinuing.	Each reason is a dummy variable that takes the value of one for that particular reason and zero all else
MPCE Quartile: Below 20 per cent, 20-40 per cent, 40-60 per cent, 60-80 per cent, 80-100 per cent	Each of these expenditure quartiles are dummy variables that takes the value of one for each quartile and zero all else
Household Type: *Rural*- self-employed in non-agri., agri. Labour, other labour, self-employed in agri. *Urban*- Self-employed, causal labour, other labour	Each of these household type is dummy variable that takes the value of one if the household belong to that particular type and zero all else.

SECTION-B

Empirical Results

Tables 7.3 and 7.4 present empirical results of two logistic regression models on the basis of coefficients and corresponding marginal effects for both rural and urban India separately. The type of institution last attended (i.e., govt./private) is found to be only significant for the urban sample. The results indicate that a student whose last attended institution is government is more likely to complete higher education *vis-a-vis* a student whose last institution is private in urban India. An additional student whose last attended institution is government has higher probability of completing higher education by 1.7 per cent compared to a student whose last attended institution is private in urban India. Even though many private higher educational institutions in urban places are mushrooming day by day, the role of government in providing mass higher education has well been visualised to provide quality and subsidised education for poor and ensure degree completion. For instance, nearly 71 per cent students whose last attended institution is government are from families with less than Rs 3000 per capita household consumption expenditure in rural areas and the same figure for urban India is 68.5 per cent with per capita household consumption expenditure less than Rs 6000. In addition to the above reasons, high fee structure, strict curriculum and examination patterns, lack of teacher student and peer interactions etc. in private institutions are other reasons responsible for lower completion rate of higher education.

The marital status of the student is significant for the urban sample but insignificant for the rural sample. The probability of not completing higher education for currently married and widowed/divorced is 3.8 per cent and 26.7 per cent respectively higher compared to a student who is not married in urban India. In other words, compared to a student who is not married, the probability of completing a higher education degree is reduced by 3.8 per cent points and 26.7 per cent points respectively, if we add one student from each marital category of 'currently married' and widowed/divorced from urban India into the sample. The findings here are closely associated with the assumptions of existing theories on sociology and gender studies on marriage who in a nutshell claim that due to various commitments connected with marriage (the extent of commitments in case of married, frustration due to loneliness in case of widowed/separated etc. differ for both newly married and widowed/divorced and therefore the differing coefficients), it is less likely that a married person/couple and divorced/separated would complete higher education compared to an unmarried student enrolled in a degree in higher education.

The religious background of students found significantly influencing the probability of not completing higher education and is only significant for rural India in our analysis. A student from Islamic background has higher probability of not completing higher education compare to a student from Hindu background in rural India. In the case of other religions, the probability of completing a higher education degree is higher compared to a student either from Hinduism or Islam background. While an additional student from Islamic background will add the risk of not completing higher education by 7.2 per cent; an addition of a student from non-Hindu/Islam others religious background will raise the probability of completing higher education by 2.2 per cent and both are in comparison to students from Hinduism background. This finding is therefore validated by the findings of the Sachar committee report [Government of India;

2006] which provides date the various deprivations and under-development of Indian Muslims in social, economic and educational indicators.

The social background of students does influence the probability of completing a higher education degree and the influence is dissimilar in rural and urban India. A scheduled tribe student has advanced the probability of completing higher education compared to a non-SC/ST/OBC others category student in rural India. On the other hand, both SC and OBC students have a lower probability of completing higher education compared to non-SC/ST/OBC others students in rural India. While an additional student from ST group in higher education will increase his/her probability of completion by 1.9 per cent, an addition of each of an SC and OBC student will reduce the probability of completing higher education by 2.3 per cent and 5.3 per cent respectively around three per cent higher probability of not completing for OBC compared to SC students in rural India. The results for ST need to be used cautiously since there are few cases from ST category in our sample of rural India. Moreover, both SC and ST coefficients are not significant for rural sample. In Urban India, on the other hand, the probability of completing higher education is lower among SCs, STs and OBCs compared to non-SC/ST/OBCs other category students and the results are statistically significant for all social groups. In other words, an addition of a ST student will increase the probability of non-completion by 9.2 per cent; nearly three per cent and seven per cent more compare to the probability of non-completion for SC and OBC respectively in urban India. While the probability of not completing higher education is higher for OBCs in rural India, in urban India more number of ST students is less likely to complete higher education compared to all other social groups.

The variable land possessed [in hectares] by the household is significant for both rural and urban samples. In rural India, a student from the household possessing less than 0.005 hectare of land is more likely to discontinue higher education compared to a student coming from the household possessing more than one hectare of land. An additional student in higher education from a household possessing less than 0.005 hectare of land will add the risk of non-completion by 2.6 per cent compared to a student from the household possessing more than one hectare of land keeping all other things constant. In urban India a student from household possessing less quantity of land is more likely to incomplete higher education.

Types of education pursued are found to statistically and significantly influence the probability of completion in higher education in both rural and urban samples. A student pursuing a professional degree course is more likely to complete higher education (marginal effect is by one per cent) compared to a student pursuing a degree in general stream in rural India. On the other hand, the probability of completing higher education for students pursuing vocational higher education is less compared to students pursuing general higher education. The marginal effect in this case indicates that an additional student pursuing vocational higher education will add to the risk of non-completion by 17.8 per cent compared to the addition of a general stream student into the system. Unlike in rural India, the probability of completing higher education for both professional and vocational stream students is high compared to general stream students. The probability of completing a professional degree is 4.9 per cent and completing a vocational degree is 1.3 per cent higher compare to completing a general higher education degree in urban India. Keeping all other things constant, while a professional stream student is more likely to complete his/her degree across rural and urban India, the probability of not completing a vocational degree is only true in urban India.

With regard to the various reasons responsible for students not completing higher education, we found all most all of the reasons are positive and significant in the model in both rural and urban India. Keeping all other things constant, reasons like 'not able to cope with or failure in studies', 'institution is far off', 'student is not interested in studies' and 'mismatch in the timings of educational institution' are significantly contributing to non-completion of higher education in rural areas. An additional student in higher education who is not able to cope with educational environment and frequent failure in studies increases the probability of not completing the degree by 85 per cent compared to financial related reasons that lead to withdrawing from studies. Moreover, the marginal effect of each of the reasons for non-completion indicates that the probability of not completing a degree for students when the institution is far off is 62.2 per cent *vis-a-vis* a student not completing a degree because of financial problems. Further, adding a student who is not interested in studies will increase the probability of dropping out by 55 per cent compared to adding a student who has financial problems to continue with higher education. Apart from the significant effect of the above factors, for a student who helps the household enterprises the probability of not completing higher education is increased by 31.2 per cent. A student whose parent is not interested in his/her education contributes to his/her dropout by 19.2 per cent. Moreover, a student who participates in other economic activity contributes to non-completion by 14.3 per cent and a student who works for regular wage/salary contribute to non-completion by 7.8 per cent all in comparison to a student who has dropped out because of financial difficulties. In summary, the magnitude of impact on a student who finds himself/herself unable to cope with the academic environment and/or experiences in failure of studies is highly positive and significant with regard to incompletion of the degree, followed by a student who finds his/her college/university in a far off place. Following this, a student who encounters timing problems is highly and more likely to discontinue followed by the student who finds little or no interest to study in higher education.

For urban India, the reasons responsible for student non-completion in higher education are categorically merged into four key variables for ease of analysis[1], i.e., domestic/familial/parental related reasons, financial constraints, and institution/academic related reasons and reasons related to the participation in economic activity.[2] Compared to the reasons associated with the family of the student, the financial, institutional/academic related reasons and reasons associated with participation in economic activity are found to positively and significantly influence student non-completion in higher education. A student who has financial constraints is less likely to complete their programme of study and the magnitude of effect is around 14.8 per cent compared to 79.8 per cent and 5.9 per cent for institutional/academic reasons and reasons associated with student participation in economic activity. In other words, while financial, institutional/academic and participation in economic activity related reasons influence students not to complete higher education, the magnitude of effect of the institutional/academic related problems highly and significantly (compare to all other problems) contribute to students' withdrawal from higher education. Thus, in a way a large part of student droppingout behaviour is explained by the problems connected with or derived from the educational institutions themselves. It is towards understanding educational institutions in a more in-depth manner, that we have undertaken analysis of primary data collected at university level.

A student from lower rung of monthly per capita household consumption expenditure [MPCE] of his/her family is more likely to discontinue higher education compared to a student with higher MPCE of family. For instance, keeping other things constant a student whose family's MPCE is below Rs 4000 and Rs 6000 in both rural and urban areas respectively, his/her probability of not completing a higher education degree increases by six per cent for a student in rural area and five per cent in urban area compared to a student from higher MPCE quartile in both locations. A linear relationship is in that it is revealed that the probability of not completing higher education is significantly more with a student who is at lower rung of their family's MPCE and *vice-versa*.

The probability of not completing higher education for a student belonging to lower occupational status of the household, i.e., 'agricultural labour' and 'other labour' is high compared to a student belonging to a household engaged in self-employed or non-agriculture activity in rural India. The magnitude of effect of not completing HE is higher for the student belonging to agricultural labour household 9.1 per cent compared to a student belonging to a household engaged in other labour 7.7 per cent. In urban India, a student belonging to both causal labour and self-employed household has higher probability of not completing higher education vis-a-vis a student from regular wage and salaried household. The magnitude of effect of household occupation on students not completing higher education is higher in case of a student from causal labour household which is 9.6 per cent and then self-employed households by one per cent both in compare to regular wage/salaried households in urban India.

Table 7.3: Determinants of Students of Age 5-29 Years who were Ever Enrolled but Currently are not Attending (Completed) Higher Education (Rural India)

Dependent variable	*Whether Completed! (Yes/No)*		
Variables	*Odds Ratio*	*Standard Error*	*M.E. (dy/dx)**
Column (1)	*Column (2)*	*Column (3)*	*Column (4)*
Sex	0.939	0.137	-.008
Type of Institution last attended	0.963	0.133	-.004
Never Married	Reference Category		
Currently married	1.083	0.143	.010
Widowed/Separated/Divorced	3.643	4.522	.244
Hinduism	Reference category		
Islam	1.612**	0.398	.072
All Other (Religion)	0.836	0.215	-.022
ST	0.853	0.228	-.019
SC	1.184	0.254	.023
OBC	1.479***	0.216	.053
All Others	Reference category		
Land < 0.005	1.213	0.317	.026
Land 0.005 to 0.01	0.442***	0.124	-.085
Land 0.02 to 0.40	0.858	0.167	-.019
Land 0.41 to 1.00	0.853	0.156	-.020
Land 1.01 to 8.00	Reference category		
Types of Education-General	Reference Category		
Types of Education-Professional	0.928	0.287	-.009
Types of Education-Vocational	2.726*	1.649	.178
Parents not interested in studies	2.923***	1.029	.192
College/University is far off	19.540***	9.679	.626
To work for wage/salary	1.676**	0.390	.078
For participating in other economic activity	2.375***	0.517	.143
Look after younger siblings	2.741	1.895	.179
To attend other domestic chores	3.557***	0.977	.235
Financial Constraints	Reference category		
Timings of education institution not suitable	13.838*	19.861	.562
For helping in household enterprises	4.906***	1.302	.312
Student not interested in studies	13.524***	3.318	.550
Unable to cope up or failure in studies	232.17***	100.16	.850
Expenditure Quartile (Below 20 per cent)	1.636**	0.359	.073

(Contd.)

(Contd. Table 7.3)

Dependent Variable	*Whether Completed! (Yes/No)*		
Variables	*Odds Ratio*	*Standard Error*	*M.E. (dy/dx)**
Column (1)	*Column (2)*	*Column (3)*	*Column (4)*
Expenditure Quartile (20 per cent-40 per cent)	1.857***	0.392	.094
Expenditure Quartile (40 per cent – 60 per cent)	1.419*	0.267	.049
Expenditure Quartile (60 per cent – 80 per cent)	0.936	0.168	-.008
Expenditure Quartile (80 per cent – 100 per cent)	Reference Category		
HHT- Self-employed in non-agriculture	Reference Category		
HHT- Agricultural Labour	1.799**	0.463	.091
HHT- Other Labour	1.658*	0.479	.077
HHT- Self-employed in Agriculture	0.966	0.164	-.004
CONSTANT	-2.53***	.259	
Log Likelihood	855.13		
Pseudo R2	0.277		
No. of Observations	2401		
Predicted probability of whether completed			.155

*Note: ***p<.01 (2-tailed), **p<.05 (2-tailed), *p<.10 (2-tailed).*

Table 7.4: Determinants of Students of Age 5-29 Years who were Ever Enrolled but Currently are not Attending [Completed] Higher Education [Urban India]

Dependent variable	*Whether Completed! (Yes/No)*		
Variables	*Odds Ratio*	*Standard Error*	*Marginal Effect (dy/dx)*
Sex	1.099	0.129	.006
Type of Institution last attended	0.794**	0.089	-.017
Currently Married	1.678***	0.187	.038
Widowed/Separated	6.260***	4.468	.267
Islam	1.283	0.230	.019
All Others (Religion)	0.864	0.168	-.010
ST	2.505***	0.558	.092
SC	1.995***	0.362	.063
OBC	1.320**	0.164	.021
Land 0.005 to 0.01	1.259*	0.166	.017
Land 0.02 to 0.40	1.352**	0.193	.023

(Contd.)

(Contd. Table 7.4)

Dependent variable	*Whether Completed! (Yes/No)*		
Variables	*Odds Ratio*	*Standard Error*	*Marginal Effect (dy/dx)*
Land 0.41 to 1.00	0.730	0.257	-.019
Land 1.01 to 8.00	1.451	0.349	.030
Types of Education- Professional	0.049***	0.094	-.049
Types of Education- Vocational	0.818	0.620	-.013
Financial constraints	3.627***	0.610	.148
Institutional/academic reasons	87.264***	23.853	.798
Participation in Economic Activity	1.988***	0.265	.059
Expenditure Quartile (Below 20 per cent)	1.043	0.279	.003
Expenditure Quartile (20 per cent-40 per cent)	1.906***	0.482	.060
Expenditure Quartile (40 per cent – 60 per cent)	1.999	0.210	.013
Expenditure Quartile (60 per cent – 80 per cent)	1.109	0.145	.007
Self-employed	1.158	0.129	.010
Casual Labour	2.700***	0.693	.106
CONSTANT	-3.303***	0.175	
Log Likelihood	-1341.40		
Pseudo R2	0.181		
No. of Observations	4904		
Predicted probability of whether completed			.078

*Note: ***p<.01 (2-tailed), **p<.05 (2-tailed), *p<.10 (2-tailed).*

SECTION-C

Findings, Discussion and Conclusion

Socio-economic Characteristics

Despite years of policies and programmes for better access, participation and completion of weaker sections in higher education, the probability of completing a higher education degree remains dim for SCs, STs and OBCs compared to non-SC/ST/OBC others both in rural and urban India. The magnitude of deprivation is higher for SCs compared to STs and OBCs in both rural and urban regions of India. Students from these three categories do not face similar problems in higher education. While caste-related factors are significant for SCs, geographical-cultural isolation/distance is the outcome of STs under-development. On the other hand, many believe OBCs as a group is a political outcome at some period of Indian political history that substantially shifted policy attention on weaker sections to a more well-off section. Moreover, these groups are not homogeneous and graded diversities exist in their objective situations. These differences and diversities are importance explanations of why SCs, STs and OBCs differently perform in different contexts with regard to their participation in higher education.

The religious identity of a student holds significant with regard to the probability of continuing and completing a higher education degree in rural areas. Students belonging to the Muslim minority community are more likely to discontinue their higher education compared to Hindu community students. On the other hand, the probability of completing a higher education degree is higher for non-Hindu/Muslim other religious minority communities. Alarmingly the low completion rate of Muslim minority students in rural areas suggests that the pattern and expectations and belief system of Muslims have not substantially changed as is seen in the case of the urban Muslim community. Young generations from this minority community prefer to work and earn in unorganised sectors; [e.g., mostly in small-scale industries, factories, garages etc.] rather than the continuing or complete higher education. Though the majority of the Muslims stay in urban and semi-urban areas, the problems of participation in higher education in rural areas do need critical policy attention that matches with their religious and cultural expectations.

Across the two parameters, i.e., family consumption expenditure [64th round NSS] and family income [student survey in two universities], students belonging to the lower rung of both expenditure as well as income are more likely to dropout from higher education compared to students belonging to higher rung of income and expenditure of their household. This conveys the fact that poor among the marginalised as well as non-marginalised sections do face problems in sending their son/daughter to higher education. Again, if they are able to send than they are less likely to persist in the system without supportive financial mechanisms. Expenditure is largely a function of household income and less the expenditure more the likelihood that a poor student from that household will face problems of retention and persistence. Lower expenditure or income of the household suggests lower economic/financial potentials which have significant bearings on whether or not a student from that household would persist in the system of higher education.

Parental Education and Occupation

Both in rural as well as urban India the probability of completing a higher education degree lean towards students whose parents are highly/salaried and are employed in non-agriculture. For instance, findings from 64th round NSS reveal that the likelihood of not completing a degree is higher for students belonging to agricultural household and the same for urban students is casual labour and/or self-employed households. This suggest the fact that students from lower educational [i.e., low educational attainment level] and occupational [i.e., agricultural household, casual labour etc.] status of their parents have to go through several difficulties inside the institution as well as in their own families. It also indicates the conditions framing the student's pre-university studies: the education, occupation and income of parents are strong determinants of their children's educational opportunities. For example, patterns and traditions of family structure mean that in rural villages, and even urban areas, it is likely that the students were managing their studies and helping their parents in agricultural production and this would have necessarily impacted upon their opportunities to study effectively. Importantly, familial circumstances also frame the students' understanding of what it is reasonable to value and to expect (Bourdieu and Passeron, 1977; Bourdieu, 1997).

Marital Status

Compare to a student who is not married, probability of completing a higher education degree is reduced by 3.8 per cent points and 26.7 per cent points respectively, if we add one student from each marital category of 'currently married' and 'widowed/divorced' from urban India into the sample. The findings here is closely associated with the assumptions of existing theories on sociology and gender studies on marriage who claim that due to various commitments connected with marriage [the extent of commitments differ for both newly married and widowed/divorced], it is less likely that a married person/couple and divorced/separated would complete higher education compare to an unmarried student.

Dropping out behaviour of students are found to be statistically and significantly associated with the types of education being pursued by the students. The probability of completing a higher education degree is much higher for students pursuing professional education degree compare to general education degree both in rural and urban India. On the other hand, completing a vocational degree finds it difficult in rural India compare to urban India. The emerging patterns of course type and droppingout behaviour of students may imply that a professional degree course is well-planned by the student and his/her family with practical considerations on private expenditures and the likelihood of market efficiency of the course in getting a job after completion. On the other hand, both a general education and vocational education degree is generally considered as courses chosen as last option or more practically having very little or no marketability. Even when one considers marketability of vocational courses, [for instance, vocational training is intended to provide hands-on experiences for short term employment in workplaces and industries] the short-term, fragile nature of such jobs may be one reason that explains why students pursuing these courses are less likely to complete their degree.

Reasons for Droppingout

Against the much expected and generally perceived reasons that hinder students to complete higher education, factors connected with the institution are potentially responsible for student dropout. Researches previously had revealed that lack of income of the family or not providing financial assistance to the student is one of the substantial reasons why student leave their education half-way. However, the results now indicate a divergent trend in that the educational institution itself responsible for predominant share of dropout decision made by the students. Institutions with their processes of teaching, learning, assessment, peer and teacher interactions etc create conditions that hinder marginalised students to cope with and/or failure in their studies. For instance, results from 64th round of NSS data reveal that a student who is not able to cope with the institution/academic expectations is significantly and more likely to dropout compare to a student who has financial problem. While inability to cope with the dominant academic culture suggest a lack of cultural code specifically require to participate in higher education which in turn suggest lack of socio-cultural capital on the part of student. On the other hand, there can be the case that marginalised students are specifically targeted may be because they belong to identically an inferior social community and because that they receive benefits of affirmative action. There are many instances of discrimination and neglect in the universities specifically done to weaker sections by expecting them to behave in a particular way or secure/debate up to never-reach-expectations of teacher. In the process, these expectations are placed in such a manner in curricular processes that these students find it beyond their scope and ability to meet them and the end result is that they leave the system.

Quite a large number of students decide to dropout because they personally are not interested in studies. Yet others decide to dropout because they find their parents are not interested in their studies. In both cases, the decision to dropout suggest lower socio-economic development of the family, lack of expectations of parents on student education and lack of confidence on the part of student herself to excel in higher education. This is pertinent to note that lack of interest in higher education is not a problem by itself or an independent problem, rather it is the outcome of lack of facilities and opportunities that the student require to participate in education effectively. Lack of interest for higher education on the part of parents and students do reveal a complex and unequal structure of familial and social demand and expectations for and out of higher education. For example, a rural remote agricultural parent might find it reasonable to be disinterested in their children's education if the poverty level of the family is so intense and that demand the student to work for wage and livelihood. Yet in many other cases, the prospects of a student to continue and complete higher education is jeopardised by the conservative baggage being carried on by parents on the possible role that higher education can play to solve various socio-economic issues they meet in their daily life. In other words, many parents stop sending their children to higher education may be because they doubt the potential that higher education can offer in solving problems of the poor.

Yet other reasons for which students dropout from higher education are connected to a whole set of economic/income/wage related activities. There are large numbers of students who help their parents in their own household enterprises and others do leave their studies they have to earn soon for their family.

Notes

1. Reasons for droppingout are; parents not interested in studies, college/ university is far off, to work for wage/salary, for participating in other economic activity, look after younger siblings, to attend other domestic chores, financial constraints, timings of education institution not suitable, for helping in household enterprises, student not interested in studies.

2. *Domestic/familial/personal reasons include*; parents not interested in studies, to look after younger siblings, to attend other domestic chores, student not interested in studies. (2) *Institutional factors*; institution is far off, timings of educational institution is not suitable, language and medium of instruction not familiar, unable to cope up or failure in studies and unfriendly atmosphere in institution. (3) *Financial factor*; financial constraints. (4) *Reasons connected to the participation in economic activity*; to work for wage and salary, for participating in other domestic activity, for helping in household enterprises.

References

———— (1965), '*The Problem of Teaching, Conference of Australian Universities*', The Australian University, 3, 3.

—— (1969), The Educational and Vocational Development of College Students, Washington: American Council on Education.

—— (1972), College dropout: A National Profile, ACE Research Reports, Washington DC. : American Council on Education.

———— (1977) , Preventing student from droppingout, San Francisco; Josrey-Bass Publishers.

———— (1981), '*A long Way to go: Report on a Survey of Scheduled Caste High School and College Students in fifteen States of India*, Allied Publishers, New Delhi.

———— (1987), Leaving College: Rethinking the Causes and Cures of Student Attrition. Chicago: University of Chicago Press.

————(1988), Stages of student departure: reflections on the longitudinal character of student leaving. J. Higher education, 59, 438-455.

————(1997), Classrooms as communities: exploring the educational character of student persistence. J. Higher Educ., 68, 599-623.

Ahuja, G. C. (1980), Educational Wastage and Stagnation among Tribal Children, *Journal of Indian Education*, 6 (1), 58-70.

Aitken D. Norman (1982), '*College Student Performance, Satisfaction and Retention: Specification and Estimation of A Structural Model' The Journal of Higher Education,* 53, 1, 32-50.

Astin, A.W. (1964), Personal and Environmental Factors associated with college dropouts among high aptitude students, Journal of Educational Psychology, 55 (4), 219-227.

Bayer, A. (1968), '*The College Dropout: Factors Affecting Senior College Completion*', *Sociology of Education*, 41, 305-16.

Bean, J.P. (1979), Dropouts and Turnover: The Synthesis of a Causal Model of Student Attrition, *Dissertation Abstract International*, 39 (8), 4750-A.

Blanchfield, W.C. (1971), College Dropout Identification: A Case Study, *The Journal Of Experimental Education*, 40 (2), 1-4.

Bourdieu, P. (1997), The Forms of Capital. In A.H. Halsey, H. Lauder, P. Brown, and A. Stuart Wells (Eds) *Education: Culture, Economy, Society*, Oxford, Oxford University Press.

Bourdieu, P. and Passeron, J. C. (1977), *Reproduction in Education, Society and Culture* (London and Beverly Hills, Sage Publications).

Bragg, Emma W. (1956), '*A Study of Student Withdrawal at 'W. U.*', *Journal of Educational Psychology*, Vol. 47 (4), 199-202.

Chapman, D. W., and Hutcheson, S. M. (1982), '*Attrition from Teaching Careers: A Discriminant Analysis*', *American Educational Research Journal,* 19: 93-105.

Chitnis S. (1972), '*Education for Equality: Case for Scheduled Castes in Higher Education*',

Cliff, M. (1962), An Investigation of Factors Associated with Dropout and Transfer by Scholarship Applicants, *Journal of Educational Psychology*, 55 (4) 219.

Donovan R. (1984), '*Path Analysis of a Theoretical Model of Persistence in Higher Education among Low-Income Black Youth*', *Research in Higher Education*, 21, 3, 243-59.

Economic and Political Weekly, 7, 31-33, 1675-81.

Edelbrock, G.R. (1975), '*Personality Characteristics of Selected Community College Dropouts*', *Dissertation Abstracts International*, 36, (7-8), 4900-A.

Forster, M. (1959), *An Audit of Academic Performance*, Queens University, Belfast.

Grace, H.A. (1957) ,'Personality Factors and College Attrition', Journal of Peabody Education, 35, 36-40, In *Journal of Educational Psychology*, 1964, 55 (4), 219.

Hammond, S.B. (1957), '*Draft Report of First Year Student Survey, 1955-56*', Mimeo, University of Melbourne.

Holmes, C.H. (1964), '*Why They Left College and University*', *Journal of Educational Psychology*, 55 (4), 220.

Jackson, C.M. (1978), '*A Follow-Up Study of Educational Opportunity Fund Students: Graduates and Dropouts*', *Dissertation Abstracts International*, 39 (3), 1369-A.

Kamat, A. R. and Deshmukh, A. G. (1963), *Wastage in College Education*, Poona: Asia Publishing House.

Karandikar, S. P. (1975), '*Problems and Conditions of Students in the Poona University Area*', Ph.D. Thesis, in M.B. Buch, Second Survey of Research in Education, Faculty of Education and Psychology, Baroda, 1972-78, 521.

Khan, M.Z. and Singh, D. R. (1978) ,'*College Youth and their Course of Study and their View of Society*', *Journal of Higher Education*, 4 (1), 57-66.

Kohen, A. I., Nestel, G., and Karmas, C. (1978), '*Factors Affecting Individual Persistence Rates in Undergraduate College Programs*', *American Educational Research Journal,* 15: 233-252.

Kumar, E. R. (1980), '*Dropouts, 'Dilemma*', The *Illustrated Weekly of India*, 23 (3), 29.

Loeb, J. and Duff, F. (1974), '*Graduate Student Cohort Data for Individual Advising and Resource Allocation*', *Research in Higher Education,* 2: 325-340.

Lunneborg, C. E., and Lunneborg, P. W. (1973), 'Doctoral Study Attrition in Psychology', *Research In Higher Education*, 1: 379-387.

Malik, Y. (1984), 'A Study of the Attitude of Students of Jawaharlal Nehru University Towards Higher Education', *Unpublished M.Phil. Dissertation, JNU, New Delhi.*

Mary Ott et al. (1984), '*Logit Analysis of Graduate Student*', *Research in Higher Education*, 21, 4, 439-460.

Mathews, T.H. (1957), *Academic Failures: Canada's Crisis in Higher Education*, University of Toronto Press.

Maxwell, M.J. (1960), '*An Analysis of the California Psychological Inventory and the American Council of Education Psychological Test as Predictors of Success in Different College Curricula*', *Journal of Educational Psychology*, 55 (4), 219.

McCloy, C. H. (1980), '*A Study to Determine the Factors that Cause Students to become Dropouts at Chattanooga State Technical Community College*', *Dissertation Abstracts International,* 40 A (9), 4864-A.

Munro, B. H. (1981), '*Dropouts from Higher Education: Path Analysis of A National Sample*', *American Educational Research Journal*, 18: 133-141.

Naylor, P. D., and Sanford, T. R. (1982), '*Intra-Institutional Analysis of Student Retention Across Student Levels*', *College and University,* 57: 143-159.

Peng, S. S., and Fetters, W. B. (1978), '*Variables Involved in Withdrawal During the First Two Years of College: Preliminary Findings from The National Longitudinal*

Study of the High School Class of 1972', *American Educational Research Journal,* 15: 361-372.

Phadke, J.K and Shukla, R.C. (1980), Educational Waste— A Study in Dropouts among Scheduled Tribe College Students in Vyara, Vyara Institution of Tribal and Rural Development and Research.

Rawat, P. L. (1970), *History of Indian Education*, Agra, Ram Prasad & Sons.

Reddy, Y.M. (1971), '*A Study of Adjustment Problems of Adolescents in Relation to Their Fathers' Occupation'*, Research Bulletin of the Department of Psychology, 6, 34-41.

Rong Chen (2008), '*Financial Aids and Student Dropout in Higher Education: A Heterogeneous Research Approach*', in J.C. Smart (Eds.) *Higher Education: Handbook of Theory and Research,* XXIII, 209-40, The Netherlands: Springer.

Rumberger, R. W. (1983), 'Dropping Out of High School: The Influence of Race, Sex, and Family Background', *American Educational Research Journal,* 20: 199-220.

Schonell, F. J. (1962), *Promise and Performance: A Study of Student Progress at University Level*, University of Queensland and University of London Press.

Sewell H. Williams and Shah P. Vimal (1967), '*Socioeconomic Status, Intelligence, and the Attainment of Higher Education*', *Sociology of Education*, 40, 1, 1-23.

Sharma, S. (1972), '*Sex and Caste Affiliation, a Source of Variation in School Achievement of Adolescents'*, *New Trends in Education*, 3 (2), 28-32.

Singh, A. and Sharma, G.D. (1981), *University and College Finances*, New Delhi; Association of Indian Universities.

Slocum, W.L. (1964) ,'Social Factor in Academic Mortality', College and University, 1956, 32, 53-64, In *Journal of Educational Psychology*, 55 (4), 220.

Smith P. Jeremy and Nayar A. Robin (2001), 'Droppingout of University: A Statistical Analysis of the Probability of Withdrawal for UK University Students', *Journal of The Royal Statistical Society Series A (Statistics In Society),* 164, 2, 389-405.

Stork, D., and Berger, P. D. (1978), 'Attrition in The Liberal Arts College of a Major Metropolitan University' *Research in Higher Education,* 9: 281-289.

Terenzini, P. T. And Pascarella, E. T. (1977), 'Voluntary Freshman Attrition and Patterns of Social and Academic Integration in A University: A Test of a Conceptual Model', *Research in Higher Education,* 6: 25-43.

Terenzini, P. T. and Pascarella, E. T. (1978), 'The Relation of Students' Precollege Characteristics and Freshman Year Experience to Voluntary Attrition', *Research in Higher Education,* 9: 347-366.

Thomas L. (2002), '*Student Retention in Higher Education: The Role of Institutional Habitus*', *Journal of Education Policy*, 17, 4, 423-42.

Tinto, V. (1975), Dropout from Higher Education: A Theoretical Synthesis of Recent Research. Rev. Educ. Res., 45, 89-125.

Turkel B. Susan and Abramson T. (1986), '*Peer Tutoring and Mentoring as a Drop-Out Prevention Strategy*', *The Clearing House*, 60, 2, 68-71.

UNESCO (1965), *Access to Higher Education: The International Study of University Admission,* Vol. 11, National Studies, Paris, International Association of Universities.

Yoshino, I.R. (1964), 'College Dropout at the end tf the Freshman Year', in *Journal of Educational Psychology*, 55 (4), 219.

8

Education Status of Scheduled Tribes in Andhra Pradesh: A Case Study of Lambada Tribe

Bikku

Abstract

Education is the process of instruction aimed at an all-round development of individuals, it provides the necessary tools and knowledge to understand and practice in day to day life. For many, education is understood to be a means of overcoming handicaps, achieving greater equality and acquiring wealth and status. It helps every individual to develop fullest potential (Sargent, 1994). The formal education among the tribal in India is low. The dropout rates are very high in the primary and secondary schools level, especially girls are higher compared to boys though various policies and programmes have been implementing by the government and other Non-governmental Organisations (NGOs) and others. The literacy rate of Scheduled Tribe (ST) in India is 47.1 per cent according to census 2001.

The Lambada Tribe are semi-nomadic residing in the various states of India, having different names like, Banjaras, Brinjaris, Lamans, Lambanis, Sugalis (Thurston, 1909), in the south India they are the more populated especially they constituted majority among all tribal community in Andhra Pradesh. The present study is carried out from fieldwork among the Lambadas of Zaheerabad Mandal of Medak district in Andhra Pradesh. The paper is an attempt to discuss about the education status and dropouts which linked to a set of relationships in the social, cultural and economic aspects, through anthropological perspective.

Key Words: *Education, Status, Scheduled Tribe, Literacy, Lambada, Andhra Pradesh.*

Introduction

The education is an important parameter to measure any society or community development, that is how much that society got educated and has literacy rate? Education cannot be the only literacy but it is in much broader sense much more than the literacy. Man thinking and behaviour has always been influenced by the education, the process of man evolutions him-self occurs through the process of education, in this process and the education shape the man and society. It enriches the knowledge in human being through which mans present and future will be decided. Education is important and one of the most powerful means of bringing about socio-economic development in the society. Education is the process of instruction aimed at an all round development of individuals, providing the necessary tools and knowledge to understand and participate in day to day activities. Education is the only wealth which cannot be stolen. It builds character, provides strength of mind and increases knowledge. Education sustains the human values which contribute individual and collective well-being. It forms the basis for life-long learning and inspires confidence to face challenges. It provides the skills to become more self-reliant and creates awareness of opportunities and rights.

As John Dewey (1921), said that in his book Democracy and Education: An *Introduction to the Philosophy of Education* "Education, in its broadest sense, is the means of this social continuity of life"

According to a philosopher of education George F. Kneller (1941), education "in its broad sense, education refers to any act or experience that has formative effect on the mind, character, or physical ability of an individual ... In its technical sense, education is the process by which society, through schools, colleges, universities, and other institutions, deliberately transmits its cultural heritage at its accumulated knowledge, values, and skills from one generation to another".

Moreover, Emile Durkheim, a prominent figure in the area of sociology of education in his book titled *Education and Sociology* wrote in 1956 defined education as "Education is the influence exercised by adult generations on those that are not yet ready for social life. Its object is to arouse and to develop in the child a certain number of physical, intellectual and moral states which are demanded of him by both the political society as a whole and the special milieu for which he is specifically destined".

In socialisation process the education play vital role, so individual and communities live dignified life with education. As India is diverse country in which there are more than 550 tribal communities, as these tribal communities are backward in terms of economically and politically. Then there is need to stress on, how the education playing role in this tribal communities overall their development? Another question on which this paper will focus is why there is lack of education among the tribal communities?

Universal primary education is a constitutional directive. Article 45 of the Directive Principles urges all states to provide 'free and compulsory education for all children until they complete the age of fourteen years' within a period of ten years from the commencement of the constitution. The right to education is recognised as fundamental in the 83rd constitutional amendment, but the goal of universal education has remained a distant dream to these tribal communities.

The term Scheduled Tribes first appeared in the Constitution of India. Article 366 (25) defines Scheduled Tribes as such tribes or tribal communities or parts of or groups within such tribes or tribal communities as are deemed under Article 342 to be Scheduled Tribes for the purposes of this Constitution Article 342 prescribes the procedure to be followed in the matter of specification of Scheduled Tribes.

The NPE, 1986 and the Programme of Action (POA), 1992, recognised the heterogeneity and diversity of the tribal areas while underlining the importance of instruction through the mother tongue and the need for preparing teaching/ learning materials in the tribal languages. A working group on Elementary and Adult Education for the Tenth Five Year Plan (2002-07) emphasised the need to improve the quality of education of tribal children and to ensure equity as well as further improving access. In general, the tribes that remain geographically isolated are able to retain their traditional cultures and religions longer. On the other hand communities that are either nomadic or live in the periphery of civilised life are prone for drastic changes (Manjunatha B.R. and Annapurna M. 2012). Fifty-four years after Independence on November 28, 2001 the Government enacted the 93rd Amendment to the Constitution making the Right to Education a Fundamental Right. It puts the onus of sending children to school on parents rather than the State. It is not enough to talk of fundamental rights and fundamental duties of the citizens. It is equally necessary to dwell on the fundamental duties of the government. The extent to which this enactment will be increasingly backed by resource allocation will be the test of the seriousness of purpose of the government to implement the law.

Objectives

1. To study the educational status among the Lambada tribe.
2. To understand the dropouts related to socio-cultural and economic aspects.

Methodology

This paper is based on the both primary and secondary data source. Primary data has been collected from the fieldwork. The field work techniques were included unstructured interviews (including with school teachers), observation, group discussions; these are the conventional random samplings. The secondary data includes books, journal articles, news papers and government records and census, etc. The primary data collected from four

Lambada Thandas namely Hothi (K) Thanda, Vittu Nayak Thanda, Govindpur Thanda and Jamgar Baudi Thanda in Zaheerabad Mandal of Medak district of Andhra Pradesh.

Tribal Education in Indian Contest

There are nearly 600 tribal communities in India which consists of 8.2 per cent of total population in India. However, traditional tribal societies are undergoing a rapid change with the mainstreaming policy of the Indian government. For the tribal communities the process of becoming a part of the mainstream has meant a declining control on their resources and erosion of their cultural heritage. The major issue affecting the tribals in India is displacement: not merely displacement by large projects but resource displacement, thus violating the basic survival rights of tribal communities. Tribal areas reveal a high degree of land alienation. Non-tribals have invaded tribal protected areas. Deforestation, mainly due to exploitation of forests for industrial purposes, is another manifestation of resource displacement. This has resulted in decreasing access to forest resources by tribal communities. With increasing globalisation and privatisation, the land rights of tribal areas is under even greater threat since these are regions, which have a high natural resource base and has tremendous potential to meet multiple market demands. Added to resource displacement is project displacement where development projects have threatened the livelihood needs of tribal communities. More than 40 per cent of displaced persons of all large development projects are tribals. There is proper rehabilitation and resettlement of displaced people led them more dropouts.

More importantly displacement has been accompanied by erosion of the identity of tribal communities, which is being subsumed within the dominant culture. There is a breakdown in their own community institutions, which hitherto safeguarded their resources, traditional practices and values. In the process the richness and wealth of their knowledge systems, identity and survival with integrity is being destroyed.

The Educational Context in the Tribal Areas of Andhra Pradesh

In Andhra Pradesh there are nearly 35 different tribal communities living, According to 2001 census the total tribal population in Andhra Pradesh 50,24, 104 (male 2548295 and female 2475809) against total population 7,62,10,007 which consists of 6.59 per cent. The highest population of district is Khammam which consists of 26.47 per cent (6,82,617) and least populated district is Hyderabad which consist 0.90 per cent.

Lambada Tribal Education Status in Andhra Pradesh

The Lambadas are a scheduled tribe inhabiting throughout Andhra Pradesh. They are also known as Sugalis or Banjara. They are the largest tribe in Andhra Pradesh. They Lambadas also inhabited in several states in India such as Karnataka named by Lambani, Maharashtra, Lambani, Banjara, Gujarat Banjara, Rajasthan Banjara, Gouar. But they called themselves Goar Banjara or Goar Mati. Lambadas are dependent on agriculture. The Lambada tribal population consists about 20,77, 94 (40 per cent above) (10,71,589 of males and 10,06,358 of females) against 50,24,104 of all tribal communities in Andhra Pradesh. They live in exclusive settlements of their own called Thandas, usually away from the main village, tenaciously maintaining their cultural and ethnic identity. Tribal literacy rate is about 5, 81,334 which consists of 35.74 per cent (4,10,888 (50.57 per cent) of males and 1, 70,446 (12.19 per cent) of females.

In Medak district the according to 2001 census the literacy rate 28.08 per cent (41.06 of male and 14.26 per cent female). In the case of Zaheerabad Mandal the tribal literacy rate is 32.31 per cent (47.52 of male and 15.96 per cent of female.

There are 42 villages and nearly 40 Lambada tribal Thandas are located in Zaheerabad Mandal in Medal district of A.P. In this mandal majority of population are Lambadas and others are Yerukula tribes and few of koyas. The total tribal population is 10, 574 (5, 458 males and 5,116 females) and the literacy rate is 32.31 per cent (47.52 per cent of male and 15.96 per cent of female) as per 2001 census. There are 25 private high schools and 14 government high schools, and there are more than 90 primary schools in this mandal.

Lambada tribes in the four Thanda are all homogeneous communities. The Hothi (K) Thanda total population consists of 383 out of 54 households and literacy rate 44 per cent. Govindpur Thanda has 89 households the total population is around 650 and literacy rate 42 per cent. Vittunayak Thanda has nearly 320 household's population around 3000 and the literacy rate 32 per cent. Jamgar Baudi Thanda has nearly 55 households and total population in this village is nearly 450 and the literacy rate is 32 per cent.

Schools and Colleges in Zaheerabad Mandal

Table 8.1

	Primary Schools	*High schools*	*Junior Colleges*	*Degree and PG College*
Govt.	40	14	1	1
Private	3	25	6	3
	Primary Schools	High schools	Junior Colleges	Degree and PG College
Govt.	40	14	1	1
Private	3	25	6	3

Education

There is one school in the Hothi (K) Thanda that teaches up to 5th standard. It is a Government school; medium of education is Telugu. There are two teachers in this School. Out of the total population of 283, only 126 males and females have attended school. There are 92 educated males (32.5 per cent of the men) and 34 educated women (12 per cent of the female population) in the Thanda. When they settled in this Thanda, educated people were rare. Among educated persons 49 are educated upto primary only. Banjaras of this Thanda send their girls to school to pursue education till primary and upper primary levels. After that most of girls get engaged in house work, cattle raring and helping their parents in the agriculture work, financial difficulties, and general apathy of parents towards formal educations. In this Thanda only two girls are studying higher education, one girl is doing B.Ed (bachelor of education) and another girl is studying in a nursing school.

Education Level in the Hothi (K) Thanda

Table 8.2

Education Level	*Male*	*Percentage of male*	*Female*	*Percentages of female*	*Total of male and female*	*Percentages of total male and female*
Primary	31	10.95	18	6.36	49	17.31
Upper Primary	13	4.59	9	3.18	22	7.77
High-School	24	8.48	5	1.76	29	10.25
Inter(10+2)	15	5.30	0	0.00	15	5.30
Degree	7	2.47	0	0.00	7	2.47
Masters	1(MCA)	0.35	0	0.00	1	0.35
Others	1(IT Diploma)	0.35	2(1 B. Ed, 1 Nurse)	0.70	3	1.06
Total	**92**	**32.50**	**34**	**12.00**	**126**	**44.50**

The Banjaras of Hothi (K) Thanda have a positive view towards urban culture for education. Traditionally Banjaras are illiterates. After the independence, the Central and State Governments; provided free education to them. Zaheerabad is a town (now a growing urban area) about four kilometers away from Hothi (K) Thanda. In the urban area they get education facilities from primary school to degree colleges and some private colleges also boys till matriculation. There is one school in this Thanda up to 5th class. It is government school. Medium of education is Telugu. There are two teachers teaching in this School. Out of the total population of 283 there are 126 males and females who attended school. There are 92 educated males in percentage of 32.50 and 34 women are educated. The percentage of educated women is only 12 per cent in the Thanda. Among the men and women, 49 people are educated till primary level.

Andhra Pradesh Tribal Educational Dropouts

On November 20, 1989, the United Nations (UN) General Assembly adopted the Convention on the Rights of the Child (CRC), a historic document for

Table 8.3

Sl. No.	*District*	*I - V (6-10 Years)*			*VI - VII (11-12 Years)*			*VIII - X(13-15 Years)*		
		Boys	*Girls*	*Total*	*Boys*	*Girls*	*Total*	*Boys*	*Girls*	*Total*
1.	Srikakulam	122.34	115.16	118.77	103.39	82.75	93.00	69.21	50.42	**59.77**
2.	Vizianagaram	251.41	233.52	242.55	137.13	101.03	118.99	79.12	64.02	**71.55**
3.	Visakhapatnam	348.04	341.79	344.98	226.45	166.67	196.76	128.85	88.82	**109.01**
4.	East Godavari	85.33	86.11	85.71	70.34	68.14	69.24	37.50	37.80	**37.65**
5.	West Godavari	58.07	61.65	59.83	37.02	35.66	36.34	24.06	23.87	**23.97**
6.	Krishna	67.54	68.52	68.02	35.84	30.38	33.14	25.92	17.11	**21.57**
7.	Guntur	114.17	112.81	113.51	53.76	36.56	45.22	31.90	18.75	**25.39**
8.	Prakasam	114.09	107.63	110.95	40.48	29.61	35.12	21.58	14.15	**17.93**
9.	Nellore	204.93	201.49	203.24	77.88	67.67	72.81	43.03	34.06	**38.59**
10.	Kurnool	57.05	56.53	56.80	36.80	36.62	36.71	25.68	22.81	**24.27**
11.	Anantapur	74.45	74.43	74.44	61.99	56.05	59.08	47.91	36.85	**42.51**

(Contd.)

(Contd. Table 8.3)

Sl. No.	*District*	*I - V (6-10 Years)*			*VI - VII (11-12 Years)*			*VIII - X(13-15 Years)*		
		Boys	*Girls*	*Total*	*Boys*	*Girls*	*Total*	*Boys*	*Girls*	*Total*
12.	YSR Kadapa	70.79	65.60	68.27	43.31	34.09	38.76	25.17	18.89	**22.08**
13.	Chittoor	81.96	80.91	81.45	60.96	49.74	55.39	32.48	26.23	**29.39**
14.	Ranga Reddy	175.57	170.09	172.95	109.97	76.90	93.91	59.69	37.11	**48.74**
15.	Hyderabad	40.60	39.46	40.06	24.93	21.67	23.36	15.09	12.92	**14.05**
16.	Nizamabad	205.54	191.20	198.41	131.97	76.20	103.84	69.06	30.35	**49.57**
17.	Medak	183.30	173.19	178.38	86.88	46.27	66.83	45.56	17.94	**31.95**
18.	Mahabubnagar	255.85	223.66	240.20	138.85	65.29	102.58	68.04	26.54	**47.62**
19.	Nalgonda	293.14	261.30	277.70	182.25	118.89	151.10	102.86	54.77	**79.26**
20.	Warangal	395.22	405.36	400.15	250.35	188.28	219.72	138.36	93.30	**116.16**
21.	Khammam	579.12	593.40	586.08	506.09	456.44	481.56	280.49	212.11	**246.77**
22.	Karimnagar	95.13	92.21	93.69	58.20	45.68	51.94	32.71	23.10	**27.92**
23.	Adilabad	513.80	504.34	509.16	327.74	266.74	297.39	135.69	103.19	**119.55**
Andhra Pradesh		**176.91**	**172.23**	**174.63**	**112.61**	**86.73**	**99.80**	**62.40**	**43.34**	**52.99**

Source: Directorate of Economics and Statistics, Hyderabad.

children all over the world. By providing a legal framework to the 'rights of a child' it holds the governments accountable for enforcing these. In the Indian

Table 8.4: Dropout Rates of Scheduled Tribes (2005-06)

Sl. No.	*District*	*Class I – V*			*Class I – VII*		
		Boys	*Girls*	*Total*	*Boys*	*Girls*	*Total*
1.	Srikakulam	27.80	32.90	30.34	63.80	68.73	**66.20**
2.	Vizianagaram	15.13	24.05	19.52	58.20	68.83	**63.46**
3.	Visakhapatnam	46.90	52.88	49.82	59.99	70.07	**64.98**
4.	East Godavari	27.95	26.44	27.22	57.01	56.55	**56.78**
5.	West Godavari	34.12	28.27	31.20	59.10	58.10	**58.61**
6.	Krishna	33.21	39.83	36.49	62.71	70.98	**66.89**
7.	Guntur	50.22	53.85	52.00	69.89	81.11	**75.40**
8.	Prakasam	46.84	51.18	48.97	79.96	85.62	**82.66**
9.	Nellore	41.89	38.52	40.27	78.03	79.69	**78.82**
10.	Kurnool	32.07	33.54	32.77	58.68	57.77	**58.25**
11.	Anantapur	17.80	20.74	19.25	46.78	50.10	**48.37**
12.	YSR Kadapa	24.50	26.89	25.64	53.64	61.17	**57.17**
13.	Chittoor	13.42	15.72	14.55	51.40	58.14	**54.65**
14.	Ranga Reddy	53.15	60.00	56.48	75.88	81.21	**78.31**
15.	Hyderabad	23.02	48.50	35.95	35.46	48.11	**41.93**
16.	Nizamabad	58.91	62.69	60.71	80.23	87.23	**83.41**
17.	Medak	66.37	73.10	69.48	80.19	86.73	83.00
18.	Mahabubnagar	63.54	71.07	67.04	82.84	90.99	**86.45**
19.	Nalgonda	58.37	68.13	63.06	77.89	84.19	**80.74**
20.	Warangal	62.80	65.75	64.28	81.04	85.24	**83.09**
21.	Khammam	32.86	35.27	34.05	61.62	66.60	**64.09**
22.	Karimnagar	46.21	51.35	48.69	70.52	73.67	**71.99**
23.	Adilabad	39.02	45.14	42.10	77.78	83.01	**80.38**
Andhra Pradesh		**47.46**	**52.13**	**49.73**	**72.16**	**77.50**	**74.71**

Source: Directorate of Economics and Statistics, Hyderabad.

context, the Convention has come under criticism because of its distance from the actual situation of children along with there being very little awareness about the rights of the child among children, social activists working for the rights of children and even those responsible for making child rights a reality offer science subjects at master level. Hostel accommodations are provided to girls and in India, the problems faced by children, especially in the rural areas and more so by the girl child, are manifold and most of the times situation specific. Children are involved in various kinds of activities ranging from working in fields or cottage industries (carpets, matches, firecrackers, bidis, bangles, traditional handicrafts, etc.) alongside their parents, on tea plantations, tend cattle, fetch water and wood, as domestic servants, rag pickers, helpers on construction sites, in tea stalls, as apprentices, in stone quarries, and many others. Most of these activities go unreported as they are not in lieu of wages and thus do not get covered under the official definition of work. Most of these children also get left out of the education system as the schools that they would need to go to, would have to be flexible and suited to their work schedules. (Usha, 2001)

Dropouts Levels among the Tribal in Andhara Pradesh

In Andhra Pradesh the percentage of dropouts among the STs are more at high school levels, According 2005-06 report there 49.73 per cent (47.46 per cent of boys and 52.13 per cent of girls) dropouts at primary educational level. In the case of high schools level dropouts is 74.71 per cent (72.16 per cent boys and 77.50 per cent of girls). In Medak district there are nearly 18 tribal groups which consists 1,34,533 populations are living, the Lambada tribe is majority which consists 1,18,642 population. The dropout rate is 83 per cent (86.73 per cent girls and 80.19 per cent are girls) in I-VIII the class in the Medak district.

The Reasons for Dropout

(A) Economical Aspects

1. One of the main reasons for dropout of children from Lambada community is due to prevalence of wide spread poverty.

2. Many children are enrolled as unemployed for MGNREGS, (Mahatma Gandhi National Rural Employment Guarantee Scheme) to work for this scheme to earn money they are skipping the school.

3. Their agriculture is depending on rainy season, if there is low or high rainy rain then their crops will get spoil, so they will migrate to cities like Hyderabad, Mumbai, Pune, etc., for work. When they migrate to cities they will take their children with them, this also one of the main reasons for dropout.

4. The crop failure also impact on agriculture labourers, this lead to agricultural labours migrate to the cities.

5. There is stigma that government school are not good, so as they cannot send their children to the private school due to high fee and costly education,

so they think that sending them to government school in no use. This reason for more dropouts from government school.

6. Some of the families are sending their children to the private school till fifth or six class, but after that they cannot offer fees of school.

7. Children are going as wage labour for their family burdens.

8. During the agriculture or crop season, due to scarcity of labour children are going for work to help parents, and those who are poor they think that this is the season to earn the money, so they will take their children for work.

9. Especially among the Lambada community there is prevalence of seasonal migration to other regions and cities, e.g., paddy harvesting, sugar cutting.

10. Money lender is the main reason because they lent money with high interest, and government is not proving the loans, so due to high interest they have to work. Thus it leads to bounded labour and migration, this also leading to the child labours.

(B) Socio-cultural Aspect

1. One of the social reasons for dropout is early marriage to the children or child marriage.

2. Due to the family burden children are living the school.

3. Now there exist wrong belief among the people is that though you study high, you will not get jobs, so they are starting work in the early stage only.

4. One of the main reasons for dropout is due to the language problem, as they speak Lambada language, so they are getting communication problem.

Conclusion

There is need to bring awareness among the tribal communities about the education and its fruits. In order to do this state must plays active role to provide education as well. There is need to provide informal education and training to uplift to the tribal communities. It is not only the state but responsibility lies on all of us to bring awareness among tribal communities that they can realise that with education they can live with dignity.

References

1. Bakshi, P.M (2010), "*The Constitution of India,*" Delhi: Universal Law Publishing Co. Pvt. Ltd.

2. Bikku (2010), "*Urban Impact, Cultural Adaptation and Persistence of Traditional Values and Customs among the Banjara of Hothi (K) Thanda of Andhra Pradesh*" M.Phil dissertation submitted in University of Hyderabad, Hyderabad, India.

3. Dewey, John (1921): "*Democracy and Education: An Introduction to the Philosophy of Education*", New York: The Macmillan Company. p. 3.

4. Educational Statistics of Andhra Pradesh (2011 – 2012), *"Commissioner and Director of School Education State Project Director RVM (SSA)"*, Hyderabad: AP Government Publication.

5. George F. Kneller (1941), "*The Educational Philosophy of National Socialism"*, London: Oxford University Press.

6. Government of India (1992), "*National Policy on Education 1986" (Programme of Action 1992),* New Delhi: Ministry of Human Resource Development.

7. Jayachandran, Usha (2001): "*Taking Schools to Children 'Bhonga Shalas*'", *Economic and Political Weekly,* September 1, pp. 3347-50.

8. Manjunatha B.R. and Annapurna M. (2012): "*An Investigative Study on School Dropouts in Tribal Settings: A Case of Three Selected Tribes in South Karnataka*", *Antrocom Online Journal of Anthropology*, Vol. 8. No. (2), pp. 421-427.

9. Nambissan, Geetha B (1994), "*Language and Schooling of Tribal Children: Issues Related to Medium of Instruction*" *Economic and Political Weekly,* October 15.

10. Ramachandran, Vimala (2004), "*Is Schooling for the Poor on the Government Agenda?*", *Economic and Political Weekly*, July 24.

11. Rao. Vasanta Sriniva (2009), "*Lack of Community Participation in the Sarva Shiksha Abhiyan: A Case Study*" *Economic and Political Weekly*, Vol. XLIV, No.8. February 2.

12. Sargent, M. (1994), "*The New Sociology for Australians",* Melbourne: Longman Cheshire.

13. Thurston, Edgar (1909), "*The Caste and Tribes of South India*", A-B. Madras: Government Press.

9

Development and Displacement–A Question of Human Right: A Case Study of POSCO Project in Odisha

Chitta Ranjan Mishra

Introduction

After the independence with an objective to achieve to speed economic growth many developmental projects have taken in our country for our nation building. These projects placed in second five year plan in our country. These projects include construction of megadams, powerplant, largescale industries, and mining.Though these developmental projects have provided irrigation to thirsty lands, energy for the growing industries, and brought about the economic prosperity for the country but in another side these projects leads towards the displacement of large number of people in our country. Among the people displaced by various developmental projects a large number of people from schedule tribe, schedule caste or other indigenous people. Mostly developmental projects were took place in tribal areas and they suffer more in this model of development. In the name of development the poor people often pay a very heavy price which not only involves the simple loss and destruction of goods and property, but people's lives and ultimate source of substance. Development does not benefit to all people, it is only for small number of people in our country. But such consequences in the path of nation's development are often deliberately ignored and authorities continue to remain tight-lipped, trying to camouflage vices under the lofty banner of national growth and development (Dutta, 2007). Various studies conducted by scholars show that as many 75 per cent of displaced people have not been rehabilited

(Fernades,1991). In the absence of proper resettlement and rehabilitation pushed them in to impoverishment, marginalisation and more backwardness. Michael M. Cerenea (1995) has rightly pointed out that development induced involuntary displacement leads to eight impoverishment risk, i.e., Landlessness, joblessness, homelessness, marginalisation, food insecurity, increased morbidity and mortality loss of access to common property and social disarticulation of the displaced population. With the following the old colonial rules of Land acquisition policy government now acquire the Tribal land in the name of "Public interest". When people resist against this in human activities government use brutal force to depress their voice which leads towards the violation of the democratic or human rights of the tribal or indigenous people in our country. This paper mainly studies the industrialisation with reference to POSCO project in Odisha. This paper mainly studies the discourse of development and displacement and aspect of human rights of indigenous people in our country with relate to Odisha.

Overview of Development and Displacement in India and Odisha

The process of socio-economic development stated soon after the independence of India under the successive five year plan. Government established many developmental projects which lead towards the large displacement in our country. Industrialisation is one of the strategies for development. So both Central and State governments established many industries after the independence for economic development. But it displaced many people from their native home, from their livelihood and their also their lives. Tribals or indigenous people were affected more through this projects. Industrialisation proved good for the nation but disastrous for the Tribal. A conservative estimate of the number of people displaced from 1950-1991 was about the 2,13,00,000 (Fernades,1991). As per the government records at least 75 per cent of those displaced are still not resettled. Historical evidence suggests that in first half of the 19th century a major wave of development displacement took place between 1830 and 1842. British government passed Land Acquisition act in 1894 which taken as a legal instrument of economic control over the people of India. By using the concept of "public domain" the British were able to theorise and legitimise their control over land. After the above the 60 years of the independence India following the same shame full policy for land acquisition which leads towards problem for the poor indigenous tribal people in our country. It maintains social in justice till today. Odisha is identified as the natural resources based state in our country which invited various companies to invest this place. There is an estimate that around 10 lakhs people have been physically displaced and 60 lakhs people have been disposed from their land. Displaced tribals who constitute more than 40 per cent of the total displaced population in Odisha are worst suffer. In Odisha project based development began in late 40s but gain momentum in the 50s after the implementation of the five year plan. The major developmental projects undertaken in the 50s were the Rourkela steel plant and Hirakud Dam project. During the 70s several multipurpose Dam likes Rengali, Upper Kolab, Upper Indrâvati and Subarnarekha were stated in the state. The Thermal Power Station (ITPS), Talcher Super Thermal Power project (TSTP) and the National Aluminium Company (NALCO) came up in the eighties. These projects were established in the resource rich highland districts of Odisha, which are predominantly inhabited by Tribals and other indigenous people in the state. These large projects left a massive effect towards the inhabitants in that place. In order to economic development the government of Odisha has launched a massive programme for industrialisation in post economic refòrm phase. In this phase Odisha has attracted investment of 41 lakhs crores (The Economic Times, 2007). In 2005 alone the state government has signed as many as 43 MoUs with various corporate bodies for setting up their industrial units at an investment of Rs 1,60,000 crore (Mishra and Maitra, 2007), POSCO was among them which was signed MoU with state government in 2005 to establish Steel plant in Jagatsinghpur. Odisha like other developing economics has however faced peoples protest during its industrial process. In last few years it has faced a number of protests against setting up of industries like Vedanta Alumina limited in Langigarh, Tata Steel at Kalinganagar and now POSCO in jagatstinhapur. The Kalinganagar incident is part of serious resistance of the people threatened with displacement by mega project.

Development, Displacement and Discourse

Development means making a better life for everyone. In common parlance the term development implies some shorts of advancement in positive direction (Martinussen, 1997). Views of development are inevitably linked to some idea of progress, which involves change from one state to another (Harrison, 1989). But after some days it changes its connotation.With the rise of capitalism and industrial system in western countries the concept of development changes and only one way of development is developing of GNP or per capital income. The meaning of development gained momentum in 1950s after the independence of third world countries from the British rule. Many third world countries follow the one way of development that is modernisation and western path of development to strengthen their economy.The third world became the favoured recipient large shift of foreign from the western countries and western technology and follow the industrialisation as their development strategies. So development became strong economy related after the independence of third world countries and it became strong as to synonymous with economic development. The development defined in terms of economic growth was the core development thinking in the 1950s. Unlike other third world countries India also followed the same model of economic development. At that time there were two version of economic development, one was Gandhi's village economy model and other was Neheruvians western model. Gandhi was against the industrialisation and western model of development and he clearly put it on his most popular book "*Hind Swaraj*". But in another side Nehru was against the Gandhi's views on economic model of development and advocated that it leads towards the slow growth of country's economy and western model of industrialisation leads towards the high growth of economy in the country. So Nehru in second five year plan placed industrialisation as his model of development. Development was inclusively defined in terms of growth of GNP. But this development was not for all. Though it helps India to become an economic healthy country but it leads towards the inequality and huge displacement of large section of society, among them mostly Tribal or Indigenous people. It leads towards the violation of human rights. They became poorer after displacement of their native place. This development model raises question that development for whom in our society? The indigenous or tribals deprived from their own land. During the current time around five lakhs people displacing in every year in the name of development (Medha Patkar, 2000). The issue of development and displacement now became question of national importance.

Scheduled Tribes and Human Rights

The great gift of classical and contemporary human thought to culture and civilisation is the notion of Human Rights. Human rights include, right to life, right to an adequate standard of living, freedom from all type of torture and other ill-treatment. Human rights in general are those minimum rights which every individual being a member of human family must possess consideration of other enjoy. To protect the Human rights of tribal or indigenous people United Nation announced different declaration like Universal Declaration of Human Rights in 1948.This declaration provides that right to live, right to liberty and security. Article one of the Universal Declaration of human rights provides right to equality. In 1966, United Nation Declaration on the Right to Development adopted by the General Assembly on 4th December, 1986 which deals with that development should participatory. International Labour Organisation (ILO) has also defended the social and economic rights of indigenous people (J. K. Das, 2001). United Nation has commemorated the year 1993 as the International Year for the World's Indigenous people. Another positive step towards the promotion of the rights of indigenous peoples is that the UN General Assembly in its resolution 48/163 of 21st December, 1993 proclaimed the UN International Decade of World's Indigenous people (1995-2004) which commenced on 10th December, 2004. Indian Constitution also provides many rules to protect the interest of the Tribals in our country. Fifth and sixth schedule of our constitution deals with the schedule tribe and schedule caste in our constitution. Currently India passed law regarding the Scheduled Tribes and other Traditional Forest Dwellers (Recognition of Forest

Rights) Act 2006 to reserve or protect the forest for the Tribals. It empowered the Gram Sabha which represents the Tribal people.

POSCO Project and People's Protest

South Korean Pohang Iron and Steel Company Limited which known as POSCO India has signed a MoU with the state government of Odisha to establish Steel plant, an Iron-Ore mine and a port in Jagatsinghpur district, which will be the largest investment 12 billion dollars) foreign company in our country (The Times of India, 2007). It requires 12,000 acres land. Government agreed to provide land in three packages like, 25 acres of land in Bhubaneswar, 4,000 acres in Jagatsinghpur for plant and 2000 acres for township, port and also remaining for other purposes (The Sambad, 2008). It will displace around the 613 families in plant areas which is matter of concern. In the purposed areas people farming the betel vine and other vegetables for their occupation which will be destroyed after the establishment of company.

People's Protest

People's agitation is continuing against this project because, it will deprived them from their native place, livelihood. There are some fact that they earn 14,000 to 20,000 as their earnings from betel and also other people earning the healthy money from the fishing. Among them some are Tribals and Indigenous people. More than 8,000 people depending on this livelihood. So they are agitating against this project or land acquisition. Women, children and social activist are participating in this protest. POSCO Pratirodha Sangrama Samiti (PPSS) leads this protest with the leadership of Abhaya Sahoo. People claim that government acquires land with the brutal force. It is also violating the Forest Right Act, 2006, because purposed areas are included in forest reserve areas according the act. Though company promised to give compensation to affected people but it will not sufficient for the people. Centre also made different committee on this. Saxena Committee suggest Central government for withdrawing the support from that are, because it violates the Forest Right Act and without concerning the Gram Sabha government acquires lands from the people violates their rights but Meena Gupta Committee was for the project.

Government now able to acquires land for its first phase production. Agitation now only exists in Dhinkia.

Conclusion

New development paradigm leads towards the large problems for the people, mainly the indigenous Tribal people. They are getting nothing but only losing everything in the name of development. This development not for the all section of the society. It is only for the some section of the society. Due to the weak policy of government larger section suffer more and they protest. But the government depresses them with using brutal force which leads towards the violation of the human rights of the poor, indigenous and Tribal people in our country. Government should follow the proper policy for this and should follow proper rehabilitation policy.

References

Barnett, Tony (1988), *Sociology and Development*, London: Htchinson Press.

Chakravorty, Sanjoy (2013), *The Price of Land: Acquisition, Conflict, and Consequences*, New Delhi: Oxford University Prcss.

Das, J.K. (2011), *Human Rights and Indigenous Peoples*, New Delhi: APH Publication.

Dewet, Chris (2001), "*Economic Development and Population Displacement: Can Everybody Win*?" *Economics Political Weekly*, Vol. 36(50), 15th March.

Dhagamwar, V. and Verma, N. (2003*), Industrialisation Development and Displacement: The People of Korba,* New Delhi: Saga Publication.

Dutta, Ashirbani (2007), *Development-Induced Displacement and Human Rights*, New Delhi: Deep and Deep Publications.

Kannongo, Sanghamitra (2011), *Tribal and Human Rights*, Delhi: Swastik Publication.

Madangopal, Dakshyayani (2010), *Marginal Zones: Development–Induced Displacement in Mumbai*, Bangalore: Books for Change Press.

Mishra, Banikanta (2011), "Paan or POSCO?", *Economics Political Weekly*, Vol. xlvi(27), 25th June.

Mishra, Sudarsan (2008), "POSCO Project in Orissa", *The Times of India*, Bhubaneswar, 8th March.

Mohanty, Biswaranjan (2001), "Displacement and Rehabilitation of Tribals", *Economics Political Weekly*, 40 (13), 26th March.

Parida, Jayanta (2006), *Tribals: Development, Displacement and Rehabilitation*, New Delhi: Classical Publishing Company.

Patekar, Medha and Bhaduri, Amit (2009), "Industrialisation for the people by the people, of the people", *Economic s Political Weekly*, 40(12), 13th January.

Pati, Sikta (2012), *Industrialisation and Displacement: An Economic Impact*, New Delhi: Concept Publication.

Peet, Richard and Hartwick, Elaine (2009), *Theories of Development: Contentions, Arguments, Alternatives*, New York: The Guilford Press.

Sachan, A.K. and Jaiswal, B. (2005), *Development Induced Displacement and Rehabilitation,* New Delhi: Alpha Publication.

10

Development Induced Displacement of Tribals in Odisha: Issues and Concerns

Dasarathi Bhuiyan

Development, through industrialisation, science and technology, has become a major concern *vis-à-vis* livelihood of the people. Today in many parts of the country, there is a strong opposition against dams, industries and other such development related projects. This understanding of development is being questioned at the grassroots level by various struggles from the standpoint of tradition and culture. It is in this context, that this paper discusses the anti-industrial movement in Odisha and attempts to understand the various debates emerging from the movement. The key questions examined here are as follows: First, on what basis is the movement opposing the industrial project? Second, if the movement is opposing modernisation and industrialisation, then is it free of modernisation? And, how does the movement look at such developmental projects: as a blend of "development and resistance" and "tradition and modernisation", or something else? Accordingly, the information collected about the movement during the field visit and through secondary sources is analysed within the framework of Development and Resistance: Encounter between the State and Communities. [1]

Development and Displacement in Odisha

Odisha is one of the backward States of the country. It however possesses vast deposits of various valuable minerals and other resources, which remained unutilised and underutilised due to various reasons. The State saw the setting up of large development projects like multipurpose river valley projects- Hirakud Dam, Rengali, Upper Kolab, Indravati, Subarnarekha etc. Large industries — Rourkela Steel Plant, NALCO, HAL, POSCO and the like. Besides several private sector projects have either set up or signed MoUs with the State Government to start their units which include industrial giants Tata, Jindal, Birla, POSCO and others. But what is painful is the large-scale involuntary displacement of weaker sections, particularly the tribals. Statistical data indicates that a large portion of the project affected families belong to the tribal group. Since the tribal belt is invariably rich in mineral deposits, they are affected much by the ongoing power, mining and industrial projects. Therefore, these weaker section communities are opposing the ongoing projects. As a result, there emerges an encounter between the State and affected Communities.[2]

Objectives of the Study

Keeping the aforesaid objectives in view and the tribals in particular an empirical study was undertaken to find out the status of Development and Resistance between the the displaced tribal families and government. However, the broad objectives with which the empirical study was undertaken are the following: Assess the status of the displaced tribals: (i) Find out the extent of livelihood restoration of those affected (ii) Identify the factors responsible for resistance against development (iii) Recommend on the basis of research findings specific critical areas that need to be looked in to by the policy makers and implementing agencies for more effective resettlement and rehabilitation measures for the displaced persons in general and tribal displaced persons in particular in development projects.

Geographical Coverage of the Study and the Sample

The study on the basis of which the present report is based has been undertaken on the sample displaced tribal families in various projects located in the tribal Pocket of Odisha.

Methodology

For collecting empirical data a number of sociological and anthropological research tools were used. Some of the major research tools used for the study are:

(i) Interview schedule
(ii) Focus Group Discussion
(iii) Participatory Rural Appraisal
(iv) Case Study

Possible Areas for Exploration

The larger political and economic forces isolate, bypass the local governance during the process of establishment of any proposed projects. Weather it is Tata, Jindal, POSCO, Birla or the State Government authority almost all the forces have neglected the local governance while establishing their major establishments in the weaker sections habited regions.

Even the tribal regions which fall under PESA, both the government and the industry have collaborated to negotiate directly with people without engaging village panchayats in the tribal areas. Therefore, it is an important area of research relating to exclusion of panchayat institutions in situations of political conflict or economic contestation. Research needs to address this field to generate insights on what happens to inclusion when local governance institutions themselves get excluded from the processes of development and governance.[3]

Case Studies

In this context this study explores two case studies. To a greater extent the Tribals of Odisha are driven by traditional way of life. Though Odisha has been subject to many new projects, dams or minings they are opposing the mega projects and tribals are the active supporter of this movement. Some Tribals have been actively engaged in the operational setup of the Naxal movement in Odisha which involves it damaging the property of multinational companies those are working in the tribal areas for their development.[4]

Conflict over the mining of bauxite in the Kashipur region of Rayagada district in southern Odisha had taken a violent turn with the killing of three innocent tribal people. On December 16, 2001 two platoons of armed police entered Maikanch village in Kashipur block and opened fire at the residents. Abhilas Jhodia (25), Raghu Jhodia (18) and Jamudhar Jhodia (43) died and eight others sustained serious injuries.[5]

Ever since the entry of multinational companies for bauxite mining and processing in 1993, the tribal people of Kashipur and Laxmipur blocks of Rayagada district, Dasmantpur block of Koraput district and Thuamulrampur of Kalahandi district have been apprehensive of displacement and loss of livelihood.[6]

Odisha is known for its rich mineral deposits. The assessed reserves of chromium and nickle ores and bauxite in the state constitute a substantial proportion of the total deposits of them in the country. Taking advantage of the process of liberalisation and the opening up of the economy, private companies set their sights on the Kashipur region, which has considerable concentration of bauxite. In the region, the Baphilimali hill is estimated to have a deposit of 1,957. 3 lakh tonnes of bauxite, Kadingamali 914 lakh tonnes, and the Sasubohumali hill 860 lakh tonnes. The Katuramali hill in nearby Thuamularmpur block has a deposit of 400 lakh tonnes. Utkal Alumina, a consortium of Indian Aluminium Company (INDAL) (now owned by HINDALCO, part of the Aditya Birla group), the Tatas (they pulled out in 1998), Hydro Aluminum of Norway (or Norsk Hydro) and ALCAN (Aluminum Canada), are in the forefront of the mining-related activities. The Odisha Mining Corporation, the state government organisation, has been sidelined in the process. In the case of Utkal Alumina, it is estimated that, 1,750 hectares of land will be required for mining, the plant site, a township and dumping spots. Apart from this, a stretch of land approximately 20 km long and 50 meters wide will be required for conveyer and corridor maintenance. The entire project is 100 per cent export-oriented.[7]

Unaware of Government rules, most of the tribal people do not register their land rights. In these areas land is broadly divided into two categories – forest and unsurveyed upland (Dongar). Upland constitutes about 60 per cent of the total land in tribal-dominated areas such as Rayagada, Koraput and Kondhamal. Such upland is considered unsuitable for cultivation and a record of right is not allowed in its case. Although the tribal people in the lowland areas own land, their rights are either not recorded or are recorded in the names of others. Illegal transactions of land are common and the tribal people are often at the receiving end.

Since the finalisation of the proposal, the Odisha government has actively tried to hand over the land to the companies. Government officials now say that the transfer of land has been made and that the tribal people have to vacate. Encouraged by the support from the State government and the local authorities, corporate houses claim that they are the real owners of the land.[8]

Displacement of populations, loss of livelihood and damage to the environment and ecology of the region, which have been the consequences of mining and industrial activities, were kept hidden from the outside world or presented in a misleading manner.

Concerned over the prospect of having to leave their hearth and home, people started organising themselves. Road blockades, demonstrations and dharnas were organised in front of government offices at Kashipur and Rayagada. Survey teams of the companies were denied access to the area. Day and night vigil was maintained to prevent the entry of the government and company officials.[9]

The responses of the tribal people were co-ordinated by organisations such as the Prakrutik Sampada Surkhya Parishad, the Baphilimali Surkhya Samiti and the Anchalika Surakhya Samiti. Every village had a resistance body.

The Administration visited Kashipur, Maikanch, Kucheipadar, Tikir, Rayagada town and other places and met a number of people. Meanwhile, under the direct patronisation of the companies, a pro-project group had also been formed. Those who fight for the rights of livelihood and against displacement were branded as people who oppose industrialisation and development. The pro-project group propagated the idea that the mining of bauxite was the only means for the area to cross the boundaries of backwardness. The tribal people were advised to sacrifice their "petty" rights in the "interest of the nation."[10]

The pro-mining group, which included professionals, traders, contractors and others, feel that the tribal people would have gained enormously with the implementation of the projects. The government machinery, which is supposed to protect the interests of the people, were not perceived as such but were identified with the strident moves of these groups, which were not affected by the projects.

The state machinery in Odisha appears to have capitulated to the designs of the companies. All the major political parties, the local administration and the police apparently act in concert to help them. "All-party committees" have been floated, with parties such as the Biju Janata Dal (BJD), the Bharatiya Janata Party (BJP) and the Congress (I) on them. Political leaders, police and administration officials visit the tribal areas; the tribal people alleged that they create panic among the residents.[11]

The December 16 incident was preceded by certain actions of an 'all-party committee", which the tribal people looked at with suspicion. On December 15, under the leadership of N. Bhaskar Rao, Rayagada district president of the BJD, and Krishna Mohapatro, a former block chairman of Kashipur, a group of people reached Maikanch and allegedly tried to disrupt a gathering of tribal people who were to discuss a "road blockade" (Chakajam) programme at Rafkana junction, 30 km away from Kashipur, scheduled for December 20. The Paribesh Sampad Surkhya Parishad planned the programme. The companies and the State administration obviously wanted to foil it.[12]

The people resisted the efforts to disrupt the meeting. On December 16, armed with a First Information Report (FIR) filed at the Kashipur police station, two platoons of armed policemen led by Circle Inspector Subash Swain and Kashipur Block Development officer (BDO) Golak Mohanty reached Maikanch. The policemen allegedly beat up the women and asked for the whereabouts of the men, who were hiding in the nearby hills, Hearing the commotion, the men returned from the hills. It was alleged that as soon as the policemen noticed the men, they opened fire.[13]

The version of the police and the administration was that the police party went to Maikanch to investigate the "attack" on Bhaskar Rao on December 15. Residents of the village attacked the police party by means of bows and arrows and threw stones at them, and this forced the police to open fire, it says. Several political parties, such as the BJD, the BJP and the Congress (I) and the State administration allege that a non-governmental organisation, Agragamee, which has been working among the tribal people of Kashipur, for about 20 years, and its director Achyut Das are inciting the tribal people to resort to violence and refuse to vacate the area. It is alleged that Agragamee planned the attack on BJD leaders. The BJD organised rallied and meetings at Rayagada demanding the arrest of Achyut Das and a ban on Agragamee. It is a fact that Agragamee played a role in raising the consciousness of the people, uniting them and making them aware of their rights.[14]

A three-member delegation of Left parties, comprising Ali Kishore Patnaik, member of the Odisha State secretariat of the Communist Party of India (Marxist), Pradipta Panda, CPI(M) Member of Legislative Assembly (MLA) and Biswanath Sahoo, former Communist Party of India (CPI) MLA, visited the area on December 19 and 20. It also met the Collector and District Magistrate at Rayagada.

On December 21, at a press conference convened in Bhubaneswar, the team members described the police firing as "pre-designed murder" to crush the movement against displacement. It was "murder" because all the three people who died received the bullets above the chest, they said. It cannot be disputed that the police opened fire as soon as they saw people coming down from the nearby hills because three cows and one buffalo that were grazing on the hillock also died. Naveen Patnaik government ordered an inquiry into the firing, which was conducted by a senior civil servant, Sanjeev Kumar Hota. Several organisations had protested against the killings and supported the tribal residents right to livelihood. At Berhampur, a daylong dharna was organised in front of the office of the Revenue Divisional Commissioner (Southern Division) by the Adivasi Dalit Vikas Manch on December 23. At Bhubaneswar similar protests were held by various NGOs. The resistance to the alumina project and the police firing had important implications.[15]

Ever since the entry of multinational companies, the tribal people of Odisha have been apprehensive of displacement and loss of livelihood. It has been a surprise for many that Odisha, which is so well situated and blessed with mineral riches, should be one of the poorest states in the country. In terms of industrialisation, it ranks below many of its smaller and less endowed neighbours. Odisha is the richest mineral state in the country. Therefore, Odisha is surely getting attention from big industries. Mineral rich Odisha has been demanding a second steel plant in Odisha after the Rourkela Steel Plant, which was set up in the fifties.

Since the finalisation of the Mega projects, the Odisha government has actively tried to handover the land to the companies. Encouraged by the support from the state government and the local authorities, corporate houses claim that they are the real owners of the land. Displacement of tribal populations, loss of livelihood and damage to the environment and ecology of the region, which have been the consequences of mining and industrial activities, were kept hidden from the outside world or presented in a misleading manner. Concerned over the prospect of having to leave their hearth and home, the tribal people started the organising road blockades, demonstrations and dharnas. On December 16, 2000, two platoons of armed police entered Maikanch village. In Kasipur block and open fired at the tribal. As a result, three innocent tribals died and others sustained serious injuries. Conflict over the displacement of the tribals in Kalinga Nagar region of Jajpur district in Odisha had taken a violent turn with the killings 12 tribals in January 2006. At the centre of controversy is a mega steel plant project, which is being persuaded by TATA steel.[16]

However, tribals of Odisha who stand to lose their homesteads, think differently. Livelihoods are closely tied with land in this region. Compensation could conceivably be awarded for homesteads that are lost at the projects. But these schemes are rather skewed in their application. Private land can be compensated for, but common and forest lands are not deemed to warrant material orders. Odisha also has a curious law, which holds that land situated on a gradient would not be eligible for compensation. But in order to ensure sustained development through a participatory and transparent process, Government of Odisha has framed a comprehensive resettlement and rehabilitation policy in 2006 after the Kalinga Nagar incident.

In the Kalinga Nagar incidence more than 11 tribals were killed opposing to industrialisation by the Tata group of companies. Also, it is natural that a closer contact with the masses would help the Maoists to engineer the economy of the area.

The land of tribals, for instance, in Odisha is owned through customary right. Ownership documents exist mainly for the plain lands and only customary rights are there for the land in the hill slopes, which means they do not have 'legally' defined ownership. Thus, even in the wake of proper compensatory measures, many of the tribal people would be left out from the compensation, as they do not have 'legal' ownership. On the other hand, land is seen as inalienable resource for the livelihoods of the tribal people. Apart from providing them with sustainable livelihood, the land also provides them with freedom to work independently according to their needs. This dependence on land and forest produce has relatively isolated the tribal people from the mainstream economy. In other words the absence of modern legal system denotes the weak penetration of modernisation in this region. In recognition of this tradition, the Indian state provides statutory guarantees under V Schedule of the Constitution; where in tribal land cannot be sold or bought by a non-tribal. However, in UAIL case the rule was bent to suit the needs of industrialisation and development.[17]

The tribal people generally cultivate both plain and hill lands to enable them to different crops. Land forms a very important and crucial aspect of tribal life – land is the basis for the formation of their culture, economy, society and their polity. To quote:

"Our life, culture, and employment everything revolves around the soil. In the month of Asadha (signifying the rainy season) we have Kulimaruparba, we get the root of the crop home and worship it. In the month of Bhoda (the following month) we worship maize. From making the plough to agriculture work, we do everything together. So there is peace in our village. But once industrialisation starts, our festivals will vanish and our region will be destroyed.... We will get jobs, but who will do the cultivation? People will eat money or what? We cultivate; therefore we eat." (Buka Miniaka, a tribal of Kashipur says,)[18]

The tribal people believe that they can be free and independent as long as they own the land. Dangar is the widely practised mode of cultivation.[19] They grow different varieties of paddy, maize, and various types of pulses and oil seeds like, *kandul, masur, mung, chana, alsi, castor, mustard*, etc. As most of the villages are surrounded by perennial springs on all the four sides, water is available throughout the year. Their food habits are in tune with the crops that they cultivate. In the morning, generally, they have *mandia paej* (gruel prepared out of *ragi*), which is also their staple food. Rice with some cereal forms is another major part of their food. However, since the last one decade, there is also increase in the cultivation of various vegetables. As a result something or the other is available around the year. Apart from this, they also grow various roots and tubers in their kitchen gardens, which also form their staple food. Whatever is available through agriculture activity is not accumulated in the modern sense, but exchanged in return for other goods.[20]

Whose Development…?

The state in India looks at the development process, particularly, as a part of modernisation.[21] Hasan (2000) argues that the Indian state pursued twin goals through the process of development: unifying the nation and social transformation. These two objectives were crucial as the Indian state was formed on modern premise with a traditional society as base. On the other hand, the movement by way of questioning the process of development appears to be also questioning the basis of modernisation itself. But the question remains whether the movement is articulating tradition against modernisation or is it just struggling for alternative notion of development that is inclusive of tribal identity and culture within it.[22]

"We have seen big projects in our Odisha like Indravati project and NALCO project. We have heard about Hirakud and Upper Kolab hydro projects. We have seen deprivation and sorrow of local people caused by these development projects. In our view development means that all should live peacefully and happily. But that some should die for development – we do not require this kind of development." This is the opinion of Bhagaban Majhi: a tribal of Kashipur.[23] Thus, any meaningful development needs to recognise the rights of the tribal people over land, forest, and other resources that are related directly and indirectly to their livelihood. To sum up, in the words of one tribal woman: What is development? Whose development? Does development imply cars and vehicles for everyone? The Chief Minister and others may need cars but why does everybody need it? Is it possible to give cars and vehicles to everyone? We don't need cars and motors. We are people of the soil and our lives revolve around the soil (Bulka Miniaka).[24] Thus for the tribal people development is something that has livelihood, land, water, forests, culture, identity, history, community, freedom, as the key ingredients.[25]

Why Encounter between the State and Tribal Communities?

PESA Act 1996 (Panchayat Extension to Scheduled Areas Act) extends Panchayats to the tribal areas of eight states of India namely, Andhra Pradesh, Bihar, Gujarat, Himachal Pradesh, Maharashtra, Madhya Pradesh, Odisha and

Rajasthan with the intention to enable tribal society to assume control over their own destiny to preserve and conserve their traditional rights over natural resources.

However, most states have been indifferent to the Act as well as corresponding transfer of powers the tribal population (to access and utilise natural resources for consumption and livelihood). Women, dalit and tribal have suffered social and economic marginalisation for a long time and therefore are considered for affirmative action. Particularly in the rural setting, the socio-economic hierarchies are inter-related. Hence, the groups who occupy low position in social hierarchy such as dalit, women, and tribal also invariably occupy low position in economic hierarchy.

The larger macro political and economic context in which local governments operate:

How local governments can or cannot promote inclusion in the contexts of (a) violent conflicts and political unrest, and (b) neo-liberal economic growth, globalisation and commoditisation of commons such as land, water and forests.

(a) Despite India being a stable democracy, political conflicts have festered in specific regional contexts. Two types of conflicts have been most visible and have escalated in the recent times—the armed conflict in the North Eastern region which has taken the shape of separatist movements; and conflicts between the state and the Maoist groups (popularly known as Naxalites) in Chhatisgarh, Jharkhand, Odisha and Andhra Pradesh where the Maoist groups claiming to be supporters of the poor have launched violent assault against the government. It is imperative to explore how political contexts as described above affect the functioning of local governments and implications of this for the resource poor communities and those considered being most vulnerable to unrest such as poor and women.

(b) Economic conflicts between those whose resources are threatened by rapid economic growth agenda of neo-liberalism and globalisation, and those who are actively pursuing these have intensified in recent times.

In pursuing economic growth panchayats as local decision-making institutions are either bypassed or co-opted by the economically powerful forces in executing their agenda. In many parts of India this has resulted in contestations spearheaded by those who are threatened with loosing the resources on which their survival depends. Examples include Singur and Nandigram in West Bengal and Kalinga Nagar in Odisha where the Special Economic Zones are contested by people; in tribal areas of Odisha mining operations by multinationals have faced opposition from local people. In other parts of India, it is not entirely unknown for financial incentives in the short run inducing a peaceful cooption of the panchayats in the neo-liberal agenda of the state but in the long run carrying with the possibility of the communities losing control over their natural resources.[26]

Impact of Development Projects on Displaced Tribals

On the basis of the empirical study conducted on the displaced families, the following are some of the important impacts that have been revealed from the analysis of data by the researcher:

1. *Decline in Joint Family System:* The pre-displacement level of nuclear and joint families was changed in both tribal and non-tribal families showing the same trend of breaking down of joint family to nuclear families. This is a general feature noticed in most of the development projects.

2. *Landlessness:* India being a farm dominated society with agriculture as the main occupation, displacement from land, removes the main foundation on which people's productive systems, commercial activities and livelihood are based. Unless this foundation is reconstructed elsewhere or replaced by steady income-generating employment, landlessness sets in and the affected families are impoverished. In most of the cases/ projects, land for land, norm could not be followed. But cash compensation is inadequate to make up for the loss of land. This impact has serious implication in the current project under study and therefore needs special consideration by the project implementing agencies in general and the policy makers formulating strategies for the impacted people of development projects at government level.

3. *Joblessness and increase in the proportion of workers:* When people were displaced from their habitat, they lose their means of livelihood. Creation of new jobs or alternative sources of income for them becomes very difficult since the oustees do not possess any skill to learn new methods of earning their livelihood. Hence those who were owners of the means of production before displacement have now become daily wage earners. In these projects, taken up for the study, though the project authorities followed the policy of providing a job to each displaced family, the other members of the displaced families remained jobless. The policy also discriminated against the landless labourers, artisans, share croppers and petty businessmen among others.

4. *Homelessness:* Loss of house and shelter may be only temporary during the transition period for most of the displaced. But for some, homelessness remains a permanent feature. The project authorities only provided homestead plots while the displaced persons have themselves built their houses. Again when a split occurs in the family, those who leave the family become homeless.

5. *Food insecurity:* Forced displacement increases the risk of chronic food insecurity. In India, crops are grown to provide food to the family while vegetables are grown in the kitchen gardens that take care of the food needs of the family. Surplus is also sold in the market. But forced displacements deprive the oustees from their former resource of livelihood rendering them landless. Even when homestead land was provided, the oustees could not properly reclaim and level the hilly area. In the LB Valley project, the displaced families have to buy everything including food items from the market.

6. *Loss of access to common property:* For the poor people, particularly, the landless and otherwise asset less people, loss of access to common property (forest lands, water bodies, grazing land, etc.) leads to a major deterioration in their income and livelihood levels. Such lost resources are rarely compensated by the Government in the relocation sites. There are also frequent conflicts between the host population and new settlers over the use of forest land and other government land. As a result, the resettler do not get fuel wood and other minor forest produce, which they used to collect from the forests in their old habitat.

7. *Social Disintegration:* Forced displacement tears apart the social fabric of the oustees. Production systems are dismantled, kinship groups and family systems are often scattered and cultural identity of the people is under threat. Social and community networks that help people to cope with poverty through exchange of food and clothing, mutual help with farming, building houses and caring children are disrupted. Social disintegration has been a major impoverishment risk in all the projects undertaken. In the LB Valley project, the mutual help arrangement and other socio-economic relationships have been totally disrupted.

8. *Increased Morbidity and Mortality:* Loss of ancestral and homestead land, less no access to health care facilities, the psychological trauma caused thereby and the food insecurity together often leads to serious diseases. There is also the danger of parasitic and vector born diseases in the relocated sites because of unsafe water, poor sewerage etc. In fact, lack of food, unhygienic living and environmental degradation in the new place were found in the project area to have a serious impact on the health of the oustees. In these projects, pollution caused by coal dust and frequent blasting has caused skin diseases, eye irritation, gastric disorders, diarrhoea and other ailments. Though medical centers have been opened in the resettlement colony they are dysfunctional in the absence of the doctors. The findings of empirical study in the project resettlement areas and the analysis of the empirical data gathered from the study reveals that the following situation prevails in the resettlement area and to the displaced people in general and the tribal displaced families in particular (as majority of the sample households were tribals): [27]

- The general socio-economic condition of the oustees has deteriorated significantly.
- Socio-economic inequalities have widened.
- The cropping pattern has changed drastically.
- Dependence on trees and livestock has reduced substantially.
- Increase in the proportion of agricultural labourers.
- Increasing trend towards nuclear family.
- Poor dwelling conditions of the oustees.
- Improper use of compensation money.
- Rise in the incidence of indebtedness.

• Drastic reduction in the socio-economic condition of women in the PAFs.

Conclusion

In view of these after effects of displacement, especially on the tribals it is necessary not only to identify, avoid and mitigate risks in each development project that entails displacement, but also to focus on benefits over and above compensation and rehabilitation for damages as well as benefit sharing arrangement. A prudent approach demands long term commitments, financial and institutional guarantees and the use of professional approach in dealing with the issues of social development of indigenous people. Constant monitoring by technically competent independent observers can go a long way in ensuring more effective resettlement and rehabilitation arrangements in case of the displaced families which can end up in not only restoring the pre-displaced living condition of the millions of displaced families but also in substantially bringing in improvement in their socio-economic condition in the post-project period.

Notes

1. Rajashree Mahanty. "Impact of development project on displaced tribal: A case study of a development project in Eastern India". Odisha review, Sep-Oct 2011, pp. 67-68.
2. Alcan, (2006), "Backgrounder: The Utkal Project", http://www.business-humanrights.org downloaded on 07-05-07.
3. Syed S. Kazi, "Displacement and Rehabilitation", in civil services chronicle, (English monthly), Vol. XVI, No.12, New Delhi, Jun. 2006, p. 26.
4. Adivasi, Journal of the Scheduled Castes and Scheduled Tribes Research and Training Institute, Bhubaneswar, Vol. 46, No. 2, December 2006, Editorial page.
5. Nair, Suresh, "AV Birla group begins work on Utkal project", Economic Times, April 14, 2004. Norwatch Newsletter, 1-96 at www.norwatch.no
6. Bulliyya, G. J. K. Nayak and G. Mallick, (2005), "Forest Habitat and Tribal Subsistence Economy Rights in Scheduled Tribal-Domain State of Odisha", Man in India, 85, (3 and 4), pp. 125-139.
7. Das, Achyut and Vidya Das, "Chronicle of a Struggle – the Kashipur Anti-Mining Movement", <http://www.sanctuaryasia.com> downloaded on 07-05-07.
8. Prafulla Das, "Odisha the fight continues" the Hindu Survey of the Environment (Annual Issue 2006), New Delhi, p. 100.
9. Manoranjan Mahanty, "KBK to Kalinga Nagar a Dangerous Drift for Odisha and India", in main-stream (English Weekly), New Delhi, Vol. XLIV, No. 43, October 13-19, 2006, p. 25.
10. Dr Snehalata Panda, "Socio-economic profile and Development of tribals in Odisha", in Kurukshetra, (English monthly). Vol. 55, No. New Delhi, August 2007, p. 32.

11. Prafulla Das, "Odisha the fight continues" the Hindu Survey of the Environment (Annual Issue 2006), New Delhi, p. 100.

12. Trilochan Sahoo, "Industrialisation and Displacement in Odisha", Adivasi, *op. cti.*, pp. 133-134.

13. Mahapatra, L.K. (1991). "Development for Whom? Depriving the Dispossessed Tribals's." Social Action, 41(3): July-Sept, pp. 271-288.

14. Ramesh, K.S (1998). "Resettlement and Rehabilitation of Family Displaced by Development Projects: Corporate Social Responsibility." ASCI Journal of Management, 28(1): pp. 29-36.

15. R.C. Pandit, "Development vs. Displacement of Tribals people in india and problems and prospects". New Delhi, 2009. p. 179.

16. Fernandes, Walter (1996). "Land Reforms Ownership Pattern and Alienation of Tribals Livelihood." Social Action, 46(4): Oct-Dec.

17. Rajashree Mahanty. "Impact of Development Project in Eastern India. Sep-Oct 2011 (Odisha Review), p. 68.

18. Buka Miniaka, a tribal of Kashipur says Dangar is slash and burn cultivation. Each village has a traditionally demarcated area for dangar use of the people of that particular village. If the possessor of the land does not use it for consecutively for two years, then the village community will decide about its redistribution.

19. Syed. S. Kazi, "Displacement and Rehabilitation," in civil services chronicle, (English monthly), Vol. xvi, No. 12, New Delhi. June 2006, p. 26.

20. Hasan, Zoya, ed., (2000), Politics and the State in India: Readings in Indian Government and Politics-3, New Delhi: Sage Publications.

21. Hasan, Zoya, ed., (2000), Politics and the State in India: Readings in Indian Government and Politics-3, New Delhi: Sage Publications.

22. Bhagaban Majhi: a tribal of Kashipur.

23. Bulka Miniaka: a tribal of Kashipur says.

24. Samal, K.C. (1998). Poverty Alleviation after liberalisation: Study of a Tribals Block in Odisha. EPW, Vol. XXXIII, No. 28, July 11, pp. 1947.

25. Indian People's Tribunal Report on Environment and Human Rights, (2006), Kashipur: An Enquiry into Mining and Human Rights Violations in Kashipur, Odisha, IPT, Mumbai.

26. Mishra, Banikanta (2006), "People's Movement at Kalinganagars; An epitaph or an Epitome?" Economic and Political weekly, Vol. XLI. No. 7, Feb 18, pp. 551-554.

27. Pathy, Jaganath, (1992), "Articulation of Capitalism and Destitution of the Scheduled Tribes of India", in Buddhadeb Chaudhuri, ed., Tribal Transformation in India: Economy and Agrarian Issues, Vol-I, inter-India Publications, New Delhi, pp. 488-495.

11

Ramoshi the Denotified Tribe in India: Understanding their Struggle and Politics of Exclusion

Dattatary Bhandalkar

Abstract

This paper is a sincere attempt to bring to the forefront the voices and experiences of the Ramoshi tribes in Maharashtra about being "Denotified" in society. The 'Ex-criminal Tribes' of India, now referred as 'Denotified' tribes, comprise a significant population who were once declared as 'Criminals' by the British with the enactment of Criminal Tribes Act, 1871. They continue to remain stigmatised and discriminated by dominant sections, deprived of access and excluded of opportunities to exercise the basic human rights. Caste as a character of societal structure played a significant role. The interplay of caste and power relations in society affected the community in context of livelihood, access to common resources in villages, employment opportunities, ownership of land, participation and representation in village panchayat.

The paper interestingly shows how ancestral labelling gradually affects their lives in context of acceptance, being viewed as 'Others' in society and follows with occupational crisis, under representation in local self-governance, resulting into poverty and marginalisation of the population. The paper is a reflection of the field reality of the Denotified tribes and explains their situation through their lenses. The paper emerged out of an empirical research, with a qualitative approach, exploratory research design, undertaken with the Ramoshi tribes in Maharashtra. It highlights the politics of exclusion experienced by the tribes from treatment by dominant others in society to participation in village, experiences of land alienation, displacement and migration over years to ill-treatment by police officials. The paper exemplifies the existence of power relations and interplay of caste politics with the reality of being treated unfairly and indifferently in society. It reflects on the historical background of the tribe and how it is still affecting the community eventually leading to construction of labeling and exclusion of the tribe.

The Denotified Tribes in India– A History of Exclusion

The tribal of our nation are known for their diverse and rich culture and practices. However, the reality of the tribes in our country has gradually changed over the years. Among many tribal communities in India a significant population of marginalised tribal communities were once classified and declared as 'Criminal Tribes' with the declaration of Criminal Tribes Act in 1871. With the enactment of the Act, these tribesmen were registered and notified as 'Criminals' in society. Their movements and actions were restricted by the British government; elaborate arrangements were made for their supervision and settlements were made in different corners of the country to separate them from other sections of society. A majority of this tribe still exhibit their primitive and ethnic traits. Many of them still live in tribal groups, wander from one place to another in search of livelihood and they do not have any permanent home of their own. They have specific rituals, beliefs, religious practices of their own and those are unique to themselves. Neither globalisation, liberalisation nor any social advancement could improve their conditions to a significant extent. Although the government of independent India officially 'Denotified' these tribes in 1952, it made no provisions for improving their situations. The CTA gave the police arbitrary powers to even kill members of the declared 'criminal' tribes. Although the notified criminal tribes were 'denotified' the communities are not categorised under the constitutional schedules like the scheduled caste and scheduled tribes. Some de-notified and nomadic communities have been included in the respective state lists of SCs and STs. However, there is no uniformity in the status of these tribes across the country. The human rights violations against the DNTs are not covered by legislation such as the Scheduled Castes and Scheduled Tribes (Prevention of Atrocities) Act (1989) that protects the SCs and STs. The DNTs do not possess traditional land rights or house titles. The tribal population being majorly nomadic in nature yet; is not included in the census of the country. They remain denied of citizenship rights including voting rights. They are mostly engaged in informal means of livelihood. Presently, there are 198 denotified tribes in India, with 14 such communities in Maharashtra (Rathod, 2000). These groups of communities are scattered in nature and mostly situated in the drought prone areas. These tribesmen are not just a neglected section of our society but a complex one as well. Their problems are not only grounded in contemporary reality, but also deeply rooted in history. They have suffered injustices at the hands of both polity and society; their issues have not been sufficiently redressed as well. They are still being treated as criminals by birth and subjected to harassment and perscecution at the hands of the police and the state machinery. In the backdrop of prolonged conflict in context of caste system in India, a significant population group has been oppressed; they are subject to stigma, discrimination and their social, economic and political rights have been violated strikingly. There is an immense need to explore and understand the issues of the de-notified population in India and address them to ensure justice to these ethnic groups.

The *Ramoshis* of Maharashtra

The *Ramoshi* tribe is one among many tribal communities who were declared as "criminal tribes" in Maharashtra and further classified as 'Denotified tribes' in post independence era. The *Ramoshis* were known as 'warrior tribes' and were majorly a wandering population with their traditional occupation being hunters, gatherers and guardsmen. These tribes primarily belonged to Karnataka, Madhya Pradesh, Andhra Pradesh and Maharashtra. The *Ramoshis* in Karnataka and Andhra Pradesh were referred as *Berad* and *Boya.* The *Ramoshis* in Maharashtra are majorly concentrated in areas of Satara, Solapur, Sangli and Purander Taluka in Pune. With the declaration of the Criminal Tribes Act, 1871, the *Ramoshis* along with many other tribal communities were notified as criminals in society. Although post-independence, the tribes were decriminalised, they were further classified and notified as 'Habitual Offenders' with the declaration of the Habitual Offenders Act, 1959 and later notified further as 'Denotified tribes'. The process of labeling and notifying the *Ramoshis* continued even after decriminalisation. The tribe remains identified as 'Criminal tribes' even today and face stigma and exclusion both in the hands of polity and society.

The *Ramoshis* were warrior tribes and were associated with many empires and majorly used to work as warriors fighting battles, as hunters, protecting watchmen and guards for properties of emperors. They were often referred as '*Bedar*' meaning fearless. The *Ramoshis*, once included in the Criminal Tribe category of Bombay Presidency, were involved in uprisings against the British. The tribe primarily used to reside in the forests, away from the villages. They were known for their valor during the Maratha Empire. The changes of the British National Forest Policy during the early nineteenth century created conflicts over forest use. The *Ramoshis* with their traditional occupation on force of arms and with poor skills to earn livelihood were forced into criminal livelihoods. The tribe organised themselves and revolted against the British. The rising protest and fight against the British alarmed them and eventually the Criminal Tribes Act, 1871 was declared. As per the Census of 1901, their population was 60,555 of which 31,444 were males and 29,111 were females

(Singh, 2004). The *Ramoshis* were the first among many other de-notified tribes in Maharashtra, who started settling down in villages post independence era. Some of them continued staying in the settlements, while others started migrating to other places in Maharashtra in search of their livelihood. They were majorly an unsettled population then, without lands and without any means to earn their livelihood. However, although over the years the tribe gradually settled in the villages, the stigma of criminality attached to the community continues and the tribe continue facing stigma and exclusion in the hands of the polity and society.

The Unheard Voices

The Denotified tribes are indigenous population and are distinguished in relation to their ancestry, their livelihood patterns, their nomadic nature and many other distinct features. The tribes before the colonial era were distinguished by such features, but during the colonisation period with the declaration of Criminal Tribes Act (CTA), 1871, the tribes were classified and tagged as 'Criminal' in society. The tribes were majorly engaged in hunting before the British colonisation, but with the changes of the British National Forest Policy, their livelihood was compromised. The tribes lacked any other skills for earning their livelihood. Their revolt against the British led to declaration of the CTA to get control over movements and actions of these tribes and settlements were built to capture them and keep in isolation, segregated from rest of society. This was the turning point which affected not only the existing population at that point of time but continues to influence the tribal population even today. The act of declaration and tagging a large group of tribal population resulted into restriction in movement and freedom of the tribes; people started perceiving them differently in society. The tribe began to be seen as 'Others' in society.

Interplay of Caste and Power

The Caste System in India is unique to our country which classifies individuals before their birth. This classification started with the Varna system which classified people based on their occupations and tagged them as 'lower' and upper' castes. The occupation based caste system in India had fixed job for all in society based on the caste they are born with. The denotified tribes majorly wandering in nature had hunting as their primary occupation. An elderly village member who belonged from outside the tribal community added that—

According to *Balutedari* (*Jajmani* system) there were fixed jobs for each community but not for the *Ramoshis*. So they started stealing for upper caste communities, providing them security, guard them from other powerful people in society and others. In British era the *Ramoshis* used to work for *sahukar*, rich people of the village. They used to plunder rich travelers, rich people of other villages and they used to offer the entire wealth to the *sahukar*. The *sahukars* in return used to give grains and other groceries for their family.

The participant's response reflects the struggle of the tribe for basic necessities like grains, groceries for their families and how for earning the basic necessity the tribe indulges into criminal activities. Livelihood crisis at a large level leads to poverty which in turn compels their involvement in many other illegal activities like production of illegal liquor, smuggling of river sands etc. With great despair one of the participants reflect —

"Each family has three or four children, how would they feed them? Now here in these villages if you see, our community is majorly engaged in illegal liquor business".

The tribe remains in the circle of poverty and marginalisation due to several social, economic and political factors playing in the situation. A majority of the respondents shared experiences that how their family has been affected due to nomadic nature and historical background of the tribes. The tribesmen in recent days are also involved in illegal ways of liquor production in villages. They are quite often arrested by policemen. In such cases their wife and children continue the business. Due to nomadic lifestyle and criminalisation of the community, children also face discrimination in schools. This affects their education. Some of the respondents said that due to high consumption of alcohol among youth, death at an early age is also common. The wives are left alone at a very early age with children. Hence the historical background of the community, recent business involvement in liquor production, habits of alcohol consumption affects the family system of the *Ramoshis*.

An old man belonging to *Ramoshi* community remarked with great annoyance about the condition of the tribe and how Caste as a dominant factor interplayed in the situation of the Denotified tribes.

We were not criminals. For earning our livelihood we used to work for upper caste. At times due to extreme livelihood crisis we used to get involved in crime. The upper caste people took this opportunity and forced us for all kinds of illegal activities, theft, plundering, crime etc. But we have to change and society should accept us as we are. Police played the biggest role in the criminalisation of *Ramoshis*. Still our people go for petty work at their home; we have to come out of this '*gulami*'. They also took our land from us but still we are working for them.

The response shows his annoyance. He emphasises by saying that they are not criminals and the livelihood crisis compelled their involvement in crime. He clearly mentions about how the dominant upper castes interplayed into the situation leading to increased involvement in crime. The power dynamics existing in the village affected the *Ramoshi* population not only in terms of their livelihood but also access to common resources in villages, employment opportunities, ownership of land, participation and representation in village Panchayats. The responses of the participants show that the tribe also experienced land alienation and hence had no opportunity of cultivation to earn their livelihood. In many cases the participants reported of their land being taken away by the dominant sections in the village and the tribe continued working as wage labourers in their lands in exchange of grains for their families. Some of the participants also reported of being displaced of their own land and they were forced to stay outside the main territory of the village. The researcher also observed that the location of houses of the *Ramoshi* community were outside the village territory, separate from all other houses in the village. The oppression was not only from the dominant castes of the village but also the police personnel. Other responses of the participants indicate that the treatment of police personnel towards the tribes were also to dominate, marginalise and stigmatise them rather being just to their concerns. Many times the tribesmen are arrested only on basis of suspicion by virtue of being labeled in history as 'Criminal Tribes'.

Perception as 'Others' in Society

The treatment of police personnel and other dominant castes resulted into building up of a negative image of the tribe in society. The tribe was perceived as different from others; others who have a criminal involvement and hence they have been identified as 'Criminals' in society. The demonstration of this image is visible in everyday acts of their lives like the location of their houses being outside the village territory, no involvement in village activities, no participation in Village Panchayat, no participation in village meetings and other decision making processes. These actions due to dominance of upper castes and ill-treatment of police personnel create also a perception of 'them' among the tribes. The tribesmen start perceiving themselves as 'others' different from the rest in society. It leads to formation of a self-concept and they construct an identity of themselves as deviant in society. With a deep sigh, the participants respond that their being deviant in society earns their livelihood, gets those grains from the upper caste.

Struggle for Constitutional Status

The several versions of the Criminal Tribes Act never recommended any provision for the betterment of the tribe, rather continued classifying and re-classifying them. No efforts have also been taken over years to develop a means to protect these tribes form atrocities. No special constitutional remedies have been suggested so far for the 'Denotified' tribes as a special group. In some state they are included in scheduled caste, some in scheduled tribes, majorly in other backward classes. In Maharashtra, a special group has been created as 'Denotified and Nomadic' (DNT) community classified as '*Vimukta Jati*'. Due to the wandering nature of the community and hunter and gatherers being primarily their traditional occupation over years, the tribe is not house listed and in most cases do not have any proof of identification losing their voting rights. As responded by one of the participants, they are treated as 'un-registered citizens' who have no access to exercise their basic rights.

For years many non-governmental organisations along with several commissions set up by government have been trying to put forth the major concerns of the tribal population with recommendations to make special provision for the Denotified population. With special constitutional remedies, safeguards the core issues of the tribe could be addressed; their issues of stigma, discrimination, ill treatment by police personnel, domination of other castes, livelihood crisis, problems of unemployment, poor skills, low income etc., could be holistically addressed. The atrocities with the de-notified tribes is also very high, however no safeguards in forms of laws are available to the tribe. Their cases are not registered, rather they are often arrested on cases not proven guilty based only on suspicion of the police by virtue of belonging to the tribes.

Living with Exclusion

The responses about the historical background of the community across the case studies suggest that the Criminal Tribes Act 1871 played a significant role in the lives of the *Ramoshis*. It was a turning point in history of *Ramoshis* since they were declared legally as criminals in society by the British. This action imposed the Label of criminal upon *Ramoshis*. This labelling began in history with the declaration of the Act which continued over the years.

The voices of the participants reflect interestingly the *emergence of themes* like History of the community, involvement in crime, occupational crisis, treatment of Police officials, stigma and discrimination leading to formation of perception among others and them and under representation in local self-governance. The reflections from the field elaborate the cycle of life of the *Ramoshis* beginning from criminalisation due to ancestral labeling, leading to stigma and discrimination in society, following with occupation crisis and involvement in crime, with poor participation and no representation in village decision-making leading to exclusion of the population from the society. Exclusion is a complex and multi-dimensional concept associated with several other structural problems in society like poverty, inequality, discrimination and marginalisation, etc., power is an important aspect which interplays between groups leading to exclusion. The process of exclusion involved two groups – the one who holds the power to exclude and the other who is excluded. This process works through systematic way through the agencies of society like state, police, courts etc. This further leads to cumulative form of exclusion.

The responses of the participants about the background of the community emphasised that due to wandering nature of the tribes and occupation based caste system adhered to the tribe, they were majorly involved in occupations like watchmen and guards post independence. They used to work for the upper dominant castes in guarding their properties etc. During the struggle for freedom with the British, the tribe was involved in the uprising against the British in the leadership of *Umaji Naik.* They also worked as brave warriors in the Maratha leadership. However post independence, after the repeal of the Criminal Tribes Act and enactment of the Habitual Offenders Act, the tribesmen were distributed with lands, decriminalising them but further classifying them into 'De-notified' tribes. The lands given were majorly in hilly areas and not fertile enough for cultivation to earn their livelihood. They continued remaining stigmatised and were often compelled by the dominant sections to work for their personal advantages.

The history of the community eventually led to entanglement in criminalisation of the tribe and their occupational patterns were compromised. The occupation based caste system played a significant role in shaping the occupational pattern of the *Ramoshis.* Regarding the present occupation status of the *Ramoshis*, the responses of the participants highlight that some of the Ramoshis work as cheap agricultural labors in the fields of other dominant castes in the villages, some of them run illegal liquor business and are themselves victims of substance abuse. The participants report of experiences of land alienation and how they are forced to live outside the village territory. Being forced to stay outside the village territory, they are also excluded from involvement and participation in village activities, meetings etc and have no voice in the village Panchayat. The participants report that the *Ramoshi* tribe was majorly nomadic in nature and post-declaration they were imprisoned in settlements where they had hardly any freedom. The tribe soon ran away from the settlements. They did not have any specific skill and according to the Jajmani (Balutedari) system prevalent during that period, all castes had specific jobs to earn their livelihood. Once labeled, it was difficult for them to get employment and they started working for upper caste communities, who used them for personal purposes. The *Ramoshis* involved in criminal activities like theft, plundering, kidnapping, blackmailing etc. The Policemen and other dominant sections in the villages continued oppressing them. They used to offer food grains and crops in exchange of criminal activities. The *Ramoshis* in order to feed their family continued their involvement in crime.

The location of houses of *Ramoshis* in villages was majorly outside the village, away from the main village. The responses of the participants emphasised that this was majorly due to low acceptance of the community in the village. Being located outside the village also restricted involvement of the *Ramoshis* in village activities. Thus the occupational pattern, oppression by upper castes, the general perception of people from other communities contributed significantly in stigmatising the community. They continue being subject to discrimination even today. Some of the participants expressed that sometimes even though the *Ramoshis* are not involved in agricultural theft, they were observed suspiciously by other communities. Even policemen arrest them without any formal procedure but on prior assumptions based on their historical background.

The involvement in village activities and representation in panchayat meetings or bodies were merely there. They were not included in any village meetings and hence had no voices in decision making process of the village. There was no representation of the tribe at the Panchayat level. Their voices remain unheard even today. Under representation in Panchayat levels as well as in village meetings prevents their issues to be brought up and discussed in society at large. Although days have passed, times has changed, the label of criminal is still attached to the community affecting their everyday lives. The reality of being 'un-registered' as citizens due to lack of proof of identification makes them vulnerable in the hands of the police and other state machinery. They have no voice in democracy due to no or poor representation in the political system. They are majorly scattered population and move around from one village to the other in search of livelihood. There is a need to mobilise them as groups to represent their population and voice their opinions. However being less mobilised and scattered in nature, their participation in democracy is lost. Their voices still remain unheard.

Conclusion

The Denotified tribes in India, although have been decriminalised post-independence with the repeal of the CTA, 1871, the population continues to live with stigma and exclusion even today. The population got deeply affected due to the history attached to the community during the British colonisation period. The changing law and order during the British period affected not only the livelihoods of the population then, but continues to affect the present generation of denotified tribes in terms of their education, employment, livelihood, acceptance in society and denies their basic rights. Although the population was decriminalised post-independence, no efforts were taken to improve the situation of the tribes with any amendments in the constitution providing safeguards considering them as separate groups. The process of ancestral labeling began with declaration of the CTA and the process continued affecting the population over generations. The responses of the participants elaborate on the ill-treatment of the local police officials and other dominant castes in the village towards these tribes. However no provision has been made so far for protecting the population from the atrocities. The population being wandering in nature traditionally continues to move from one to the other even today. Those who have gradually settled down in villages majorly reside in hilly or drought prone areas. The responses of the participants also report of land alienation and hence either they work as cheap labourers in their own lands or keep wandering for earning their livelihoods. They are not house listed and remain excluded from the census. They lose their voting rights and their voices are hardly reflected in the democracy. Representation of the population even at Panchayat levels is very poor. They live in temporary huts or sheds outside the villages and not much involved in the village activities or Panchayat meetings. They under-representation in governance even at village levels restrain their opinions being considered in democracy. The population continues to struggle for earning their basic livelihoods and entitlement of the rights of the de-notified population is still a far achieved dream.

References

Abraham, Susan (1999), Steal or I'll call you a thief 'criminal' Tribes of India, economic and political weekly.

Bates Crispin, (1995) '*Race, Caste and Tribe in Central India: the Early Origins of Indian Anthropometry*', International Standard Book Number.

Bharal, G.P. Denotified Communities and their Problems of Rehabilitation, Indian Journal of Social Work, Vol. 28 (4), 1968, pp. 353-362.

Bokil, Milind (2002), De-Notified and Nomadic Tribes: A Perspective, Economic and Political Weekly, Vol. 37, No. 2 (Jan. 12-18), pp. 148-154.

Dandekar Ajay, (2009), '*Disenfranchised by History: The Tribes and their Narratives*'. Publisher: Muukt-Saad.

D'souza, Dilip. (2001), Branded by Law, Penguin Books India, New Delhi.

Draxe, P. B. (2005), Afailed Revolt against the Raj: the Rebellion of the Berad, A Criminal Tribe, under the Leadership of Umaji Naik. Sage Publication.

Criminal Tribes Act, 1871: Act XXVII. British Library, Oriental and India Office Collections, Shelfmark V/8/42.

Jha, Arvind Kumar, (2010), Formal Education and Pardhi Tribe's Culture in Mulshingi of Kolhapur, Maharashtra, Afro Asian Journal of Anthropology and Social Policy Vol. 1, No. 2, July- December, 161-165.

Mackintosh, Captain Alexander, (1833), '*An Account of the Origin and Present Condition of the Tribe of Ramoossies*'. American Mission Press, 1883.

Mehta, B. H. Ex-Criminal Groups in India, Indian Journal of Social Work, Vol. 16 (1), 1955, pp. 10-18.

Radhakrishna, Meena (2006), Criminal Tribes and the Debates on Criminal Law Criminal Tribes Act, 1871: The Construction of an Indian Criminal, working paper of social sciences.

Ratthod, Motiraj (2000), Denotified and Nomadic Tribes in Maharashtra, The Denotified and Nomatic Tribes Rights Action Group Newsletter Published by DNT Rights Action Group.

Simhadri, Y. C. Differential Association and Denotified Tribes, Indian Journal of Social Work, Vol. 39 (2), 1978, pp. 161-174.

Simhadri, Y. C. Caste and denotified Tribes, Indian Journal of Social Work, Vol. 37 (4), 1977, pp. 373-383.

Simhadri, Y. C. Ex-criminal Tribes and Criminological Theories, Indian Journal of Social Work, Vol. 34 (2), 1973, pp. 107-112.

Simhadri, Y.C. (1991), Denotified Tribes, Classical Publishing Company, New Delhi.

Singh, K.S. Bhanu, B.V. (2004), '*Anthropological Survey of India, People of India: Maharashtra*', Vol. 3. Popular Prakashan.

12

Social Exclusion and Marginal Communities: Some Reflection on Development Induced Displacement in India

Niharranjan Mishra, Dinabandhu Sahoo

Abstract

The uprooting of millions of people to new unknown places is a matter that is now becoming increasingly a continuous issue. Forced displacement results from the need to build infrastructure have raised major issues of social justice and equity. With the onset of economic reform in 1990s the State led development seems to have negotiated with corporate at the cost of natives. The resource-centric development approaches being sponsored by State and Central Government has changed the physical ecosystem and has destroyed the age-old livelihood source of marginal communities especially the tribal communities who lives in resource reach areas. As it is reflected in most of the literatures that the reasons for displacement vary, in a large majority of the cases the rehabilitation and resettlement has only left bitterness for the displaced populations. There are hardly any cases to cite as successful rehabilitation programme. The State which is worried about development has ignored the rights of marginal communities and has thrown them in cross road with lots of promises. The displaced communities are looking for the ways to come out from the clutch of exploitation. They are in dilemma where to go-be happy with the compensation given; join hand with activists to fight for their right; support what their political leader says; leave everything and search for a new life; or give an end to their life. In view of this, taking some literatures into account the present paper has made an attempt to answer following questions.

Can development provide justice to the marginal communities? Can State bring the so-called development ignoring the voice of poor? Why always marginal communities are being affected due to the State-led development initiation? Can we bring a solution to all these problems? Can a Government bring an inclusive growth for these displaced people who have sacrificed a lot for the cause of country's economic development? Can we really restore the livelihood of marginal communities who are displaced?

Introduction

Development-induced displacement is not a new and recent phenomenon. The evidence of land acquisition for the development of towns is found in ancient period between 7th and 4th century B.C, in the Mauryan period (321-181 B.C) and its state control over economy and other aspects, in the Gupta age (3rd- 6th century A.D), Khalsa lands (lands reserved for the state) in Medieval Muslim rule. It seems to be extended under Mughal rule. Another example, in 18th century the Jai Samand Tank near Udaipur in Rajasthan displaced many people (Ganguly Thukral and Singh 1995). The process got intensified in the colonial age in early 19th century when coal mining began in Raniganj and extensive irrigation started in North India, coffee plantation in Mysore, tea gardens in Assam, reconstruction of Grand Trunk Road, Major Irrigation Works in South India, construction of railway lines, irrigation system in Bari Doab, beginning of Scientific Forestry, establishment of Iron and steel plant in Jamshedpur and beginning of countless such Projects (Mankodi 1989:141-143). However, in those days displacement was not a problem because of adequate availability of land and low density of population. But recently displacement has been a concern especially for developing countries because of neo-liberalism and its policy of 'accumulation through encroachment'.

In the last decade, the magnitude on which displacement of peasant communities has occurred in Africa, Latin America, Central Asia, South Asia including India and China is really unbelievable (Cotula *et al.* 2009 and Pearce 2012). One of a recent report put "the number of reported deals concluded worldwide between 2000 and 2011 at around 2000 covering 203 million hectares. Africa accounted for 948 acquisitions covering 134 million hectares—an area larger than France, Germany and the UK combined" (Africa Progress Panel 2012:40). In India alone in the last sixty years following independence the development projects have displaced roughly sixty million people and among them 75 per cent are adivasis and 25 per cent are Dalits (Fernandes 2008). Now the local communities finding no alternative way are either resisting or involuntarily accepting the development projects. In view of this, taking some literatures into account the present paper has made an attempt to answer following questions. Can development provide justice to the marginal communities? Can State bring the so called development ignoring the voice of poor? Why always marginal communities are being affected due to the State led development initiation? Can we bring a solution to all these problems? Can a Government bring an inclusive growth for these displaced people who have sacrificed a lot for the cause of country's economic development? Can we really restore the livelihood of marginal communities who are displaced?

Development-induced Displacement the Number Involved

Sainath (1996) on the number of displaced people from 1951 to 1990 said that over 21.6 million people are displaced by dams and canals alone, 2.1 million people are dispossessed by mining, 2.4 million people are dislocated by industries, thermal plants, sanctuaries and defence installations. Thus, around 26 million Indians have been displaced between 1951 to 1990. He calculated displaced people in terms of direct displacement, i.e., those lose their land only. His estimate leaves out many groups who are affected but do not own land. Further he states that it is not even possible to arrive at a rough figure of people displaced for the country as a whole.

The Indian Institute of Public Administration (IIPA), study estimates that one dam on an average displaces 44,182 people. Hence, in India 3300 dams would displace 44,182 times 3300 or 145 million.[1]

Countering the IIPA estimates of 145 million people as too large, Arundhati Roy (1999) puts the number of dam displaced as 50 million. Similarly, an unofficial figure pointed out by N.C. Saxena, secretary to the Planning Commission as a total of 50 million, out of which 40 million are displaced by dams.

Another estimate of World Bank (1996), if applied to India's 3300 dams, then on an average 4189 people per dam the maximum number of displaced people can be about 14 million.

The International Rivers Networks, an anti-dam organisation states that there are about 40,000 big dams in World and they displaced people between 30 to 60 million.[2] If 45 million is considered as a representative figure, then one dam on an average displaces 1125 people and India's total 3300 big dams displace 3.7 million people.

The Central Water Commission (CWC), data states that a big dam whose height is 15 m or above displaces an average of 19,425 people while a dam whose height is 25 m or above displaces an average of 22,349 people.[3]

Bhalla and Mookerjee (2001), estimated by a particular economic method put the number of big dam displaced people between 3.4 to 3.7 million or three to four million.

Fernandes (2011), criticises both Ray and Bhalla's estimate on the ground that both have taken CWC definition of all dams above 15 metres as large. They then calculated the average number of displaced people for each dam and multiplied it by the number of large dams. However, all the dams in India are not large dams, there are minor, medium and large dams. All the dams also differ in submergence, height and capacity.

Fernandes and other scholars have undertaken studies of all displacement after Independence. They combining all completed studies and partial data from some other states pointed an all India figure of 60 million DPs/PAPs till 2004 from 25 million hectares, including seven million hectares of forests and six million hectares of common property resources (2008).

From the above estimates it is concluded that there are different estimates, some are too low while some are too high. The country even after six decades following Independence does not have an accurate official database on the number of those have paid the price of development. The official data many a times have been underestimates. The country need to undertake official studies to determine the total number of displaced or affected people. Walter Fernandes and his associates studies have definitely advantages which need to be completed and extended to all states those have partial data. It also be extended from the period 2004 to the present. Besides the coming development projects require accurate calculation of DPs and PAPs by displacement specialists.

Development-induced Displacement–its Human Costs

Deprived of livelihood and income, they face penury. As their families split up and spread out, their community bonds crumble. Cut off from their most vital resources, those uprooted are then robbed of their history, traditions and culture. May be even forced to adopt an alien diet. Higher rates of disease and mortality pursue the dispossessed. So do lower rates of earnings and education. Also, growing joblessness, discrimination and inferior social status. Oddly, it all happens in the name of development. And the victims are described as beneficiaries.

—(*Sainath* 1996)

The above paragraph is a quotation from one of India's leading journalist, who over his long term journalistic career observes the costs of development India has offered to its millions of people for the greater common good.

For the last two decades, development projects have caused displacement of about 15 million people world-wide per year (Cernea 1996b). According to Francis Deng, the former representative of the UNs Secretary General on Internally Displaced persons, among the 20-25 million internally displaced people in the world, 50 per cent of them are forced migrants within African continents. The present representative of the UN Secretary General on IDPs, Walter Kalin remarked Africa's displaced persons are among the world's most vulnerable. Downing said that in India out of the 20 million people displaced since Independence, it is estimated that 75 per cent of them have been impoverished due to development projects. Walter Fernandes who is conducting an all India survey on the nature and extent of displacement and resettlement said that the number of Displaced Persons (DPs) or those affected by projects without relocation, called 'Project Affected Persons' (PAPs) has increased enormously after two decades of globalisation, but no official database exist on their total number or type. The reliable data-based studies have been completed only in 13 states that give a total of 20.42 million DPs-PAPs. Studies have not been done in the high displacement states like Madhya Pradesh, Maharashtra and Chhattisgarh. In Odisha, Andhra Pradesh, Assam, West Bengal and Tripura only around 80 per cent of the data could be accessed and in Mizoram, Jharkhand, Kerala, Meghalaya and Sikkim it was around 60 per cent. Many studies done were for 1951-1995 are being updated to 1947-2010. Extrapolation based on this research and on new case studies brings one to 60 million DPs-PAPs between 1947-2000 (Fernandes et al. 2012:17).

The discipline of 'development studies' has witnessed new development today. In the new decades of globalisation and its flows and networks, there are emerging currents that are attempting to deterritorialise development. The Welfare State is no longer the leading saviour and is seeking new partners in multilateral agencies, non-government organisations (NGOs) and local social movements as it is being confronted with a network of non-state actors like diasporic communities and transnational coalitions. Amidst these shifting transnational dynamics, development projects by the state and international agencies are being forced to factor in regard for its environmental and social costs by transnational coalitions and networks (Khagram 2004). Joseph Stiglitz (2002) views that the 'the new development paradigm' as a real societal transformation. Besides, minimalist, residualist and welfarist approaches of dealing with displaced populations are gradually giving way to the Realisation that Resettlement and Rehabilitation (R&R) process needs to be seen as a development project in its own right (Mathur and Marsden 1998). But what needs more attention today is 'managing resettlement' rightly and efficiently (Mathur 2006).

The most widespread consequences of DIDR is impoverishment risks of a large segment of population (Cernea 1996, 2000; Mahapatra 1999b; Mathur and Marsden 1998). The concept 'Risk' refers to the possibility that some course of action will trigger future injurious effects-losses and destruction (Giddens 1990). Luhman (1993) says that risk postulates as a counter-concept to security. John Adams (1998) says that the higher the risks, the lower the security of the displaced populations. Risks are often directly perceptible and can be measured through science as they have objective reality. The term 'Impoverishment' refers to a situation in which people's welfare and livelihood worsen as a result of specific intervention. The concept impoverishment in many sense is related to the concepts like 'absolute poverty' 'relative poverty' 'the ultra-poor' and 'the assetless'.

The chief identifiable impoverishment risks that displaced population many a time suffers are: 1. landlessness, 2. joblessness, 3. homelessness, 4. marginalisation, 5. food insecurity, 6. increased morbidity and mortality, 7. loss of access to common property resources and 8. Community disarticulation.

Bondage Labour

Displacement and resettlement sometimes turn many DPs into bondage labour. Some 30,000 out of the 150,000 construction workers of the Asiad facilities in 1982 were slave labourers from Odisha and Chhattisgarh, brought by labour contractors with promise of job in Baghdad. They were the oustees of Hirakud dam and other projects. Today such people form a large proportion of construction and brick kiln workers (Fernandes *et al.* 2001).

Impact on Children

Displacement sometimes results child labour, when parents do not have access to work, they are forced to push their children into labour. The 56 per cent of all displaced families in Assam and 49 per cent in West Bengal were forced to pull their children out of school and turn them into child labourers in order to earn an income for the family (Fernandes, 2008). Many a time due to lack of school facility or long distance to school, children deprive of their school education.

Impact on Social Structure

Felix Padel and Samarendra Das (2011), highlighted that the social structure of a village is radically altered and dismantled as a result of displacement. The economy is completely transformed when people who have essentially been cultivators are uprooted from their land and pushed into the industrial labour. Food security disappears and money takes a greater importance in defining relations between people.

The material culture of the village is changed beyond recognition. From making most of their own food, tools and houses, villagers have to depend on factory made goods. The influx of cars, buses and trucks into their area makes life more dangerous and pollutes the atmosphere, as do the industries that become the centre of the local power structure.

People's identity is radically altered. From being largely self-sufficient for their basic food wants and material needs, they become dependent on a hierarchy outside their control for jobs and every aspects of life. Their lands and houses that were made by their parents or forefathers, so losing their land and ancestral village creates a traumatic break with previous generations.

People's religious life is also transformed. The outsider tear apart the natural surroundings, engage in blasting rock formations and cutting down trees to make profit, undermines people's sense of sacredness in nature, which lies at the heart of traditional tribal religion. A women in Vedanta's refinery project in Lanjigarh said '*Amoro deveta bi nasht kole*' that means "they even ruined our deities" referring to the *Darni Vali* (Earth goddess stones). Similarly, the Hirakud and Indravati reservoir displaced say that their 'deities were drowned'.

Cultural Genocide, Felix Padel and Samarendra Das opined is another phenomenon which is often least recognised, but perhaps most painful aspect of displacement due to the drastic drop in the quality of life of people and the disruption and dismantling of a culture.

Impact on Women

Forced displacement is more severe for women than men, because of difference in caste, class, religion or region. Everywhere women bear the brunt of the forced move a lot more than the male counterparts of their families. Resettlement marginalises women in various ways (Mehta 2009). Displacement forces the women into a double bind in two ways. First, the widespread nature of male biases in Indian society perpetuates gender inequality in terms of unequal resources allocation and distribution and also legitimises the silencing of women's interests. Second, biases within state institutions, structures and policies help perpetuate the societal inequalities. This is the double bind that displaced women often face due to displacement and resettlement (*ibid*).[4] The gender bias is evident in law and is also present in displacement policies. Project authorities rarely consult women on their problems and needs while designing resettlement plans. Under the land acquisition law, it is men as owner of land who get the compensation amount, not women (Basu, 2006).

Women's position is also badly affected, even where education, health centres and self-help groups (SHGs) are provided for oustees. The reason for this is that in a village, women often retain a large degree of control over their own labour, working essentially for themselves and their families, at times of their own choice. Even when they do coolie labour, this tends to supplement work on their own land as they see fit. Losing their land, they become more dependent on their husbands and often bear the brunt of men's frustration, in a situation where work ceases to be on their own terms. Tribal women who retain their land go to market to sell their own produce. The dignity from this self-sufficiency is destroyed by displacement. Many studies show that prostitution grows enormously after displacement, because men do not have work and so also women, they view their body as a resource for the present.

Development-induced Displacement and Marginal Community

While there is absence of official data on the magnitude of displacement, some non-official studies have estimated displaced persons since Independence at about 60 million till 2004, of which 40 per cent are tribals (Fernandes 2006 and 2011). Another official report by the Expert Group on Prevention of Alienation of Tribal Land and Restoration puts the number at 47 per cent (MoRD 2004). Of the total tribal victims of displacement around 75 per cent have not been rehabilitated (Fernandes 1991 and 1998; Planning Commission 2003).

Tribals are victimised as a result of development because of multiple causes. The tribals suffer displacement due to their powerlessness and having no voice in the decision-making process, for example the transfer of army firing range from Bihar to Jharkhand (Fernandes, 2008).[5] Besides politics often mediated in the process of site selection (Balagopal 2007). The tribals suffer extensive displacement due to a factor which termed as the process of sequential exhaustion in the context of forests (Gadgil 1989). Due to this process, the contractors expliote the forests which constitute the lifeline of tribals living in the vicinity for commercial and industrial use. These agencies exhaust forest resources near tribal villages and then in the interior forests and replacing with commercial plantations. A similar process is observed in the case of dam construction, which in early phase acquires the non-tribal dominated developed agricultural lands and exhausting these sites the focus shifted to hilly areas inhabited by tribes (Fernandes, 1991).

In the tribal areas the lands held by tribals is not transferable due to legal restrictions on its alienation. The market value of land in tribal areas in comparison to non-tribal areas is too low. So the cost of acquiring in terms of compensation is low. The obligatory criteria to rehabilitate the tribals are also low. This is the reason why much more land is acquired than is actually necessary and later lavishly utilised by project authorities for township, housing, infrastructure and other institutional needs unrelated to the project. For example, Arcellor Mittal Steel Limited applied 7750 acres of land to Odisha government for its steel project in Patna Tahasil in Keonjhar district, while it does not applied any land for its R and R colony establishment. Similarly Tata Steel in Kalinga Nagar has acquired 3500 acres. The amount of land applied shows much larger amount than is actually needed. However, the former has cancelled its project due to varieties of reasons. This is not part of present discussion.

The literacy and level of awareness among the tribal people are considerable low. The tribals have been politically marginalised and there is lack of empathy for their suffering in the larger society. There is no sustained protest for land acquisition due to these reasons and their protests are easily subdued by the local officials with the use of force.

The effect of multiple displacements is another phenomenon for tribal marginalisation. Once a tribal area is declared for industrialisation, numerous industries follow. Some are ancillary industries while others are attracted by infrastructure boom resulting from the setting up of industry. As a result additional lands need acquisition, which further displaces the tribals and huge influx of manpower takes place in the area for supply of labour and services which pushes the magnitude of displacement far beyond the level caused by the formal land acquisition. The tribals become the easy victims of these developments due to their social fragility against the dominant groups and political marginalisation (Saxena, 2012).

Provision of Justice

The Constitution of India has given social justice and special provisions to the tribes and their habitations. Besides provisions relating to the fundamental rights and the Directives of Principles of state policy which provide entitlements to all citizens, Articles 244, 244A, 275(A), 342, 338(A) and 339 deal exclusively with the tribals. These include, among others, reservation of seats in legislature, public services and educational institutions.

Special provisions are given to 'Fifth' and 'Sixth' schedule areas. In case of Fifth schedule areas, the governor of the state, who has special responsibility in respect of these areas, has powers to stop, amend or modify the operation of any central or state law. The governor is required to send a report regarding this schedule area every year to the president. Besides Article 238(2) authorises him to make regulations for peace and good governance of the scheduled areas. This power can be used to restrict transfer of land by or among the members of the scheduled tribes, regulate allotment of land and money lending. There is a provision for constitution of a Tribal Advisory Council in the Fifth schedule areas which the governor is required to consult in discharge of his responsibility for the welfare of the tribes. Similarly, the Sixth schedule contains provisions for the administration of tribal areas relating to the specified states including in it. The laws enacted by the state governments to prevent alienation of the tribal land to the non-tribals continue to operate (Saxena 2012).

PESA Act (Panchayat Extension to Scheduled Areas Act 1996) has extended to Panchayati Raj Institutions to scheduled areas under which *Gram Sabha* has been granted special powers relating to the land acquisition, grant of prospecting license and mining lease, minor forest produce and protection against alienation of land. This law recognises village community's competence to manage natural resources in schedule areas and consultation of *Gram Sabha* mandatory relating to these subjects. The Supreme Court in a land mark judgement, *Samatha Vrs* the state of Andhra Pradesh, has prohibited transfer of leasing of tribal land to the non-tribals or private industries in scheduled areas (Balagopal 2007). Reservation of seats for the tribals in panchayats and chair persons of panchayats has also been mandated.

The Denying Justice

It is true that the Constitution of India has given a lot of social justice measures for the protection, survival of tribal people. But the question arises "whether the constitution or any respective states are abiding these rules?" or "Are they violating these in favour of development?" Some Fundamental Rights are being violated and compromised in case of development-induced displacement. For instance, the right to reside and settle in any part of the territory guaranteed under Article 19(1-C) of the constitution is ignored when people are involuntarily shifted from their existing habitat. The right to live with dignity in terms of Article-21 gets violated by the forced deprivation of the means of livelihood and life supporting resources to these displaced.

Right to equality and equal protection is denied since development projects lead to unequal distribution of benefits and suffering. The Directive Principle of State policy particularly enshrined in Article 39(b) and (c) are sidetracked. The special protection given to 'Fifth' and 'Sixth' schedule areas in the Constitution are infringed as development projects lead to eviction of the affected tribes from these areas (Saxena 2008). The adverse consequences unleashed by development projects force the tribal people to migrate to other areas where they face hostility and face further marginalisation as a community and lose their identity and benefits as schedules tribes. The PESA Act 1996 is violated and its provision of *Gram Sabha* is formally held or manipulated in favour of the corporation. The *Samtha* judgement no longer comes to practice when huge lands being transferred to private corporate industries.

The ILO Convention 107 (1957), dealing with indigenous people in which India is a party is also not observed when displacement occurs (Mahapatra, 1999). Article II of this convention prescribes the recognition of collective ownership of land and 12.2 and 12.3 about provision of land to oustees, both of which have been ignored in the process of resettlement (Saxena, 2008). Displacement therefore denies justice to the marginal communities and fundamental rights and forces them to exclude from the mainstream of the community.

Conclusion

The foregoing discussion makes it clear that there is no respite for the tribal communities the burden of displacement. Today the marginal communities are facing more complex problems emanating from various issues like globalisation, apathy of state apparatus, inactive civil society and the defective policy formulation. The tribals have been victimised against the ideology of development and for the national interest for inclusive development, which is based on new liberal policy of 'accumulation through encroachment'. The new policy paradigm on the other hand brings on its fold displacement, human suffering, human rights violation, misery and social exclusion. The tribals have no power in politics or mediation which can reduce the magnitude, scale and pace of displacement. They have little support from the mainstream society and political establishment to provide them proper rehabilitation and resettlement. The grand provisions for their protection and the vibrant democracy with a lot promises and assurance by the ruling political elites provide no comfort to them in the coming future.

Notes

1. Bhalla, S. Surajit and Arindam Mookerjee. 2001. "Big Dam Development: Facts, Figures and Pending Issues"
2. Taylor and Francis Ltd. 17(1) 89-98. doi: 10.1080/713672558.
3. *Ibid.*
4. *Ibid.*
5. This was spoken in an address by Walter Fernandes at the release of Social Development Report 2008 at the Council for Social Development, New Delhi on 18th September, 2008.

References

Adams, John. 1998. *Risks in a Hyper-Mobile World*. London: Geography Department, University College, Africa Progress Panel 2010

Balagopal, K. 2007. "*Impact of Grants to Industries.*" *Economic and Political Weekly* 42 (39).

Balagopal, K.2007. "*Illegal Acquisition in Tribal Areas.*" *Economic and Political Weekly* 42 October.

Basu, Malika. 2006. "*Gender Focus in Resettlement Planning.*" *In Managing Resettlement in India: Approaches, issues, experiences,* edited by Hari Mohan Mathur. New Delhi: Oxford University Press.

Cernea, M.M. 1996b. "*Public Policy Responses to Development-induced Population Displacement*" *Economic and Political Weekly* 31, 1515-1523.

Cernea, M.M. 2000. "*Risks, Safeguards and Reconstruction: A Model for Population Displacement and Resettlement*" *Economic and Political Weekly* 35(41): 3659-3678.

Fernandes, Walter. 1991. "*Power and Powerlessness: Development Projects and Displacement of Tribals.*" *Social Action* 41(3): 243-270.

Fernandes, Walter. 1998. "*Development-induced Displacement in Eastern India.*" pp. 217-300 in *Antiquity to Modernity in Tribal India Volume 1*, edited by S.C. Dube. New Delhi: Inter- India Publications.

Fernandes, Walter. 2006. "*Liberalisation and Development-induced Displacement*" *Social Change* 36 March.

Fernandes. Walter 2008. "*Sixty years of Development-induced Displacement in India: Impacts and the Search for Alternatives.*" in *India Social Development Report 2008: Development and Displacement,* edited by H.M. Mathur. New Delhi: Council for Social Development and Oxford University.

Fernandes, Walter, Nafisa Goga D'Souza, Arundhati Roy Choudhury and Mohammed Asif. 2001. *Development-induced Displacement in Andhra Pradesh 1951-1995: A Quantitative Study of Its Extent and Nature.* New Delhi and Guwahati: North Eastern Social Research Centre.

Fernandes, Walter.2011. "*Development-induced Displacement in the era of Privatisation.*" pp. 301-316 in *Resettling Displaced People: Policy and Practice in India*, edited by Hari Mohan Mathur. New Delhi: Routledge Taylor and Francis Group and Council for Social Development.

Fernandes, Walter, Shanti Chhetri, Sherry Joseph and Satyen Lama. 2012. *Progress: At* Whose Cost? Development-induced Displacement and Deprivation in West Bengal 1947 2000. Guwahati; North Eastern Social Research Centre.

Gadgil, Madhab.1989. "*Forest Management, Deforestation and Peoples' Impoverishment.*" *Social Action* 39 (4).

Giddens, Anthony.1990. *The Consequences of Modernity*. Stanford: Stanford U.P.

Khagram, S. 2004. *Transnational Struggles for Water and Power*. Ithaca: Cornell University Press.

Kothari, S. 1996. "Whose Nation: The Displaced as Victims of Development." *Economic and Political Weekly* 31(24): 1476-1485.

Luhman, Niklas.1993. *Risks: A Sociological Theory*. New York: Aldin de Gruyter.

Mahapatra, L.K. 1999a. *Resettlement, Impoverishment and Reconstruction in India*. New Delhi: Vikas Publishing House.

Mahapatra, L.K. 1999b. *Resettlement, Impoverishment and Reconstruction in India: Development for the Deprived*, New Delhi: Vikas Publishing House.

Mathur, H.M, ed. 2006. *Managing Resettlement in India*. New Delhi: Oxford University Press.

Mathur, H.M. and David Marsden, eds. 1998. *Development Projects and Impoverishment Risks: Resettling Project Affected People in India*. New Delhi: Oxford University Press.

Mehta, Lyla. 2009. "Introduction." *In Displaced by Development: Confronting Marginalisation and Gender Injustice,* edited by Lyla Mehta. New Delhi: Sage Publications.

Ministry of Rural Development (MoRD). 2004. *Report of Expert Group on Prevention of Alienation of Tribal Land and its Restoration*, New Delhi: Government of India.

Padel, Felix and Samarendra Das. 2011. "Resettlement realities: the gulf between policy and practice" in *Resettling Displaced People: Policy and Practice in India*, edited by Hari Mohan Mathur. New Delhi: Routledge, Taylor and Francis Group and Council for Social Development.

Saxena, K.B. 2008. *Development, Displacement and Resistance: The Law and the Policy on Land Acquisition*. New Delhi: Council for Social Development.

Saxena, K. B. 2012. "Development is War; Underdevelopment is Benign: Political Economy of Tribal Displacement in India." pp. 26-79 in *The Other Side of Development: The Tribal Story,* edited by A. K. Ghosh and R. D. Munda. New Delhi: Konark Publishers Pvt Ltd.

Stiglitz, J.E. 2002. *Globalisation and its Discontents*. U.K: Allan Lane, The Penguin Press.

World Commission on Dams (WCD). 2000. *Dams and Development: A new framework for decision-making*. London: Earth scan Publications Ltd.

13

Status of Schedule Tribes in Andhra Pradesh: With Special Reference to Educational, Economical, Socio and Political Contexts-A Brief Review

C. Rama Mohan Reddy, T. Sasikanth Reddy

The Constitution of India does not define Scheduled Tribes as such; Article 366(25) refers to scheduled tribes as those communities who are scheduled in accordance with Article 342 of the Constitution. According to Article 342 of the Constitution, the Scheduled Tribes are the tribes or tribal communities or part of or groups within these tribes and tribal communities which have been declared as such by the President through a public notification. The Constitution of India incorporates several special provisions for the promotion of educational and economic interest of Scheduled Tribes and their protection from social injustice and all forms of exploitation. These objectives are sought to be achieved through a strategy known as the Tribal sub-plan strategy, which was adopted at the beginning of the Fifth Five Year Plan. The strategy seeks to ensure adequate flow of funds for tribal development form the State Plan allocations, schemes/programmes of Central Ministries/ Departments, Financial and Developmental Institutions. Schedule Tribes (ST's) are Indian population groups that are explicitly recognised by the Constitution of India order 1950. The order lists 744 tribes across 22 states in its first schedule. In Andhra Pradesh 35 types of Schedule Tribes are living in eight districts. ST's are 6.6 per cent are in total population of Andhra Pradesh.

Historical Facts

From the 1850 ST community is referred to as the depressed class. During British period the Minto-Marley report, Montague-Chelmsford reforms report,

Simon Commission, etc., proposed the issue of reservation of seats for depressed class (SC & ST's) in provincial and central legislations. In 1935, British passed the Government of India Act 1935 in which reservation of seats for depressed class was incorporated into the Act. After independence the constitution assembly continued the prevailing definition of Schedule Tribes and gave the president of India and governance of states responsibility to compile a full listing of tribes and also the power to edit it later as required. The actual complete listing of tribes was made with the Constitution (Schedule Tribes) Order 1950. Article 366(25) of the Constitution of India refer the Schedule Tribes as those communities, who are scheduled in accordance with Article 342 of the Constitution. The essential characteristics of Schedule Tribes are identified by the Locur Committee. Indications of primitive tribes, distinctive culture, shyness of contact with the community at large, geographical isolation and backwardness are most identified features of ST's community. There is 7.5 per cent reservation facility for employment opportunities and they are experiencing political reservations also at present based on their population.

Tribes in Andhra Pradesh

As per 2001 in India the population of tribes is 8.2 per cent. In Andhra Pradesh 6.6 per cent tribes population exists. In the state, Tribes are of two groups. One group is at presently across the hilly tract of the Deccan Plateau and by the rivers Godavari and Krishna. The second group is present along the extended areas between the river Krishna and Godavari. According to ST order Act 1976 there are 33 types of Tribes in eight districts and other 50 lakh nomads are surviving. In overall of the state, in Coastal Andhra 5.96, in Rayalaseema 2.86 and in Telangana 8.87 Tribal population exist. The prominent tribes are *Khonds, Kholamis, Nayakpods, Koyas, Konda doras, Valmikis, Bhagats, Savaras, Jatayus, Godabas, Yanadis* and *Chenchus*. 76 per cent of Tribes are covered by Sugali (4.4 per cent), Koya (11.3. per cent), Yanadi (9.2 per cent), Yerukula (8.7 per cent), Gonda (5 per cent) and remaining 24 per cent of population belongs to small tribes. Nomadic tribal are—*Pichukaguntulu, Balasanta, Saradakandru, Veeramustivaru, Bhavaneelu, Birannalavaru, Golla Suddulu, Pasaralu, Jangamulu* and *Kommuvaru,* etc., are other tribes surviving in Andhra Pradesh. They don't have scripts for their language. They follow their customs and traditions strictly. 92.5 per cent population is living in rural areas. Their livelihood based on the occupations like making of toys, baskets, mats, cosmetics and collection of leaves, honey etc. The life style of tribes has been changing gradually after initiation by the government contribution. Reservation in education, employment and in legislative assemblies and local bodies are changing the life style of the tribals.

Constitutional Safeguards

The Constitution of India mentioned development of schedule tribe in Directive Principles. The Constitution (Schedule Tribes) Order 1950 identified schedule tribes' population-based some peculiar characteristics. Those communities are in accordance with Article 342 of the constitution. Some other safe guards are there in the constitution of India. Articles 23 and 24 mentioned social safe guards. Articles 244 and 275(1) referred special economic safe guards. Education and cultural safeguards are referred by Articles 15(4), 29(1) and 350(a). Political safe guards are mentioned in accordance with 164 (1), 330, 332, 334, 243(0), 371(A), 371 B, 371 C, 371 F etc. Service safe guards are mentioned by articles 16(4), 16(4A), 16 (4B), 335, 320(4) etc. Article 335 puts limitations for reservations, Article 338 emphasis appointment of special officer whenever necessary regarding tribe matters. Article 339(1) refers establishment of commission on tribal issues by President of India. But it is the responsibility of state to look after the benefits which are available from these articles.

Educational Status

In Andhra Pradesh literacy rate is 60.4 per cent. But, the literacy of schedule Tribe is 37.04. After 30 years also illiteracy rate is 63 per cent. In rural areas the illiteracy rate of ST's is 70 per cent. For the improvement of literacy the Andhra Pradesh Government has started hostels for boys and girls. Residential schools, vocational training centers etc. National Policy of Education (1986 and revised Policy in 1992) suggested the following programmes for education of tribal people.

1. Opening primary schools in Tribal Areas
2. Need to develop curricula of their language
3. Promoting schedule tribes youth to work as teachers
4. Ashram schools, Residential schools should be established in large scale in Tribal areas.
5. Incentives to encourage their life style through education.

Problems

To promote education in schedule tribes two types of problems are there. Internal problems like school system, content, curricula, medium, pedagogy, academic supervision, etc., and external problems like education policy, planning, implementation and administration, etc., are influencing education in tribal areas.

Economic Status

In the state, agriculture labour of ST's is 10.3 per cent. In the state 115.31 lakh land holdings are there. Among them ST's have only 7.5 per cent of holdings. In total land of Andhra Pradesh ST's have only 8.2 per cent of land. So there is need for distribution of land for tribes. In total employees, STs are representing 4.9 per cent. As literacy rate is 37 per cent the work participation rate (WPR) is 53.9. Male work participation is 55.7 per cent and female work participation is 52. A report in 2000 said that 45 per cent of Rural ST population is below poverty line and in urban areas 35.6 per cent is under below poverty line. According to National Sample Survey Organisation 61st round estimates, in India monthly per capita expenditure of tribes is Rs 426.19. In Andhra Pradesh monthly per capita expenditure is Rs 420.01. Less population is able to use schemes of government for their opportunities. Majority population survive on their traditional occupations like making of toys, baskets, mats, cosmetics and collection of leaves, honey, shifting, agriculture etc. The main obstacles to Economic Development of Schedule Tribes are destruction of forests, illiteracy, indebtedness lack of awareness about the schemes for them, strict follow of traditions and customs, in effective implementation of schemes etc. Though there is an improvement of conditions of Schedule Tribes, it is not at desired level. So, much more measures to be taken by the governments.

Social and Political Status

The article 338A relates the population ST's. Before and after Independence ST's as vulnerable section were given reservation to enter into Parliament and legislative assemblies, but this facility is not applicable to Rajya Sabha at present. After 2002, separate National commission for schedule Tribes was started and came to effect from 19th February 2004 due to 89th amendment. Priority was given to protect the culture, traditions and customs by the constitutions. To protect their rights and to avoid suppression from other communities. Prevention of Atrocities Act was formed in 1989. The ministry of tribal affairs was constituted in October 1999 with the objective of development of Schedule Tribes in a coordinated and planned manner. This is also a significant step to lift the tribal communities. In Andhra Pradesh fourteen MLA's three MP's belongs to ST communities. The implantation of political reservations should be reviewed and revision as per their population. The health policy 1983 emphasis improving tribal health especially through detection and treatment of endemic and other diseases specific to tribes.

Schemes for the Prosperity of the Scheduled Tribes

For the development of Schedule Tribes Special Central Assistance grant has been released under 275(11) Article of Indian Constitution. Investment share, price support, village, train, bank scheme, etc., are introduced. Besides this National Schedule Tribe Financial and Development Corporation was established with 500 crore authorised capital. Integrated area development and modified area development were introduced. The following are important land marks in Tribal development:

1. Programmes were designed with as special fusion ST's (1951).
2. Adoption of Panchsheel principles for process of tribal development (1956).
3. Opinions of multi-purpose tribal development blocks for intensified development of ST's 1961.
4. Introduction to strategies of TSP and SCA for tribal development (1974).

5. Expansion of infrastructure facilities for poverty alleviation in 1985.

6. Setting up of tribal co-operative marketing development federation 1987 and Finance Development Corporation in 1989.

7. 73 and 74 amendments and Panchayat extension to Scheduled Areas Act.

8. Sections up on separate ministry of Tribals 1999 and National Schedule Tribes Finance and Development Corporation 2001.

The Following are Recent Measures taken by the Government

1. Recognition of forest Act 2006 will be administered by the Ministry of Tribal affair to protect interest of the Tribals in forests.

2. The scheme of vocational Training Centers has been revised as vocational training in Tribal areas with effect from 01-04-09.

3. During 2009-10 the ministry has founded 14 education complexes under the scheme of strengthening education among schedule tribe girls in low literacy districts.

4. Under the scheme of grant-in-aid to voluntary organisation durings 2009-10. The ministry funded about 237 projects covering schools, hostels, libraries etc.

5. Under the scheme of development of particularly vulnerable Tribal groups, the ministry released Rs 40.43 crore for six states.

6. Under the scheme of Market development of Tribal products/produce ministry released Rs 9.68 crores. But states have to take responsibility to give fruits of the schemes.

Measures to be Taken for Prosperity of Scheduled Tribes

Many programmes helped tribal to improve their conditions. The following are important for further improvement.

1. Strict implementation of reservation of seats in public sector employment.

2. Proper looking into reservation of seats in institutions of higher learning.

3. Formulation of proper welfare schemes for prosperity of Tribals based on fact data.

4. In private sector also these should be reservations for schedule tribes.

5. The present 7.5 per cent of reservation for government services should be increased whenever necessary.

6. Destroy of their habitations should be reduced because, major projects, SEZs and other projects are causing for migration of ST's.

7. Their habilitation (Thandas) should be converted into gram panchayats.

8. Development of forest villages is needed for Tribal prosperity.

9. Empowering Tribals in governance is the most needed one.

10. During every plan review and revision is must to alter policies.

11. Stopping of corruption and ineffective work progress in the implementation of schemes belonging to Schedule Tribes.

The directive principles of Indian constitution referred the development of Schedule Tribes in the society. Though policies are vast implementation is not proper so both state and Central government have to take proper steps. Since 1951 governments are implementing number of programmes and schemes for the development of Schedule Tribes. But the implementation is not effective. Besides this, lack of awareness about the programmes is also strong factor due to illiteracy among tribes. Therefore, there is need for extension of contribution from government side and other voluntary organisations and likeminded NGOs for effective implementation of programmes and bringing awareness among Tribes. Then only the future of the Schedule Tribes will be in good prosperity.

References

1. K. Sunitha Rani (2006), *Struggle for Survival - Tribal of Andhra Pradesh* Fifty Years of Andhra Pradesh CDRC: p. 469.
2. K. Sujatha (1992), *Study of tribal teachers working in tribal areas*: Journal of educational planner and administrator: Vol. 6, No. 4.
3. N.K. Acharya (2006), *Reservation for SC, ST's, OBC's*, Fifty Years of Andhra Pradesh CDRC: p. 461.
4. Sachchidananda and R. R. Prasad (1998), *Encyclopaedic Profile of Indian Tribes with Maps and Photographs*: Discovery Publishing House, New Delhi.
5. www.planning commission.nic.in.
6. www.nhrc.nic.in.
7. www.tribal.gov.in, Annual Report 2009-10 of Ministry of Tribal Department.

14

Policies against Tribals: A Study of Displacement through Development Projects

Johani Xaxa

The process of change and development in India has not only been technological and economic, but also has been a political struggle, related with the changes in the power relations and decision-making process within the system. Since independence, India was engaged in nation-building or modernisation process and fast development of infrastructure and economic conditions of the people, and the country as a whole. But the question arises whether development should mean profit for capitalists or protection of the rights of the people (Indigeneous) and the prosperity or greater good far the larger numbers? However, the pursuit of development adversely affected the marginalised sections causing deprivation, displacement and devastation and invariably led to the 'disempowerment of the tribes' (Xaxa, 2001:206). Further, question arises for development, for what and at what social cost (Baboo, 2002:195). When the nation developed it was at the cost of the marginals. When the majority developed in the country, the marginals excluded systematically. The development projects are meant for the development of the country, and ultimately of the people as a whole, but it is resulted in displacement of lakhs of people and forced them to leave their home and land to struggle for livelihood.

There are two faces of the "temple of modern India", one, the glorification of development, the other fact that like monuments of the past. These present-day temples too are built on the blood and sweat of million of people, whilst slaves and prisoners built the former, today's farmers and others who live off the land, forests and other resources are being impoverished in the name of 'development' (Fernandes). Nations are thus not only oppressive to others but can be brutal to its own people. In this way the whole issue of displacement takes place as a result of development projects where the majority of the development-displaced are tribals and landless dalits. Odisha's tribals are also not excluded from it. This paper intended to focus on the problems of displaced poor, down trodden tribal's tragedy in the state of Odisha.

The State of Odisha occupies a unique place amongst the undeveloped States of India, because of it's large concentration of tribal population in one hand, and on the other, the people are poor but their land is rich in resources. The Scheduled Tribe constitutes nearly 22.5 per cent of the total population of Odisha. (Indian Census Report 2011) 62 tribal communities has been designated as Scheduled Tribe of which 13 recognised as Primitive Tribal Group (PTG). Nearly half of the State's area (45 per cent) is under 5th Scheduled of the Indian Constitution. Odisha is one of the poorest States in India, with an estimate of 47 per cent of its population living less than a dollar a day (Haans & Dubey, 2003). In 1999-2000, 37 per cent of the Scheduled Tribes in Odisha were Below Poverty Line as compared to 55 per cent and 33 per cent respectively for Scheduled Castes and General Castes (Haans & Dubey, 2003). The populations in the Scheduled areas are comparatively much poorer than the population in non-Scheduled areas. In South Odisha the situation is even worse with 87 per cent of the Scheduled Tribes below the poverty line.

Tribals are agriculturists by their occupation; hence land is the main source of their livelihood. But in the Scheduled areas of Odisha, an average 74 per cent of the land is categorised as State land (forest land and non-forest land). Thus, three-fourth of all land in the tribal dominated districts belong to the State. However, most of the tribals in these areas are either landless or marginal landowners. They own only 4.8 per cent (in standard acres) of agricultural landholdings with an average holding of only 0.44 standard acres. Thus, more than 50 per cent of all Scheduled Tribe landowners in Odisha are marginal landholders and another 20 per cent at least are landless.

In context of landownership, the communal landownership and swidden/shifting cultivation was never settled with respective tribal communities. These lands were, if settled then, settled either as forest land or as government revenue land. In practice much of the customary owned land is still under cultivation of tribals and is treated as encroachments. As all customary tribal lands are government land, the state government found it very easy to divert customary tribal lands for development projects and forcibly ousted them from their land and inhabitat, carries with it the risk of becoming poorer than before displacement. Michael Cernea, a sociologists has identified eight interlinked potential risks intrinsic to displacement such as; Landlessness, Joblessness, Homelessness, Marginalisation, Food insecurity, Increased morbidity and morality, loss of access to common property, and Social Disintegration (Cernea, 1999).

Odisha is extremely rich in minerals, most of which lies in the tribal districts. The hilly terrain and availability of water also makes them suitable for reservoirs and dams. The major dams taken up in Scheduled areas are the Machhkund, Salandi, Balimela, Upper Kolab, Indrawati and Mandira etc. The major industrial projects taken up in Scheduled areas have been the Rourkela Steel Plant, NALCO's Alumina Refinery at Damanjodi, Hindustan Aronetic Limited (HAL), Sunabeda. Large numbers of industrial projects are under implementation as proposed in Scheduled areas including the alumina refineries of UAIL (Utklal Alumina India Ltd.) in Kashipur, Vedanta at Lanjigarh, Tata Steel Plant at Kalinganagar in Jajpur, POSCO Steel Plant at Paradeep in Jagatisinghpur. The richness of forests and wildlife has also led to increasing number of protected areas (Wild life Sanctuaries and National Parks) in the Scheduled areas of Orissa. Such protected areas have created a major problem as the rights of the inhabitants in and around these areas in the forest and forest land is being extinguished, affecting their livelihoods and sometimes leading to displacements.

Most of the minerals are deposited in Scheduled areas. The most important mining zones within Scheduled areas are iron ore and manganese mining in Sundargarh and Keonjhar districts, coal in Sundargarh district, bauxite in Kalahandi, Koraput and Rayagada districts. Apart from displacement, mining and industries lead to large scale influx of non-tribals, this often leads to Social and Political marginalisation of the tribals. The environmental impacts are drastic and affect much larger number of people than directly displaced.

The liberalisation of mining and industrial policies which allowed for direct foreign investments, facilitated number of mining and industrial projects located in Scheduled areas. Some of these propose mining areas are inhabited by Primitive Tribal Groups, such as Paudi Bhuiyans in Keonjhar and Sundargarh districts. Almost all the iron ore mines deposits in Odisha are located in the Scheduled areas of Keonjhar and Sundargarh districts. The life of the inhabitants (tribals) are already disturbed with massive mining, leading to displacement of tribals, destruction of their livelihood, support system including forests and water resources, large scale air and water pollution and cultural genocide through massive influx of outsiders, and also entry of giant factories as POSCO, Jindals, Tata Steels etc. The mining areas were originally inhabited by Scheduled Tribes, especially PTGs and whose livelihoods have been destroyed completely. Bauxite are also located in Scheduled areas in Kalahandi, Rayagada and Koraput districts with the major mining being done by NALCO in Koraput district. These has been a major source of controversy with the local tribals opposing proposed mining projects tooth and nail, and the state government using all possible strategies, including coercion and repression to make these deposits available to mining multinationals. The resistance of Kashipur tribals against UAIL's mining project and alumina refinery has been going for over 10 years now. Similarly, flashpoints building up near proposed bauxite mining on

Niyamagiri by Vedanta, Sunger by L & T, Kodingamali by Aditya Aluminum and Maliparbat by Hindalco. The bauxite deposits are all located on top of the highest mountains in South Odisha which are called Malis and are sacred to tribals as they are often the only source of water of drinking and irrigation of fields in summer season, and sustain local agricultural economy. This reality of tribals has created massive resistance against bauxite mining amongst tribals.

In Kashipur and Lanjigarh the tribals organised continuous resistance against displacement from mining and the environmental impacts of mining. Similar situation is now emerging in all tribal areas where industrial projects are being planned. Part of the reason for the strong resistance is bitter experience of the tribals of Koraput and Rayagada with the earlier projercts such as Upper Kolab, Indrawati, HAL, NALCO, etc., which has led to destitution of a large number of tribals and destruction of their livelihoods base and their culture. Another important reason is that inspite of most of the land in the area proposed to be acquired being categorised as Government, are under cultivation by the tribals. Thus, in Lanjigarh, while acquiring land for Vedanta, the local tribals cultivating government land were simply evicted without compensation, destroying their livelihoods. In Lanjigarh, for instance almost 64 landless Kondh households (Scheduled Tribes) had been cultivating Revenue Land for the last 30-40 years. When the Revenue Department, filed the case against those people, the notice showed, the physical possession of lands for at least seven to eight years. However, the tribals claimed that even their forefathers were cultivating the land. Both as per the principle of adverse possession and as per the section 7(a) of Orissa Prevention of Land Encroachment Act, 1972, such land should have been settled with the landless persons to the extent of one standard acre (equivalent to 4.5 acres to uplands), when the tribals tried to get the land regularised in their name prior to this issue, they were asked to pay bribes up to Rs 5000 per acre, which they could not afford. In 2003, instead of settling this land with the tribal cultivators cultivating the lands, the district administration evicted these 64 families by force without compensation, there by taking away their main livelihoods. By law, this action of administration violated the protection provided to the Scheduled Tribes in Scheduled V of the Constitution, and the Section 3 (iii) of the OSATIP Regulations (1956) by turning Scheduled Tribes effectively landless. Therefore, it is correct to comment that "industrialisation is necessary evil". As for the development, industrialisation is necessary, but at the same time industries requires the minerals and both mining and industrialisation caused displacement of millions of poor tribals.

As a consequence of development projects, the tribal people in Odisha have become poorer than before. Partly this is due to a process of alienation of the rights over land, forests, water bodies and other resources. Although these rights guaranteed under 5th Scheduled of the Indian's Constitution, the State Governments including Odisha, are not inclined to recognise them and, are in fact, looking for an escape route. Odisha government has also not considered the rights of the tribal people to be consulted on matters concerning the acquisition of land for project purposes, which the Panchayats (Extension to Scheduled Areas) Act, 1996 (PESA) has specifically conferred on them.

The displaced poor tribals have scarified more than the benefits they got from the development projects. The development projects become curse to them, as it has convert them to homeless and landless and place them to zero stage. It is evident from the Government's development programs that, Government's policies are against tribals life. The problems they facing are:

- First of all, they lost their home and community villages with which they were emotionally attached. Though poor, they usually have 2/3 living rooms of mud walls and home-made tile roof, sufficient area for garden, cow-shed, goat-shed, pig-shed, etc., when they displaced it is very difficult to build a new set of house in a new place. The displacement reversed their life to years back to improve.
- When they moved to government's resettlement and rehabilitated colonies, which allotted with small houses like Indira Awas. It is very difficult for them to adjust there.
- From several study it has been revealed that in most cases the government failed in giving sufficient compensation to displaced tribals. They also do not know how to utilise the money properly.
- Most of the times, the government instead of giving compensation, evict them forcefully, as they do not have legal documents (Legal land patta). Because, most of their lands are unauthorised occupation. Hence they get no compensation and become landless and marginal labourers.
- When they have been given compensation of land for land, the lands more often the barren lands in lieu of their fertile land, which take them back to some more years to develop (thus it is right to say, government's development policies led to disempowerment of tribals).
- The displaced families have been thrown out at resettlement colonies without basic amenities of life. Some time places are arid and hilly regions, Roads and Communications, Schools and Colleges, Markets, Hospitals, Wells and Tanks and drinking waters, etc., have not been provided to resettlement and rehabilitated colonies.
- The displacement not only disturbed their economy but also social, cultural and educational rights. Socially, they preferred to live together in their community. Through their social and religious customs and traditions, they protect and maintain their tribal Culture and Identity. For the matrimonial relations, they need their own community. Thus displacements have shattered their Culture and Identity.
- Educationally, too, their children suffered a lot because they have to go to school for four to five kilometers. In some places they have to go through jungles, have fear of wild animals. Therefore, their children do not go to School in due time, and starts school in late age, or drop out from school.

• In the resettlement colonies hardly they can get electricity. Those who sacrificed their every comfort to illuminate the urban towns, live in darkness.

• Medical facilities are not provided to them. They have to depend on herbal medicines. Due to lack of medical facilities, they died without medical aid or because of rough communications; the critical patients die before reaching hospital.

• The PESA Act is openly violated by the state government. In the scheduled Area, the State government has to consult the Gram Sabha or the Panchayats at the appropriate level, before acquisition of land for development projects. But the State never consults the Panchayats and, thus violating the right to decide their own priorities as a part of right to development as an inalienable human rights.

The development projects as adopted by Odisha Government with a desire to bring national development has not only worsened the life of the tribal population but also denied their basic rights to livelihood and substance, culture, land, common property resources employment and participation. A State's prime duty is the welfare and protection of its all citizens, but it has turning the tribals life into refuges and foreigners in their own country. The acquisition of tribal land in the name of development has evicted them from their home state and deprived them of a decent living, which is marked by widespread poverty, hunger and starvation death, migration to neighbouring States in search of a minimum livelihood. Thus, development policies of the Government directing against tribal's development.

Suggestions

• The Central Government as well as the State Government should stop alienation of land inhabited by the tribal people. It must correct the loopholes in existing lows and take steps to restore lands transferred from tribals to non-tribals and register land records for tribal land.

• In the Scheduled Areas under Fifth Scheduled, Government should adhere to PESA Acts. According to this Act, it is mandates that Gram Sabha or Panchayats should be consulted before acquiring the land for development projects.

• After the use of land for project purposes, the surplus lands should takeover by the government and return them to landless tribal families and also other landless families. It has been seen that, the Government had sold the surplus lands (acquired from tribals) to non-tribals.

• Before displacement, the government must be developed the resettlement colonies with all amenities required by the tribals as par their original place. The settlement colonies must have educational institutions for tribal children. The road communication must be developed, so that they can easily move from resettlement colonies to nearby cities. The medical facilities must be well developed. The proper water supply and electrification should be provided to each and every house.

• The poor tribals have no knowledge of monitoring the compensation money. Hence, the government, instead of giving lump sump money as compensation, should give them facilities of fixed deposits or else help them to start any kind of business.

• Those who, do not want money as compensation, should be provided with farming land, having equal fertility status and equal gross yield as their own lost land.

• Dam construction for irrigation purpose need not be of great heights, because greater the height of the dam more will be the encroachment of land by the water. For the purpose of Hydro-Electricity, the heights of dams ought to be high but it is not so in case of irrigational dams.

Lastly, the final view is that Development work of the country should not be stopped, it is necessary but not in the cost of tribals.

References

1. Xaxa, Virginius. 2001. *"Empowerment of Tribes"* in Singha Roy, Debal K (ed.) Social Development and the Empowerment of the Marginalised Groups: Perspectives and Strategies, New Delhi: Sage Publication, p. 205.
2. Baboo, Balgovind. 2002. *"Dams, Displacement and Violation of Human Rights: Case of Harked Dam in Orissa"* in Katare, P.M. and B.C. Barik (eds.) Development, Deprivation and Human Rights Violation, New Delhi: Rawat Publication, p. 195.
3. Fernandes, Walter. "*Paying the Price for Someone Else's Displacement*" http:/intochangeindia.org/agenda/migration-a-displallcement/payingf the.
4. Cernea, Michael. 1999. "*When Economic Analysis is Essential to Resettlement: A Sociologist's View*" in Michael Cernea (ed.) The Economics of Involuntary Resettlement: Questions and Challenges, (Washington, D.C., World Bank).
5. Census Report India, 2011.
6. Sharma,, R.N. 2003. "*Involuntary Displacement: A few Encounters*" *Economic and Political Weekly*, March 1.
7. Bandopadhya, D. 2004. "Rayagada Story Retold: Destitutes of Development" *Economic and Political Weekly*, January 31, Vol. XXXIX, No. 15.
8. Das, J.K. 2001. *"Human Rights and Indigenous Peoples"* New Delhi: A.P.H. Publishing House, pp. 58-93.

15

Tribal Land Alienation

Palla Trinadha Rao

This article presents the problem of tribal land alienation in the Scheduled Areas of Andhra Pradesh. The chapter examines the causative factors for tribal land alienation and its varied dimensions. Historically tribals owned the land in their own customary rights. Their entire life process was centered and built upon two major means of production, i.e., the forest and the land. Both land and forest lands are slipping from their control due to multiple interventions. Historical evidences are ample which reveals the uneven structural changes that have taken place from time to time due to the commoditisation of the tribal economy in which land plays a critical and predominant role. This chapter argues that the laws which have been promulgated to protect the tribal land interests are not effectively implemented resulting in external appropriation of tribal lands in the Scheduled Areas.

Introduction

Scheduled Tribes (STs) account for 8.6 per cent of India's population. 35 tribal communities are notified in Andhra Pradesh as STs and their population is about 59.18 lakhs as per the 2011 Census reports. The Tribal Sub-plan area extends over 31,485.34 sq. kms. in the districts of Srikakulam, Vizianagaram, Warangal, Visakhapatnam, East and West Godavari, Khammam, Adilabad and Mahaboobnagar districts constituting the traditional habitat of nearly 30 tribal groups. The tribal groups of Yerukula, Yanadi and Sugali or Lambada live mainly in the plain areas outside the Scheduled Areas.

The question of land tenure has been a pivotal and sensitive political issue in the context of Scheduled Areas of Andhra Pradesh. Agriculture continues to be the main source of livelihood for majority of the tribals.[1] However, large tracts of tribal land are concentrated in the hands of predominantly elite non-tribal sections of society. Consequently, tribals are marginalised and deprived of their traditional land rights. The alien systems of land tenure introduced during colonial times have had far reaching adverse effects depriving tribals of their dignity and their access to land justice.

The 'alienation' of humankind in a fundamental sense refers to the loss of control; its embodiment in an alien force which confronts the individual as a hostile and potentially destructive power. When Marx analysed 'alienation' in his Economic and Philosophic Manuscripts of 1844, he indicated four principal aspects—the alienation of human beings from nature, their own productive space, as a member of the human species and from each other.[2] Alienation, in the Marxist conception of man in the capitalist society, is the process that facilitates the exploitation of many by a few.[3]

Seen from the tribal point of view, tribals may be thought of as an alienated group. They suffer from several forms of alienation since, 'in a system of cumulative inequalities privileges, property and power are combined in the certain individuals and while the socially underprivileged are economically and politically deprived'.[4] Alienation of land itself, however, constitutes just a small component of this entire process of alienation, albeit an essential one. It is therefore, imperative to view this single phenomenon, within the holistic context of tribal existence and tribal cultural ethos.[5]

The 'alienation' of tribals from their traditional habitat is caused due to the policies of the State. The process of induction of non-tribal population into these Scheduled Areas was expected to bring progressive assimilation of the local tribals into the new socio-economic order of the immigrants, while raising their income, productivity and standard of living. 'However, often the outcome has been contrary to the above expectations, reducing the share of tribals in the gross regional product, substituting one institutional exploitation by another, uprooting them from their native land and reducing them to the status of aliens on their own soil.'[6]

In the early years of the 20th century, many tribal communities lived by and large freely, in pre-capitalistic socio-economic formations.[7] This is because the community ownership of land in India was not commoditised prior to the British rule. Tribals in their pre-capitalistic socio-economic formations had not regarded land as a commodity as it was freely available to them for cultivation. Thus, the concept of alienation with regard to the problem of land alienation in tribal areas can be understood in relation to the concept of private property relations, commoditisation of the means of production as land, labour and capital and the very process of penetration of the private sphere by the state capital.

The loss of private holdings by tribals, despite a number of laws being passed by both the pre-colonial as well as post-colonial state to check land alienation, has been a cause of concern. These laws had many shortcomings and were unable to check the transfer of land from tribals to non-tribals.[8] Even where legislation is designed to protect tribal land interests, such as restricting alienation of tribal land or ensuring that tribals receive the benefit of land tenure reforms, the results have been disappointing.[9]

Several legislations have been passed since Independence but 'despite the legislation in force against alienation of land from tribals to non-tribals, a fair proportion of them have either been dispossessed of their land or have parted with their land due to some other reason.'[10]

Tribal Identity and Land Rights

Tribals share a symbiotic relationship with natural resources. Agronomic practices and their relationship with land are based on the nature-man-spirit complex and sustenance of the economy which is unique to tribal cultures in many parts of the country.[11]Traditional communal Land tenure systems continue to exist even where formal land tenure systems emphasise on individual property rights.[12] In the predominantly agricultural societies, the importance of land cannot be over-emphasised. It is a symbol of security, the main source of income and wealth, as well as of social, political and economic power. 'The land tenure system reflects social class structure and class relations, as they represent an array of legal, contractual or customary arrangements whereby people engaged in cultivation gain access to productive opportunities linked with land and thereby income.'[13]

The British legal concept of individual private property destroyed the tradition of collective ownership and sharpened tensions within the Adivasi society while eroding their relationship with nature. These same tendencies are visible today in various developmental policies that are being implemented in the country in the post-independence era. It is the primary cause of conflicts between the tribals and the larger non-tribal society. The entire worldview of Adivasis is situated around their land. They cannot imagine their physical existence apart from it and therefore eviction from their land or encroachments by outsiders has resulted in resistance and even armed struggles in Andhra Pradesh ever since the British era.[14] There have been and continue to be, several rebellions across the country. Prominent among them in Andhra Pradesh are Alluri Seetarama Rao's armed resistance in Visakhapatnam Agency and the Gond Rebellion led by Komram Bheem in Adilabad Agency in Nizam state.[15] The Rampa Rebellion (1922-23) from East Godavari to Vizianagaram under Alluri Seetarama Raju was in protest of the Madras Forest Act of 1882 which placed restrictions on the free movement of tribals in the forest areas and prevented them from engaging in their traditional practice of *Podu* or slash and burn cultivation.

Post–independence, tribal unrest has been primarily on issues relating to restrictions on *podu* cultivation and encroachment of non-tribals in large numbers into Agency areas (tribal areas), posing threat to the existence and identity of tribal society. Special laws to protect the tribals from land alienation have been violated and about 48 per cent of the land in Agency areas is formally owned by non-tribals. Large scale manipulations during the Survey and Settlement period of 1970-76 led to grant of land entitlements of tribal land as settlement *pattas* in the name of non-tribals. According to the Koneru Ranga Rao Land Committee Report, 'Every year more and more land is passing into the hands of non-tribals and if not checked with a very strong executive force, very soon the tribals may not have any land at all.'[16]

The historical and legal perspective is that land in the Scheduled Areas once belonged to tribals. Until and unless the contrary is proved, the land in occupation by non-tribals shall be deemed to have come through a transfer from tribals. So the burden of proof lies on the non-tribals to legally prove that the land in their possession had been with them even prior to the Andhra Pradesh Agency Tracts Land Transfer Act of 1917, which restricts land transfer between the tribals and the non-tribals. The tribals have customary boundaries to the village and land is a community asset rather an individualised economic asset. The object of the Fifth Schedule and the Land Transfer Regulations is to preserve tribal autonomy and their culture, to help in their economic empowerment, to ensure social, economic and political justice for preservation of peace and good governance in the Scheduled Areas. The word 'regulate' in the allotment of land to members of STs in the Scheduled Area must be read as an endeavour to ensure regulation of the land only for and among the members of the STs in the Scheduled Area.[17]

Non-tribals and the State in Scheduled Areas

Land of the tribal communities in this region has been taken away by the non-tribals who have penetrated the region for economic gains. The penetration of non-tribals was aimed at gaining access to forest and land to exploit them as economic resources, mainly for the market, thereby undermining the traditional subsistence economy and society of the tribals.[18] This penetration was engineered by the British to serve their own colonial interest. Otherwise, there was no reason as to why a mass of non-tribal people should suddenly begin encroaching upon tribal land, something they had not done in the past. The newly imposed British land system was radically different from that prevalent among many tribal groups.[19]

The colonial period witnessed a progressive and aggressive monetisation of the economy of the tribal region for revenue generation, making dependence on the forest ever more precarious and thus destroying tribal self-reliance. Moreover, as the forests were taken over by government agencies and commercial interests, the tribals were forced more and more to live by farming the land, where they were progressively pushed into bonded labour by exploitative landlords, moneylenders, government officials and other outsiders. The creation of private property rights over land was an equally disastrous break with tribal tradition in which land was always held by the community even when it was assigned to private use.[20]

The first phase of migration of non-tribal peasants from the plains occurred around 1820 when a number of *zamindaris*, either whole or in part, came into the auction market and the highest bidder got the rights of ownership. This auction process was initiated to raise revenue. But it paved the way for the non-tribals to infiltrate tribal areas. The administration made further steady inroads for the control of the productive resources of the tribals by passing forest laws in 1882 and *abkari* laws in 1864 .These laws were meant to regulate the forest usage and consumption of toddy or alcohol.[21] The Godavari River facilitated the movement of non-tribals from the widely populated plain areas of East and West Godavari to the sparsely populated tribal areas, by country craft, mechanised boats and launches.[22] Towards the end of the nineteenth century, the British began leasing out the rights to extract bamboo and timber from the forests on both sides of the river to the non-tribal merchants of Rajahmundry. When motor boats were introduced in the second decade of this century, a larger number of merchants and their agents moved into these settlements.[23]

The huge influx facilitated further opening up of tribal areas intensifying the demand for land for diverse purposes—housing, infrastructure, business and social utilities which further led to the dispossession of the tribals. For instance, if one travels by road through the long stretch from Bhadrachalam in the Khammam district of Andhra Pradesh to Raipur in Chhattisgarh, a distance of about 550 kms and almost entirely a Fifth Schedule region where tribal land may not be sold or passed on to the non-tribal people, yet, one can see that most of the shops and land along the roadside are owned or occupied by non-tribals. This blatant encroachment upon tribal land is overlooked by a largely non-tribal government that accepts tribal people's displacement as a precondition for development.[24]

Yet, another form of land alienation is when the States promote development projects as hydroelectric power stations and mining and industries. These developmental activities do not confer any benefit on the tribals directly and render them landless.[25] The construction of irrigation dams and industrialisation are the major reasons for massive and irreversible deforestation and subsequent land loss of the tribal communities. In the last sixty years, in the new era of development, tribal communities have been displaced on a large scale. Displacement has taken place as an offshoot of the economic development by the State itself and, in particular, its industrialisation and irrigation policy.[26] For instance, there are eighteen major dams in Andhra Pradesh and six of the large ones alone have been responsible in displacing about half a million people. The proposed Indira Sagar Project (Polavaram) threatens involuntary displacement of 2.37 lakh people from 276 villages in the Scheduled Areas of Andhra Pradesh, 55 per cent of them being tribals. It will result in the submergence of 94,357 acres of land situated in the Scheduled Areas, of which 29,852 acres are *poramboke*. In addition to this, the Polavaram Project will submerge 3,223 hectares of forest.[27]

Tribals suffer from physical displacement in several parts of the country due to development projects initiated by the government.[28] Displacement among the tribals is on a massive scale and often with adverse implications on the communities, mainly due to laws that do not recognise the communal and customary rights of tribal people over their territories. Resettlement literature is replete with case studies on development projects that ignore the customary rights of the tribal people and treat them as illegal occupants of government land. Such an approach invariably leads to the impoverishment of once well settled communities; precisely the opposite of what development promises.[29]

Loss of Tribal Land during Survey and Settlement Operations

After abolition of intermediary land tenure systems, survey and settlement operations work was undertaken in the Scheduled Areas of Srikakulam, Vizianagaram, Visakhapatnam, East Godavari, West Godavari, Nugur and Bhadrachalam taluks of Khammam district of the Andhra region.

The survey and settlement operations are covered by Andhra Pradesh Regulations 1/69, 2/69 and 2/70, to settle the land occupations of both the tribals and non-tribals. Three tenures viz., *malguzari, muttadari* and estates prevailing in these areas were converted into *ryotwari*. The intermediaries *mahaldar, muttadar* and *zamindar* between the government and ryots were abolished.

All the Settlement Regulations referred above in fact dilute the letter and spirit of Land Transfer Regulations 1 of 70 by enabling non-tribals to claim patta over land situated in the Scheduled Areas, in effect negating the presumption that unless and until contrary proved, the land in occupation by non-tribals would be deemed to have come from the tribals through a transfer.

The Expert Group on Prevention of Alienation of Tribal Land and its Restoration, Ministry of Rural Development, Government of India, headed by the Planning Commission Member, B.N. Yugandhar has also cast a serious doubt on the settlement *patta* throughout Schedule Five areas. Similarly, the denial of *pattas* to the tribals is the other side of the coin of Settlement *Pattas*, which calls for a scrutiny of the rejection orders.[30]

As per the 1990 Report of Neerabh K Prasad, an IAS Officer, entitled 'Protection of Tribal Land' in the Settlement Regulations 2/69 and 2/70, it has been stipulated that the non-tribals had to prove eight years of continuous possession of land prior to 1969 and 1970 and an absence of any prohibited transfer as per Land Transfer Regulations, to be eligible for a grant of a *patta*. Further, it states that norms were openly flouted by the non-tribals. False receipts were created by the *mutta* clerks or estates clerks showing payment of taxes. The tribals were driven out by creating terror through organising police raids, thus making it convenient for the non-tribals to get the tribal land measured in their names. In a specific case at Nelakota village of East Godavari District, the village abuts a huge inland tank by the name of Ramavarapu Ava and gets irrigation from the same. The non-tribal residents of the adjacent villages, especially Ramachandrapuram, dubbed the tribals as naxalites (post-1969 Srikakulam Naxalite Movement period) and organised police raids. The tribals had to flee from the hill tops and stayed there for more than a month. This period was used by the non-tribals to get the land surveyed and settled in their favour. Land with rich forest growth was taken as *patta* even though tribals were never in occupation of the land; obviously with an eye to the rich timber. The cases of Jangalthota and Chintalpudi of Y. Ramavaram Mandals of East Godavari are glaring examples of these. The tribal claims were never properly examined and were largely unaware of the settlement operations. By the time the tribals realised that their land was being granted as *pattas* to the non-tribals, it was too late for an appeal. As a result of these dubious measures, the land holdings of the non-tribals jumped from 9,805 hectares before 1969 to 16,789 hectares by 1976 in the Scheduled Area of East Godavari District. [31] The non-tribals in three Agency mandals of West Godavari District hold *pattas* for over 53,719 acres, while tribals have *pattas* for over 37,042 acres only in the Scheduled Area as per the Minutes of the Cabinet Sub-Committee circulated on 24th July 1997:

Just before the abolition of the Estates, the landholders accelerated issuance of *pattas* in several cases even with regard to the waste land in the estates by receiving paltry sums. So the Settlement Officer is directed to reopen all the *pattas* that were granted till now under the provisions of Ryotwari Settlement Regulations 2 of 1970, observed by Justice BSA. Swamy while dealing with a case in relation to land disputes in West Godavari District Agency Areas.[32]

In Bhadrachalam division in Khammam district, 8,297 non-tribals were granted *pattas* for 29,554.16 hectares according to the Report of Secretary to Government (1992). Expressing concern over the grant of *ryotwari* settlement *pattas* to non-tribals in the Scheduled Areas during the survey period, the Secretary to Government, Govindarajan (1992) reports two cases have come to the attention of the Government during the course of verification by special officer for survey of tribal land and assignment to tribals in Khammam district in the month of July 1990. In one case five non-tribals were granted *ryotwari patta* in respect of an extent of 30 acres of land while the tribals are in possession and enjoyment of the said land. In another case, non-tribals have obtained *ryotwari pattas* in respect of an extent of 101 acres where as the tribals are in continuous occupation and enjoyment of the said land.

During 1996-1997 when land disputes erupted in tribal areas of West Godavari District, one of the major contention of the tribals was that they should be given possession of land as per the 1902 Resettlement Register (RSR) and the non-tribals who were occupying land classified as tribal or government in the 1902 Resettlement Register should prove that they had got hold of the land in a legal manner. The Resettlement Register of 1902 is currently not even available with the offices of the Commissioner, Tribal Welfare or the district.[33]

Extent of Tribal Land Dispossession

Dispossession of land for a variety of reasons is evident, including for mines, industries, hydro power, and irrigation projects resulting in both direct and indirect eviction of the tribal communities.[34] The decline in the percentage of cultivators among the ST households from 45 per cent to 35.4 per cent during the period 1994-2005 indicates the loss of land and their increasing dependency on agricultural labour which increased from 37 per cent to 43.7 per cent during the period 1994-2005. The percentage of population depending on agricultural labour increased only in the case of STs, while it has declined for the Scheduled Caste. [35] Even the existing land holdings of the marginalised have been alienated, in spite of score of laws in force for ensuring protection of the land rights of the marginalised, especially the Adivasis.[36]

Had history been otherwise, nearly five lakh tribal families living in the Scheduled villages of Andhra Pradesh would have presently together been the proud owners of 18,48,209.30 acres of land with an average household landholding of 3.69 acres. But instead, presently more than 48 per cent of this land is cultivated by the non-tribals. In some districts as Warangal, Khammam and Adilabad, more than 50 per cent of the land in the Scheduled villages is held by the non-tribals. The pernicious poverty of the tribals has led them to become victims of schemes of non-tribal money lenders, thus resulting in indebtedness and consequent alienation of land. To check the land alienation, several Land Transfer Regulations including 1 of 59 as amended by 1 of 70, were created prohibiting the transfer of land between tribals and non-tribals, and among the non-tribals since 1917. In spite of these restrictions, land alienation is still prevalent amongst the Adivasis. [37]

Implementation of Land Transfer Regulations

In 1917, soon after a two year long hit-and-run tribal insurgency in the Godavari Agency, the British enacted the first Agency Tract Interest and Land Transfer Act, to prohibit land transfers between hill tribes and non-tribals without prior permission from the District Collector. Subsequently, Land Transfer Regulations 1 of 59, as amended by 1 of 70, were made. Despite these being in force for long, 56 per cent of the cultivable land in the Scheduled Areas (about 8.7 lakh acres) is owned by the non-tribals, while the extent of land restored to tribals under these enactments is only nine per cent of this area (about 80,000 acres).[38] And, if anybody can ever manage to estimate the extent of agricultural land that is supposedly owned by tribals but in reality is being held and cultivated by the non-tribals, then these statistics would reveal an even more unequal state of affairs.[39]

There is another important legislation in respect of lands in the Telangana area of the State. The Andhra Pradesh (Telangana Area) Tenancy and

Table 15.1 : Outcome of Cases under LTR at SDC Courts as on 31st January, 2010

Sl. No	*District*	*Cases detected*		*Cases Disposed*		*Cases Decided in favour of STs*		*Cases Decided in favour of Non-STs*		*Land Restored to Tribals*		*Balance cases at the end of the month (col. 3-5 and 4-6)*	
		Nos	*Extent (Acres)*	*Nos*	*Extent (Acres)*	*Nos*	*Extent (Acres)*	*Nos*	*Extent (Acres)*	*Nos*	*Extent (Acres)*	*Nos*	*Extent (Acres)*
	1	2	3	4	5	6	7	8	9	10	11	12	13
1.	Srikakulam	462	1100	453	1024	296	538	157	486	250	522	9	76
2.	Vizianagaram	1364	7544	1343	7501	955	5631	388	1870	850	5498	21	43
3.	Visakhapatnam	5708	22731	5480	22087	4359	17721	1121	4366	3029	13944	228	644
4.	East Godavari	8485	49637	8264	48768	3751	19667	4513	29101	3392	17685	221	869
5.	West Godavari	11611	62121	11477	60820	2584	11082	8893	49738	2451	10081	134	1301
6.	Khammam	33582	126713	33325	125834	15514	52192	17811	73642	12750	41662	257	879
7.	Warangal	7289	15784	7052	15218	4865	8964	2187	6254	4865	8964	237	566
8.	Adilabad	8245	54008	7564	51543	4175	27839	3389	23704	3305	23606	681	2465
9.	Mahbubnagar	16	61	15	57	13	49	2	8	13	49	1	4
	Total	**76762**	**339699**	**74973**	**332852**	**36512**	**143683**	**38461**	**189169**	**30905**	**122011**	**1789**	**6847**

Source: Office of the Commissioner of Tribal Welfare, Hyderabad, Admin. Report, Jan. 2010.

Agricultural Land Act of 1950 classifies all tenants into ordinary and protected tenants. The Act further stipulates that if the tenant personally cultivated the land continuously for a period of six years during a stipulated period, he shall be deemed to be a protected tenant. As a protected tenant he reserves the right to purchase the land from the owner. This Act was also in force in the tribal areas of Telangana region. The non-tribals who gained access to land from tribals through clandestine and dubious methods were protected by the legislation. There was no law strictly prohibiting the transfer of land between tribals and non-tribals till 1963 in the Telangana region barring a revenue division Bhadrachalam in the Kammam district. The land reforms which were introduced by the State of Andhra Pradesh protecting the tenancy was made applicable to tribal areas without taking into cognisance the tribal interest.

The greater part of land alienation occurred after the 1940s. There are several loopholes in the existing Land Transfer Regulations 1 of 70. For instance, the law does not act retrospectively and thus cannot be applied to land transfer deals between the tribals and the non-tribals prior to the enforcement of the Act. Therefore, the exploitative relations in Agency areas still dominate the social structure. Hence, the problem of land alienation becomes part of the bigger problem of the existence of unequal class relations between the tribals and the non-tribals in the present day society.[40]

The suo motu power given to the government to proceed against non-tribals without waiting for a complaint from a tribal seems to be an ideal arrangement, but in the given administrative culture, it has perhaps been more of a boon to the non-tribals than to the tribals. In proceedings taken up suo motu by the government, the non-tribal faces only the government. The government does not take the trouble of finding out who among the local tribals may have a claim to the land. It does not publicise the enquiry in the village. The officer hearing the cases, designated as Special Deputy Collector, merely looks into the documents provided by the non-tribal, and if they appear reliable, he approves the right of the non-tribal over the land.[41]

Of 76,762 cases covering an extent of 3,39,699 acres of land, 74,973 cases covering an extent of 3,32,852 acres were disposed off by the SDC Courts in the State of Andhra Pradesh by the end of January 2010. The courts decided 36,512 cases covering an extent of 1,43,683 acres of land in favour of the tribals. However, the enforcement machinery set up under the regulations could only restore 1,22,011 acres of land pertaining to the 30,905 cases out of a total of 36,512. On the contrary, the non-tribals were able to secure orders in their favour in 38,461 cases and retained 1,89,169 acres of land in their possession.

Table shows that the success rate for land acquisition is 49 per cent in the case of tribals, and 51 per cent in the case of non-tribals. Tribals were able to regain land possession from non-tribals only to the extent of 43 per cent of the total extent of land, covered by cases disposed off, while the non-tribal could retain 57 per cent of the disputed land. Due to the failure of the implementing machinery in implementing the orders passed by the SDC Court in favour of the tribals, only 85 per cent of the total cases were disposed off in favour of the tribals, and only 85 per cent of land extent was physically handed over to them. This shows the failure of the administrative machinery in executing orders passed by the court in the favour of tribals. The non-tribals continued to possess land even when the eviction orders were passed against them.

The Scheduled Areas is to ensure justice to tribals, their survival and livelihood. But as K. Balagopal pointed out:

It is not enough if a disadvantaged class of people are endowed with legal rights. Legal instruments created for the benefit of the socially privileged can be expected to find their way to implementation without anything else. This is not the case with legal rights enacted for the benefit of the disadvantaged.'[42]

Conclusion

The extent of land alienation in the Scheduled Areas is a cause for public concern. The process of land alienation has not stopped even after the promulgation of tribal protective land laws due to weak enforcement of the laws. Tribals have lost their land due to multiple attacks, including the exploitative mechanism compounded by forcible acts of the non-tribal settlers and the interventions of the state in dispossessing their land. The tribal land alienation issue is further complicated by the mainstream political parties due to their tilt towards the non-tribal vote bank policies. The special protection extended for tribal rights through various legislations with the support of main opposition parties are part of the welfare measures of the State, but without the political will to actually convert them into a reality. As a result of land alienation, the tribals have lost livelihood and their cultural linkage with the natural resources. Perhaps, the tribal belt will experience more and more incursions of the non-tribals and industrial interests in future and lose its character despite the Fifth Schedule of the Constitution. The magnitude of the problem is of national importance and needs to be tackled and solved through Parliamentary intervention and effective enforcement of the laws.

Notes

Abkari tax	:	Excise Tax.
Koneru Land Committee	:	Koneru Land Committee headed by the State Minister Koneru Ranga Rao was constituted in 2005 to study the tribal land problems and give recommendations, followed by discussions held between Maoists and State of Andhra Pradesh.
Mukhasa	:	Mukhasa is a village or land assigned to an individual either rent free or at a low rent, on condition of services.
Mutta	:	A village or group of villages held by a Muttadar.
Muttadar	:	A person who holds Mutta under a Sanad granted by the Government subject to payment of a fixed amount of land revenue

		and who assists the Government in maintaining law and order in the Mutta.
Patta	:	Land entitlement deed.
Pattadar	:	The Ryotwari proprietor is usually termed as pattadar.
Poromboke	:	Poromboke is a land belonging to Government which is not *prima* facie available for assignment.
Proprietor	:	Land lord or Land holder of villages held by Estate, Mutta, Mukasa.
SDC court	:	Special Deputy Collector (Tribal Welfare) is a designated enquiry officer under Land Transfer Regulations to conduct enquires for restoration of lands from the possession of non-tribals in the scheduled areas. The court is manned by SDC.

References

1. Ambagudia, Jagannath. Tribal Rights, Dispossession and the State in Orissa, Economic and Political Weekly, 14th August 2010, Vol. xlv, No. 33, 2010.

2. Areas of Srikakulam, Vijayanagaram, Visakhapatnam, East and West Godavari, Kammam, Warangal and Adilabad districts were notified by the President of India under Fifth Schedule to the Constitution of India.

3. Arnold, David. Rebellious Hillmen: The Gudem Rampa Rising 1839-1924 in Ranajit Guha (Ed.), Subaltern Studies I, OUP, Delhi, 1982.

4. Ashokvardhan, C. Tribal Land Rights in India, Centre for Rural Studies, LBS National Academy of Administration, Musoorie, 2006.

5. Balagopal, K. Foreword to book Land Rights of Adivasis by P. Trinadha Rao (2004) Laya Publication, Visakhapatnam.

6. Balagopal, K. Land Unrest in Andhra Pradesh – III – Illegal Acquisition in Tribal Areas, Economic and Political Weekly, 6th October 2007, p. 4031.

7. Balagopal, K. Pitting the Tribals against the Non-tribal Poor, Economic and Political Weekly, 27th May 1989, p. 1151.

8. Beteille, Andre. (1974). Studies in Agrarian Social Structure. Oxford: Oxford University Press.

9. Burman, Roy B.K. Communal Land System of the Tribals and Problems of Institutional Finance in Manipur and Tripura, Delhi, 1986.

10. Draft National Policy on Tribals, Ministry of Tribal Affairs, GoI, New Delhi, 2004.

11. For details see, Patnaik, S.C. and S. Patel. Impact of Modernisation on Tribals: Economic dualism and path of change (A case study of Malkangiri sub-division in Koraput district), paper presented in the Seminar on 'Prospectus of Economic Development of Tribal of Koraput District held in October (Mimeo), 1982, pp. 2-14.

12. For instance Vidyarthi, LP (1963) The Maler: The Nature-Man-Spirit Complex in a Hill Tribe introduces the concept of 'nature-man-spirit' in anthropology and Bharath Bhushan M and Satyamohan PV (1990) study of the tribal scenario in Andhra Pradesh The Koyas - A Study of Nature–Man-Spirit-Complex among the Koyas of Bhadrachalam (mimeograph) explains the inseparable link of land with tribal

life. The ethnographic film in Search of Ethnic Dimension - The Koyas made for the University Grants Commission deals with the nature-man interaction and the associated belief system. It examines the features of the environment in relation to the Koya economic system. Also see http://video.google.com/videoplay?docid= 12041 6098650145419&hl=en#.

13. Girglani Commission. J.M. (2005), Committee Report of Ministry of Rural Development (Government of AP).

14. Godavari district Gazetteer, Government Press, Madras, 1907, p. 101.

15. Heredia, Rudolf C. Tribal History, Living Word or Dead Letter, Economic and Political Weekly, 29th April 2000.

16. Istvan Meszaros (2006), "Marx's theory of Alienation". Aakar Books, New Delhi.

17. Mohan Lal, Morley. Poverty Alleviation: The Indian Experience. Delhi: Himalaya Publishing House, 1988, p. 386.

18. Nath, N, D.K. Behera, and Sarkar, R.M. (Eds.). The So-called Development, Displacement and Dispossession: An Analysis on Land and Forest Rights of the Project Affected People. Land and Forest Rights of the Tribals Today, Serials Publications, Delhi, 2006.

19. Note on Land Problems in Agency Areas of West Godavari, Social Welfare (TW) Department, Government of AP, Hyderabad, 1997.

20. Gangamma P.Vs. Vasudha Misra and another. 1998(2) ALD 35.

21. Philip Viegas (1991), Encroached and Enslaved, Indian Social Institute Publication, Delhi, p. 32.

22. Pinto, Ambrose. Fillip to Land Transfers Land Acquisition Bill, Economic and Political Weekly, 5th December 1988.

23. Ramnath, Madhu. Surviving the Forest Rights Act: Between Scylla and Charybdis, Economic and Political Weekly, 1st March 2008.

24. Ranga Rao, Koneru. The Land Committee Report - 2006, GoAP, Hyderabad, 2006, p. 57.

25. Rao, Trinadha P. Tribal Development in Question, Laya Publication, Visakhapatnam, 2004.

26. Rao, Trinadha P. Nature of Opposition to Polavaram Project, Economic and Political Weekly, 15th April, 2006.

27. Rao, Trinadha P. Persisting Alienation of Tribal Land, A.P. Social Watch Report, Hyderabad, 2007.

28. Rao, B. Janardhana. Land Alienation in Tribal Areas of Andhra Pradesh, Kakatiya University, Warangal, 1987.

29. Rao, B, Janardhana. Adivasis in India – Characterisation of Transition and Development, Adhyayana Publications, Warangal, 2000.

30. Rao, Jayaprakash P. The Struggle for Land: Tribal Revolts in Two Villages, in K. Murali Manohar, P. Ramaiah and C. Sivaramakrishna Rao (Eds.) Political Economy of Tribal Development, Indian Institute of Public Administration, Warangal, 1985.

31. Reddy, Subba N. Sword of Damocles over Tribal People of Andhra Pradesh, Economic and Political Weekly, 1st July 1989, pp. 1442-3.

32. Report of Commissioner for SC and ST (Fifth Report), Ministry of Tribal Affairs, GoI, Delhi, 1982-83, p. 28.

33. Report of Ministry of Rural Development Department of Land Resources, Govt. of India, Delhi, 2000.

34. Report on Human Development, CESS, Begampet, Hyderabad, 2007.

35. Samata Vs. State of Andhra Pradesh AIR 1997, p. 3301.

36. Sastry, VNVK. Between Gonds Rebellion, Udyama Publications, Hyderabad, 1989.

37. Satyanarayana, K. A Study of History and Culture of the Andhras, People's Publishing House, New Delhi, 1975, p. 44.

38. Shah, G. Social Movements in India: A Review of Literature, Sage, New Delhi, 1990.

39. Sharma, T.R (1979), "Karl Marx: From Alienation to Exploitation", Indian Journal of Political Science. Vol. 40, No. 3rd September.

40. The Twenty-Ninth Report of the Commissioner of Scheduled Castes and Tribes (1990) says that even though tribal people form about 7.5 per cent of the population, over 40 per cent of the people displaced till 1990, belonged to these communities. A report of the Official Working Group on Development and Welfare of Scheduled Tribes during the Eighth Five-Year Plan (1990-1995) on the rehabilitation of tribal people, based on a comprehensive study of 110 projects, has concluded that of the 1.694 million people displaced by these projects, almost 50 per cent (814,000) were tribals.

41. Tribal Welfare Department, Government of Andhra Pradesh, Land Reforms and Land Transfers, Report of Tribal Welfare Department, Hyderabad, 1995.

42. Trivedi, H. Tribal Land Systems Land Reform Measures and Development of Tribals, Concept Publications, New Delhi, 1993.

16

Governance in Tribal Areas in Contemporary Time: Tribal Peoples' Voice and Livelihood from Chhattisgarh

Pradip Kumar Parida

Key Words

Ecology vs. Economy, Right to Life with Dignity, 'People's Voice in Development, Tribal Development, Crisis in Governability, Law and Order Problem-It's Socio- Economic Roots.

Abstract

In the name of good governance the Indian state has molded contemporary economic policy in such a way that it creates question mark not only on the environmental issues but also the very existence of certain section of society. The trajectory path of development in India is producing 'forced migration' as well as 'development refugees'. People are becoming refugee in their own land. This is a process of further marginalisation for the already marginalised people and also accelerating the process of 'alienation' among the tribal's of the country. When people protest against these types of activities, it is termed as movement against the state. What about the 'life' and 'livelihood' of a citizen from the point of view of 'human security'. What about the right to life with dignity? What about ecology of the society and the involvement of the community in terms of maintaining their livelihood vs. the economic development of the state and the security of the individuals, i.e., life and liberty. Can the state sacrifice the environment justice in the name of market driven development paradigm?

Introduction

There is a rough consensus among all of us that, the movement towards good governance must include initiatives to strengthen the institutions of government and civil society with the objective of making government more accountable, transparent, open, democratic, participatory as well as promotion of law. The word 'Governance' dates back to origin of civilisation, to the pre-historic period. Since then the growth of civilisation though has undergone a zigzag motion, 'governance' has remained the key to 'state structure' in terms of its relationship with citizens, irrespective of region, religion, social structure, level of economic development as well as the nature of political regime. Etymologically 'governance' means, how to govern oneself—for example, the citizens in a state. In other words, governance is a process and government is an agency of governance where the citizens are the primary stake holders in this larger picture.

As a matter of fact, 'governance' legitimises the actions and duties as well as responsibilities of a 'citizen' in a given 'state structure'. As per the law of the land 'what is the entitlement of a citizen', keeping in background the political history, socio-economic development, resources available with the government at that particular point of time, social structure, cultural factors, level of participation of the people etc. Hence, providing the space for legitimate entitlement of a citizen in a state and creating a conducive atmosphere to realise the best potential within the individual concerned are the two key tasks with the government, as far as governance is concerned. This spreads into all the aspects of society—social, economic, political. This spreads from individual to local to district to regional to national to global level. It also clovers the arena of State, Civil society and Market. All of them influence the decision making process and behaviour of the individual— 'citizen'. It is perceived that 'accountability and transparency' will be at the heart of 'governance'. This is a broader term than 'government' and refers to traditions, norms, institutions, practices, space to the citizens and the procedures by which individuals and groups exercise power in public decision making. It also gives more space to the citizens by making them actively involved in implementation of various programmes. However accountability may not necessarily be considered as accountability from government side to people. It is also other way round, which means people should be accountable to other fellow citizens as well as government, for the day to day actions in a true civic sense, by maintaining the true spirit of democracy.

Contemporary Situation across the Globe

How the citizens participate in the governance process at the local level and more particularly the local bodies' there—be it political, economic, cultural activities, taxation system or decision making process. There is no short cut to it. But it becomes questionable, when there is lack of transparency and accountability from the local bodies/local government in terms of sharing power or resources with the common citizens—which otherwise is the crux of the 'decentralised democracy'- 'empowerment of people'—the basic philosophy and objective behind formation of 'local self government'—'self-ruling institutions'. Millen Development Goal (MDG) of the United Nations categorically mentions about the minimum amount of development standards or parameters a country must achieve in this millennium, so that there will be universal minimum standard of living across the globe. How does one achieve that goal? What are the mechanisms? When we talk about "*Dignity with Development*", how much dignified our public policy in terms of giving the space to citizens. What are the alternatives before us at the present juncture? *As we know the economic development will lead to more and more social opportunities* and will widen the scope of human civilisation in terms of sustenance. How one can come to such a conclusion, giving the background of governance in our country today. These are the questions before us.

As a matter of fact 'Government' is one of the most powerful institutions in our society in any system of governance. But free market, privatisation, structural adjustment, deregulation and decentralisation, the traditional role of 'government', has changed a lot. The actors of governance, Corporate Sectors in 'market economy' and Civil Society in 'development sectors' are playing important role in this scenario. Hence, naturally the question comes to us, is governance becomes 'good' with the minimum role of government in policy matters. The proponents of neo-liberal favours minimalist role of government and prefers market can do everything on the basis of principle of market economy. The most important point is people in a democracy are not merely 'customers' or 'clients', of the government, rather they are also 'subjects', and 'citizens' are also bounded by mutual obligations and are entitled to enjoy public infrastructure provided by the government, such as roads, ports, communications, court of law, monetary system, public sanitation etc.

In this context, it is argued by many that the pure private sector management model cannot cater to the needs of the citizens. As a matter of fact private goods are necessary. But they are worthless without public goods—such as policing and economic policies, meant to protect citizens. For example, media, it must not be fully under government control nor should be it is entirely in private hands. However, the objective of democratic government is to create a conducive environment and protect free people, not free private groups, and institutions supporting them. Hence we can say that attacks on government are attacks on the very fabric of society.

Environmental and Livelihood Issues

'Sustainable development' has become the key word in the contemporary discourse in development. The way natural resources are being exploited for the consumption purposes, that is not only giving a space for indiscriminate use of natural resources, but also creating problems for lives and livelihood of thousands of aboriginal people who are original inhabitants of this country, who are primarily residing in forest, i.e., so called adivasis (tribal's). Forget about future generation, even we are not considering our present generations. Otherwise, we would not have exploited our recourses in that fashion. Above all the natural resources are not infinite in nature. There is certain limit to it. What about the blue print on it. For example, what is the amount of natural resources, where are they located, exact amount, its utility at present and in future, modality of extraction, who will extract—whether private or government, what is the mechanism for that,—all these issues, are they are in public domain.

If we will look into the industrialisation process carried out in contemporary times across the globe, we will find not only natural environment is getting polluted but also the socio-cultural practices, economic issues (livelihood) political factors (people's protest against this), legal issues (who is the original owner—is it the state or people who are enjoying the nature for centuries and generations) are intimately involved in this. Particularly in India, since the new economic policy (NEP) started due to the onslaught of globalisation and opening of the whole market for private players (be it local industrial houses or MNCs), the people's displacement is becoming rampant, without proper rehabilitation policy. Their resettlement is becoming more problematic. People are becoming 'refugees' in their 'own home land'. What type of development is this? If we will examine these issues more minutely, whole social movements in the last two decades across South-Asia including India is primarily concentrating on control over natural resources—*Jal, Jingle* and *Jamin* (water, land, forest). All these are part of the local ecology, where an individual is leading his day to day life on the lap of nature.

On the name of industrialisation where market economy determines everything, who cares about the lives and livelihood issues of innocent tribals? Are the industrial houses getting clearance from the tribal's panchayats (as per PESA Act) genuinely or in fraudulent manner? What is the proper mechanism to get the approval of tribal people? What about the Environment/Social Impact Assesessment? What about placing it in public domain? Who are the gainers and who are the loosers at the end of the day? These are very important issues in this context. When we talk about industrialisation, do we give also equal importance to our fellow citizens' 'right to lead a life with dignity'? Today we found the undercurrent of a strong Maoist movement in the certain states of central India, where the exploitation of natural resources and displacement of tribal's due to it has taken to the maximum extent. This symbolically reflects something very serious.

The Stories from a Tribal Belt of Chhattisgarh

The fundamental question is why this is happening in such a manner today? Though that part of Chhattisgarh is full of natural resources, forests, minerals, the tribal's are at the bottom of everything. Hardly any parameter of the so called 'development' has reached to them, i.e., primary schools, primary health centres, land holding for them who has accepted agriculture as occupation—whatever miniscule it may be, village networking roads, all these are lacking. A tribal is not feeling as a part of the state system. *Their alienation from the State and the larger society is increasing day by day including land alienation*. The massive exploitation by petty contractor, forest mafia, usurping land by big industrialists at a nominal price or free of cost, creating suspicion in the minds of a tribal. What about his expectations from the state? Who is reaping the benefit? For example, though the Bastar region has abundance of mineral resources, i.e. Bailadila mines and large forest tracts and one Railway line—Kirandul exists, has it given any benefits to the tribal's? The iron ore being expropriated from Kirandul has been exported to Japan. No industry has been established there. At present whatever industry is being established, the land is taken without their permission, even if it comes under PESA and so also as far as jobs are concerned tribal's are only given as unskilled labourers.

There is lack of proper implementation of any development programmes, for example, recently enacted NREGA (according to many fact finding reports from the field including the report of Prof. Jean Dreeze). Has it any impact on tribals of Bastar. I think, a well documented and focused research is needed to come out for a conclusion. What about their livelihood pattern in a changing economic scenario? The tribal's who were dependent on forest resources and rivers for centuries, generation after generation are deprived of all these due to increasing state control as well as 'privatisation of water', timber, forest resources. Hence their grievances, frustration is taking another channel, where Naxalism is getting the chance to breed. Nothing new in it. The tribal's found a hope to express their hopes as well as frustration. Hence there is a clear cut vacuum in the governance system of the state, which is now occupied by Naxalites. But to stop it the state is responding in a more fascist way. (As an academician and researcher I am not supporting violence at any cost by any logic. As violence breeds violence). But what is the alternative for tribal's in such a situation.

Fundamental Rights of an Individual in a given State Structure

What are the rights of a 'citizen' in such a situation? As a 'citizen' in a 'democratic state', where is the space for me to ventilate the grievances within the 'state structure' itself? Where is the channel of communication between the government and people? What is the alternative mechanism to address these problems? Is the naxalite movement is simply a 'law and order' problem or it has certain larger socio-political and economic dimensions involved with it? Is it SPO-private militia is the solution to curb the violence by Naxalism. By the way Naxalite were ideologically in favour of militant armed struggle against the state, to abolish the state structure and transfer the state power. How to stop the violence created by them? It has its root in socio-economic issues, underdevelopment, bad governance system etc. Hence it is also a socio-economic problem which has culminated into a political problem having symptoms like law and order problem in the present context. Hence, it has to be tackled at political level, which is totally undermined today. Where is the space for dialogue, discussion, debate with those groups, who are against the state in armed struggle?

Findings from Tribal Belts across the Country

There is a need of changing paradigm of public policy to address these types of challenges. Not only Chhattisgarh, the other tribal belts of the country, i.e., Nagaland, Bodoland, Gorkhaland, Mizoram, Tripura, Jharkhand, some part of Orissa, Andhra Pradesh, Madhya Pradesh is witnessing this problem. Personally I feel, it is global phenomena, where the movement of the global political economy is controlling everything today. Whatever might be the circumstances and causes of problem, ultimately it is the innocent tribals are the worst sufferers. 'Human Security' is affected to a larger extent. The right to life with dignity is undermined at any cost. The aftermath of neo-liberal regime in the context of globalisation is witnessing these types of phenomena all over the world, across the globe. The reason being when market economy determines the state policies, particularly public policies, rights of the citizens, particularly 'human rights' takes a back seat. In this context the most vulnerable sections are – 'the sub-alterns', i.e., dalits, tribals, minorities and other socially marginalised sections. The present scenario of Chhattisgarh is classic example of this. However the commonality among all the movements of aboriginals across the world is who controls the natural resources and why the state is taking decisions in an arbitrary manner rather taking the affected into confidence.

Conclusion

We must have to have a paradigmatic shift from social science perspective to understand this to relate an individual and state in terms of the 'rights' of the tribal's of the country. When the fundamental rights of the people is violated (i.e., right to life with dignity, right to livelihood etc.) which are guaranteed by the constitution, what is the remedy for that. Even if some rights are not guaranteed by the constitution but enjoyed by the human beings because they are part of human civilisation. When these are violated, affected people protest against it. But if it does not stop, they protest it violently. How the solution can be arrived in this case? What about dialogue, debate and discussion in this scenario? Where is the space for democratic process? Government is a product of historical evolution. The basic argument is that government as an instrument of governance is indispensable. The 'state' came into existence due to certain rationality. Hence, the 'state' has certain activities for the citizens that are protection of life, liberty and creating a conducive atmosphere for their development and maintenance of law and order. In that context it can be argued that if the state fails to fulfill its obligation, the tribal people have every right to question the actions of the government, particularly, when their life and livelihood is at stake, they must revolt against the state, otherwise their voice will be unheard.

References

1. Bhaduri Amit and Deepak Nayar, *The Intelligent Persons Guide to Liberalisation*, Penguin, New Delhi, 1996.
2. Soros George, *On Globalisation*, Viva Books Private Limited, New Delhi, 2004.
3. Mathur, Kuldeep, *From Government to Governance*, NBT India, New Delhi, 2008.
4. Bhagwati Jagdish, *India in Transition*, Clarendon Press, Oxford, 1995.
5. Basu, D.D., *Constitution of India*, Prentice Hall India, New Delhi, 1998.
6. Bhaduri Amit, *Dignity with Development*, NBT, New Delhi, 2004.
7. L.P. Vidyarthi and Binay Kumar Rai, *The Tribal Culture of India*, Concept Publishing Company, New Delhi, 1976.
8. Dhebar, U.N.: "*Dhebar Commission Report*".
9. Ghurye, G.S.: "*The Scheduled Tribes*", Popular Book Depot, Mumbai, 1959.
10. Majumdar, D.N.: "*Affairs of a Tribe*", Universal Publishers, Lucknow, 1953.
11. Sachidanand: "*Culture and Change in Tribal Bihar*", Bookland Limited, Calcutta, 1964.
12. Elwin, Verrier: "*Nagaland*", Research Department, Advisor's Secretariat, Shillong, 1961.
13. Srinivas, M.N.: "*Social Change in Modern India*", Allied Publishers, Bombay, 1961.
14. Srivastava, S.K.: "*The Tharus A Study of Culture Dynamics*", Agra University Press, Agra, 1958.
15. Rao, V.K.R.V: "*Social Change and Tribal Society*", Journal of Social Research, Vol. IX, No. 2nd, September 1966.
16. Vidyarthi, L.P.: "*Ghaghra-A Village of Chhotanagpur*", Manager Publications, New Delhi, 1966.
17. Sundar, Nandini. *Subalterns and the Sovereign.*
18. Chakravarty, Sudip. *Traverse in Red Corridor.*
19. Planning Commission Report on Naxalite Affected Areas.
20. Supreme Court, High Court and other tribunal judgments related to the above mentioned issues.

17

Environmental Approach to Tribal Development

Satchidananda Misra

Our so called development projects push the tribals out of their natural habitat. Most often new development experiments result in tribal displacement by new migrants. We presume that tribal population benefit by the general development programme. But the hopes in this regard were belied as the benefits of the development programme did not percolate to the tribals. The task force on development of tribal areas observed that factors for the failure of tribal development programme include non-involvement of tribal people in the process, attitude of planners and decision-makers towards the tribals.

The present scenario demands a revitalising of existing development strategies and new orientation to the perspective of tribal development. Environmental approach to the tribal development can solve a lot many problems of the tribals. The tribal man puts least pressure on nature for his subsistence. He is the— 'noble savage', the natural and the 'primitive' idealised by many thinkers. An insight into the tribal culture and their way of life can vindicate the environmental dimension of development. Development becomes a myth without tribal upliftment. A development project which creates a lot of deforestation and environmental hazards bring endless miseries for the man in the forest.

All round development of tribes is possible through environmental conservation. The tribe must be allowed to participate in the process of decision making. During last century the erosion of tribal rights in land and forest resources has led to tribal resistance in different parts of the world. Despite a plethora of legislations, special safeguards and other development programmes, tribal right in land and forest resources, large scale displacement, increasing inequalities and poverty, degraded social states causing tribal tensions, identity crisis have emerged as baffling problems. The beauties of the country landscape and virtues of simple tribal life are to be celebrated in contrast to the growing urbanisation. A time has come to extend the benefits of globalised world to him through development projects without jeopardising the pristine nature which alone can assure them a good life. Environmental approach to tribal development can alone achieve this objective.

Environmentalism has given a new perspective to the tribal problems. Environmentalism and tribalism are very closely related. Hills and Forests, the very natural habitat of the tribes are the store house of experiments for the environmentalist. The causes of basic problems of the tribal people like alienation, poverty, starvation, malnutrition, poor health are attributed to environmental hazards.

With the advent of globalisation world is shrinking. The difference between 'we' and 'they', the 'non-tribals' and 'tribals' narrows down. Over the years as a result of culture contact with globalised modern societies, the primitives have been deprimitivised. No longer the tribes reside in pristine serenity. Concept of 'noble savage' is becoming meaningless. Scholars in this area have observed that the people whom we study are no longer hidden, forgotten, lost or cloistered.

Malinowski's Concept of practical anthropology has become very important for the present day planners and policy-makers of a welfare state. They tend to use anthropological knowledge to diagnose the problem and to suggest remedies for the social, economic and cultural problems. The administrators are getting themselves trained in the use of these practical methods to cope with the problems in general and in the field of tribal development in particular. India has the largest concentration of tribal people anywhere in the world except in Africa. 2001 Census keeps the tribal population somewhere around 84 millions. It has identified 698 Scheduled Tribes. 75 out of 698 tribes have been identified as primitive tribal groups.

Hence development policies and process emphasise the need of tribal development. Sachchidananda in one of his articles 'Tribal Development: Challenges in the Nineties' mentioned— "Promotion of the economic interest of the tribals has been one of the basic planks of planned development. It was presumed that the tribal population benefit by the general development programmes in the normal course. Besides this, provision was made through special central assistance to supplement these efforts. This was to speed up the process of development so that they could be brought on par with the rest of the people in the shortest possible time. But the hopes in this regard were belied as the benefits of the general programmes did not percolate to the tribals and the supplementary programmes in fact supplanted them." Singh (1977: 242) rightly said ... "Tribal development is at crossroads. Objectives have been planned and declared. Financial resources have been garnered and earmarked. The planning process, set in motion has proceeded far. If we fail to achieve the objectives, tribal expectations having been aroused, we shall succeed in generating frustrations."

Wherever new development experiments are conducted in tribal areas, the tribal people are losing land and are being pushed back from wherever new opportunities are arising. They are pushed back by new migrant. They lose their land as it is taken by new establishments. The task force on 'Development of Tribal Area' observed that one of the factors for the failure of the development programme is that the Scheduled Tribes and tribal areas have been looked upon as a 'Welfare' problem. Another reason for the failure of development schemes for tribals is that the tribal are not involved in the process. Something like a so-called development is imposed on them. As the problem of the tribals are unique, it is not only essential that they are actively involved in planning as well as implementation of the programme but also create confidence among them in the policies of the Government. Same mechanism must be evolved in order to bring them closer to the mainstream. The process of tribal development should be participatory.

Another important area of study is the tribal rights. During the last century, the erosion of tribal right in land and forest resources has led to movements of tribal resistance in different parts of India and world. The notion of human rights in one of greatest gifts of classical and contemporary human thought to culture and civilisation. These rights to life, right to adequate means of livelihood, freedom from exploitation. The question is to what extent the society has become able to extend these rights to the tribals who live mostly in isolation from mainstream. Despite a plethora of legislations, special safeguards and other development programmes tribal rights in land and forest resource, large scale displacement, increasing inequalities and poverty, degraded social status causing tribal tensions, identity crisis have emerged as baffling problems.

'Development' is not a linear process of creating economic abundance. It is a holistic process. Creative participation of all the members of the society is mandatory in order to bring alround amelioration for all sections of the society. Emphasis on 'Creative participation' of the members and institutions implies minimisation of the entropy or disorderliness in a social system and maximisation of creativity. The problem of distributive justice is also associated with tribal development.[1] Problems like poverty alleviation, land alienation, health and disease, displacement are the consequences of so-called development models for tribals. Most of the tribal development projects have cosmetic approaches rather than the real intentions of providing genuine remedies to the problems of tribes. A report of Planning Commission of India states that a large majority of India's population is denied access to natural resources. These natural resources rather are diverted towards the urban centre to support luxury consumption.[2] The biggest failure of models for development of tribals is that it has disintegrated the symbiotic relationship between man and nature through its overemphasis on econocentrism and consumerism. Hence, the desired goal i.e., enduring and sustainable development for the tribal is defeated.

S.N. Tripathy, a researcher in the field of tribal studies has tried to find out the characteristic features of tribal economy and attempted at evaluating the government policies in connection with tribal development. He has observed that the backwardness of tribal regions widespread poverty of the tribal and problems of integrating them with the mainstream of modern civilisation are great hindrances in the path of tribal development.[3] During the British reign because of the policy of 'leave them alone' tribals were left out of the process of development. Even though this policy of isolation was meant for retention of distinct tribal lifestyle and culture, impoverishment continued. After independence Indian planning aimed at the protective and development aspect of tribal development. The protective aspects aimed at preservation of their unique cultural traits and development aspects aim at bringing about various welfare measures for them. In various five-year Plans due attention was given for tribal development. The objectives of these plans are to (i) give priority to agriculture and rural development with a view to generate adequate productive employment and eradication of poverty, (ii) ensure food and nutritional security for all particularly the vulnerable section of society, (iii) accelerate growth rate of tribal economy with stable prices (iv) provide basic minimum service like safe drinking water, primary health care facilities etc. (v) ensure environmental sustainability of development process (vi) strengthen efforts to build-up self-reliance, etc. The Annual Report of Ministry of Welfare, Government of India (1995-96) exposes the disadvantages and handicaps of the tribes. The strategy for tribal development should be devised in such a way that it can solve perpetual deprivations of the tribes without jeopardising the eco-system.

Viewing the deteriorated socio-economic conditions of the tribal people as a result of their contact with non-tribal cultures one school of thought advocates measures to put a stop to culture contact and to preserve the tribes in their pristine purity. But the second school of thought advocated policy of complete assimilation of tribe with neighbouring non-tribal cultures.[4]

One of the most exciting areas of research today is tribal development. The study of tribes becomes still more interesting with the present day environmental crises in the background. Anthropological studies of aboriginal tribes include areas like tribal rituals, culture, customs, history etc. Tribalism has evoked a lot of debate between the 'isolationists' and 'assimilationist'. One group attempts to protect the tribal interests and rights through a policy of isolationism. It feels that tribes need to be protected from outside interference. The other group wants to protect the tribal culture through the process of assimilation with the mainstream.

The policy followed by the Government for the development of the Scheduled Tribes in independent India bears a strong imprint of the colonial legacy. The immediate task before the Government of free India is to remove the communication gap between tribals and regional community in the framework of national integration, to protect the resource base and to initiate measures to meet the immediate needs of the tribes.

Four phases of the development policies regarding scheduled tribes can be identified in the post-independent period—(a) Provision of immediate relief in terms of amenities and building up the productive infrastructure for future growth (b) emphasis on resources mobilisation and provision of social service infrastructure (c) reduction of disparity and growth with justice and (d) participatory development with focus on self-management harnessing of productive forces for meeting the basic needs as well as to contribute to self-reliant growth.[5]

The tribes live in intimate relationship with forests and their entire existence has been linked with forestry due to historical and environmental factors. The life of the tribes rotate around the forests. Hence forest policies of the state have a direct bearing on tribal development. The National Forest Policy 1952, 1980, Recommendation of Debar Commission, B.K. Ray Burman Committee, National Committee on Development of Backward Areas (1980) are of relevance in context of tribal development. The new forest policy categorically stated that rights and concessions enjoyed by them should be fully protected. Their domestic requirements of fuel wood, fodder, minor forest produces and construction of timber should be allowed to be fulfilled through forest products. But an analysis made by Nadeem Hasnain has exposed the inadequacies of the National Forest Policy of 1988 in catering to the needs of the tribes.[6]

Development involves change in land and water use patterns. Since independence the five-year plans resulted in displacement of many tribals. The more unfortunate event is multiple displacement. The tribal groups are displaced several times due to development projects. If displacement is inevitable, resettlement must include reconstruction of production system, raising standards of living and minimising, the conflict with host community. "The commitment therefore has to be not just for resettlement but for rehabilitation which should be an entitlement and not an act of reluctant generosity." (Smith Kothari, 1995)

Apprehensions are expressed that modern development programme and projects for the tribes may be injurious to their culture. The development perspective has to consider preservation and promotion of the essential components of the cultural heritage of the tribes. Preserving the cultural heritages on the one hand and working out a process of development on the other may be guided by certain principles. (i) The cultural principles without which the oustees will loose their identity and cultural heritage should be identified and their positive and negative impacts on the society as perceived by the people themselves should be critically examined and enumerated. (ii) The changes the oustees welcome after critical assessment of the situation due to resettlement should be examined. Researches should be conducted regarding the identification of the tools of developments and to ascertain how these could be used for the formulation of the programme of tribal development while presenting their cultural milieu.[7]

The strategy of sustainable development can be successful when the development programmes selected and implemented are consistent with the cultural heritage and cultural dynamics. The programme should be based on right type of tools of development, mostly eco-friendly tools identified for the tribal community.

Scholars observe that the programmes of tribal development are so far like 'straight jacket', generic and universal packages which are delivered at the threshold of tribal communities. The programmes like IRDP, ICDS and JRY must be added with an environmental dimension in order to increase their acceptability before the tribal communities. The environmental approach to tribal development emphasises the role of NGOs working in a tribal belt. They work as agents of change for them and act as bridges between the tribes and non-tribes. The success of resettlement and rehabilitation programmes depends largely on these voluntary groups which are the harbingers of tribal movement. Sometimes the tribal development programmes are pursued keeping political goals in view. This will not help much.

The present scenario demands a revitalising of existing development strategies and new-orientation to the perspective of tribal development.

Some suggestions are extended by the scholars working in this field for ensuring development for the tribes.

(a) The complex problems facing the scheduled tribes can be tackled more smoothly if we empathise with them and take a holistic view of life. The tribals can avail of the welfare and development programmes only if the anti-exploitative measures are effectively implemented.

(b) Instead of Tribal sub-plan, a separate plan for tribal areas in each state should be formulated. On the basis of the allocation of funds area specific and people specific tribal plans may be formulated.

(c) Another important job is to assess the state of culture and developmental needs of a group. A thorough survey is to be conducted in order to obtain quantitative data on educational and economic level. More education facilities should be provided which can open up scope to understand the world around.

(d) Awareness drive has to be accelerated in the tribal areas about tribal rights, participatory process.

(e) Forest Conservation Act should be relaxed as to ensure subsistence to tribals in general and 'Primitive' tribal groups in particular.

(f) Priorities are not be set by planners (outsider) but by the tribes as they are the clientele.

(g) Quite a number of the so-called primitive tribes particularly those who depend upon forest resources for their livelihood, have often had their way of life disrupted by a drastic change in the ecology. Sufficient awareness is to be created among the non-tribals about environmental conservation.

(h) This concern for environmental conservation in my view is the most important thing which can go a long way in protection of tribal culture and right. The rest of this article shall throw some light on the link between tribal development and environmental conservation.

The development paradigm which has direct bearing on tribal people's problematique has an anthropocentric tinge and a reductionist perspective of natural world. This has destroyed the ecological resource base and caused inroads in the customary tribal matrix of harmonious equilibrium between nature and man. The doctrine of individualism and statist ideology being crucial of capitalistic and neo-colonialistic development stigmatises and severely impairs the collective identities. The dominant notion of development is gradual triumph of rationality and value-neutrality. Hence, it has cultivated a contempt towards tradition, values. The development projects in a nutshell do not pay any need to the culture and ecological complexities prevailing in tribal areas. The tribal get marginalised in the process. Their customary, holistic and anticipatory conception of nature, generic and corporate character of land, community oriented values and collective identities, self-management systems, cognitive heritage, unique. Socio-cultural-linguistic framework and consensual decision-making process are derecognised and castigated resulting in a silent and subtle form of ethnocide.[8]

The tribal man puts least pressure on nature for its subsistence. Rather it is a glory for him when he identifies himself with nature. A man who stands in the globalised society is the consumer that strains the nature around him. It overuses nature. His attitude is the attitude of domination over nature. His approach is anthropocentric. With the advent of science, technology and globalised market economy he becomes highly competitive. He justifies his action by quoting Francis Bacon—that the conquest of nature is the goal of science, and 'Knowledge is power'. Civilised man interprets that political order is designed primary to protect right to life, liberty and estate. John Locke's writings endorsed individualism, the accumulation of wealth and subjugation of nature. To the so-called leaders of industrial revolution the environment was primarily a source of raw-material, along with rising standard of living came increasing burden on environment. Technological optimism gave rise to environment degradation and the innocent tribe is the first prey.

To other attitudes are 'unity, with nature' and 'stewardship of nature'. To save the tribe, we must save environment. The idea of unity with nature is somewhat opposed to domination over nature' when we will have an insight into the tribal life-style and culture, we may feel that tribal attitude is more or less close to 'unity with nature' attitude. The eastern and western religions, the romantic movement in literature and philosophy, evolutionary biology and ecology put emphasis on this attitude. This view stresses humanity's harmony with nature. For Blake, Wordsworth and Goethe nature is not an impersonal machine but an organic process with which humanity is united. They idealise 'the noble savage' and exalted the 'natural' and 'primitive'. If we view tribalism with this view we can find the natural and the primitive in the tribals. We can advocate for wildernсss preservation in the same tone with John Muir. Features like totemism of the tribal trend minus its superstitions dimension can help shaping this attitude that respects nature.

Some of such attitudes have become the attributes of youth counter culture of 1960s which has been disenchanted with technology. Our globalised outlook and preoccupations with efficiency and productivity has alienated the primitive society from nature. Our so-called developed projects pushed the tribal out of their natural habitat. Steps like deforestation have brought endless miseries for the man in the forest, since forest constitute the only source of livelihood for them.

Development is a myth without tribal uplift. A holistic perception will help us in this regard. The twentieth century science of ecology implies the ecosystem concept emphasising the interdependence of all form of life. Some authors have found more specific, ethical guidance in ecology. Rachel Carson's early writings combined scientific knowledge with a sense of spiritual unity with nature. In her book *Silent Spring* (1962) the call for an ecological conscience was tied up to scientific studies of the effects of pesticide on bird population.

An insight into tribal culture and way of life can vindicate the utility of ecological development in bringing about all round amelioration of the tribal communities. The development programmes all over the world and in the third world countries in particular were monopolised by economist and politicians. Now cultural anthropology dominates. The understanding of the culture and social relationship that prevail in the underprivileged weaker society like the tribal society is of utmost importance in designing development policies. It is clear that culture impinges on development in all its aspects. Since ultimate values belong to the realm of culture, questions like what is development? Change in what direction is to be regarded as development? or what are the objectives of development are people-related.

The real development for the tribes can be achieved with ensuring quality of life for them. Sometimes the tribal habits smack of ignorance or too much of innocence and barbarism. That drag them to a state of superstitions. An ecological model of development shall put emphasis on the training of the tribes for wise use of nature. Gifford Pinchot has thought of scientific management of natural resources or stewardship of nature. The biologist Rene Dubos extends a philosophy of respectful use of nature and creative intervention. The practices of '*Podu*' and 'Jhum' cultivation can be given a new touch to devoid them of the destructive impacts on nature. We know the tribals have more intimate relation with the nature and animal world. This relationship can be harassed to yield positive results that in the long run can help improving tribal life.

Another dimension of tribal development is participation of tribal people in the process of development. Environmental Conservation fosters the concept of sustainable development. Sustainable growth itself is complete only when people for whom the development is meant are taken into confidence and involved in the process of decision-making. Strategies and concerted action are best implemented if the affected people are allowed to see their own interests. The focus should be on strengthening local capacities for planning and implementing development activities. In case of tribal development, this experiment of course is difficult. To sensitise the innocent, native tribes in the process of development is extremely difficult as they most often view the non-tribal would with suspicion. The government official and NGOs implementing tribal development schemes must exercise caution and work with patience. In some tribal pockets these activities may be slightly easier, where some tribal organisation easier, where some tribal organisation, customs and rituals thrive on community participation. Some studies have been conducted on this front in the context of Chipko movement (in hills of UP), the Gonds of Adilabad (Andhra Pradesh), Jharkhand. Chipko movement particularly extends a platform where dwellers of hill forests were united under the banner of environmental conservation. Even the tribal awakening at the foothills of Kerandimal of South Orissa provides an interesting case-study for scholars in this field.

The environmentalists have distanced themselves from the political movement in Adilabad and Jharkhand. But they have identified overwhelmingly with the Chipko movement. Chipko movement particularly has become a symbol for the world—an environmental icon. Today few environmentalists remember that the villagers were just not against tree-felling. They also fought for greater control over forest resources. In 1973 the Chipko movement spelt out six-point charter in a meeting in Garud of Chamoli district. The points are:

(1) Abolition of the auction/contractor system and the formation of forest labour co-operatives.

(2) People's participation in forest management.

(3) Establishment of local, small-scale forest based industries to generate employment.

(4) A new forest settlement to determine the people's right to forest produce.

(5) Assistance to village efforts for afforestation.

(6) Ban on felling green trees in areas critical for the protection of water sources and prevention of landslides.

In November 1986, the Chipko charter was reiterated by Chandi Prasad Bhatt at a meeting of national and International environmental activists at Suraj Kund. The principles are—

1. To understand what the forest itself wants and to analyse the socio-economic conditions of the people in order to establish the type of forestry required.
2. To identify and reserve areas affected by landslides and erosion or crucial for the conservation of water-resources.
3. To establish the minimum needs of the people living next to forests and an administration such that these rights may be easily exercised.
4. Complete stoppage of the contractor system and instead the people to be organised to undertake conservation, development works.
5. Trees of use to villagers to be planted near the village so that people need not enter reserve forests.
6. Village industries based on minor forest produce to be set up to prevent migration.

Two leaders of Chipko movement Bahuguna and C.P. Bhatt hold two different stands of environmental activism. Bahuguna finds the outside elements like forest official and contractors responsible for the degradation of Himalayan eco-system whereas C.P. Bhatt does not deny the native's role in deforestation but holds that his has been a result of separating the local population from management of forest wealth. Further Bhatt argues, both forest officials and commercial forestry are merely agents of development process, biased in favour of the urban-industrial complex and against local needs. He is also sharply critical of the growing separation between the state and the people, as clearly manifest in the framing of development schemes by urban-centered technocrats that have little relevance to the realities of tribal rural India". (Unquiet Woods - R.C. Guha).

It is not suprising that tribals in many pockets of the country indulge themselves in some act like tree felling, Podu cultivation etc. which causes environment hazards. But it is more due to ignorance. And they do it for subsistence not for luxury.

The ethos, modern science and technology holds is different from the value systems of so-called primitive tribal societies. They view the eco-system in its totality, thereby ensuring a rational and sustainable use of resources. What helps more the tribal natives is appropriate rural technology than modern technology that alienates itself from the local needs. Appropriate technology is eco-friendly and it promotes self-reliance (both in terms of invoking mass participation and using local resources). It reduces inequality and builds itself upon the traditional skills of the native. Thus native skills are reinforced (not neglected.)

Tribal indigenous knowledge of nature has something which can strengthen the sense of environmentalism of the non-tribal world. There is a need to document these knowledge and make it available for future use. Environmental consciousness of the society can again be fed back to the tribal world for their sustainable development. Like the non-tribal world the tribes are confronted with the conflicting values (a) the material values like survival, health, and material welfare and employment (b) social values like distributive justice, participatory freedom, inter personal community, personal fulfillment and (c) environmental values like resource sustainability, eco-system integrity, environmental preservation etc. But the thing is that the innocent tribal man is not aware of these conflicting values. For him the material values like food, shelter and health are the immediate concerns. But environmental values add quality to the life they live.

The so-called development process has marginalised the tribal people. The tribal people are losing their land and being pushed back from where new opportunities and avenues are arising. In spite of so much of programmes of tribal development, the tribal people still remain at the bottom. Environmental ethics can go a long way in solving tribal problems. Development process inspired by environmental values can alone take cognisance of tribal values and interests. Since the causes of environmental exploitation and tribal exploitation are the same tribal development in the true sense of the term is possible through environmental conservation measures.

Any development policies and programmes for the tribal population all over the world must possess an environmental dimension if they really mean development for the tribes. With globalisation we are urbanised. But the pastoral motif must continue. The beauties of country landscape and the virtues of simple tribal life are to be celebrated in contrast to the growing urbanisation. A tribal man standing in the midst of uncorrupt nature is the greatest ecologist. A time has came to extend the benefits of globalised world to him and allow his spirit to guide our actions in pursuit of material happiness in the modern world. Environmentally sensitive development projects for the tribes are the only answer. The development programmes can be effective only when based on tribal values inculcated by the tribes in the wilderness which is a 'sacred space'. In this wilderness we rediscover our primeval intuitive capacities long suppressed by calculative rationality.

References

1. Anand Kashyap, Parameters of Tribal Development: Some Key Conceptual Issues, Tribal Situation in India, p. 29, Rawat Publication, New Delhi, 1998.

2. Pandey Deep Narayan (1995), The 'Problem' Seminar, No. 426, p. 13.

3. S.N. Tripathy, Dynamics of Tribal Migration, Sonali Publication, New Delhi, 2006, p. 127 (Chapt. V)

4. S.H.M. Rizvi and Shibani Roy, Scheduled Tribes, B.R. Publication (Delhi) 1998, pp. 18-19.

5. A. Kumar, Tribal Development in India, Sarup and Sons, New Delhi, 2002, p. 226.

6. Nadeem Hasnin, Tribal India, Palaka Prakashan, Delhi, 2005, p. 220.

7. W.S.K. Phillips; Perspective in the development of the tribals affected by the Sardar Sarovar project, Tribal situation in India, Rawat Publication, New Delhi, 1998, p. 246.

8. Jaganath Pathy, Impact of Development Project on Tribals, Tribal Situation in India, p. 282.

18

Adivasis from Public Policy Perspective in India

Satyam Sunkari

Abstract

Public policy is whatever governments choose to do or not to do (Thomas R, Dye, 1972:3). David Easton defines public policy as "the authoritative allocation of values for society" (1953:48). In contemporary democratic and political arrangements of India, policies obviously are being made by political system. In such political spheres, policies for the Adivasis are governed by the state's power elements rather than people's needs though the Constitution of India has clearly laid down the principles in its document for the just society with special arrangements. My paper argues based on empirical studies that policies have been formulated and operationalised since long back but outreach of its objectives have not been perpetrated in terms of financial allocation and distribution, reaching targeted people and finally changing their socio-economic conditions which were essentially suppose to be brought changes.

Adivasis – Socio-economic and Political Set Up

Inequality among Adivasis remains an important aspect of social sciences' research in Indian academics. Societal and political issues like denial of equality, accessing developmental and welfare measurements—education, employment, livelihoods, natural resources (land, water and forest resources) political participation, and political leadership are still rampant. Adivasis communities are characterised by geographical isolation, lack of socialisation at larger social context, and socio-economic backwardness in political context. They have their own and unique lifestyle, having an inherent set of cultural and religious beliefs. India has about 8.2 per cent of the Scheduled Tribes of the total population (Census, 2011). Most of Adivasis have close association with natural resources like land, water and forests for their livelihoods. Of the total, more than 93 per cent of Adivasis are settled in rural areas and only six per cent are living in urban areas. Demographically, Adivasis are largely distributed in the states of Madhya Pradesh, Maharashtra and Orissa and in some extent of populated states are Andhra Pradesh, Assam, Bihar, Gujarat, Kerala, Madhya Pradesh, Orissa, Rajasthan, Uttar Pradesh and West Bengal. Sparsely, with an about ten per cent people, belonging to this community distributed in states like Karnataka, Maharashtra and Tamil Nadu. While some of the states—Haryana, Punjab, Chandigarh and Union Territories like Delhi and Pondicherry have not accounted a single Scheduled Tribe (Census, 2011).

Geographically, central India consists of Madhya Pradesh, Maharashtra, Andhra Pradesh, Orissa, Chhattisgarh and Jharkhand is unique in terms of homelands for majority of Adivasis. There are about 100 districts of all central Indian states with around 55 million Adivasis which are accounted for more than 70 per cent of India's tribal population. The region is home to one of the largest concentrations of rural poverty in the world even though the area is with the rich vegetation and good rainfall. Notwithstanding favourable resource conditions, Adivasis regions have been neglected in terms of infrastructure, agriculture, education, health, housing, food security and almost all human development indicators (International Water Management Institute, 2007). A large number of Adivasis in rural areas are still dependent on forests for their livelihood. In the forest based Adivasis economy provisions for basic necessities like food, fuel, housing material, etc., is made from the forest produce (ftp://ftp.fao.org, *2011).*

Concerning Adivasis social and economic development, recent Human Development Report of UNDP stated that majority of Adivasis are multidimensionally poor (UNDP Human Development Report, 2010). Human Development Report further elaborated multidimensionally poor in terms of "poverty go far beyond inadequate income—to poor health and nutrition, low education and skills, inadequate livelihoods, bad housing conditions, social exclusion and lack of participation. A household is multidimensionally poor if it is deprived in at least two to six indicators involving cooking fuel, toilet, water, electricity, floor and assets, nutrition, child mortality, children enrolled in school and years of schooling" (UNDP Human Development Report, 2010).

As regards the availability of amenities such as percentage living in pucca houses, percentage having toilet facilities and percentage using PDS, access to protected water and electronic connections, STs are relatively disadvantaged when compared to other general populous (ftp://ftp.fao.org, 2011). Further, some of the Scheduled Tribes are categorised into 'Primitive Tribal Groups' (PTGs) by the Government of India in 1975 based on more backwardness among the tribal population groups. So far seventy-five tribal communities have been identified as 'primitive tribal groups' in different States of India. The special development packages for PTGs have been provided to the Indian States and Union Territories since fifth five year plan period (1974-1979) apart from Special Central Assistance (SCA) to Tribal Sub-Plan (TSP).

Keeping in view of disgusting situations of Adivasis, Government of India has initiated 'Affirmative Actions'. Generally, affirmative action is understood as a mechanism to do away with socio-economic, political and cultural inequalities as quoted by Leaber (1991). "The aim of affirmative action is to protect or promote the welfare of a person or a group who/which was previously marginalised, suppressed or discriminated" (Leaber, 1991 quoted by Uddhab Pd Pyakurel, 2011). As pointed out by Thorat, S.S. *et al* (2005) "Bhimrao Ambedkar suggested four or more remedies to be employed in combination to ensure equal opportunity as well as fair access and participation of the marginalised sections in the social, political and economic process in the society. These included equal rights, legal safeguards against violation of rights in terms of punitive measures, measures to ensure equal access and participation through reservation policy in civil, political and economic spheres, and a definite strategy by the state for the development and empowerment of marginalised to compensate for exclusion in the past" (Thorat et, 2005 quoted by Uddhab Pd Pyakurel, 2011). Such ideological, philosophical foundations and situational social and political complexities have led to formulate welfare and developmental policies for integrated development of Adivasis by the Government of India.

Objective

In this context, the paper intended to explore policy based outcomes, and issues and challenges in reaching objectives of welfare and developmental policies to targeted communities (Adivasis) based on empirical studies from the selected areas. The following sections elucidates policy's objectives, outreach and grass-root issues critically keeping in the minds of targeted goals.

Methodology and Area of the Research Study

According to Thomas R, Dye (1972), policies can be evaluated and studied in different forms like hearings and discussions on the programmes within administrative circles, programme measures by government agencies on policy output, comparison with professional standards by guessing ideal levels of benefits and services, evaluation of citizen complaints, before versus after comparisons, projected trend-line versus post programme comparisons, comparisons between jurisdictions with and without programmes and comparisons between control and experimental groups before and after program implementation (Thomas R, Dye, 1972). The present study followed the policy form of evaluation of citizen complaints in which issues and critics were brought into limelight. But, it sometimes fails to bring what actual changes are there in society rather convey what are the issues are in ongoing programmes. In present study, I have brought mostly representation of public views and their opinion.

As regards to the methodology of the paper, I have selectively done fieldwork which I have conducted in different areas and periods on different policies. For instance, policy based study on drinking water and sanitation, primary education, empirical study was done in eight villages – Shettihadpanur, SC Guda, Patel Guda, Pataguda, Kallur Guda, Rajula Guda, Bimangutta and Shivaguda — of Narnoor mandal, on Mahatma Gandhi National Rural Employment Guarantee Programme (MNREGP) and Agricultural Inputs, Subsidy and Farmers' Debt Relief Scheme, selected villages were Chenchupalugu, Rangapur, Bolketpali, Bonala and Billakal villages of Achampet mandal of Mahabubnagar district. Further recent forest and landbased policies like Forest Rights Act (FRA) and Forest Development Agency (FDA) were conducted in four Adivasis habitations—Lokonda, Kittalapadu, Mamidijola and Jagannathapuram (Heeramandalam mandal), of Srikakulam district. The main criteria for selection of different habitations for different policies are to gain more and in-depth understandings on respective policies in this study.

Since this paper confined to target oriented concerning individual's social welfare and changes of the community, policies like PESA and other rights based issues were not covered in this study. The period of this paper was June 2010 to December 2011. During this period, extensive field visits were done in exclusively in Adivasis habitations for the research and other developmental activities purposes and specific issues relating to welfare and developmental policies of Adivasis were captured and analysed in systematic way so as to meet the present research paper's objectives.

Limitations of the Study

Since the study focussed on major policy interventions of Adivasis, I have selected different study locations to assess welfare and development-oriented policy initiatives from the people's point of view and uniform field selections were not followed to avoid narrow or uniform views. That was the reason I have tried to understand and evaluate each programme from different locations to absorb diversified views on the presently implementing welfare and development policies. Further, qualitative arguments were only documented and presented and quantitative analysis was maximally minimised in this paper. It was also essential to note that the study had not focused on the Panchayats (Extension to the Scheduled Areas) Act, 1996 (PESA) since it was exclusively initiated to enable Adivasis to assume control of its own destiny to preserve and conserve the traditional rights over resources, due to its broad area and targets, i.e., community based intervention, so the paper confined only to the programmes which were targeted to enhance living standards of Adivasis.

Policy Based Explorations

According to David Easton, a political system works through three types of elements— demands, support and outputs. In such system, demands emerge from the open environment (society), supports comes from within the system through organised institutions or political originations and outputs of the political system framed by authority in terms of decisions and policies. Finally, in political system, political decisions or policies have materialises to adjust the system (society) (David Easton, 1953). Thus, David Easton defines public policy as "the authoritative allocation of values for society" (David Easton, 1953 quoted by Maheshwari, S.R. 2006:48). In terms of Thomas R, Dye, public policy is whatever governments choose to do or not do and further he asserted that "policy analysis encourages scholars and students to attack critical policy issues with the tools of systematic enquiry. He asserted that policy analysis is 'thinking man's response' to demands that social science become more 'relevant' to the problems of society" (Thomas R, Dye, 1972: 7). In contemporary democratic and political arrangements of India, policies obviously being made by political system in which different forces try to influence policies. Here in this paper, an attempt was made to understand the causes and consequences of public policy and drawn the research findings based on empirical explanations.

The significant policies of Adivasis are—Community Development Projects (including Adivasis and other rural communities and it was initiated during First Five Year Plan), Special Multi-purpose Tribal Blocks (SMPT–was given special focus in areas with prominent tribal population [Second Five Year plan (1956-1961), Tribal Development Blocks (SMPT was renamed as TDBs), Tribal Development Agencies (TDA's were established on similar pattern of Small Farmers Development Agency [SFDA] to address the problems of the tribal people), Tribal Sub-plan [TSP] (it was adopted during the Fifth Five Year Plan and it aimed at to provide mechanism for integrating the developmental activities of the government and the semi-government organisations by financing through the Integrated Tribal Development Projects [ITDP]) and Integrated Area Development Plan (this focused on was on the specific problems of the area and the tribal people in each ITDP) (Mehta P.C. 2000 and Planning Commission reports [First Five Year Plan to 11th Five Year Plan]). During the Fifth Five Year Plan, Special Central Assistance (SCA) to Tribal Sub Plan (TSP) and Grant-in-Aid under Article 275(1) of the Constitution were adopted to provide additional funds flow to TSPs for income generating activities, infrastructure development and administrative reinforcement (Planning Commission, 2012, http://tribal.nic.in, 2012).

Importance was given to community-based economic activities in the Sixth Five Year Plan (1980-85). A 'Modified Area Development Approach' (MADA) was adopted for Adivasis concentrated pockets of 10,000 populations with at least half of them being STs. Primitive Tribal Groups (PTGs) were also given emphasis for their overall development. Supportive financial institutions at national like Tribal Cooperative Marketing Development Federation (TRIFED) as an apex body for State Tribal Development Cooperative Corporations and

National Scheduled Castes and Scheduled Tribes Finance and Development Corporation (NSFDC) were set up to provide remunerative price for the Forest and Agriculture Produce, credit support for employment generation and skill development of Adivasis during the Seventh Five Year Plan (1985-90).

The Ninth Five Year Plan (1997-2002) approach envisaged advancement of STs through a process of (i) Social Empowerment, (ii) Economic Empowerment and (iii) Social Justice for socio-economic development. An exclusive Ministry of Tribal Affairs was set-up in 1999 for a focused approach to the development and welfare of the Adivasis in the country. Centrally sponsored schemes supported by the Ministry of Tribal Affairs and other Central Ministries and Departments were continued in the 10th Five Year Plan (2002-07). The 11th Five Year Plan was given much focus on educational, economic and social development. One of the highlights of the plan was the proposal made to set up a Commission on Land Reforms to specifically look into issues of land. Another important pro-active policy is the Scheduled Tribes and Other Traditional Forest Dwellers (Recognition of Forest Rights) Act, 2006 (henceforth FRA) which has been in operation since 2008 to recognise and regularise the land entitlement to Adivasis. Apart from specific targeted policies, major rural poverty alleviation programmes classified into three major categories—first one is wage employment programmes, second category is area development programmes and third one is social assistance programmes.[1] After Community Development Programme (CDP 1952), specifically focused programmes were initiated along with specific programmes of Adivasis. Accordingly, empirically observed outcomes and issues of policies concerning Adivasis are presented in the following sections.

Drinking Water, Sanitation, Health and Primary Education

As keeping in mind that safe drinking water is a birth right of every individual, water supply and sanitation were given due priority in the national agenda during the first five-year planning period (1951-1956), consequently increasing investments have been made in subsequent plans. Since the issue of sanitation and providing drinking water was aired as politically debatable and academically interpretative with social policy perspective, it is indispensable to note down on. Keeping in view of issues on drinking water and sanitation, programmes like Accelerated Rural Water Supply Programme (ARWSP 1972-73), National Drinking Water Mission (NDWM 1986) Central Rural Sanitation Programme (CRSP 1986), Rajiv Gandhi National Drinking Water Mission (NDWM was renamed as RGNDWM in 1991) and National Water Policy (2002) were initiated to improve the standards of sanitation and dignity to women including Adivasis' populated areas (Department of Drinking Water Supply—Ministry of Rural Development, 2002:1, Planning Commission, 2002).

It is observed in the policy notes that preference was given to the Scheduled Castes and Scheduled Tribes. I have analysed existing and available drinking water facilities keeping in the mind that whether water policies reached to the Adivasis habitations or not based on empirical investigation in these specific study locations. In this state of policy affairs, I would like to present a case study analysis from Adivasis habitations of the mandals of Utnoor, Narnoor which was done during the summer season of 2010. Water and Sanitation issues were analysed based on the empirical study done in Sirpur-U Mandal and health and education issues were drawn from Sedwai, Admiyan, Gadiguda and Rampur villages of Narnoor mandal.

Empirical Investigation on Water and Sanitation

The present analysis is completely based on empirical investigation. In fact, in the summer season (April) of 2011, I have extensively visited tribal habitations which were presented in the Table 18.1 of Sirpur-U mandal of Adilabad district to understand the severity of drinking water scarcity, irrigation and livelihoods of respective local people. Simultaneously, I have also documented all the social and economic issues including drinking water sources.

Drinking Water

Table 18.1: Revenue Village - Shettihadpanur

S.No.	*Name of Habitation*	*Water Resources*	*Total Households*
1.	Shettihadpanur	• Well – 1 and Hand pump - 1	36
2.	SC Guda	• Well – 1 and Hand pump - 1	43
3.	Patel Guda	Well – 1 and Hand pump – 1 (not working) Submersible pump set (only works in rainy season)	87
4.	Pataguda	• Well – 1 (Kunta)	23
5.	Kallur guda	• Well – 1 and Hand pump – 1 (not working)	36
6.	Rajula guda	• Well – 1 and Hand pump – 1 (not working)	187
7.	Bimangutta	• Well – 1 and Hand pump – 2	210
8.	Shivaguda	• Hand pump-1	N/A

Source: Information is based on Field Visits, as on April 2011.

The field studies has been carried out in Shettihadpanur revenue village of Sirpur –U Mandal. Shettihadpanur revenue village has seven other villages and views and data collected from these habitations to substantiate my argument in this regard. The data of Table reveals that all habitations have dependent still on traditional wells along with hand pumps. It can be also observed in the Table 18.1 that of the total eight hand pumps, four were physically verified and indicated that they were not in proper working conditions and reasons are lack of technical personnels. Habitation named Pataguda is still depending on traditional well (or pit) but not it exactly well, it's local name is a kunta (pit) and it has highly chances to contamination of drinking water. If we look at household wise drinking water resources, in Shettihadpanur habitation, there are 36 households and only one hand pump and one traditional well for their regular water consumption and in the same way, in SC Guda, 43 households are there but drinking water sources only one hand pump and well. And it can be seen similar situation in all habitations. The same conditions were evident in other field studied locations.

Responses on severity of water scarcity was drawn from 16 respondents from eight selected villages and data shows that 81.25 per cent respondents said "there is severe problems in accessing minimum water for drinking, 18.75 per cent replied "need urgently drinking water facilities". The responses clearly indicated to respond positively to address the problem from existing water policies. If we observe the present situational analysis on this part we would come to know what actually has been going. Being policy oriented analysis, it would be essential to present down to earth aspects of the connected issues. Hence, rapid action is required. It is obvious based on the field data many of the schools located in these mandals have poor hygienic conditions or do not have water, sanitation and hand washing facilities at all. Along with physical observation, I have also interviewed community members, local leaders and elected representatives including sarpanch. The elected sarpanch of Grama Panchayat is woman named Parwati Bai, elected from habitation of Bimangutta. She said that the officials of concerning departments like Panchayati Raj, Irrigation and Rural Water Supply cannot respond immediately to solve the problems. Further she said that "they, generally, says reasons for delay that shortage of adequate technical and other administrative staff, and very pressure from other villages".

Again she suggested some measures to deal with the problems, in her opinion, "there should be efficient mechanism to handle problems aroused in our habitations because we have just dependent on hand pumps, that too, our habitations are located in different distances. In addition, in our mandal, setting of all habitations is similar. So we need exclusively one technical persons to handle and solve repairable problems of our hand pumps because we completely dependent on them. But, in every summer season, we bring drinking water from natural stream. We also know that many human and animal improper disposals of wastes including feces contaminate water sources. Many ignorant people improperly dispose of urine, feces, and kitchen wastes close to our streams. Even then, we have to use such water because we do not have any alternative". Another woman, named, Rupa Bai, aged 26, shared her regular experiences with relation to water need in her home. She said that she does wake up early morning 4 am to bring water for drinking and cooking purposes far away from at least 200 meters and again at 6 am she goes for water for the purposes of bathing and washing. Thus, she has to do regularly and has to, again, involve in labour works after completion of all such domestic works. Though the policy of *drinking water supply under the programme of* National Rural Drinking Water (NRDWP) which was initiated in 2008 and it is targeted to ensure availability of potable drinking water on sustainable basis in SCs/STs dominant habitations has exclusive focus on tribal habitations and also allotted substantial financial resources. But it is lacking with committed bureaucratic personals at grass-root and intermediary level.

Sanitation

Case study analysis on sanitation was also done in Shettihadpanur revenue village of Narnur mandal. The seven villages of Shettihadpanur revenue village– Shettihadpanur, SC Guda, Patel Guda, Pataguda, Kallur guda, Rajula guda, Bimangutta and Shivaguda. The responses shows that 34.8 per cent of the respondents accepted that sanitation is essential for better health by facilitating proper bathrooms, latrines and proper water supply, 51.4 per cent have raised their voice on insufficient water and strongly responded as water is essential for maintenance of sanitation but unsurprisingly, 13.8 per cent gave answers that 'what is sanitation and is it essential to construct bathrooms and latrines, we have been following our own practices with our existing knowledge'. A case study presented here to make clear the existing experience.

A woman named, Rukma, aged 42, from the same habitation, expressed her problems with regard to Sanitation (bathroom and latrine) and water for household needs. In her words, "We have been thinking to construct a bathroom with the help of government's scheme, but there is no any option to get water connectivity. Even in midnights also we (women) go for nature calls to far away from my house. My daughter also got some health problem of urinal infection due to lack of space for proper bathroom and toilets. So if we get individual taps we will construct the bathroom and our long awaited problems may be solved". This is her opinion and expression which says severity of water and sanitation needs for household consumption. It is obvious that sanitation and drinking water scenarios are yet to be developed in more holistic approach so as to change present situations at habitations of Adivasis and need to improve habit of the importance of sanitation and hygienic conditions at their surroundings.

Health Issues

The Government of India has launched the National Rural Health Mission (NRHM) in 2005 to provide accessible, affordable and accountable primary healthcare services to poor households of rural India in 2005 (Gill Kaveri, 2009). One of the major important aspects of this policy is the creation of female health activists (ASHAs) and involvement of grass-root committees like village health and sanitation committees (VHSCs) and convergence with PRIs to reach promptly the desired objectives. But, it is obvious from the field areas that the functioning of ASHA was not evident, according to the women belongs to the villages of Shettihadpanur, SC Guda, Patel Guda, Pataguda, Kallur guda, Rajula guda, Bimangutta and Shivaguda and the responses emerged that 92 per cent viewed that "they are not actively working with proper facilities. They contact us only for the sake of name" and remaining were not replied positively regarding health and sanitation committees which are important to campaign health issues among the members and community. They have experienced distinctive health problems in last rainy season governed by their habitat, difficult terrains and ecological conditions. It is understood that the utilisation of government provided healthcare services at grass-root level is relatively low. Primary Health Centers have not yet opened.

Primary Education

Regarding primary school, observatory statement and people's opinion was documented. The primary school was located in the village of SC Guda. The school, at the time of my interview with community, was occupied with two bullocks. I immediately asked the people who were there at that point of time with me that why were there bullocks in the school? "School was not running and teacher comes periodically, not regular and local assistant prepare meals and arrange for the students" replied 92 per cent of the people (there were 25 people at that point of time) and remaining said that "teacher comes occasionally, especially at the time of supervision by higher officials". Here, I would like to raise a question that why rigorous and thorough supervision has been neglecting and why mass campaign to enhance the student's enrollment in schools was not taken comprehensively. The questions need to be seriously looked in. The proper function of primary schools at grassroots level is essential to promote equitable social development and bring justifiable society. Since the upgrading the class of the student from lower level to further levels is perfectly connected with the school which has proper function system. But, in the Residential School's system, the system of school education in some extent is acceptable in terms of regular functioning, teacher attendance, meals, supply of books and supervision. Issues like irregular teachers and students and proper maintenance of the school premises were observed in other non-residential (primary and upper primary levels) schools like Shettihadpanur, Patel Guda, Pataguda, Kallur guda, Rajula guda, Bimangutta and Shivaguda.

Rural Housing

Empirical study was conducted in the habitations of Hemayikuntan (Indravelli mandal), Rampur (Narnnor mandal), Bimangutta (Sirpur -U Mandal) to evaluate the housing scheme (Indiramma housing scheme) and PDS. It was seen that most of the houses were still in semi-completed condition and most of houses were stopped at basement stages. Surprisingly, opinions on housing scheme and its implementation process was collected from recent beneficiaries and leaders each four respondents from Hemayikuntan, Rampur and Bimangutta and thus total twelve responses collected on the process of housing scheme. Data shows that 84 per cent aware about middlemen involvement and reluctance of officials in proper implementation was viewed by remaining sixteen per cent. It was clearly mentioned by respondents that benefits of the houses were taken by the middlemen those who were engaged in sanctioning house and very less amount was given to house beneficiaries for their signatures on the loan amount papers. Unfortunately, the overall process of housing loans and its sanctioning process were still not understood by the community members. Their unawareness and lack of information properly, procedures were helped middlemen and officials to interrupt implementation process.

Public Distribution System (PDS)

Views on appropriateness of PDS and needs of Adivasis' families were collected from (Hemayikuntan (Indravelli mandal), Rampur (Narnnor mandal), Bimangutta [Sirpur-U Mandal]) the selected 30 women respondents while focusing on the issues like adequate food grains, irregular distribution and malpractice. It is clear from three habitations that all the households have white ration cards and availing the benefits of PDS. But contrast views were emerged on accuracy of implementation process. Majority respondents (73 per cent) were opined that regularly inadequate and irregular supply of food grain is caused to really hunger of their children because "we engage mostly in labour works and we cultivate cotton and cultivation of paddy crop is very less" replied by local women members. 27 per cent accepted with a view of malpractice in PDS in terms of diverting food grains and illegal selling of rice and sugar. It is understood that adequate food grains supply with proper distribution system is essential to achieve desired results of PDS.

Views on Social Assistance Programmes

Observations on the National Social Assistance Programmes (NSAP) were drawn from Hemayikunta of Indravelli mandal, Rampur of Narnnor mandal and Bimangutta of Sirpur-U Mandal.[2] It was clear by women of these habitations that the objectives of the programmes are good and really helps us if regularity maintains in implementation. A pregnant woman from Bimangutta said that "still corruption by local officials is continuing, whenever we go to them we have to pay and process is very long. In maternity cases the amount is very low but in case of Family Benefit Scheme, they asks large amount to sanction the loan". "Recognition and application of Old Age Pension is taking long time and we have to visit the offices of concerned very frequently" replied by woman from Rampoor. According to study's field data, 26.32 per cent (of the total 30 respondents) felt that awareness on the programmes is not communicated to us (women of these habitations) and nearly 53.33 per cent of the VSSs agreed with the view that delay in process and identification of the beneficiaries even though higher officials ordered to identify and distribute the benefits. Remaining was not responded to these responses.

Mahatma Gandhi National Rural Employment Guarantee Programme (MNREGP)

Opinions, activities and livelihood promotions through Mahatma Gandhi National Rural Employment Guarantee Programme (MNREGP) were collected from the selected members (one woman and one man from each habitation) of five Adivasis's habitations—Chenchupalugu, Rangapur, Bolketpali, Bonala and Billakal villages of Achampet mandal of Mahabubnagar district. Thus, total 10 members were interviewed in this specific issue.

Table: 18.2

S.No.	*Statement of Response*	*Percentage of Responses of members of VSS*
1.	Soil and Moisture Conservation	44 (88)
2.	Plantation	3 (6)
3.	Nurseries/regeneration	3 (6)
4.	No works	0 (00)
Total		**50 (100)**

Source: Field Study Interviews.

The types of activities taken up under MGNREGA were presented in Table 18.2 based on the field based interviews. The data shows that 88 per cent of respondents replied that the activities like soil moisture and other environmental related works taken up and 12 per cent viewed 'plantation and regeneration works' were taken for the livelihood creation in selected five habitations. Further, I have evaluated on whether MGNREGA was promoted or increased livelihoods or any change was taken place.

Table: 18.3

S.No.	*Statement of Response*	*Percentage of Responses of Members of VSS*
1.	Livelihoods improved	13 (26)
2.	Reduced Work days	0 (00)
3.	No Change	8 (16)
4.	Reduced Migration	29 (58)
Total		**50 (100)**

Source: Field Survey in five Habitations.

The perceptions on changes in livelihoods were presented in Table 18.3. Only 26.31 per cent of the respondents have agreed with a view that the works under MGNREGA have improved livelihoods and 16 per cent opined 'no change' was seen through this programme. Most importantly, responses emerged to substantiate with a view that the programme has reduced migrations in these specific habitations during the period of implementation.

Agricultural Inputs, Subsidy and Farmers' Debt Relief Scheme

The study on Agricultural Inputs, Subsidy and Farmers' Debt Relief Scheme was conducted in Chenchupalugu, Rangapur, Bolketpali, Bonala and Billakal villages of Achampet mandal of Mahabubnagar district from the state of Andhra Pradesh based on high dependency on agriculture comparatively with other Adivasis habitations. These villages are called as forest fringe villages according to Forest Department since they have located nearby forest. From each village, two farmers with the size of two-three acres were selected and thus, ten members interviewed on the issues like subsidised fertilisers, availability of crop loans, and distributional pattern of seeds and beneficial pattern under the scheme of Farmers' Debt Relief Scheme. In this connection, the question was asked "have you received subsidised fertilizers?" Responses emerged from farmers, as many as, 90 per cent of the respondents gave as 'not received' and remaining ten per cent did not answer either way. Respondents felt that subsidised products are available at mandal headquarter. Some farmers said "soon after we reach to the office of fertilizers stock, nothing left there. Then, we go for private shops to buy fertilizers".

An attempt was made to know the opinion on crop loans. In this regard, it was asked "have you received crop loan for your agricultural purpose?" The answers show that 80 per cent replied 'no' and only 20 per cent farmers have availed crop loans. The reason is that lack of proper titles of the lands. The study also tried to find out whether 'Farmers' Debt Relief Scheme' was reached or were they utilised this scheme? As regards to this question, 60 per cent of the respondents replied that "the scheme was helped to those who were taken loans and who were not paid for long, but, we used to pay loans regularly, some of us were not into that scheme". Very few (40 per cent) have said that "the scheme was really helped in overcoming our burden of debt in bank". The responses on availability of subsidised seeds show that only 30 per cent (not in regular seasons) have got such assistance and remaining (70 per cent) were not received from that initiation. Adivasis farmers detailed their experience that "the officials concerning subsidised seeds waste so much of time in the process of distribution of seeds" and very few people get subsidised seeds. Sometimes, it was understood that farmers had failed to get subsidised seeds due to heavy rush at the counters. It was also observed that, most of the times; stocks of seeds were inadequate and moreover unreasonably distributed, experiences of farmers disclosed.

Forest Rights Act (FRA)[3]

FRA has aimed at to ensure, recognise and regularise Adivasis rights over land by granting legal entitlement to those millions of families who are today seen as encroachers and thus empower and improve livelihood chances of a historically marginalised people. The Act has taken an initiative to correct the historical injustice of Adivasis. In this backdrop, the study examines the challenges and problems of tribal people with relation to implementation of FRA. The study tried to bring the issues in implementation of FRA based on empirical investigation. For this purpose, an empirical study was conducted in the study was done in four Adivasis habitations – Lokonda, Kittalapadu, Mamidijola and Jagannathapuram (Heeramandalam mandal), of Srikakulam district. From each habitation, four eligible claimants and sixteen respondents were interviewed and interaction was also held with Chief Functionary of an NGO-Samyogitha, which is located at in these field locations. In this study, policy process was evaluated based on the implementation process in connection with the eligible claimants (beneficiaries). Awareness, Formation of Forest Rights Committee (FRC), The Process of Verification, Composition of FRC, FRC—Preparation of record of claims and evidence, problems with Forest Department Officials and Sub-Divisional Level Committee (SDLC).

It is observed in the forest fringe villages of that most of the respondents (87.5 per cent) have had not aware about the Act. The objective of the Act is to ensure livelihood and food security of Adivasis, but only 12.5 per cent of community leaders were aware about the Act and its implementation process. The Forest Rights Committee (FRC) was, according to the local people, influenced by Forest Officers in formation process along with the Gram Sabha where it has to be formed by Grama Sabha.[4] Since Grama Sabha is organising at Grama Panchayat, actual voice of the Adivasis was not reflected because Grama Sabha consists of all sections of village. They demanded Grama Sabha should be organised in their habitations as a unit. This was also accepted by local NGO functionary (Samyogitha).

In the process of verification by Forest Rights Committee, it was found that in some hamlets the verification is not properly conducting and some areas, verification is taking place in nominal way; effective participation of people in verification is not there in the study areas. In practice, the members of FRC are not intimated about the verification. No intimation to members of FRC on meeting is found, sometimes informally giving, there is no evidences of issuing notices of the meetings. It has to intimate the members while specifying the purpose of the meeting, date, time and place. Other issues like proper preparation of consolidation of claims list, submitted claim forms, Village Map, Forest map to help in identifying the forestland or status of land applied by claimants was not observed and respondents were said that such information is only available at the Tahasil (Mandal Revenue) Office and the Divisional Forest Office (DFO). This observation indicates that thorough awareness programmes and interface with other developmental departments and programmes are essential to achieve desired outcomes of the Act.

Some important issues were also emerged from these habitations that there is lack of data on claims (facilitate and submitted), status reports at FRC, no registers and authentic seals at FRC level, conflict between the forest department and community on forest and agricultural land issues, delays in distribution of individual titles even after of sanctions, discouragement by forest officials (especially forest guards) in submitting claims, overriding bribes by forest department, unnecessary deadlines by government to submit the claims (even today, people are not even able to understand the process of implementation) and most importantly the land distributed under this Act were not recognised by the local banks to support or sanction crop loans.

Forest Based Afforestation Scheme under Forest Development Agency (FDA)

National Afforestation Scheme is aimed at to develop the forest resources with people's participation, with focus on improvement in livelihoods of the forest-fringe communities, especially the poor.[5] The scheme is targeted to support and accelerate the ongoing process of devolving forest protection, management and development functions to decentralised institutions of Joint Forest Management Committee (JFMC) at the village level, and Forest Development Agency (FDA) at the forest division level. The components under the scheme are Aided Natural Regeneration, Artificial Regeneration, Bamboo Plantation, Cane Plantation, Mixed Plantation of trees having MFP and medicinal value, Regeneration of perennial herbs and shrubs of medicine value, Pasture Development/ Silvipasture, Soil and Moisture Conservation and Entry Point Activity for village development and Fencing, Monitoring and Evaluation, Training, Awareness raising in JFMCs. The study was done in similar villages of study on FRA. In this study, open discussion was held with chairpersons, vice-chairpersons and presented members of committees from these villages. The issues like awareness, people's participation and pattern of funds flow were discussed.

It was observed that awareness levels on institutional framework and it's functioning like regular meetings, trainings, activities suppose to be taken, whether trainings were held or not, whether there is relation between Gram Panchayats and FDA, and election process. It is obvious from these habitations that training activities were communicated only to the members who have regular connections with concerned officials, which in turn objectives of trainings were, in large extent, not reached. Trainings on forest regeneration activities were not produced desired and expected outcomes. "Relation between the FDA's and Gram Panchayats was not clear. In addition, guidelines were not issued or some times, guidelines were kept with the officials only and this led to gap between the targets and outcomes of the FDA" responded by members of these habitations. Some of the respondents (members) replied that meetings supposed to be held at Grama Panchayat level but these were taken at Forest Offices only with few people and signatures were collected through respective chairpersons.

Moreover, "members of these committees felt that activities under FDAs are not at all a source of regular incomes, but, if the government officials, especially concerned Forest Department's officials seriously focus on the proper functioning of JFMCs, definitely there would be better chances to earn better incomes" expressed by one chairperson who was, in some extent, in support of community members. It was observed based on the financial transactions by the Bank Account that there was evidence of funds flow for livelihood activities. Contrarily, "funds were used only by few members and misuse of funds was proved in general body meetings, but, this issue was managed by some concerned officials. There was always skepticism about financial transactions. There should be appropriate and accurate mechanisms with trained personalities at grass-root level. Another important issue in this policy context which needs to be discussed was representation of women in the committees. Though there is policy level measures to encourage women participation and representation, inadequate representation of women in General Body (GB) meetings and Executive Committees (EC), was quite visible. The reasons were varied as women of Adivasis were greatly involved in diversified activities like farming, labour, domestic and other non-farms.

Conclusion

The present analysis brought some issues based on empirical investigation. Though policies targeted to ensure availability of potable drinking water on sustainable basis in SCs/STs dominant habitations, the study found issues like lack of committed bureaucratic personnels to achieve desired policy outcomes at grassroots level. It was clear on sanitation and drinking water issues that there should substantial policies to focus on community health, sanitation, drinking water, education and housing. In case of PDS, still malpractices like diverting food grains and to open markets were evident. Some of the issues like corruption of local officials and regularity in reaching assistance were missing though social assistance programmes were targeted to reach desires of the people. Some of the programmes like Mahatma Gandhi National Rural Employment Guarantee Programme (MGNREGP) and Agricultural Inputs, Subsidy and Farmers' Debt Relief Scheme were yet to reach targeted communities and delay in process and low outreach in implementation led to inequality of benefits sharing.

Concerning on FRA, data on claims, status reports, conflict between the forest department and community on forest and agricultural land issues, delays in distribution of land holding claims, discouragement by forest officials (especially forest guards), overriding (invisible) bribes and non-recognition of distributed land for crop loans under FRA were mostly seen in the study. And National Afforestation Scheme is being implemented to develop the forest resources with people's participation, with focus on improving livelihoods of poor, low level of awareness, irregular meetings, improper training calendar, and deficient institutional relations between FDA's (village level committee) and Grama Panchayats were for the most part playing in derailing expected outcomes. And important aspect like creation of sustainable livelihoods through natural resource regeneration process is in some extent neglected by the concerned officials. In views of Adivasis, inadequate and irregular incomes, scrawny standards of health and nutrition, low level of educational standards, and inadequate livelihoods, improper housing conditions, lack of participation were clearly visible. According to UNDP's Human Development Report (2010), Adivasis are still in multidimensional poverty based on the indicators stipulated by it.

Notes

1. Wage employment programmes - Integrated Rural Development Programme, Training of Rural Youth for Self Employment (TRYSEM), Development of Women and Children in Rural Areas (DWCRA), Supply of Improved Tool Kits to Rural Artisans (SITRA) and Ganga Kalyan Yojana (GKY) were introduced as sub-programmes of IRDP, Swarnajayanti Gram Swarojgar Yojana (SGSY), National Rural Livelihood Mission (NRLM), The Food for Work Programme (FWP 1977), National Rural Employment Programme (NREP, 1977), Rural Landless Employment Guarantee Programme (RLEGP), The Million Wells Scheme (MWS), Jawahar Rozgar Yojana (1989), The Employment Assurance Scheme (EAS), The Jawahar Gram Samridhi Yojana (JGSY, 1999), The Sampoorna Grameen Rojgar Yojana (SGRY, 2001), National Food for Work Programme (NFWP 2004), Mahatma Gandhi National Rural Employment Guarantee Act (MGNREGA 2005).

II. Area Development Programmes - Intensive Agricultural District Programme, Drought Prone Area Programmes (DPAP), Desert Development Programmes (DDP), Hilly Area Development Programmes and Tribal Area Development Programmes), Special-Group Development Programmes (Small Farmers Development Agency (SFDA) and Marginal Farmers and Agricultural Labourers Agency [MFALA]), Minimum Needs Programme (MNP), Watershed Development Programmes (1990), National Watershed Development Projects for Rain fed Areas (NWDPRA), Integrated Wastelands Development Programme (IWDP 1989-90), and

III. Social Assistance Programmes - Public Distribution System (PDS), Rural Housing (Indira Awaas Yojana), Pradhan Mantri Gramodaya Yojana (2000-01), Pradhan Mantri Gram Sadak Yojana (2000) and National Social Assistance Programmes (NSAPs) like National Old Age Pension Scheme (NOAPS), The National Family Benefit categories – first one is wage employment programmes, second category is area development programmes and third one is social assistance programmes. After Community Development Programme (CDP 1952), specifically focused programmes were initiated along with specific programmes of Adivasis. Accordingly, empirically observed outcomes and issues of policies concerning Adivasis are presented in the following sections.

Scheme (NFBS), The National Maternity Benefit Scheme (NMBS), Antyodaya Anna Yojana, The Annapurna, Farmers' Debt Relief Scheme,

Pradhan Manthri Adarsh Gram Yojana and National Rural Health Mission (NRHM 2005).

2. The National Social Assistance Programme (NSAP) "comprised National Old Age Pension Scheme (NOAPS), National Family Benefit Scheme (NFBS) and National Maternity Benefit Scheme (NMBS). These programmes were aimed to provide social assistance benefit to the aged, the BPL households in the case of death of the primary breadwinner and for maternity" (Ministry of Rural Development [http://rural.nic.in/sites/programmes-schemes-NSAP.asp], 2012).

3. The Scheduled Tribes and Other Traditional Forest Dwellers (Recognition of Forest Rights) Act, 2006 (in brief - FRA) has been in operation since 2008 to recognise and regularise ground reality by granting legal entitlement to those millions of families who are today seen as encroachers and thus empower and improve livelihood chances of a historically marginalised people. Further, it is claimed that the Act will reduce social conflict. The Act also ensured the tribal people to involve meaningfully in the protection and management of forests and wildlife. In addition to all, the Act has taken an initiative to correct the historical injustice of the tribal people.

4. Forest Rights Committee (FRC) is required to initiate the process of verification of claims on individual and community forest rights mentioned in Section 3 of the Scheduled Tribes and Other Traditional forest dwellers (Recognition of Forest Rights) Act, 2006. The FRC, constituted by Gram Sabha, is responsible for initiating the process of verification of claims on behalf of Gram Sabha after due intimation to the concerned claimants and the Forest Department.

5. Ministry of Environment and Forests was operating four centrally sponsored afforestation schemes during the 9th Plan, i.e., Integrated Afforestation and Eco-development Project Scheme (IAEPS), Area Oriented Fuelwood and Fodder Project Scheme (AOFFPS), Conservation of Non-Timber Forest Produce including Medicinal Plants (NTFPS), and Association of ST and Rural Poor in Regeneration of Degraded Forests (ASTRPS). The Mid-Term Evaluation of the projects under these Schemes recommended a decentralised approach and speedy fund transfer mechanism. Taking cue from these recommendations, a Pilot Scheme, Samnavit Gram Vanikaran Samridhi Yojana (SGVSY) was launched in 2000-01 utilising the delivery mechanism of Forest Development Agency (FDA) and Joint Forest Management Committee (JFMC). As per Tenth Five Year Plan document of Planning Commission (the Forests and Environment sector), the National Afforestation Programme (NAP) Scheme was initiated by scaling-up the SGVSY project experience and converging all afforestation schemes of the Ninth Five Year Plan period to avoid duplicity or redundancy, and at the same time keeping in focus the decentralisation agenda of the government. NAP is being operated as a 100 per cent Central Sector Scheme".

References

The Hindu Editorial, Where There is a Will, 5th December 2012, p.10. http://www.hindu.com/2010/10/20/stories/2010102050560300.htm, viewed on 5th December 2012.

Government of India, Ministry of Environment and Forests, National Forest Policy (1988), http://envfor.nic.in/divisions/fp/nfp.pdf, viewed on 5th December 2012. www.aptribes.gov.in/html/guidelines/13-1-FP-1%20to%206.pdf, 11/3/2011).

Department of Environment, Forests and Wildlife, Circular No. 13-1/90-FP of Government of India, Ministry of Environment and Forests, dated 18.9.90, http://tribal.gov.in/index1.asp?linkid=360&langid=1, viewed on 27/11/2012.

Sarkar, R.M. 2006, Land and Forest Rights of the Tribals Today, Eastern Book Corporation, Delhi, p. 275.

Vidyarthi L.P. and Binay Kumar Rai, (2000) Tribal Culture of India, New Delhi: Concept Publishing Company.

Office of the Registrar General and Census Commissioner (Ministry of Home Affairs, Government of India), Census Report 2011, http://censusindia.gov.in/2011-prov-results/prov_results_paper1_india.html, viewed on 11/6/2012.

Kunharnan, M. (1997) Tribal Development in India - Retrospect and Prospect, Budgeting for whom. Update quarterly, No. 1, April-June.

Kulkarni, P.D. (1964) "Tribal Welfare Some Problems of Implementation", Published in Souvenir: National Seminar on Welfare of Tribes and Denotified Communities with Reference to Fourth Plan, Bhopal, 1964, p. 122.

Prakash, C.M. (2000) *Tribal Development in 20th century,* Udaipur: Siva Publishers.

Planning Commission, Government of India, First Five Year Plan, (1951-1956) New Delhi, pp. 636-640.

Bhownick, P.K. (1981) "Reports of Scheduled Tribes an Appraisal" in Vidyarthi, L.P. (ed.) *Tribal Development and its Administration,* New Delhi: Concept Publishing Company.

Planning Commission, Government of India, Approach Paper for Ninth Five Year Plan (1997-2002).

Thakur, R.N. (1997) "Tribal Development Need for a Fresh Perspective", *Kurukshethra,* March-April.

Uddhab Pd Pyakurel, (2012) "A Debate on Dalits and Affirmative Action in Nepal", *Economic and Political Weekly*, October 1, 2012, Vol. XLVI (40), pp.71-78.

Deb, Kaushik, (2004), *Reforms in Drinking Water and Sanitation*, New Delhi: Teri Press.

Climate Institute, Water, http://www.climate.org/topics/water.html, viewed on: 14/10/2011.

Grail Research, (2009) Water - The India Story, http://grailresearch.com/pdf/ContenPodsPdf/Water-The_India_Story.pdf, viewed on: 10/10/2011.

Indira Khurana, Romit Sen, (2008) Drinking water quality in rural India: Issues and approaches, www.wateraid.org, viewed on: 1/10/2011.

Ministry of Planning and Programme Implementation (Department of Statistics), 1997 Compendium of Environment Statistics. New Delhi: Government of India.

Ministry of Rural Development (Department of Drinking Water Supply), 2010 Rajiv Gandhi National Drinking Water Mission, National Rural Drinking Water Programme - Movement towards Ensuring People's Drinking Water Security in Rural India: Framework for Implementation, New Delhi: Government of India. http://www.ddws.gov.in/sites/upload_files/ddws/files/pdf/RuralDrinkingWater_2ndApril_0.pdf, viewed on: 15/09/2011.

Muralidharan, D., R. Rangarajan and GBK. Shankar, 2011 "Scientific Correspondence- Vicious cycle of fluoride in semi-arid India – a health concern", *Current Science*, Vol. 100, No. 5, pp. 638-640.

Hedstrom Peter, Richard Swedberg and Lars Udehn (1998) "Poppers's Situational Analysis and Contemporary Sociology" Online Journal of *Philosophy of the Social Sciences*, 28 (3): 339-364.

Planning Commission (Government of India), (2002) India Assessment, *planningcommission.nic.in/reports/genrep/wtrsani.pdf,* viewed on: 4/9/2011.

Panda, R.C. (2003) "Drinking Water Mission - Drinking Water Quality and Related Health Impact in Rural India" presented in the 3rd World Water Forum, Kyoto. www.cerna.ensmp.fr/Documents/cerna_globalisation/maria-delhi.pdf, viewed on: 9/9/2011.

Easton, David (1953), *The Political Systems: An Enquiry into the State of Political Science*, Calcutta: Scientific Book Agency.

Dye, Thomas R. (1972), *Understating Public Policy*, Englewood Cliffs, N.J.: Prentice Hall, Inc.

Prakash C.M. (2000), *Tribal Development in 20th Century*, Udaipur: Siva Publishers.

Planning Commission (Government of India), First Five Year Plan, (1951 - 1956) New Delhi, pp. 636-640.

Planning Commission (Government of India, 1997-2002), Approach Paper for Ninth Five Year Plan.

International Water Management Institute (2007) Rethinking Tribal Development: water management strategies for revitalising tribal agriculture in central India, *Water Policy Briefing*, http://www.iwmi.cgiar.org/publications/Water_Policy_Briefs/PDF/WPB27.pdf, viewed on: 9/9/2011.

May 2007 – A policy briefing based on research presented in the book titled "Mainstreaming the Margins: water centric livelihood strategies for revitalising tribal agriculture in Central India, 2005 and a paper titled.

Phansalkar, S.J., Shilp Verma, (2004) Improved Water Control as Strategy for Enhancing Tribal Livelihoods, *Economic and Political Weekly*, 31st July, pp. 3469-3476.

Planning Commission (Government of India) (2010), Mid-term Appraisal Report of the 11th Five Year Plan, http://planningcommission.nic.in/plans/mta/11th_mta/MTA.html, viewed on: 5/9/2011.

Gill Kaveri, (2009), A Primary Evaluation of Service Delivery under the National Rural Health Mission (NRHM): Findings from a Study in Andhra Pradesh, Uttar Pradesh, Bihar and Rajasthan, Working Paper 1/2009 – PEO, New Delhi: Planning Commission of India, May, http://planningcommission.nic.in/reports/wrkpapers/wrkp_1_09.pdf, viewed on: 5/9/2011.

Gopalakrishnan Shankar, (2010) India: Social Development Report 2010 – The Land Question and the Marginalised (Council of Social Development), New Delhi: Oxford University Press.

Maa Adavi (Vanasamakhya [in Telugu]), Atavi Hakkula Chattam Sakramanga Amalu Ayenduku Injadri Krushi, Vol.19, March 2010, p. 4.

19

Awareness of Human Rights among Tribal and Non-tribal Higher Secondary Students – A Comparative Study

KV Sridevi, Asha BN

Introduction

Human rights—the rights related to life, liberty, equality and dignity of the individual–are the very essence of rule of law. They comprise civil, political, social, economic and cultural values. It is the peculiarity of the Indian situation that the issue of human rights has come into public focus rather in a negative way. Human rights have become a matter of public concern in the view of:

(i) increasing incidents of arbitrary arrest and custodial violence.

(ii) Other abuses of power resorted to by the law enforcement agencies especially in states affected by terrorism and insurgency.

The entry of Human Right issue into public consciousness coincides with the growth of terrorists and separatist movement in Punjab and Jammu and Kashmir in mid 80s and early 90s. The issue has also acquired importance due to the attempts of the US and western powers to link the international aid to the developing nations with their Human Rights Record on the ground that Human Rights situation in any country in today's world is not a domestic matter but the legitimate concerns of the international community. The proliferation of Human Rights NGO's and other groups especially in the areas affected by militancy in the recent years has also added to the popularity of the subject.

The important dimensions of human rights that are usually considered for evaluating the awareness of the same are–law and administration of justice, equality of opportunity, history, civil and social rights and responsibility, consumer rights, violence and identity.

Human Right Education in India

In 1964 the first commission of SC and ST, Government of India traced the progress of Education in tribal areas after independence and pointed out that the state of education among the tribes is not seen satisfactory in different parts of India.

Kothari commission (1966) in its report devoted high attention for tribal education. It made thirteen recommendations on various aspects such as wastage and stagnation, hostels, scholarship and shortage of teachers, etc.

The National Policy of Education, 1986 laid down for the first time in the history of Indian Education, a national curriculum framework as the basis for building national system of education. Most of the core elements identified in the policy are related to one or the other dimensions of Human Rights Education: The history of India's freedom movement, constitutional obligations, and other content to nurture national identity. It has been laid down that "these elements will cut cross subject areas and will be designed to promote values such as India's Cultural heritage, Egalitarianism, Democracy, Secularism, Equality of sexes, protection of Environment, Removal of social barriers, Observance of small family norms and inculcation of the scientific temper". NPE also recommended that Human Rights Education should be promoted by:

- Identifying and culminating from the school system all that is prejudicial to human rights.
- Bringing to Human Rights Education a greater conceptual clarity and sharper focus and
- Articulating general guidelines to translate conceptual clarity and focus on each stage and for various subjects.

Objectives of the Human Rights Education

- To advocate and promote availability of all physical and cultural inputs needed for healthy children such as minimum caloric requirements, education toys, play grounds to all children of preschool age free or subsidised.
- To promote the goal of equal educational opportunities.
- To promote the realisation of goal of free and compulsory education up to the age of 14 especially by allocating funds and facilities for disadvantaged and backward groups.
- Advocate the affirmative action for weak social sectors including relaxation in admissions.
- Promote education to all levels and humanistic education ideas and models conducive to the inculcation of the values of freedom, equality and dignity at all.
- To wipe out class discrimination and class disparities especially in rural areas.

Human Rights Education at Higher Secondary Stage

NCERT has recommended a core course in general studies compulsory to all students. This includes the study of Human Rights in historial perspective, universal declaration of Human Rights, Human Rights Conventions, the states of Human Rights, racism and apartheid and struggle against them; unequal international economic relations and world economic development, social structure and social justice, social and economic equality, economic exploitation and atrocities against the weak, child labour, status of women and dynamics of the quest for equality, national unity, communalism, revivalism, castism and various kind of the chauvinism and respect for diversity. The course also recommends placing local problems within the broad framework of those themes.

The Common Wealth Study on school-based understanding on Human Rights in four countries India, Botswana, Zimbabwe and Northern Ireland has been published as an educational research paper no. 22. The result of the study on young people are acquiring basic concepts in different dimensions of Human Rights indicated that in India students have got solid understanding about all these aspects. The study conducted by READ (Rehabilitation Education and Development) in 30 villages of Karnataka also inferred that the general public is not much aware of human rights; even it is true in the case of tribal people.

Tribes are indigenous people; it is indeed a shameful fact that their education and living are still in poor condition even after decades of the independence. One cannot expect them to be aware of Human Rights since they are educationally and culturally backward. In Kerala literacy rate of tribes is about 30 per cent. The tribes in the State constitute 1.03 per cent of the total population. Wayanad is one of the districts of Kerala which is considered as an educationally backward area. In this area the tribal students constitute a major part of the student community.

Article 46 of Constitution of India states that "the State shall provide special care, the educational and economic interest of the weaker section of the people".

One of the guiding principles of the Constitution of India is that 'rights and duties' of citizens co-exist. Higher secondary schools are the workshops where the molding of new generations—*who determines the future of the nation*—is being done. In order to meet the ends, it is very much essential to have awareness about human rights at the right time. It is in this context the investigators made an attempt to study the awareness of higher secondary students' awareness of Human Rights among tribal and non-tribal higher secondary students of educationally backward district Wayanad of Kerala. In this area a major part of the students constitute tribal students who live in deep forest and high hills without being greatly disturbed by the overwhelming changes in the outer world. Human right violations are usually occurring in every field of this district. The dropout rate is very high as both the parents and students are not interested in education.

It should be noted that the higher secondary students have to cast their votes just after one year of completion of their course. They are inevitable part of the largest democracy of world. So their awareness towards constitutional and society issues has got a great significance.

There were many studies carried out to find out the educational level or academic achievement (Aruna, 1981; Varma, 1985; Amarjan and Thimmappa, 1986; Srikanthan Nair, 1987); socio-psychological variables like intelligence, self concept, achievement motivation, emotional adjustment, perception of environment etc. (Anita, 2000; Dutt, 1983; Kaul, 1983; Chand, 1983; Fatmi, 1986; Sing,1981; Gator, 1992, Rosily, 1994). Very few studies were conducted on human rights awareness among tribal population especially people and higher secondary students of Wayanad District, Kerala. Hence this study was taken up.

Objectives of Study

1. To compare Human Rights awareness between tribal and non-tribal higher secondary students.
2. To study the difference in Human Rights awareness between tribal and non-tribal higher secondary students with respect to their
    - Gender
    - Stream selected

Hypotheses of the Study

1. There is no significant difference in the Human Rights awareness between tribal and non-tribal higher secondary students.
2. There is no significant difference in Human Rights awareness between tribal and non-tribal higher secondary students with respect to their
    - Gender
    - Stream selected

Methods

It is a descriptive study and survey method is used to collect data.

Sampling Procedure

The population for the present study was higher secondary school students at Wayanad District in Kerala. Cluster random sampling technique is followed for the selection of tribal students and non-tribal students.

Sample of the Study

The total sample was selected from both tribal and non-tribal higher secondary schools in Wayanad district, Kerala. A total number of 240 sample were chosen, 120 each from tribal and non-tribal. Due care was taken to have equal gender representations as well as from stream selection (Science and Humanities).

Instrumentation

Human Rights Awareness Test: A test developed by Chandran A G in 2002 is used in the present study. The test comprises 40 objective type questions. The split half reliability for the test is 0.93.

Personal information Blank: This has been developed to collect the data regarding background variables of the students.

Statistical Treatment of Data

After the collection of data, all the response sheets were scored with the help of scoring key. Each correct answer was assigned one mark and each wrong answer fetched zero. Thus, obtained raw data was set for analysis using statistical techniques such as "t" test. The results of the analysis are tabulated in the following table:

Table 19.1: Statistics for the Whole Data

Variable	*Groups*	*N*	*Mean*	*SD*	*'tvalue'*
Overall	Tribal	120	21.92	4.71	2.33*
	Non-tribal	120	23.33	4.67	
Gender	Girls	107	22.49	4.67	0.48*
	Boys	133	22.21	4.26	
Stream Chosen	Science	120	22.33	4.95	3.71*
	Humanities	120	25.17	6.72	

*Significant at 0.05 level.

From the Table 19.1 it is clear that the mean score on human rights awareness test of non-tribal students (23.33) is more than the tribal students (21.92). The t-value obtained (2.33) is found to significant at 0.05 level. In other words non-tribal students have better awareness on Human Rights when compared to tribal higher secondary students.

Table 19.2: 't' Values of Human Right Awareness between Various Groups

Variable	*Groups*	*N*	*Mean*	*SD*	*'t-value'*
Tribal (Gender)	Boys	85	22.0	4.90	0.43*
	Girls	35	21.6	4.56	
Stream opted	Science	60	21.35	5.00	0.08
	Humanities	60	21.42	4.83	
Non-tribal (Gender)	Boys	48	27.69	4.64	5.03*
	Girls	72	23.0	4.68	
Stream opted	Science	60	22.25	4.90	2.66*
	Humanities	60	24.41	3.96	

*Significant at 0.05 level.

The Table 19.2 even indicates that girls have better awareness towards human rights when compared to the boys in general (t-value 0.480 is found significant). The students with Humanities background were found to possess better awareness than their counterparts from science background (as the t-value 3.70 is significant).

From the Table 19.2 it is clear that the mean score on human rights awareness test of tribal boys (22) is more than the tribal girls (21.6). The t-value obtained (0.43) is found to significant at 0.05 level. In other words tribal boys have better awareness on Human Rights when compared to tribal girls.

The Table 19.2 even indicates that there is no significant difference in the awareness of higher secondary students on Human Rights between with respect to the stream selected.

Whereas it is also evident that non-tribal girls have better awareness on human rights than the non-tribal boys. In case of non-tribal students the students who opted for science were found to possess better awareness when compared to the students who selected Humanities stream (as the t-value (2.66) is significant).

Major Findings of the Study

The following are the major findings of the present study:

1. Human Rights Awareness among the non-tribal students is found to be more when compared with tribal students.
2. Human Rights Awareness among the girls is found to be more when compared to boys.
3. Human Rights Awareness among the humanities students is found to be more when compared to science students.
4. Tribal boys have better awareness on Human Rights when compared to tribal girls. Whereas non-tribal girls have better awareness on human rights than the non-tribal boys.
5. There is no significant difference in the awareness of higher secondary students on Human Rights between with respect to the stream.
6. Non-tribal students who opted for science were found to possess better awareness when compared to the students who selected Humanities stream.

Educational Implications of the Study

1. From the present study the investigators found that there is a significant difference between tribal and non-tribal students in human rights awareness. This clearly shows that the government initiatives (with all the noise it made) in this regard, has not been successful enough.
2. The government initiatives have to be evaluated thoroughly and should see that the awareness level of tribal students is raised on human rights.

3. The study indicates that students of humanities were found to have better awareness than science students as they study in their curriculum, schools have to conduct some seminars, guest talks regarding the human rights and it is not enough having it as a compulsory subject at high school and higher secondary level.

4. To identify the relevant and significant objectives of Human Rights Education that is to be accomplished at various levels of school education as well as higher education level is the need of the hour. This is because the criteria for selecting contents of Human Rights Education are determined by these objectives. To transact the syllabus of Human Rights Education, the following steps have to be taken by the government:

- Teachers have to be specially trained to this context as a separate subject for all higher secondary students.
- Special classes are to be provided for its transaction using innovative methods of teaching at school level.
- Special education to women for awareness of elimination of discrimination against women to be provided.
- Non-formal education can be media to promote Human Rights Education to contribute to their promotion of awareness to right to education and health and an adequate livelihood including food, water and housing to just a favourable condition of work security and freedom from violence.

References

Bini Borgahan (1999). Human Rights: Social and Political Challenge, New Delhi: Kanishka Publishers.

Anita (2000). Study of achievement motivation among tribal and non-tribal secondary school pupils in Wayanad District. Unpublished M.Ed. Dissertation, University of Calicut.

Sam A Chelladurai (1999). Human rights education in India, The READ experience, HURIGHT-OSAIKA.

Rosily, NP (1994). A Study of attainment of biological concept in relation to attitude towards science and achievement motivation of tribal and non-tribal pupils of Standard VIII. Unpublished M.Ed. Dissertation, University of Calicut.

Singh (1981). Achievement of tribal students in relation to their intelligence, motivation and personality, Doctoral Dissertation, University of Bihar.

Fatmi, J M D (1986). A study of achievement related motivation among tribal and non-tribal high school students. Unpublished Doctoral Dissertation, Magadha University.

20

Working of Civil Society Organisations for Development of Tribals: A Study

BK Mahakul

In recent times, in most developed and developing countries, a Third Sector has emerged as a viable institutional framework to serve as a catalyst for development. This is in distinction to the role played by the governmental organisation as the first sector more accustomed to maintain law and order and the private commercial enterprises as the Second Sector known to exist more for profit making than for affecting the process of development. Despite the innumerable difficulties and obstacles which this intermediate zone non-governmental, non-profit organisations often classed under the collective form third sector have a surmount, it has become a major approach to encourage participation, social change and democratisation to the theory of development and to the dispersal of power is the civil society. In its various forms, the third sector is supposed to ease the burden on government expenditure by mobilising resources through other organisations in society, bringing about greater cost efficiency, higher flexibility and improved relations with beneficiaries. Due to changing role of the modern state there is no doubt that governance for the 21st century must overcome bureaucratic unresponsiveness. A modern state in our present understanding is supposed not only to protect the individual's freedom and liberty but also to guarantee social security, increasing affluence and social progress. Thus, the range of public duties has grown up over the years, which is now exceedingly wide. In order to fulfill these duties, the modern state has been encouraging the new sector, i.e., Civil Society Sector.

The tribal people have remained exploited and socio-economically backward through generation. Hence, the urgent need is to lift them up, and to bring them to the mainstream of national life through the performance of required and effective roles by both the Governmental and Civil Society Organisations.

In this benign venture, however, the role of the Government alone seems to be inadequate because participatory democracy requires active participation of citizens and Civil Society Organisations in bringing about holistic development of entire population including the socio-economically backward Scheduled Tribes as the special target groups. The scheduled tribes requires assistance of a very specialised nature, which can help them to terms with their environment and overcome their social, physical, situational handicaps and enable them to fulfill their promise and reach their full potential. The government is aware that in the area of tribal development, the support and cooperation of Civil Society Organisations is very much necessary. Since tribal development is one of the important aspects of a State's overall development the study of the phenomenon of Civil Society Organisations in tribal development have become imperative.

The present research work is intended to study the Working of Civil Society Organisations for Development of Tribals with reference to Orissa. In this research work an endeavour has been undertaken to identify the Civil Society Organisations engaged in tribal development, to enquire into the development programmes undertaken for the tribals and their perception towards the working of Civil Society Organisations.

The present research work attempts to ascertain the development programmes undertaken by Civil Society Organisations and attitudinal pattern of tribals towards tribal development. Therefore, an empirical method of study has been adopted for enquiry and analysis of the impact of development programmes and attitudinal pattern of the tribals. Both the Primary and Secondary sources were used to collect data and information relating to study. For the purpose of primary data, all these 5600 tribal beneficiaries have been interviewed on the basis of a structured interview schedule and their responses have been examined for delineating the socio-economic profile and the pattern of their attitude towards the development programmes undertaken by the Civil Society Organisations. As regards the secondary data, specifically for preparing the concepts like, tribes, development, civil society etc., a number of authoritative works as well as reports and documents have been consulted. On the whole, the method of study adopted for the purpose of this work is empirical as the study is based on facts and data collected from the respondents of the sample through personal interview.

The paper has been divided into two parts. Part-I discusses the concepts like tribes, development, Civil Society etc. from theoretical perspective. Part-II analyses the findings like socio-economic background of the beneficiaries, impact of the development programmes and perception of the tribal beneficiaries and suggestions.

PART–I

Concepts

Tribes: The term 'tribe' has no statutory definition and as such it has a wide variety of meanings. The word tribe is derived from the Latin word '*Tribus*'.

It originally meant a community of persons claiming descent from a common ancestor, definite territory and common cultural pattern. Gradually it stood for aboriginals, native and rascist stereotypes and related to the people of Africa and Asia, as also of North America and even of Australia.[1] In Indian context they are categorised as the Scheduled Tribes. The Imperial Gazetteer of India says, "a tribe is a collection of families bearing a common name, speaking a common dialect, occupying or professing to occupy a common territory and is not usually endogamous, though originally it might have been so".[2]

The constitution of India does not define the word tribe but declares that the Scheduled Tribes are "the tribes or tribal community", which the President may specify by notification. The Constitution of India empowers the President to declare any community as tribe. President of India, may with respect to any State or Union Territory, after consulting the Governor thereof, by public notification, specify the tribes or tribal communities which shall for the purpose of the constitution be deemed to be Scheduled Tribes in relation to the State or Union Territory, as per Article 342(1) of the constitution. After the lists have been promulgated any inclusion therein or exclusion there from may be made only by Parliament as per Article 342 (2). The tribals, in the context of modern Indian society, signify a group of primitive people living in the hills and forests having their own language and culture.[3]

Development: Development refers to growth, evolution advance, blossoming, elaboration, furtherance, progress, progression, unfolding, expansion, enlargement, extension, spreads, increased, improvement, maturity, flourishing, prosperity, promotion, refinement.[4] Dictionary definitions of the verb 'to develop' suggest that it means to change gradually, progressing through a number of states towards some sort of expansion, improvement, or completeness or a state in which the subject's true identity is revealed.[5] In the economic literature of the early, Post Second World War period, development was defined as "a rapid and sustained rise in real output per head and attendant shifts in the technological, economic, and demographic characteristics of a society.[6] Development, still in the sense of economic growth, came to seen as part of a much wider process of social change described as modernisation. According to Lerner "Modernisations, the process of social change in which development is the economic component".[7] The emphasis in development as modernisation is thus on how to inculcate wealth oriented behaviour and values in individuals. By the end of the 1960s, development came to be seen not simply as raising per capita income but more important, of reducing the poverty level among the masses or, as it was more picturesquely put satisfying their 'basic' needs.

Development has three important implications—first, it emphasises that development is essentially a human issue, a concern with the capacity of individuals to realise their inherent potential and effectively to cope with the changing circumstances of their live or as Cairnecross puts it, 'the key to development lies in men's mind, in the institution in which their thinking finds expression and in the play of opportunity on ideas and institutions.[8] Second, development involves the total and full mobilisation of a society. The task of changing the "institutions in which the thinking of individuals finds expression" cannot be undertaken in an ad hoc, piecemeal fashion. It has to be comprehensive and to involve total political commitment. Hence, Myrdal's definition of development as "the movement of the whole social system upwards".[9] Third, development represents a redefinition of a country's internation relation. It involves a shift from an outward oriented, dependent status to a self-centered and self-reliant position with regard not only to the processes of decision-making, but more importantly the pattern and style of production and consumption. Development is a widely participatory process of directed social change in a society, intended to bring about both social and material advancement (including greater equality, freedom and other valued qualities) for the majority of the people through their gaining control over their environment.

The above analysis on development indicate the following:

- Development as a concept is much broader than economic growth or economic development.
- It is just not to increase national income; it is also for improving the quality of life for each and every member of the society.
- It is also not just social growth or change but also is a process of bringing about, social, economic and political transformation in the life of the marginalised sections of the population.

Civil Society: The term Civil Society has been defined in a variety of ways. Originally, it meant a political community, a society governed by law, under the authority of a state. More commonly, it is distinguished from the state and the term is used to describe institutions that are private in that they are independent from government and organised by individuals in pursuit of their own ends. Civil Society therefore refers to a realm of autonomous groups and associations, business, interest groups, clubs, families and so on. Hegal defines, Civil Society is a collective body, whose members are conceived as "Self-subsistent persons".[10] In the Hegelian understanding of Civil Society, it is only an intermediary, which will ultimately lead to the formation of democratic state.

According to Michael Walzer Civil Society is the "Setting of Settings"; where people associate with each other on various grounds, but notably for the sake of realising their natures as social beings. He argues that, the picture here is a man freely associating and communicating with one another, forming and reforming groups of all sorts, not for the sake of any particular formation-family, tribe, nation, religion, commune, brotherhood or sisterhood, interest group or ideological movement— but for the sake of sociability itself for 'we are by nature social, before we are political or economic beings'.[11]

Civil Society is a collection of individual and collective for the 'Common Public Good'. In this definition, Civil Society is as linked to a public arena where the promotion of broadly defined public good is the purpose of Civil Society action. This 'Public Good' could include promotion of education, health care or sanitation; it could include prevention or pollution and deforestation, it could include protection of human rights or maintenance of peace and harmony; it could also include expression of dissent.[12]

According to conventional notions in the social science 'Civil Society' refers to that space which (1) exists between the family, on the one hand and the state on the other, (2) makes interconnections between individuals or families possible, and (3) is independent of the state. The concept of Civil Society has been viewed by different scholars in different perspective while some scholars favour a strong, vibrant and assertive Civil Society.[13] Some others favour a strong state to create Civil Society and assume that the state and civil society are intertwined concepts.[14] There are others relate civil society with the process of democratisation and for understanding the process of political change.[15] Others relate Civil Society with associations.[16]

Development Planning is essentially a mechanism to achieve improvement in the quality of life of the people. It is an umbrella concept. It has different connotation such as social development, economic development, political development and so on. Better health, education, income, information etc., can improve these aspects and thereby lead to development. These pre-conditions, aspiration and motivation of the people. Therefore, Civil Society Organisations are emerging gradually and participating actively in the process of social and economic transformation of tribals.

PART-II

Findings: The socio-economic development seems to be significantly influenced by the socio-economic characteristic of the individual, so an endeavour has been undertaken to enquire in to the socio-economic background of the tribal beneficiaries. This has been enquired into in respect of the variables of age, gender, education, income and occupation. Their attitudinal profile have been studied and analysed.

The term beneficiary applies to those respondents who are directly benefited from the services of the organisations under study.

Age: In terms of the variable of Age, the beneficiaries have been grouped under three Age Groups such as Young (who are 35 years or below), those who are between 36 years to 55 years have been grouped under Middle Age Group and those who are above 56 years of age have been grouped under the Old Age Group.

On analysing it is found that 74.85 per cent (4191) of the beneficiaries belong to Young Age Group, 9.23 per cent (517) belong to Middle Age Group, and 15.92 per cent (892) belong to Old Age Group.

Gender Groupings: In terms of the variable of gender, the beneficiaries have been grouped as Males and Females. It is found that female beneficiaries constitute 52.55 per cent (2942) and male beneficiaries constitute 47.45 per cent (2657). The reason for outnumber of female beneficiaries, the government has been giving much more emphasis on Women development/empowerment.

Education: It is found that 30.57 per cent (1711) have studied upto middle level, 22.29 per cent (1249) upto Primary level, 18.15 per cent (1017) Secondary/ Higher Secondary level, 18.47 (1024) are illiterate. 4.14 per cent (231) have studied upto graduation level, 1.60 per cent (90) upto Post-graduation level and 4.78 per cent (681) could not say about their education.

The sample is found to have been dominated by the beneficiaries attained middle educational level.

Income Groupings: On the basis of average annual income approximately, from all sources, beneficiaries have been grouped under four income range. The groups are, below Rs 3000.00 between Rs 3001.00 to Rs 5000.00, Rs 5001.00 to Rs 8000.00 and Rs 8001.00 to Rs 10,000.00

It is found that 39.50 per cent (2212) of the beneficiaries income range of Rs 5001 to Rs 8000, 22.92 per cent (1283) beneficiaries income range of Rs 3001 to Rs 5000, 22.29 per cent (1248) beneficiaries income range of Rs 8001 to Rs 10,000 and 15.30 per cent (857) income upto Rs 3000.00. It is found that maximum no. of beneficiaries belong to the income range between Rs 5001 to Rs 8000.

Occupation: In terms of the variable of occupation of the beneficiaries, from which they earn their livelihood, have been distributed occupations-wise.

It is revealed that as many as 32.48 per cent (1819) beneficiaries are unemployed and has no occupation of their own. It is followed by 28.02 per cent (15.70) reported cultivation as their principal occupation. There are 25.80 per cent (1444) beneficiaries engaged in labour followed by 13.70 per cent (767) beneficiaries reported have petty shop as their principal occupation.

The sample of beneficiaries is dominated by the dependent having no principal occupations. Hence, they intended to get benefits from the developmental schemes through voluntary organisations.

The socio-economic background of the beneficiaries has, thus been enquired in respect of the variables of age, gender, education, income and occupation. It is found that the sample, in terms of the variables of age has been dominated by the Young Age Group, in terms of the variables of education, Middle level Educated Group, female beneficiaries in terms of the variable of gender and no occupation/unemployed in terms of occupation.

Impact of the Schemes and Perception of Beneficiaries

The immense impact of the services rendered by the concerned Civil Society Organisations to the respective beneficiaries can be observed by enquiring their satisfaction. Impact can not be measured only in economic indicators, as welfare service has multi-dimensional aspects which cover material, non-material, economic and non-economic benefits. All these are inter-related and an appraisal of social welfare services involves in their collective use and application. The ultimate aim of effect of these services is satisfaction of beneficiaries. Thus, to know the impact of the services the researcher has obtained information from the beneficiaries implying economic and non-economic changes in their lives.

Classification of Beneficiaries According to Benefits

The researcher has classified the beneficiaries according to the benefits received by them.

Variable	*Groups*	*N*	*Mean*	*SD*	*'t-value'*
Tribal (Gender)	Boys	85	22.0	4.90	0.43*
	Girls	35	21.6	4.56	
Stream opted	Science	60	21.35	5.00	0.08
	Humanities	60	21.42	4.83	
Non-tribal (Gender)	Boys	48	27.69	4.64	5.03*
	Girls	72	23.0	4.68	
Stream opted	Science	60	22.25	4.90	2.66*
	Humanities	60	24.41	3.96	

- There are 28.36 per cent (1588) beneficiaries received benefits under Vocational Education and training scheme which includes computer, cutting and tailoring, embroidery, typing, stenography, craft, vegetable processing etc.
- It is followed by 20.71 per cent (1160) beneficiaries who got financial and material Assistance. Financial assistances are covered under schemes such as scholarship, pension and assistance to poor, relief, prizes and petty shops. The material assistance includes supply of uniforms, blankets, sewing machines, appliances to handicapped.
- 14.03 per cent (786) beneficiaries received health and medical benefits. They are served mainly through nature-cure, physiotherapy, eye-operation camps, ambulance services, free medical check-up and referred services.
- There are 11.45 per cent (641) beneficiaries who received services pertaining to counselling, advice and general awareness. The general awareness covered social problems, health and nutrition, communal harmony, environmental awareness human rights, right to information and need felt political guidance. Under the counselling disputes are settled and legal advice given.
- 8.59 per cent (481) beneficiaries are assisted under the scheme of education. In these cases the civil society organisations managed NCLP School, nursery, Primary education for tribal children.
- 4.14 per cent (232) beneficiaries have got the benefit of guidance in farming know-how.

- 2.86 per cent (160) beneficiaries got employment through civil society organisation in the educational institutions, small business and sale of daily products.

This analysis shows that several services, benefits assistance are arranged by the civil society organisations.

The researcher have enquired into the benefits received by the beneficiaries according to their preference with developmental schemes, in terms of variables of age, gender, education, occupation and income.

On analysing the responses of the beneficiaries in terms of age-groups, it is found that 24.69 per cent (1035) of the Young age-group has been benefited from Vocational Education and Training. 23.82 per cent (998) have been benefited from Financial and Material Assistance. Whereas 16.18 per cent (678), 10.63 per cent (445), 9.37 per cent (393), 8.49 per cent (356), 4.27 per cent (171) and 2.55 per cent (107) of the Young-age group have been benefited from health and medical assistance, education, counseling, advice and general awareness, farming guidance and employment respectively.

The Middle Age Group, it is found that 44.87 per cent (232) of the beneficiaries benefited from Vocational Education and Training followed by 13.73 per cent (71), 10.25 per cent (53), 6.96 per cent (36), 6.96 per cent (36) and 3.48 per cent (18) of the beneficiaries have been benefited from financial and material assistance, counselling, advice and general awareness, employment, health and medical services, education and farming guidance respectively.

From Old Age Group, it is found that 35.98 per cent (321) of the beneficiaries have been benefited from Vocational Education and Training, 26 per cent, 10.26 per cent, 8.07 per cent, 5.94 per cent, 3.92 per cent and 1.90 per cent of the beneficiaries have been benefited from counselling, advice, and general awareness, financial and material assistance, health and medical services, education, farming guidance and employment respectively.

Thus, it is found that in terms of age groups the beneficiaries of all age-groups have been benefited mostly from Vocational Education and Training. It would help them to be economically independent.

On analysing the responses of the beneficiaries in terms of the variables of gender, it is found that 36.89 per cent (980) male beneficiaries have been benefited from Vocational Education and Training, followed by 19.49 per cent, 11.37 per cent, 10.9 per cent, 7.38 per cent, 7.38 per cent, 3.98 per cent and three per cent of the financial and material assistance, counselling, advice and general assistance, health and medical services, education, farming guidance and employment respectively.

On analysing the responses of the female beneficiaries, it is found that 21.81 per cent (642) female beneficiaries have been benefited from Financial and Material Assistance followed by 20.65 per cent, 9.70 per cent, 4.29 per cent and 2.34 per cent of the female beneficiaries have been benefited from vocational education and training, health and medical services, counselling, advice and general assistance, education, farming guidance and employment respectively.

Thus, it is found that the male beneficiaries mostly preferred and benefited from vocational education and training programme, followed by financial and material assistance. While the female beneficiaries mostly preferred and benefited from financial and material assistance followed by vocational education and training.

On analysing the responses of the beneficiaries in terms of education, it is found that 25.91 per cent (268) illiterate beneficiaries have been benefited from Vocational Education and Training, followed by 17.21 per cent of them benefited from Financial and Material Assistance and other 17.21 per cent of have been benefited from Health and Medical Services. While 13.82 per cent, 13.82 per cent, 6.87 per cent and 5.12 per cent illiterate beneficiaries have been benefited from counseling, advice and general awareness, education and farming guidance respectively.

On analysing the responses of the beneficiaries having primary education, it is found that 25.71 per cent of them have been benefited from Vocational Education and Training, followed by 20 per cent benefited from Financial and Material Assistance. While 12.85 per cent, 10 per cent and 5.71 per cent have been benefited from health and medical services, counseling, advice and general awareness, education and farming guidance respectively.

On analysing the responses of the beneficiaries having Middle Education, it is found that 36.46 per cent have been benefited from Vocational Education and Training, followed by 27.08 per cent, 8.30 per cent, 8.30 per cent, 6.25 per cent and 4.16 per cent beneficiaries have been benefited from residential facilities, education, health and medical services, counselling, advice and general awareness and farming guidance respectively.

On analysing the responses of the beneficiaries having Secondary/Higher Secondary Education, it is found that 21.04 per cent have been benefited form Vocational Education and Training, Financial and Material Assistance, followed by 17.60 per cent, 6.99 per cent, 6.99 per cent, 3.53 per centand 1.77 per cent have been benefited from counselling, advice and general awareness, employment, education and farming guidance respectively.

On analysing the responses of the beneficiaries having Graduation level of education, it is found that 38.52 per cent have been benefited from Vocational Education and Training. While 15.59 per cent, 15.59 per cent and 7.36 per cent of the beneficiaries have been benefited from employment, financial and material assistance respectively.

On analysing the responses of the beneficiaries having Post-graduation level, it is found that 36 per cent of them have been benefited from Vocational Education and Training, while 20 per cent each have been benefited from three Developmental Programmes, i.e., financial and material assistance, health and medical services and residential facilities.

On analysing the responses of the beneficiaries having Informal Education it is found that 26.87 per cent, 26.87 per cent, 19.40 per cent, 13.43 per cent, 13.43

per cent have been benefited from vocational education and training, education, counseling, advice and general awareness, health and medical services respectively.

Thus, it is found that the illiterate beneficiaries have been benefited more from financial and material assistance, health and medical services. while primary, middle, secondary/higher secondary, graduate, post-graduate and Informal educated beneficiaries have been largely benefited from Vocational Education and Training Programme of the developmental schemes through Civil Society Organisations.

On analysing the responses of the beneficiaries in terms of Cultivation, it is found that 38.60 per cent (606) have been benefited from financial and material assistance followed by 33 per cent, 15.92 per cent, 3.38 per cent of the beneficiaries have been benefited from vocational education and training, farming guidance, counseling, advice and general awareness respectively.

On analysing the responses of the beneficiaries in terms of Occupation of Labour, it is found that 37.04 per cent (535) have been benefited from Vocational Education and Training Programme followed by 24.70 per cent, 12.40 per cent, 9.83 per cent, 7.40 per cent, 4.91 per centand 3.68 per cent have been benefited from financial and material assistance, education, counseling, advice and general awareness, employment, health and medical services respectively.

On analysing the responses of the beneficiaries who are dependent/ unemployed, it is found that 29.36 per cent (534) have been benefited from Health and Medical Services. While 21.67 per cent, 13.74 per cent, 11.70 per cent, 9.84 per cent, 7.87 per cent, 2.91 per cent and 2.91 per cent have been benefited from vocational education and training, education, financial and material assistance, counseling, advice and general awareness, employment and farming guidance respectively.

On analysing the responses of the beneficiaries in terms of Occupation of Petty shop, it is found that 25.26 per cent (199) have been benefited from health and Medical Services followed by 23.20 per cent, 18.39 per cent, 13.82 per cent, 11.60 per cent, 4.70 per cent and 2.34 per cent have been benefited from Residential facilities, Vocational Education and Training, Counseling, Advice and General Awareness, Education, Financial and Material Assistance respectively.

Thus, it is found that, in terms of Occupation of Cultivation more numbers of beneficiaries have been benefited from Financial and Material Assistance, while in terms of occupation of dependent and Petty shop, beneficiaries have been benefited from Health and Medical Services. While in terms of Occupation of Labour, beneficiaries have been benefited from Vocational Education and Training Programme.

On analysing the responses of the beneficiaries in terms of income, it is found that 50 per cent (428) whose income is below Rs 3000.00, have been benefited from Vocational Education and Training Programme. It is followed by 20.83 per cent, 14.58 per cent, 4.16 per cent, 4.16 per cent and 2.08 per cent have been benefited from financial and material assistance, residential facilities, health and medical services, education, counseling, advice and general awareness and farming guidance respectively.

On analysing the respondents of the beneficiaries in terms of income in range between Rs 3001 to Rs 5000, it is found that 30.56 per cent (392) have been benefited from Vocational Education and Training, followed by 25.01 per cent, 15.28 per cent, 12.48 per cent, 6.94 per cent, 4.13 per cent, 2.80 per cent and 2.80 per cent have been benefited from financial and material assistance, counseling, advice and general awareness, health and medical services, residential facilities, education, farming guidance and employment respectively.

On analysing the responses of the beneficiaries in terms of income in range between Rs 5001 to Rs 8000, it is found that 22.60 per cent (500) have been benefited from Vocational Education and Training, whereas 19.40 per cent, 13.70 per cent, 12.88 per cent, 12.07 per cent, 11.20 per cent, 5.65 per cent and 2.40 per cent have been benefited from financial and material assistance, health and medical services, education, residential facilities, counselling, advice and general awareness, farming guidance and employment respectively.

On analysing the responses of the beneficiaries in terms of income in range between Rs 8001 to Rs 10,000.00 it is found that 22.99 per cent (287) have been benefited from Health and Medical Services, followed by 21.48 per cent, 18.59 per cent, 12.74 per cent, 8.58 per cent, 5.69 per cent and 4.24 per cent have been benefited from vocational education and training, financial and material assistance, counselling, advice and general awareness, education, employment and farming guidance respectively.

Thus, it is found that beneficiaries have been benefited more from Vocational Education and Training Programme followed by Financial and Material Assistance Programme.

Income Before and After Taking Assistance

On analysing the information received from the beneficiaries, it is found that 22.29 per cent (1248) had annual income in range of Rs 8001 to Rs10,000, before taking benefits from the Civil Society Organisations, while 39.50 per cent (2212) had annual income in range of Rs 5001 to Rs 8000.00, 22.92 per cent (1288) had Rs 3001 to Rs 5000 and 15.30 per cent (857) had upto Rs 3000.00.

On the whole, most of the beneficiaries assisted by the Civil Society Organisations were in the low income group before taking benefits.

Inter-incomer Class Shifting

To measure the impact of the schemes of the voluntary organisations on beneficiaries, the shift ability of the beneficiaries from one income class to another have been examined. The classification of beneficiaries has been presented in income group, viz., below Rs 3000, Rs 3001 to Rs 5000, Rs 5001 to Rs 8000 and Rs 8001 to Rs 10, 000.

It is found that 91.40 per cent (5119), beneficiaries shifted to higher income group after taking assistance. This shift is comparatively higher in the income group of Rs 5001 to Rs 8000 followed by income group of Rs 8001 to Rs 10, 000.00. This percentage of beneficiaries is 83.32 per cent and 87.86 per cent of those who shifted to higher income groups from income range of Rs 3001 to Rs 5000 and unto Rs 3000 respectively.

On the whole 91.40 per cent (5119) shifted to higher income group after taking assistance through Civil Society Organisations. From this analysis it can be inferred that there is a positive impact of assistance arranged by the civil society organisations.

Increase in Income

Responses from the beneficiaries are sought to form an opinion, whether or not they feel that their income increased or no change after getting assistance through the Civil Society Organisations.

On analysing the responses, it is found that 91.40 per cent (5119) beneficiaries reported that the schemes helped them in increasing their annual income. Rest 8.60 per cent (481) felt that there is no change in their income. Those who felt that their income could not change after taking assistance mis-utilised the assistance given through the Civil Society Organisations.

Thus, it is revealed that shift in income of 91.40 per cent of beneficiaries, is an important indicator of improvement of their economic conditions.

Satisfaction with Services/ Assistance

If the beneficiaries would be found satisfied with the services rendered or assistance given by the Civil Society Organisations, it would indicate positive impact of the latter.

In this context, it is found that on overwhelming majority, that is 91.40 per cent (5119) of the beneficiaries have been responded in affirmative and are satisfied with the role of the Civil Society Organisations.

Thus, it is found that the beneficiaries are by and large, satisfied with the services rendered/assistance given by the Civil Society Organisations.

Impact on Different Aspects of Life

78.35 per cent (4388) of beneficiaries said that their income has increased, standard of living improved and socio-economic status have enhanced.

From the analysis pertaining to the nature of impact, it can be inferred that the services and assistance arranged by the Civil Society Organisations not only helped in improving their socio-economic conditions but also have strong effect on certain other aspects such as removal of physical hardships, raising confidence, moulding the attitude, raising the educational level and formation of awareness.

Thus it is found that, the developmental schemes through Civil Society Organisations have positive impact on different aspects of their life.

Perception of Beneficiaries about the Civil Society Organisations from which they Received Benefits.

The analysis of the responses of the beneficiaries show that, 46.50 per cent (2604) perceived the Civil Society Organisations role as highly commendable and valuable followed by 35.03 per cent (1962) consider it as enough to meet their development requirements. 14.65 per cent (820) reported their role in social welfare arena as good.

It is inferred from the responses that on the whole the working of Civil Society Organisations is considered by the beneficiaries as commendable and valuable, in the context of over-all tribal development.

Suggestions for Greater Tribal Development by the Civil Society Organisations

At present Civil Society Organisations are inevitable in the context of democracy. It is supposed that it is meant for educating tribal people so that they may become politically and socio-economically conscious as well as dutiful towards nation-building.

Suggestions

- Greater involvement of Civil Society Organisations in tribal development programme should be encouraged.
- Media should be to focus the achievement of Civil Society Organisations.
- More funds should be provided by the government to the Civil Society Organisations to meet the needs and aspirations of the tribal people.
- The government should have a positive stand to support the Civil Society Organisations and to boost up their moral, on recognising their achievements and contributions toward tribal development.

References

1. R.B. Jain and R.K. Nayak (1988): in K.P. Singh (ed.), *Tribal Development in India*. New Delhi, Uppal Publishing House, p. 329.
2. D.N. Majumdar (1961): *Races and Culture of India, Bombay*, Asia Publishing House, p. 367.
3. D. Thakur and D.N. Thakur (1995), *Tribal Law and Administration*, New Delhi, Deep and Deep Publications, p. 25.
4. Martin H. Manser (ed.) (2000), *Chambers English Thesaurus*. Allied Chambers Ltd., p. 202.
5. K.P. Jameson and C.K.Wilber (ed.) (1979): *Directions in Economic Development*. Notre Dame, University of Notre Dame Press, p. 5.
6. Richard A. Easterlin (1968), *Overview on Economic Growth in D.L. Sills (ed). International Encyclopaedia of the Social Sciences*, New York, Vol. 4, p. 395.
7. Daniel Learner (1968): "*Social Aspects of Modernisation*" in International Encyclopaedia of the Social Sciences, New York, Vol. 10, p. 387.

8. A.K. Cairnecross (1961), "*International Trade and Economic Development, Economia*, Vol. 28, No.106, 1st February, p. 250.

9. Gunnar Myrdal (1968), *Asian drama: An Inquiry into the Poverty of Nations*. New York, Vol. 3, p.1868.

10. G.W.F. Hegel (1953), *Philosophy of Rights*, Oxford Clarendon, p.148.

11. Michael Walzer (1998), *The Concept of Civil Society*, Oxford: Berghahn Books, pp.7-28.

12. Rajesh Tandon (2003), "*The Civil Society- Governance Interface,* An India Perspective", in Rajesh Tandon and Ranjita Mohanty (eds.), Does Civil Society Make Governance in Contemporary India?, New Delhi: Sage Publications.

13. G.E. Gellner (1994), *Civil Society in Historical Context. International Social Science Journal*, No.129: 495-510.

14. Neera Chandhoke (198), *State and Civil Society-Exploration in Political Theory*, New Delhi, Sage Publications.

15. John-Hall (1995), *"Civil Society: Theory, History, Comparison,"* Cambridge, U.K. Polity Press.

16. Gurpreet Mahajan (1999), "*Civil Society and its Avtars*: What happened to Freedom and Democracy? Economic and Political Weekly, Vol. 34, No. 20, p. 1189.

21

Empowerment of Tribal's in Assam: Role of Autonomous District Councils

Girija Brahma

Introduction

The constituent assembly felt that the unique cultural and traditional governance practices of various tribes residing in the hills of north-eastern part of the country are good enough for the effective functioning of their existing system. They believed that, the sudden disruption of village customs and ways by sudden exposure to the modern ways of administrations that is majorly based on British administrative legacy would prove to be detrimental.

This however does not negate that the other regions of the country did not have unique practices culture, traditions and governance practices. On contrary, the situation in the north-eastern region was completely different. The north-eastern India was never exposed to the British administrative apparatus as much as the other part of the country. Moreover, prior to the coming of the British, the rest of India the disputes were resolved according to principles laid down in Smriti and Dharmasutra before the coming of the Islamic invaders. After the advent of the Islamic rule certain Shariat law coexisted along with the existing Smriti and Dharmasutra.

Interestingly, all these civil codes did not make way to the hills and valley on a serious note as they were cut off from the rest of the world because of hostile climate and terrains. British policy also helped in preserving the prevailing image of uncharted territory as they did not foray into the region. The passing of Inner Line Regulation in 1873 to prohibit entry of all Britisher subjects or any class of British subjects in the area within the inner line without proper pass-issued by the competent authority was one such attempt. This was followed by the Scheduled District Act of 1874. When Simon Commission Toured India i.e., (The Indian Statutory Commission) they toured the entire British India and almost all the Hill District submitted their various demands. In 1930, Simon Commission recommended for preservation of ancestral customary rights of the tribes. Thus, the Government of India Act, 1935, section 92 enacted provisions that no act Provincial and Central legislatures can be applied to the hills areas. Thus, these hills areas were designated as backward tracts known as the excluded or partially excluded areas.

Later the Cabinet Mission under the Chairman of Sir Stafford Cripps suggested the formation of Advisory Committee on the Rights of Citizens, Minorities and tribal areas. Thus, when Constituent Assembly was set up as per the proposals of the cabinet mission, an advisory committee on tribal areas under the chairmanship of Sardar Vallabhbhai Patel to consider the problem of Assam and the tribal areas. The advisory Committee formed a sub committee under the chairmanship of Gopinath Bordoloi. He toured the entire hill region and interacted with the leaders from the various tribes, the Bordoloi committee was sensitive to the need of the growing aspirations of the tribal people. This committee was responsible for making all the possible arrangement so that the provision of Sixth Schedule that various hill tribes enjoys today could be enshrined in the Constitution.

The Idea of Sixth Schedule Area

For many, the idea of separate provision of Sixth Schedule was sown by the British rule. During the colonial Assam, the Hills district was once administered under special provision for the so called excluded areas and partially excluded areas under the Government of India Act, 1935. With Independence, the Sixth Schedule of the Constitution established autonomous district councils in the same areas, based on the premises that it would help them to maintain their distinctiveness and provide a platform for their survival.

The reason for asking autonomy is highly based on complex web of identity, ethnicity and sub nationalism. Prior to the colonial demarcation of the North-East region, there were many groups of people inhabiting specific areas with political control over a limited territory and controlled over the land and its resources that would not be termed as a nation in any modern sense. For several centuries the valleys and hills of north eastern India had witnessed waves of invasion and migration. In a true sense none of these so called ethnic groups, due to their long journey of migration, can claim racial purity. Speculation about their migrations have been widely made and widely contradicted.

Elements of Sixth Scheduled

As per the provision in the Sixth Scheduled in the Areas of north-east India. "No act of the state legislatures in respect of tribal affairs shall apply to any autonomous district unless the district councils so direct. On the other hand, these areas were given full share in the State Legislatures and State

Cabinet. The Sixth Schedule gives tribal communities residing in the hills a considerable autonomy. The role of the Governor and the State are subject to significant limitations, with greater powers devolved locally. The District Council and the Regional Council under the Sixth Schedule have real power to make laws, possibility on the various legislative subjects, receiving grants-in-aids from the Consolidated Fund of India to meet the costs of schemes for development, healthcare, education, roads and regulatory powers to state control. The mandate towards devolution, de-concentration and divestment determines the protection of their customs, better economic development and most importantly ethnic security.

Limitations Constraints

The relevance of the Sixth Schedule in the present context needs a serious review. The Schedule was specifically created to ensure the protection of the tribes from the threat of marginalisation, domination and homogenisation by the non-tribal populations and their culture in jurisdictional area of the Autonomous District Councils (ADCs). The Schedule succeeded to a great extent to preserve the distinct identity and autonomy of tribal population, yet the same provision has become subject to controversies. It has been alleged time and again that the district councils have failed to fulfil the aspirations of the people because of the lack of funds, lack of administrative and legislative powers. State government continues to pull all the strings. The funds allocated for the District Councils by the Central government are often allegedly diverted elsewhere or not released in time.

More than that, the frequent occurrence of ethic conflict in the schedule areas need a closer scrutiny. The various ethnic conflict with epicentres in these autonomous council have time and again made one ponder about the existence of an inherent ethnic polarisation and sub-nationalism and the air of mutual distrust in the air. For example, the later part of 2005, saw the Dimasa and Karbis at war. It saw the displacement of 44,016 ethnic Karbis, Dimasa and along with other tribal and non-tribal populations. Mid 2012 saw riots in BTAD, the ethic-Bodos who have political control over the area was at war against the illegal immigrants. It saw nearly four lakhs displacement within a short period of 10 days. Asian Centre for Human Rights in its study highlights the fact that in this ethnic war there was a failure on the part of administration to stop killings and arson even after one month of continuous violence. The centre also highlights the bitter reality in its study that the State government do not use the security options available at its disposal. Only after the death toll raises armies are called to aid the civilian has been the order of the day. The state which has withheld the police power and takes the responsibility to protect the lives of the citizens and people in the schedule areas have failed time and again. This results in the feeling that they are not safe and the apprehension of losing their land and identity escalates if they still become a part of Assam. The resultant is that only a separate state for them would give them fullfledged protection. Moreover the earlier move of granting of separate statehood to many of its district council those once were a part of erstwhile excluded and partially excluded areas has given them the hope that they too can get a separate state status. Well some have seen this as attempt to alter the demographic picture of the proposed homeland.

The activities of insurgent group have not been fully controlled by the State. This has proved to be a great hurdle in its peaceful existence of autonomous district council. Whether surrendered or not, whether in ceasefire or not the militants organisation has been detrimental to the achievement of schedule six areas.They all have been busy in the extortion business from the tribals as well as non-tribals that has instilled fears among the masses and have thickened the air of distrust. Various reports say that the Dimasa and Karbi conflict escalated due to the active participation of Militant Groups like Dima Halam Daoga and United Peoples Democratic Solidarity. Similarly, reports suggested the role of NDFB both talk and anti talk faction and the disbanded BLT hands in eruption of riots.

This all shows that the sixth schedule areas have proved to be incompetent time and again as it has failed to empower the tribal's with what it requires the most i.e., peace for safeguarding its distinct identity, law tradition and practices.

Moreover, the Councils are only visible to be functioning at the district level. There is no decentralisation of powers and administration to the grass root level. All it has is the all in all district council, which elects few people and they enjoy unbridled power. But democracy demands that power should not be concentrated in a few hands. Moreover unlike the Panchayati Raj Institutions and Urban Local Bodies they do not have any reservation for women and their representation in all the three district council is also meagre. In the absence of village panchayats, here a body nominated by the Council who carry out the administration at village level. As they are nominated, its defeats the very idea of democratic decentralisation. As the VCDC is nominated by the council, it is always the party member who are members of the ruling party gets a change to serve in the VCDC. The District Council is unreachable for the common masses as there have been no elections.

The Karbi Anglong experiences of autonomy under the sixth schedule tells about the lack of autonomy since its inception. However, to curtain the separatist demands Bodoland territorial council took birth and walked the same route that prevailing in Karbi Anglong long time back. It's worth pondering that the institutions those are supposed to guarantee autonomy that makes them obsolete and ineffective in one context and are sold to others as a means of conflict resolution.

I would like to conclude by saying the problems of encroachment and infiltration will be easier to handle with closer monitoring at local level, this would lessen the so called threat and local masses has to be involved in the day to day functioning of the councils and this can happen only when VCDC member is elected by the villagers by timely elections. Then only the true empowerment of tribal's will began. Moreover the right and healthy programme and policy measures by the State government is only the solution for a healthy functioning of autonomous district councils so that they can bloom to the fullest. Or else the separatist tendency to carve out a separate state in its bid to safeguard its life and property among other interest would prevail in the region. This would see bandhs and violence that would have serious economic consequences. So, to be a prosperous state, the State of Assam should not neglect the autonomous district council or else the state will sooner or later ceased not to exist because the bifurcation of the state will be the only solution left.

22

Politics of SCs and STs Conflict in Kandhamal: Failure of Indian Secularism

Himanshu Sekhar Mishra

This paper elaborates the genesis of 'Kandhas' (SCs)–'Panas' (SCs) in Kandhamal, their relation from cooperative to conflict, the politics played by Sangha Parivar in their conflict to serve their ideology and how Indian secularism becomes crony without understanding inter-religious domination and intra-religious domination simultaneously and giving scope to this kind of force to grow.[1]

In Kandhamal, on 23rd August, 2008, Sri Lakshmananda Saraswati - a leader of the Vishwa Hindu Parishad (VHP) – was murdered by unidentified gunmen under mysterious circumstances. Maoist rebels were initially blamed by the police and some Hindu organisations suspected collusion of Christian missionaries amongst the *Pana* caste. This led to large scale riots between the indigenous *Kandha* tribe (largely Hindu) and the Christian minority amongst the *Pana* caste. The underlying causes are complex and cross political, religious and ethnic boundaries. Justice SC Mohapatra said in his interim report on the violence in Kandhamal that "The violence in Kandhamal was the result of concentrated discontentment prevailing among the people since long. They relate to conversion, re-conversion; land-grabbing and non-maintenance of land records; and fake certificate issues".[2] He, however, does not elaborate on the conversion and re-conversion issues but says that "in spite of the Orissa Freedom of Religion Act, illegal conversions were taking place which created discontentment". To him, suspicion among the Scheduled Tribe and Scheduled Caste inhabitants of Kandhamal is the main cause of riots with the tribal suspecting that 'Pana' dalits are capturing their land through fraudulent means. Besides the issues of land and conversion and re-conversion, Justice Mohapatra says fake certificate is another major factor that creates discontent among 'Kandha' tribals who constitute 52 per cent of Kandhamal's population.[3] The 28 page long report says that land is being grabbed by the 'Pana'. It is a fact that a section of the 'Pana' has encroached upon the vast stretches of land which originally belong to the 'Kandhas'. As per the Land Regulation Law of Orissa, nontribal can neither buy nor take possession of land from tribal owners. Along with these lines, the report says that many 'Pana' Christians who have lost their SC tag after conversion to Christianity has managed to secure a false certificate. Some of the 'Pana' Christians also submit their fake tribal certificate for the government jobs and to grab land and reap quota benefits in education. Though in every issue, SCs and STs Conflict is manifest, but in reality it is a conflict between fundamentalist force (Hindutva forces) and secular forces which has made Indian secularism crony. This paper has three sections. First section deals with *Kandhas* and *Panas* of Kandhamal. Second section deals with the relation between *Kandhas* and *Panas* and its manipulation by the Sangha Parivar. Third section deals with crony secularism where it is elaborated how fundamentalist force strengthens itself because of the failure of secularism.

I

The present Kandhamal district has been carved out of the erstwhile Boudh-Phulbani district, consisting of two Sub-division Kandhamal and Baliguda. This District lies between 19 degree 34 minutes and 20 degree 50 minutes north latitude and in between 80 degrees 30 minutes and 84 degrees 48 minutes east longitude. It is located in the Northern extremity of the Eastern Ghats bounded by Boudh district in the north, Rayagada district in the south, Ganjam District and Nayagarh district in the east and Kalahandi district in the west. The name of the district 'Kandhamal' is derived from the name of its major inhabitants Kandhas, having total populations 6,48,201 according to the census of 2001. Out of which scheduled tribes are 3,36,809 and schedule caste are 1,09,506 and rest belong to other communities. Above all this district is predominated by the tribals. Numerically, the Kandhas constitute the largest tribe among all other tribes nearly 90 per cent of total STs and Panas are nearly 80 per cent of total SCs in Kandhamal District. Besides these SCs and STs, there are different castes such as Brahmins, Kshyatriyas, Sundhi, Karan, Kulta, Gauda, Mali, Teli, Sunari etc. From religious point of view, Hindus (incidentally the STs included despite the animistic religion followed by them) constitute 5,27,757 (82 per cent) and Christians are 1,17,950 (18 per cent) so far as census of 2001 is concerned. Besides these two major religions, there is Islam as well as Buddhist religion also.

Being Dravidians, *Kandhas* were in this hilly tract of the country before the advent of the Aryans. They have been classified under the ancient Gondid race of the Proto-Australoid group, which according to scholars like Risley, preceded the Aryans by many thousand years.[4] After the fall of Harappan culture, the ancestors of *Kandhas* with other inhabitants moved towards Gangetic valley and started their settlement at the feet of Himalayas. In due course after division they migrated to the different parts of the country. Having segregated one section of the tribe used to settle in the soil of Odisha through Vindhya Mountain. In this connection there is a folk song like "*Himalaya ra andh, binja giri ra Kandha, Athe jelen Kandhen, Basalya kalasur mandh*".[5] It is believed that the *Kandhas* migrated from Madhya Pradesh and entered into the district of Kalahandi and divided into two divisions. The branch which took southeast direction might have proceeded to Belghar region, the south-west of Kandhamal district.[6] The *Kandhas* for the first time settled their foot hold Sapangada of Tamudibandh block. There after they established their settlement at Adanga Pata and Sujunga Pata. With increase of their population, the *Kandha* classified among themselves into several sections such as *Kutia Kandha, Dangaria Kandha, Desia Kandha, Bura Kandha, Sita Kandha, Pengo Kandha, Nagala Kandha, Buda Kandha* and *Raja Kandha*.[7] The *Kutia, Dangaria* and *Desia Kandhas* play a major role in the community. The ensuing *Kandha* legend tells that prior to the settlement in this district; it was preoccupied by the 'Kurumas' who belongs to peace loving community. They were domiciled in Paberi, Ghodapathar, Linepada, Purangada, Kainjhar of Khajuripada, Chakapad and Tikabali blocks. After a little skirmish with *Kandhas*, the Kurumas were forced to oust from this land and subsequently they migrated to the neighbouring districts Ganjam and Daspalla of present Nayagarh district. Thereafter, Kandhamal became the stronghold of the *Kandhas*. Out of many *Kandhas*, *Desia Kandhas* are popularly known as Hinduised section of the *Kandha* community who are living throughout of this district.

To analyse the word *Kandha* is a difficult task. The origin of the name of *Kandha* is still not clear. Different scholars have given their different views about this. In the opinion of Krishna Sharma, "the name 'Kandha' has its origin in the root 'Koi' or 'Ku' which signifies only mountain. The Telgu 'Kodu' corresponds to the Sanskrit 'Konda' though 'Konda' in Telgu signifies only mountain and not mountaineer".[8] Another celebrated scholar P.C Ratha opines "the *Kandha*'s of natural Odisha called themselves 'Koi' or 'Koitur'. This means hill man or burn of mountain. Again some of them call themselves *Kuiloka Kuienju*".[9] To the District Gazetteer of the Boudh Kandhamal, the term *Kandha* is derived from Odia word *Kanda*, an arrow.[10] Scholar Raghunath Rath also expresses his view on the derivation of the word *Kandha*. Kangoda mandal, existed between Kalinga and Odra and bounded by the river Mahanadi on the north and Rushikulya in the south and was roughly covered the parts of modern Puri, Ganjam, Kandhamal and Boudh districts, where there were *Kandha* concentration and till now the said piece of land is the homeland of *Kandha*. Hence as the people were called by the plains people as *Kangodia, Kangoda, Kanda, Kandha* and the name *Kandh* distinguished as the name of the tribe in the later ages.[11] Scholar Sarat Chandra Mohanty opines that the hill dwellers that live on roots and tubers after collecting from hills and jungles are known as *Kanda*. Mr. Mohanty also quoted the version of famous British Linguist G.A. Grierson that, "the tribe is commonly known under the name of 'Khond', the Oriyas call them 'Kandhas' and the Telgu people 'Gonds' or 'Kods'. The name which they use themselves is 'Ku' and their language should accordingly be dominated as Kui".[12] With the march of time, though the tribes' men have accepted the name *Kond, Khond, Kondh, Kandha* as conferred upon them by non-tribals. However, the *Kandhas* identified themselves as 'Kui, Kuinga', 'Ku Enju', 'Kui Loku' or 'Koilok'.

On the other side, *Panas* are the majority community among non-tribal communities of this district. The origin of the name *Pana* is difficult to analyse. It is common belief that this caste derives its name from 'Pundrika'.[13] With the march of time the name 'Pundrika' is changed into *Topaunika, Panika, Pan and Pana*. To speak on the other words, it has been derived from Sanskrit word 'Panabika' which means drummer.[14] B.B. Mohanty in order to trace out origin and history of *Pana* quoted the opinions of Russel and Hiralal that the word *Pana* is derived from term of 'Panka', a Dravidian caste of weaver and labourers. [15]*Panas* are classified into five subcastes such as *Odia Pana, Buna Pana, Betara Pana* or *Raj Pana, Pana Baisnab* and *Patradia*. The *Panas* of this district belongs to fourteen clans such as Mahananda, Bhoina, Tandia, Dip Dohara, Bibhara, Bagha, Khura, Rana, Puda, etc., the members of the community of different clans use several surnames suffixed to their name such as Digal, Sethi, Shahani, Behera and Naik.[16]

Panas in this district are migrated from Ganjam during the time of Bhanja administration. They are very common in the district. First they acted as serfs (Agricultural labourers) of the *Kandhas*. But with laps of time, cordial relationship was established between two communities. The *Kandhas* think themselves as king and *Panas* consider as their ministers. Panas can speak Kandha language (Kui) fluently. They acted as intermediary between Kandhas and outsiders.

II

In Kandhamal, originaly the lands of *Kandhas*, the *Panas* were first brought by the Hindu king as well as *Kandha* king for rendering service to their community. Historically, *Kandhas* have control over the total land of Kandhamal and hence, they were considering themselves as *Rajas* (king) and *Panas* as their *prajas* (subjects). The *Panas* initially, worked as wage labourers on *Kandha*'s lands and provide important links between them and the outside world, as said before. They helped the *Kandhas* from tilling the lands, clearing forests for cultivation, to stealing children for human sacrifice (Bali) for which they got a very bad name as 'criminal caste' from the British Police as well as from the Hindus from the neighbouring village. British Gazettee for such records also says, in few cases, the *Panas* were forced to give their children for Bali if they fail to supply. Now, tribes after giving up this inhuman practice call this caste people as 'criminal caste' too.

However, this social solidarity between these two worlds in Kandhamal collapsed, may be due to conversions during post-1947 period or due divide and rule policy of British while capturing *Panas* to clear forests and roads, buildings, railway works or paper industries by enticing them with higher wages, or due to introducing new land relations and depriving the *Kandhas* of their traditional rights over the forest land or due to the British policy of setting up a Shiva temple in 1855 which denied entry to the *Panas*, or due to the formation of the *Babudom* (peons or clerks) among the *Panas*. In retrospect, all of these factors cumulatively contributed to the weakening relationship between *Kandhas* and *Panas*. Along with it, the flurry activities by the elements of Christian Missionaries during 1960s and the later by the Sangh Parivar in the 1970s led by the Hindu leader, Mr. Laxmananda Saraswati, their 'solidarity' began to crumble.[17]

Though there was solidarity between *Kandhas* and *Panas* once upon a time, yet, the natural rift between the two is nothing new. The *Kandhas* have the history of vociferous resistance to religious conversion by evangelists. On the other hand, over the years, a majority of *Pana* have embraced Christianity, leading to an increase in the Christian population in the district from a mere 19,128 in 1951 to 1,17,950 in 2001.[18] Though, there is a process called migration due to the expansion of modernisation, yet Migration process alone cannot explain the rise of Christian population. Conversion could have played a big role in the rise of Christian population during 1951-2001. However, the district has seen growth of church organisation run by the Catholics, Protestants (Church of North India) and Pentecostals (Baptist Church). Apart from voluntary conversion of individual families, there could be also mass conversion, so that there is such an unusual growth of Christians among *Panas*. When both *Kandhas* and the Sangha Parivar denied the *Panas* an entry to the temples as late as in 1994, *Panas* would have realised that Christianity in the district did not practice untouchability at least in the church entry issue. As a result, they might have followed mass conversion. It has played a negative role in 'Hinduisation of Dalits'. Ironically, the Parivar's policy of *Suddhi* (reconversion) does not offer a sacred thread to a *Panas* (SCs) but offers the same to a *Kandhas* (STs), thus showing an example of blatant discrimination against *Panas*. Consequently, the Sangha Parivar loses its moral right to raise any banner against mass conversion.

Bishnu Mahapatra and D Bhattacharya argue that the *Kandhas* felt threatened once the *Panas* started interacting more in market economy following British rule. After independence, they got government jobs and become money lenders with surplus money earned from jobs and business, whereas *Kandhas* decided to stay away from interaction with the British Administration over most part of 19th century.[19] However, by 2008, 20 per cent *Panas* become land owner with an average holding size of half acre of land. After independence, the money lending developed among the *Panas*. They started petty business in trading, in selling cow, hens, buffaloes, etc., to *Kandhas*. Due to the depletion of forest resources, animals have also vanished from the forests and *Kandhas* started to depend on the *Panas* for a regular supply of these sacrificial animals to satisfy their father gods and mother gods. A few *Panas* have taken advantage of money lending and got the *Kandhas* lands mortgaged and thus tribals (Kandhas) lost their land to a few *Panas*.[20] The *Kandhas* felt that the *Panas* who were their dependent minister in one time, could even become land owner. Thus, for the *Kandhas*, the *Panas* became exploiters and land snatchers. But it is not absolutely true that *Panas* has become land owner by exploiting *Kandhas*. It is also a fact that some of them are land owner due to the gifts they received from their *Kandha* king long back for rendering their service to them and helping them human sacrifice and animal sacrifice. This is true that the *Panas*, with the help of the state as well as the church, have been cornering the maximum benefits of constitutional reservation due to their educational and economic advantage. The *Kandhas,* however, allege that the *Panas* hide their Christian identity and even claim to be Scheduled Tribes (ST) or Hindu Scheduled Castes (SC) by producing forged certificates. The *Panas*, they fear, are out to dominate them economically, politically and culturally. Using this situational advantage, Parivar by generating the threat of insecurities among *Kandhas*, had entrenched itself in the district. By using the constitutional provisions for the SCs and STs and by playing with the fear of the STs in the district, the Parivar managed to draw a popular support of *Kandhas*, the late modernisers, now aspiring for modern jobs in the state sector when its space has already shrunk in the area of privatisation. However, the emergence of the *Panas* as an assertive community has become an eyesore to the upper caste Hindus, not only in Kandhamal but also in other parts of Orissa. Thus, stereotypes of the *Pana* as 'betrayer', 'cunning', 'deceitful', 'exploiter', has entered into the caste discourses in Orissa, which was skillfully used by an organised group like Sangha Parivar, to give such a negative image of *Panas* in Kandhamal.

For not depending on *Panas* for animal (meant for Bali), *Kandhas* are taught by Parivar to convince their god and goddess to follow a vegetarian strategy. For not depending on *Panas* for monetary matter, Parivar co-opted the entire road side trader, especially from outside. They were instructed by the Parivar to extend monetary help to the dependent tribe only if they give up animal sacrifice. As in some village, Christian-run NGOs concentrated services among Dalits (SCs), thus leaving out of Kandhas (STs) and OBCs; the Parivar finds this atmosphere very congenial to take *Kandhas* within its umbrella and away from the Panas and Christians in order to manipulate this Hinduised tribe as their 'foot soldier' in their battle against *Pana* Christians for the purpose of satisfying their ideology.

III

The discourses of Hindu fundamentalist and the state government on the other hand primarily discuss Kandhamal riots as ethnic conflict between the

Kandhas (ST) and *Panas* (SC). But actually, it is conflict between fundamentalist forces and secular forces. On one hand, the Hindutva forces are accused of following 'majoritarianism' which in turn has forced the religious majority and minority to resort to terrorism to make their voice felt. On the other hand, Indian secularism has been terribly confused and tries to maintain a distance from this aggressive current. But it is also accused of being complicit with 'minorityism'. There are ideologues in both the political camps who do not see eye to eye with each other.[21] Does Indian secularism have enough courage, conviction, temperance and honesty to face the religious sectarianisms and dialogue with all of them, instead of building a wall of separation? We must critically examine secularism because the weaknesses of secularism have been used opportunistically by fundamentalist forces. Constitutional orders (SC) for Act, 1950 can be taken as beginning of crony secularism in India, which provides for reservation for the Hindu SCs only, thus alluring the Hindu SCs to stay with the Hinduism. This provision got a Hindutva touch later in 1958 and 1990, when it was amended to extend reservation facility to all SCs from among the Hindus, Sikhs, Buddhists and Jains, thus refusing to recognise the existence of SC Muslim and SC Christians. This new provision reinforces a typical Hindutva agenda that claims the other two religious communities have no casteism. In Kandhamal, Sangha Parivar, by using this constitutional provision effectively, tries to convince *Kandhas* that 'Christian Panas' are no more eligible to get reservations facilities and that is why they are trying for duplicate ST certificate in order to get these facilities. In doing so, Parivar is trying to generate two feelings among *Kandha* first, hatred feeling on Christian Panas and second, a trust on itself. These activities of Sangha Parivar are generating communalism by capturing the social imaginaries especially of *Kandhas*. At the first sight, this is in fact not a success of fundamentalist force, rather the failure of secularism from the very beginning (Constitutional orders (SC) for Act, 1950). In this way, crony secularism strengthens the fundamentalist forces in capturing the social imaginaries. In Kandhamal, crony secularism in passive complicit with the Hindu fundamentalism has pushed a few Christian youth to take the shelter in the red terror camps in 2007 and 2008 which is known for retributive justice. This means more such killings are likely to follow. In Kandhamal Maoists have intervened only once in 2008. As they are weakened in Andhra, they are now trying to create a social base in Odisha. And the Sangh Parivar has offered a fertile ground for Maoism to operate in Odisha. In this way, crony secularism thus has produced varieties of terrorism from Kashmir to Kandhamal.

As most of our secular writings concentrate on the operation of fundamentalism, thereby deflating our attention from an internal criticism of secularism, we must concentrate on the serious weakness in secularism. The serious weakness of Indian secular state is its compromise with inter religious domination or intra religious domination by way of patronising elites from among all religious communities. This is how giving a scope to fundamentalist forces to entrench on either side of religious divides. In order to protect itself from cronyism, India's secularism must understand the intra-religious domination (caste and gender inequalities) among Muslim and Christians. Secondly, it must understand various forms of inter religious domination such as temple-mosque controversy or conversion-reconversion controversy. If it will understand at least these two dominations in recent future, then neither Sangha Parivar nor Christian Missionaries will find any scope in Kandhamal to divert such an ethnic conflict towards communal riots. In fact, Kandhamal needs non-intervention of fundamentalist forces and intervention of secular forces.

References

1. This term has been used by Prof Arun Kumar Patnaik in his paper called 'Choosing between Crony Secularism and Hindu Fundamentalism in Orissa: The case of Kandhamal', which had been presented by him in the workshop on "Actually Existing Secularism in India", Centre for the Study of Developing Societies, New Delhi, 10th -12th April, 2009. In this paper crony secularism has been defined is defined as a stage where state extends political, administrative and judicial support to the elites in the religious communities on cultural issues and thereby aiding the fundamentalist forces get entrenched on either side of the religious divide.
2. "Kandhamal lies nailed" Pioneer, 22nd July 2009.
3. *Ibid.*
4. "Kandhamal District" *Orissa Review*, December 2010: 131.
5. Raghunath Ratha, (1993), *Kandha Sanskrutira Analochita Adhyaya.* Koraput: Satta Sahitya Sansad. p. 2.
6. *Ibid.* p. 3.
7. STs and SCs of Orissa (2006), *Data hand book.* Complied statistical cell, Bhubaneswar: SCST RTI. p. 1.
8. Krishna Sharma (1979), *The Konds of Orissa.* New Delhi-05: Concept Publishing Company, H-13. p. 16.
9. P.C. Ratha (2008), *Foot Prints of Forgotton Genus.* Balangir. p. 293.
10. Nilamani, Senapati and D. Kunar (1983). Orissa District Gazetter, Boudha Kandhamal, Cuttack, p. 69.
11. Raghunath Ratha (2010), *The Kandhas and Kandhamal.* Bhubaneswar: Amedeus Press, pp. 23-24.
12. Sarat Chandra Mohanty (2008), Adivasi. Bhubaneswar: SCST RTI. 48(1). p. 63.
13. Nilamani, Senapati and D. Kunar (1983), *Orissa District Gazetter*, Bouda Kandhamal, Cuttack, pp. 61-67.
14. Nilamani Senapati and Durga Charan Kunar (1977), *Orissa District Gazetter*, Bouda Kandhamal, Cuttack, p. 133.
15. Nilamani Senapati and Durga Charan Kunar (1980), *Orissa District Gazetter*, Bouda Kandhamal, Cuttack, pp. 87.

16. Nrusingha Charan Behuria (1995), *Orissa District Gazetter*, Ganjam, Cuttack. p. 185.

17. Pralay Kanungo (2003), *Hindutva's Entry into a Hindu Province*: Early years of RSS in Orissa. *EPW.* 38(1): pp. 3293-3303.

18. "Kandhamal lies nailed" *Pioneer*, 22nd July 2009.

19. Bishnu Mahapatra and D. Bhattacharya (1996), *Tibal-Dalit Conflict: Electoral Politics in Phulbani*. EPW. 31(2/3), pp. 160-64.

20. See, "The Ugly face of Sangh Parivar", *http://www.humanrightsforum.org/*

21. Arun Patnaik 'Choosing between Crony Secularism and Hindu Fundamentalism in Orissa: The case of Kandhamal' (draft copy).

Bibliography

Ambedkar, B. R. (2004), *Conversion as Emancipation,* Critical quest, New Delhi.

Ambedkar, B. R. (2010), *Philosophy of Hinduism,* Critical quest, New Delhi.

Arun Patnaik, '*Choosing between Crony Secularism and Hindu Fundamentalism in Orissa:* The case of Kandhamal' (draft copy).

Behuria, Nrusingha Charan (1995), *Orissa District Gazetter,* Ganjam. Cuttack.

Bhagwati, Jagdish (2009). 'Secularism in India, why is it imperiled' in T.N. Srinivasan, ed., *The Future of Secularism*. Oxford University Press, New Delhi.

Bhargava, Rajeev (2009), 'The Distinctiveness of Indian Secularism' in T.N. Srinivasan, ed., *The Future of Secularism*. Oxford University Press, New Delhi.

Chatterjee, Partha (1998), '*Secularism and Tolerance' in Rajeev Bhargava* ed., *Secularism and Its Critics*. Oxford University Press, Delhi.

Dhyani, S.N. (1996), *Secularism: socio-legal issue*. Rawat, Jaipur.

Ferrandes, Walter (1999), 'Attacks on minorities and a National debate on conversion', *EPW*, Vol. 34, No. 03.

Galanter, Mark (1998), '*Secularism, East and West*' in Rajeev Bhargava, ed., *Secularism and Its Critics*. Oxford University Press, Delhi.

Heredia, Rudolf C. (2007), *Changing Gods: Rethinking Conversion in India.* Penguin Books, New Delhi.

India. Constituent Assembly, India. Parliament. Lok Sabha. Secretariate (1999). *Constituent assembly debate (official report), Vol-7,* Lok Sabha Secretariate, New Delhi.

Jha, Shefali (2002), '*Secularism in the Constituent Assembly Debates*, 1946-1950' *EPW*, Vol. 37, No. 30.

"Kandhamal District" *Orissa Review*, December 2010.

"Kandhamal lies nailed" Pioneer, 22nd July 2009. Kanungo, Pralay (2003). Hindutva's Entry into a Hindu Province: Early years of RSS in Orissa. *EPW.* Vol. 38, No. 1.

Kim, C.H. (2003), "*In Search of Identity: Debates on Religious Conversion in India*". Oxford University Press, New Delhi.

Mahapatra, Bishnu and D. Bhattacharya (1996), *Tibal-Dalit Conflict*: Electoral Politics in Phulbani. *EPW*, Vol. 31, No. 2/3.

Massey, James (2003), *Minorities and Religious Freedom in a Democracy*. Manohar, New Delhi.

Menon, Kalyani Devaki (2003), "Converted Innocents and Their Trickster Heroes: The Politics of Proselytising in India", in Andrew Buckser and Stephen D. Glazier (eds.) *The Anthropology of Religious Conversion,* Lanham, Boulder, New York, Toronto, Oxford: Rowman & Littlefield Publishers.

Menon, Nivedita (2004), "*The Right to Conversion*", *The Telegraph*, Kolkata, 7 May.

Mohanty, Sarat Chandra (2008), Adivasi. *SCST RTI*. Vol. 48, No. 1.

Pannikar, K.N. (1997), *Communal threat and Secular challenge*. Earthworm Books, Madras.

Pati, Biswamoy (2001), 'Identity, Hegemony, Resistance, Conversion in Orissa, 1800-2000', *EPW*, Vol. 36, No. 44.

Ratha, Raghunath (1993), *Kandha Sanskrutira Analochita Adhyaya*. Satta Sahitya Sansad, Koraput.

Ratha, Raghunath (2010), *The Kandhas and Kandhamal*. Amedeus Press, Bhubaneswar.

Sarkar, Sumit (2007), 'Christian conversion, Hindutva and Secularism' in Anuradha Dingwaney Needham and Rajeswari Sunder Rajan, ed., *The crises of secularism in India*, Permanent Black, Delhi.

Senapati, Nilamani, Durga Charan Kunar (1977), Orissa District Gazetter, Bouda Kandhamal, Cuttack.

Senapati, Nilamani, Durga Charan Kunar (1980), Orissa District Gazetter, Bouda Kandhamal, Cuttack.

Senapati, Nilamani, D. Kunar (1983), Orissa District Gazetter, Boudha Kandhamal, Cuttack.

Sharma, Krishna (1979), The Konds of Orissa. Concept Publishing Company, New Delhi, H-13.

Ratha, P.C. (2008), Foot Prints of Forgotton Genus. Balangir.

STs and SCs of Orissa (2006), Data handbook. Complied statistical cell, Bhubaneswar: SCST RTI.

23

Role of NYKS on Tribal Youth Development: A Case Study of Koraput District, Odisha

Janmejay Sahu, Ashok Behera

Abstract

Nehru Yuva Kendra Sangathan (NYKS) is a largest grassroots apolitical youth organisation under the Ministry of Youth Affairs and Sport, Government of India, working with Indian rural youth through the grassroots institutions such as Youth Clubs, Mahila Mandals and Social/Cultural Association headed by the youth. It aims to utilise the huge youth potential of the country engaging them in nation building. Today's youth is seen as 'Demographic Dividend' who has a significant role in the nation's development however the need is to shape the youth energy and mold them into the positive contribution to the society. The tribal people in India are deprived of the mainstream; particularly the tribal youth are directionless due to lack of proper education, training and employment opportunities however NYKS has been undertaking various programmes for the development of tribal youth giving them rigorous trainings, capacity building programme, field-based youth work and youth exchange programmes. Therefore, the paper tries to understand the functioning of NYKS, Koraput district of Odisha and aims to critically examine the contributions of the NYKS in Koraput district towards tribal development. Also, it attempts to study how the tribal youth of Koraput benefits from NYKS participating in various rural tribal development programmes and activities.

Introduction

In the broad sphere of Indian society, the tribal communities represent an important social category of Indian social structure. They are considered as the original inhabitants of India, who carry forward a legacy of rich and distinct cultural traits for many decades. Tribal society displays a fascinating profile of ethnic diversity. The tribal belong to different racial stocks, speak language of different families and show considerable variations in basic economy. The variation in physical and biological environment of their habitat is equally amazing. This bewildering variety in race, language, habitat and economy is fully reflected in their culture, which like a mosaic evokes the admiration of social scientists to study the dynamics of their society.

Koraput district popularly known as 'Kashmir' of Odisha, it bounds in the imprints of Odisha's glorious past. Temples monasteries and other historical monuments from the medieval period, breathtaking in their beauty and of incalculable historical importance, the art, craft and culture of the Tribals, stands as footprints of time telling the story of the years bygone. The Koraput, considered as 'Hub of Tribals' is one of the southern districts of Odisha located bordering Chhattisgarh and Andhra Pradesh. Out of total population of the district more than 50 per cent belongs to Scheduled Tribes and about 13 per cent are Scheduled Castes. They constitute 50 per cent of the total population with a sex ratio 1031 female against 1000 male.

In the recent past, this district of Koraput has gone through one of its toughest time as there have been enormous incidents of Maoist violence taken place in areas bordered with Andhra Pradesh, disrupting the normalcy, overall mood of the population, especially the younger generation. Currently, a part of the 'Red Corridor', the extreme geographic conditions, lack of health and educational infrastructure facilities makes the development of youth of Koraput more and more challengeable. Amongst the major players of youth development in the district like CAPART, NABARD, Government administration and International NGOs like Action-Aid, UNDP, Nehru Yuva Kendra Sangathan have invariably been playing a key role towards the overall development of the tribal youth of Koraput, ever since its inception. In this backdrop, a case study of Koraput has been taken where NYKS has been working with and for youth and an attempt is made to understand the broad objective of both the quantitative and qualitative aspects of NYKS achievements in the tribal youth development.

Youth and Youth Development

Youth are economic cornerstones and potential assets for the over-reaching goals of economic and social development and generally exhibit greater receptivity to new ideas and are more often innovative. Youth perspective adds value and promotes diversity of membership and representation within a decision-making. In case of tribal youth they have everything which is hidden in them therefore they need to be trained to make them capable for the nation building process. Vered Amit (1995) acknowledges that the nature of youth varies significantly according to the social context, and particularly in relation to factors such as class, gender, and ethnicity. Indeed, social historians have argued that "youth" is a relatively modern invention, which has resulted from the extension of the period of transition that lasts from the end of compulsory schooling to entry into waged labour; and this is clearly something that varies significantly between different social groups and between different cultural settings.

The United Nations (UN) broadly defines youth as those persons between the ages of 15 and 24 years. The UN proposes two categories of youth: "young people between ages 13-19 who are classified as teenagers, whilst those in the 20-24 age groups are characterised as young adults" and in promoting this definition, the UN concedes that the concept of youth hinges on "specific socio-cultural, institutional, economic and political factors" in different contexts (Word Youth Report-2006). Also, the World Bank adopts the UN definition by classifying persons in the 15-24 age groups as youth (World Bank) whereas the definition of Youth in India is cleared described in the National Youth Policy as 'the people coming under the age between 13 to 35 years old are youth'.

The American Youth Policy Forum (1995: 1) identified two premises that, they said, need to act as a foundation and guide for youth development practice: Youth development is an ongoing process in which young people are engaged and invested. Throughout this process, young people seek ways to meet their basic physical and social needs and to build the competencies and connections they need for survival and success. All youth are engaged in the process of development. Youth development is marked by the acquisition of a broad range of competencies and the demonstration of a full complement of connections to self, others, and the larger community. Confidence, compassion, commitment and character are terms commonly used to express the attitudes and behaviours that determine whether and how learned competencies will be used. Nixon (1997), too, defines youth development as a process in which all youths engage over time in order to meet their needs and build competencies. A youth-development paradigm has received worldwide recognition for its potential to transform the lives of youth. The United Nations has advocated youth development as an effective strategy for achieving both youth and community potential (World Sources Online 1999). The term youth development is enjoying greater use in practice involving youth in the United States (Networks for Youth Development 1998a). Moreover, the young people's work that focuses on individual learning and development, rather than on changing their surrounding, is not real participation-participation should not only give young people more control over their own lives and experiences but should also grant them real influence over issues that are crucial to the quality of life and justice in their communities Roman Mullahey (1999).

Nehru Yuva Kendra, Koraput

The Scheme of Nehru Yuva Kendra Sangathan was launched in the year 1972 with a vision to empower the rural youth of India by making them productive citizens, through awareness generation and capacity building programmes, NYKS become autonomous in 1987 under the independent ministry of Youth Affairs and Sports, Govt. of India. Today, it covers all the 623 districts of the country. With the amazing strength of 2.5 lakh voluntary village level youth organisations covering about 10 million youth between the age group of 15-35, NYKS stands as the largest non-political youth organisation in the Asia-Pacific region. Known as one of the oldest district branches of the country, the undivided NYK-Koraput was established in the 1973. Now, as the old district was fragmented to four i.e., Koraput, Raygada, Malkangiri and Nawarangpur, NYK-Koraput has its separate office in the district headquarter to operate with the strength of around ten thousand young people enrolled in the 265 village level Youth Organisations affiliated to NYKS, in a more confined and focused area having two sub-divisions, fourteen Blocks, around two thousand villages under 220 Gram Panchayats, covering a population of about fourteen lakhs, out of which half of the population are youth between the age group of 15-35.

Objectives and Methodology

The study was conducted with the broad objective to learn and assess the various programmes and activities of Nehru Yuva Kendra, Koraput, related to youth development in the last five years i.e., between 2008-09 to 2012-13 and to understand how NYKS creates a space for youth development among the tribal youths of Koraput district in Odisha. The methodology for this study is descriptive in nature. The collection of data was made from both the primary and secondary sources. A survey method was followed with a structured questionnaire among 100 tribal youth respondents of various stakeholders such as the Youth beneficiaries of NYK programmes/activities, student and non-student tribal youths, National Youth Crop youth volunteers of NYK, Koraput, Self employed tribal youths and Tribal opinion leaders of the Koraput districts in Odisha. Also, indepth interviews were conducted among NYK officials as well as the district level government officials to understand about the tribal development initiatives and its status. The limitation of this study is time constraint and as a small study it may not be generalised.

Koraput NYK Programmes and Activities

In the last five years, there has been a range of programmes organised by NYK-Koraput with the objective of youth development in the district, out of which the majority of beneficiaries are from Scheduled Tribes and Scheduled Castes. Following Table 23.1 shows the quantitative data of youth beneficiaries of major NYK-programmes/activities for the period 2008-09 to 2012-13.

Table 23.1: Tribal Youth Participants/Beneficiaries of NYK Programmes/Activities

Broad Category of the Programme	*Type of Activity*	*No. of Programmes*	*No. of Total Beneficiaries*	*No. of Tribal Youth Beneficiaries*		
				Male	*Female*	*Total*
Skill-Development Training Programme for Youth	Long-term and short-training on trades like Tailoring and Knitting, Embroidery, DTP, Screen Printing, Beautician course, Mushroom Cultivation, TV Repairing, Electrical and Refrigeration, Motor-cycle repairing, etc.	50	1500	150	950	1100
Youth Leadership Training Programme	In-house training and orientation for the rural youth on various skills, knowledge and applicability of various development programmes and schemes available for the rural youth.	15	600	260	100	360
Awareness Generation Campaign	Rally, meetings, workshops, seminars to sensitise the youth about their role and contribution towards the development of society, addressing core social issues and problems in their respective areas.	20	2000	1250	250	1500
Sports and Culture	Organisation of drama, folk art, dance and music, various traditional rural sports, athletics, etc.	20	10000	6000	500	6500
Youth Club Development Programme	Under this banner, a range of activities are undertaken to empower the village level youth clubs with the prime objective of making them self-sustaining units.	80	4000	2000	800	2800

(Contd.)

(Contd. Table 7.3)

Broad Category of the Programme	*Type of Activity*	*No.of Programmes*	*No. of Total Beneficiaries*	*No. of Tribal Youth Beneficiaries*		
				Male	*Female*	*Total*
National Service Volunteers/ National Youth Corps Scheme	Young people under the age 25 are given the opportunity to serve the nation under this programme to develop their skill and expertise in the areas of leadership and youth development. Rs 2500 Honorarium is given on monthly basis to the volunteers, deployed for one year in their concerned blocks.	5	150	60	30	90
Work Camps	Community assets were created by the youth through dignity of labour and volunteerism.	16	640	385	30	405
Promotion of National Integration and Communal Harmony	Various days/weeks and occasions like National Integration Camps, Youth Club Exchange Programmes were observed/organised to instill the sense of patriotism and nation building amongst the youth.	2	400	40	25	65
Incentive and Awards to Individuals and Youth Clubs	Outstanding Youth Clubs/Individuals are awarded at district level with cash incentive of Rs 10000 @ one each year	5				3

Source: Annual Progress Report, NYK–Koraput (2008-09 to 2012-13).

Evidence from the Ground

It was clearly visible from the study that the majority of the tribal youth (52 per cent) wants to contribute voluntarily towards the development of the society and stated their willingness to participate in NYK programmes and activities. Although female youth (18 per cent) is a bit shy to come to the forefront in comparison to their male (75 per cent) counterparts, the overall scenario throws a positive signal towards the NYK programmes in the district towards the youth development. Most of the government programmes are made on top-down approach, even though the need assessment survey is done on paper only. While asking whether the need and choices of the tribal youth is addressed while planning the NYK Programmes and activities, the response could reiterate the old trend i.e. the youth were unclear or confused. Only 40 per cent of the youth say that the needs like skill upgradation training and awareness on different development programmes and schemes are addressed in NYK programmes. But the tribal youth needs like income generation, employment, and entrepreneurship is still neglected in NYK Planning of programmes/activities.

Moreover, it is quite encouraging to learn that the majority of the youth (60 per cent) agreed that their lives have been improved after participating in a NYK programme. Asking the areas of improvement most of the respondents pointed out on their skill development such as communication skills, vocational skills and knowledge about government programmes and schemes have been improved through NYK programmes and activities to a considerable extent. Another remarkable improvement is visible in case of male youth (85 per cent) to improve the feeling of national integration and communal harmony through NYK programmes/activities. Responding to the question whether NYK is the right organisation to address various core social issues that affects the tribal the youth has stated a very confirmative view (65 per cent). Further, the youth (90 per cent) including both male (95 per cent) and female (83 per cent) gave an overwhelming response to skill development programmes of NYKS as it offers the scopes and avenues of employment, self-employment and income generation. 70 per cent of the youth voted for leadership and personality development training as the second most effective programme as it ensures employability among them. Other programmes like work camp, sports and cultural programmes and youth club development programmes were also highly appreciated by the tribal youth.

Through in-depth interviews with NYK and district level government officials, it is understood that set of programmes is very less in a district unit like NYK-Koraput having 14 Blocks and around 200 GPs. Even the programmes do not reach to the youth clubs who are affiliated under NYK-Koraput. The officials like District Youth Coordinator, Accountant and paid NYC Volunteers of the district too agreed upon with the statement that budget is a big concern. Moreover, it reveals that the lack of adequate staff in NYK creates a lot of constraints to organise programmes and focusses on youth development in the district. It was understandable that all officials are posted at NYK-Koraput on additional charges to undertake duties at the rate of two days only in a week. The youth too complained that it is very difficult to approach the NYK Officials due to their non-availability in the NYK branch office. Interestingly, this study indicates that the Annual Action Plan of the NYK-Koraput is not based on the need of tribal youth nor they are involved in framing it. The lack of proper coordination and linkage between the NYK-Koraput and other line departments/agencies working at district/block level is seen. It also shows that the programmes allotted by NYK-Koraput to the villages in the remote vicinity and naxal affected are insufficient to cater the needs of the tribal youth. It is revealed from the study that the attendance of the male youth in NYK programmes has been declining due to factors like migration, involvement of the youth in naxal conflict and violence, etc., however, female youth shows a positive approach towards the development programmes.

Specific Suggestions

The role and contribution of NYK-Koraput towards the tribal youth development is quite significant as the organisations stands for the youth of Koraput as a better alternative choice to the youth development. Keeping the findings of the study in the eye, the following suggestions are made may be useful for the better functioning of Nehru Yuva Kendra Sangathan such as:

- The content and approach of the NYK programmes needs to be prepared keeping in view the local needs and aspiration of the youth.
- The set of programmes is to be increased to at least cover all the 14 blocks of Koraput district with more focus on the south and west part as the border areas are much closer to the red corridor and prone to conflict and violence where the youth segment is largely drawn. Programmes like Skill upgradation training and capacity building should be organised in ample manner so that more and more tribal youth can be self-dependent.
- The NYKS should come out with Policy specific and programme specific plans for the tribal youth development.
- Adequate man-power should be given to NYK-Koraput to operate the branch in proper manner with accessibility for the youth with necessary arrangements.
- A coordination and Convergence Plan needs to be prepared by NYK and be approved by the District Committee under the approval of the Collector with responsibility-mapping and devolution. Financial institutions like Banks and DIC needs to be officially sensitised to lend money to micro-level tribal young entrepreneurs.
- The initiatives to be made for proper Monitoring and Evaluation of NYKS programmes and activities and the transparency and accountability should be ensured at all levels.

• The success stories of NYK programmes and activities in the district should be highlighted with timely its publicity through various mediums of media for mass awareness about NYKS works.

Conclusion

It was clearly established from the study that NYKS has been working with its mandate of youth development to a large extent in Koraput. Although there so many bottlenecks, the study finds NYKS has a very good relationship of the youth, particularly tribal youth of the district. The tribal youth, with their strong physique, innocence and rich cultural heritage are nothing less than human treasure for the whole nation that needs to be properly ornamented with much care and emphasis. Nehru Yuva Kendra Sangathan, being the largest youth organisation of the country should be empowered with more qualified personnel and financial strength so that it can enlarge its reach to the remote areas. However, a more comprehensive and unified approach is required to be applied in the planning, implementation, monitoring and evaluation of NYK programmes and activities. It is needless to say that organisations like NYKS should not just only be regarded as mere schemes of the Government but to be viewed as one of the most viable alternative model to counter naxal movements in the red corridor of India harnessing the youth in the manifold of the society.

References

Books and Journals

American Youth Policy Forum (AYPF). 1995. "*Contract with America's Youth: towards a National Youth Development Agenda.*" Washington, D.C.: AYPF.

Networks for Youth Development (NYD). 1998a. "*The Handbook of Positive Youth Outcomes*", New York: NYD.

Nixon, R. 1997. "*What is positive youth development?*" Child Welfare 76:571–575.

Roman Mullahey, Yve Susskind, and Barry Checkoway (1999) *Youth Participation in Community Planning*, America Planning Association, Chicago.

Vered Amit-Talai and Helena Wuff, (1995) eds. *Youth Culture: A Cross-Cultural Perspective,* Routledge, London.

World Sources Online. 1999. "*Challenges facing youth development: National and Global Perspectives*". Independent, November 19, EB 19991119460000029 10:18.

Government Reports

Draft National Youth Policy, 2012

NYKS-Odisha Zone, Annual Progress Report (2008-09 to 2012-13)

World Youth Report, 2006.

Internet Sources

http://go.worldbank.org/F6GNXM7JU0 accessed on 10th July, 2013.

http://www.un.org/esa/socdev/unyin/qanda.htm accessed on 10th July, 2013.

www. odisha.nic.in accessed on 11th July, 2013.

www.nyks.org. accessed on 12th July, 2013.

24

Political Economy of Tribal Development in Madhya Pradesh: The Case of Korku Tribe

Janmejaya Mishra

The Korku tribe

Korku is a scheduled tribe community predominantly found in East Nimar (presently Khandwa and Burhanpur districts), Betul district of Madhya Pradesh and adjoining areas in Melghat region of Amravati district in Maharashtra. The Korkus are found in highest concentration in the highland of Central India, especially in the regions surrounding the Mahadeo hill, a centrally situated peak in the Satpura mountains (Fuchs 1988). The Korkus are a branch of the great Munda tribes and are placed in the vicinity of the great tribe – the Gonds (Deogaonkar et al 1990). Korkus have derived their name from the combination of the word *'koru'* meaning man and *'ku'* which makes it plural meaning tribal men (Russell et al 1916). Korkus are believed to be a hunting gathering community dwelling in the forests of Satpura ranges on either sides of the Tapti river. They were dependent on forest-based resources and practising shifting cultivation on large scale for their livelihoods in earlier times. Eventually, they started settled agriculture. Their late introduction to settled agriculture made them less skilful in comparison to their neighbouring tribesmen of Bhil and Barela tribal communities. Besides deforestation, degradation of land and water resources was also rampant in the area. Massive soil erosion made the land unsuitable for cultivation. Further, scanty and erratic rainfall made the situation more worsen leading many water bodies to dry off. As a result of the direct consequences of degradation of land and water resources, agriculture productivity has been declined substantially over the years thus affecting livelihoods of the Korku tribe and other peasant communities. Chronic poverty, food insecurity, acute under/malnutrition and distress seasonal labour migration are the primary issues that the Korku tribe faces today.

Poverty among the Korkus

The cash flow analysis of Korku tribal households in the Khalwa block reveals many surprising features. Agriculture and manual labour work are the only sources of income for most of the households. Based on household survey data of 2008-09, average annual income of a household is estimated to be Rs 20460 (approx.), wherein the contribution of income from agriculture and labour work is estimated to be nearly Rs 14000 (70 per cent) and Rs 6300 (30 per cent) respectively. Likewise, average annual expenditure of a household is estimated to be Rs 26634 (approx). Thus, there is a net deficit of Rs 6174 per household per annum. To meet this deficit, the tribal families borrow money from informal sources i.e., local money lenders and traders at a very high rate of interest. To pay off the debt and for meeting other household expenditure, a major portion of the workforce migrates to better off areas in neighbouring state of Maharashtra and parts of Madhya Pradesh during lean seasons. Mostly engaged in agricultural labour works, they earn their livelihoods. Saving of money is found very little among the Korku families. On the other hand, expenses on social obligations like marriages, rituals and festivals are very high. Formal financial institutions like banks and credit cooperatives do not easily extend credit to them, leaving these families to depend on the mercy of money lenders and traders to fulfil their credit needs.

Average landholding size of a Korku household is 2.5 to 3 acres. Most of the farmers fall under the marginal/small holder category. Nearly, 85 per cent of the households have land and about 15 per cent are landless. Only, 12 per cent of the land owning households has access to irrigation sources mainly dug wells. Soybean, cotton, sorghum and pigeon pea are the major crops cultivated during kharif season. Wheat and gram are the major rabi crops cultivated only by those farmers who have access to irrigation. The average annual income of the households ranges from Rs 15,000 to Rs 25,000.

Debt, Exploitation and Migration

Significant changes have taken place in the cropping patterns in recent years. Cultivation of cash crops has been widely adopted by the tribal farmers in the region. Korku tribal farmers prefer to cultivate cash crops—soybean and cotton in particular on large scale basis and give less preference for cultivation of food crops such as sorghum, maize, pigeon pea and minor millets. The tribal farmers in the region have been historically exploited by local money lenders and traders. They depend on the private traders and local money lenders—mostly the upper castes for purchasing agriculture inputs such as seeds, fertilizers and pesticides required for the cultivation. However, due to lack of cash during agriculture season, the tribal farmers are compelled to take credits from the money lenders and purchase inputs from them who are also the traders running input supply shops in the name of krisi seva kendras in the local markets. The inputs purchased on credit from the traders and money lenders are very low in quality for which they are charged high price and exorbitant rate of interest. Further, most of the tribal farmers are also get into informal agreements with the traders that they would sell the agriculture produces to them during post-harvest season. As an obligation to repay the credit, the tribal farmers are further compelled to sell their agriculture produces to these traders at much lower price than the prevailing market price from whom they have taken credit during monsoon season. Thus, their continued dependency on the traders and money lenders make them prone to harsh economic exploitations and thus, the Korku tribal farmers are trapped in cyclic indebtedness year after year. Consequently, low crop productivity and negative income from rainfed agriculture and cumbersome debt force them to resort on distress seasonal labour migration. A significant portion of the Korku tribal population migrates to relatively better off areas like Akola, Jalgoan, Akot, Bhusawal, Nasik and Nagpur in neighbouring Maharashtra state and Harda, Hosangabad, Pithampur and Indore in Madhya Pradesh during off-seasons along with their entire family members. The family members of most of the rainfed farmers migrate out for 5-6 months in a year. Among the landless households, duration of migration ranges from 6-9 months. Mainly engaged in agriculture wage labour work in private farms, labour work in cotton, dal mills and construction sites they survive with bare minimum needs.

Mosse *et. al.*, also reported similar features of seasonal labour migration among the adivasis in the western Madhya Pradesh and mentioned that seasonal labour migration has become an irreversible part of the livelihoods of rural adivasi communities in western India. Labour migration is not just a means to cope with below subsistence agriculture and debt have become the only means by which valued agrarian lifestyles can be reproduced. For a few, migration is a route of upward social and economic mobility; but for the vast majority migration not only perpetuates debt and dependence, but exposes the poorest to extreme hardship and cruel exploitation (Mosse *et. al.*, 2005).

Food Insecurity

Sorghum (jowar) is the major staple food of the Korku tribal community. It meets consumption needs and is grown in nearly 20 per cent of the total area. Few farmers grow jowar in large farm lands which is confined to them only. It was also found jowar grows well in the region and gives good yield. However, the amount of jowar grown by the farmers is not enough to meet their consumption needs. Therefore, they rely on the market for purchasing jowar to meet their needs. Pigeon pea (tuar) is another important food crop grown by the tribal farmers which is grown in 14 per cent of land of the study area. It is the only food crop which gives cash income as well as kept for consumption. Tuar is cultivated with cotton as a mixed crop. The yield is around 300 to 500 kg per acre. However, it is prone to frequent pest attacks. The tribal farmers keep some amount of tuar for consumption and sell out the rest in the local markets. Cultivation of wheat is very limited to few farmers. It is cultivated only by irrigated farmers as a rabi crop. Only 10-15 per cent of the total land is under wheat cultivation. The yield from one acre of wheat is around 738 kg. Discussions with the farmers revealed that the cultivation of wheat is very recent in the region. Farmers who have access to irrigation mainly through dug wells are the ones who cultivate wheat. It was also found that those families which are cultivating wheat have shifted their food habit from jowar to wheat. Nearly, 55 per cent of the total produce is sold in the market and the rest is kept for consumption. Those families growing wheat do not face any problem of food scarcity. Seasonality is a major factor which affects the availability of food grains of the households. Discussions with the community members revealed that food grain availability gradually decreases during the period of monsoon (July-August). The stored food grains get finished and farmers have to depend on market for their consumption needs. Forty per cent of the respondents mentioned that they faced problem of food shortage during the month of monsoon. Besides these food crops, traditional minor millets like Kodo, Kutki and Sawariya are also grown in the region. These crops serve as an important source of nutrition especially for the kids and lactating women. However, the area under cultivation the minor millets have drastically decreased over the years. The tribal farmers do not prefer to grow these crops any more.

The functioning of Public Distribution System (PDS) in the study villages was found to be very poor. It was found that families having good landholding have BPL cards whereas those who deserve it most are excluded. Thirty Eight per cent of the ration card holders are BPL and the rest belong to the APL category. Nearly, 18 per cent of the households which indeed deserve ration cards do not have. Black marketing of wheat, sugar and kerosene by PDS dealers came out during discussions with the villagers. Wheat and kerosene are supplied regularly to the households while sugar, rice, salt and pulses are not. Dependency on PDS for food grain was high among the poorest families. Nearly, 32 per cent of the families are completely depended on the PDS for consumption of wheat. Further, though the Integrated Child Development Services (ICDS) is running in most of the villages, only 15 per cent of the parents prefer to send their children to the anganwadi centres. A large majority, 85 per cent of the parents do not send their children to these centres. The major reasons for not enrolling the children in the anganwadi centres are frequent migration by parents to different places in search of labour works, location of anganwadi centres from their home and poor quality of food served at the centres.

Acute under/malnutrition

Malnutrition among the children and under-nutrition among the adult members mostly women are very high in the area. Most of the children are born with underweight. Malnutrition related disease like Kwashiorkor is seen in among the children in all the villages. Nearly, 60 per cent of the children have reddish colour hair which is due to protein deficiency. Also, 15 per cent of the children suffer from skin disease which is due to the prevailing unhygienic conditions. Night blindness caused due to deficiency of vitamin A is found among 15 per cent of the children. Nearly, 10 per cent of children suffer from polio and rickets and Kwashiorkor taken together. Further, diseases like measles and diarrhea are found to be common to most of the children. Nearly, 70 per cent of the women have expressed conditions matching to anaemia. It is not only found among women but also among the adolescent girls. Anaemia is associated with deficiency of Iron in blood. Moreover, exposure to smoke while cooking also is a known risk factor of Anaemia. About, 65 per cent of the respondents perceived that anaemia is the most prevalent disease among adolescent girls. Other common ailments are fever, vomiting and skin disease. These findings were also validated through an interview with the health workers.

Nearly, 60 per cent of the women reported that they prefer to consult traditional birth attendants rather going for institutional deliveries. The remaining 40 per cent have opted for hospitals/private doctors. It was found that the incidence of infant mortality is very high primarily owing to dependency on unqualified traditional birth attendants. Further, 50 per cent of the tribal women responded that they got married at the age between 12 to 14 years, 30 per cent of women getting married at the age of 14-16 years and 20 per cent get married at the age of 16-20 years of age. In 85 per cent of pregnancy cases, the gap between two consecutive deliveries is only one year. Because of early marriages and low gap between subsequent deliveries, the growth of both children and mothers is severely affected.

AKRSP(I)'s Intervention

Aga Khan Rural Support Programme (India) – which was working in Gujarat nearly for 19 years decided to extend its work of rural development in the Nimar region of Madhya Pradesh. It started developmental interventions in the remote and poor districts of Khandwa, Burhanpur, Khargone and Barwani in south-western Madhya Pradesh after a systematic appraisal of the area in 2004-05. At present, it is working with more than 16,000 households of Korku, Bhil, Bhilala, Barela and Gond tribal communities over 120 villages in Khalwa and Pandhana blocks of Khandwa, Khaknar block of Burhanpur, Zirniya block of Khargone and Niwali block of Barwani districts in order to sustain their livelihoods through promotion of community-based institutions which are being capacitated to manage natural resources and address the core issues of poverty through improved agriculture productivity and with locally suitable off-farm activities to improving the economic conditions of poorest tribal households. The key areas of interventions are watershed development, participatory irrigation management, saving and credit services through self help groups, alternate livelihood promotion through animal husbandry, skill development and placements of rural youth.

This author directly worked in the region for three and half a years in the capacity of monitoring and evaluation specialist with AKRSP(I) being based at its regional office in Khandwa from July 2008 to December 2011. Afterwards, he was moved to its central office at Ahmedabad, Gujarat in January 2012, from where he continues to work till date.

AKRSP (I) started its interventions in Khalwa block of Khandwa district in July 2006. Participatory irrigation management, watershed development, Self Help Groups promotion and providing agriculture extension services including agriculture input supply were the major areas of its intervention in Khalwa block. As of now, more than 3000 households of Korku tribal communities in 30 villages of the block have been directly benefitted through these interventions. Broadly speaking, these 30 villages have been covered in three phases. From 2006 to 2009, 17 villages were covered under the European Commission (EC) funded SCALE project. Under this project, AKRSP (I) major thrust was reviving the old irrigation tanks and canals in eight villages which were build by govt's water resources department in 1980s. Remaining villages were covered through watershed development intervention. However, promotion of self help groups (SHGs) and providing agriculture extension services including agriculture input supply were the activities done across the 17 villages.

In the second phase, twelve villages including two old villages were selected for the Integrated Micro-plan Project (IMP) in 2010. The IMP was a newly conceived project by the State MGNREGA Council of the Govt of Madhya Pradesh under MGNREGS. The State MGNREGA Council, GoMP selected AKRSP(I) as its implementing partner for the newly launched IMP project in Khalwa block of Khandwa district and Khaknar block of Burhanpur district. It must be noted that concentration of the Korku tribe is very high in both the blocks of these two districts. AKRSP(I) followed necessary guidelines provided by the State MGNREGA Council and Jila Panchayats of respective districts to implement the projects. While implementation of the IMP project in Khaknar block of Burhanpur district went on smoothly, however, it was not to be so in Khalwa block of Khandwa district. The underlying reasons for this are discussed in detail in the following section.

Politics of Tribal Development in Khalwa Block

AKRSP(I) strictly adhered to the norms and necessary guidelines prescribed by the State MGNREGA Council and Jila Panchayat, Khandwa to implement the IMP project in Khalwa block. As the first step, it started following the set of activities for preparation of detailed project report (DPR) of the project villages. Round of meetings, discussions, PRAs, transact walks and job card verifications were held in the villages by the mid-2011. Thus, DPRs were prepared and approved by the Gram Sabhas held in the villages. All the DPRs approved by Gram Sabhas of respective villages were submitted to Jila Panchayat, Khandwa by the mid-2011. With this all the official formalities were completed by AKRSP(I) for sanctioning of the project and its subsequent implementation at village level and the villagers were promised of the project. However, AKRSP(I) has made several queries to concerned officials at Jila Panchayat, Khandwa for updates on sanctioning of the project since then. But, no clear responses were given to it. The concerned officials have just said that it will take time to move the files for sanctioning of the project which they are trying. Meanwhile, the IMP project in Khaknar block of Burhanpur district for which AKRSP(I) was also the implementing partner was sanctioned and its implementation was in full swing in 14 villages. However, in Khalwa, expectation of villagers of the 12 IMP project villages was on raise and whenever any field staff of AKRSP(I) was visiting the villages, they were increasingly finding it difficult to talk on the status of the project. Instead of waiting for sanctioning of the IMP project, AKRSP(I) started mobilising resources from other sources and implemented agriculture related intervention alongside promotion of self help groups (SHGs) in these villages. On the other hand, it continued to seek updates on sanctioning of the project to concerned authorities at Jila Panchayat, Khandwa. It was in early 2012, the Jila Panchayat officials informed that they have forwarded the files to concerned officials at Bhopal and now nothing is in their hands and the fate of the project lies with the higher authorities at Bhopal. During the same time, another project submitted to National Bank for Agriculture and Rural Development (NABARD) for horticulture promotion in Khalwa and Pandhana blocks of Khandwa district got sanctioned giving much relief to the organisation. By March 2012, the concerned authorities at Bhopal informed AKRSP(I) that now it can talk to the secretariat of the dept. of rural development on status of the project. Soon, AKRSP(I) made contacts with the secretariat of the dept. of rural development. To its surprise, concerned officials at the secretariat informed that now AKRSP(I) should forget about sanctioning of the project because, the minister of tribal development who hails from the same Khalwa region does not want this project to be sanctioned at all and he wants to meet senior officials of AKRSP(I) at his residence in Khandwa. As a follow up to this, two senior level officials of AKRSP(I) met the minister of tribal development at his residence in Khandwa. During the meeting, the minister was very calm and appreciated the organisation's interventions among the Korku tribe in Khalwa block and stated that he has nothing personal against the organisation's working in Khalwa block; that is also his constituency of state legislative assembly which he is holding for past 15 years. He further suggested that AKRSP(I) should now forget the IMP project in Khalwa and if wants can have similar projects elsewhere but not in Khalwa for which the minister can help whatever possible. The two senior staff went to meet the minister returned back in empty hands. It is now understood that why the sanctioning of the project was taking so much time which was almost 1.5 years in this case. After few days of this meeting, the district collector called on the two senior level staff of AKRSP(I) along with the district development manager (DDM) of NABARD, Khandwa to have discussion on the recent sanctioning of the horticulture project by NABARD in Khandwa district. Unlike the minister in the previous meeting, he was rude in his behaviour and asked them who gave permission to AKRSP(I) and the DDM to sanction the horticulture project in Khalwa and Pandhana blocks which was of worth Rs. 7.5 crore and told them categorically that such a situation should not be repeated in future without the permission of the district collector. Later on, it was learnt that he was told by the minister to do so. At present, AKRSP(I) mobilises funding from private sources and is implanting watershed based intervention in Khalwa block.

The minister of tribal development in Madhya Pradesh belongs to Khalwa block. He is being elected to the state assembly consecutively since past 15 years. He himself belongs to the scheduled tribe community of the Gonds. His forefathers were rulers of the erstwhile princely state which was covering Khalwa block before the independence. However, now he rules the region being a democratically elected representative of the people. He has a very good support of the masses at village level and enjoys unconditional support of the people especially the Korkus and other castes in Khalwa block. He offers occasional feasts to the community members and party workers each year and captures the votes of masses by offering populist measures before elections. He has also a stronghold among the other castes especially the Yadavs who are money lenders and traders in the region from whom the Korkus take credits and agriculture inputs during monsoon season at a very high rate of interest and sell their produces at low price and sometime sell in advance. The minister knows very well that if organisations like AKRSP(I) and others are allowed in the region, it would pose threats to his legacy of ruling the region by developing and empowering the Korku tribal community in long run. Hence, they get eliminated on the way in such manner.

Concluding Remarks

Khalwa block in East Nimar – Khandwa district of Madhya Pradesh has been in contemporary debate over development not only in the state but also in national level for many reasons and there is no irony over the fact that Khalwa has its place in the list of most backward blocks in the country. Wide spread poverty, food insecurity, malnutrition, mass scale exploitations by money lenders, traders and political leaders and gross violation of human rights in the region are the main woes to the marginalised Korku tribe of recent times. This paper only provides a firsthand glimpse of these situations. It seems that the future of the Korku tribe lies in their own hands. The sooner they understand the realities the better it is for them, which cannot happen on its own. Therefore, the role of organisations like AKRSP(I) should be making the community aware and empowering them socio-economically. Only then can there be an end to these grim situations prevailing in the region at present.

References

Deogaonkar, S G and S S Deogaonkar (1990): *The Korku Tribals.* Concept Publishing Company: New Delhi.

Fuchs, Stephen (1988): *The Korkus of the Vindhya Hills*. Inter-India Publications: New Delhi.

Mishra, Janmejaya and Raj Kumar Gupta (2010): *"Food Insecurity among the Tribals of Madhya Pradesh: Causes and Consequences"*, paper presented at Fifth Annual International Conference on Public Policy and Management held at Indian Institute of Management (IIM), Bangalore on 9th August, 2010.

Mosse, David, Sanjeev Gupta and Vidya Shah (2005): 'On the Margins in the City: Adivasi Seasonal Labour Migration in Western India' in *Economic and Political Weekly*, July 9th, pp. 3025-38.

Russel, R V and Hiralal (1916): *Tribes and Castes of the Central Provinces of India,* Vol. III, London.

Sahoo, Bijaya Laxmi (2009): *"Mapping the Nutritional Status of Tribal Communities in Khandwa and Burhanpur Districts of Madhya Pradesh"*, AKRSP(I): Khandwa.

Acknowledgements

K M Sinha, Ashok Minz, Pradeep Tiwari, Kamal Bhalray, R K Mahajan, Naveen Patidar, Devram Yadav, Gurprit Bhatiya, Chandrarekha Malviya, Sanjiv Tiwari, Sunayana Ingle, Kamlesh Panchole, Raj Kumar Gupta, Kiran Patel, Bijay Laxmi Sahoo, Bisram Patil and Ramkishan Goutam.

25

Land Alienation of Tribals in Andhra Pradesh

Justin Jos

Introduction

Land has always been a prized possession of indigenous people from time immemorial. They worship it, cultivate it, maintain it and also safeguard it but howsoever the post-colonial India has failed to adequately address the issues pertaining to the land belonging to the tribals. This has not only led to widespread alienation of acreage but has also resulted into massive displacement of indigenous people from their original inhabitation to unchartered territories resulting in disruption of their natural way of life. State intervention through constitutional means has also not afforded sufficient remedies to tribals along with unsatisfactory rehabilitation schemes and methods. Other socio-economic factors such as poverty, caste-issues, illiteracy and indebtedness etc., have been belligerent towards achieving equal status for tribals in backward regions. As a consequence of this, the overall development of a certain segment of the society in terms of social, economic, political and upward growth has been militated against. Any exclusion of indigenous people from the societal or political framework amounts to deprivation of "development"of the section as a whole and subsequent denial of equal rights of opportunity towards all aspects of human activity. The problems subsisting in tribal areas has been of utmost grievance and in the political circles however policy-makers, anthropologists and administration have deliberated that land alienation is one of the core problems prevalent in this strata of society.

The tribals present in the State of Andhra Pradesh have suffered extreme economic and collective exclusion on account of absence of social, political and fiscal mobility across the community. The Scheduled Castes and other

Backward Castes who witnessed certain degrees of progress because of protective discrimination policies of the government, the Scheduled Tribes remain abysmally backward and socially excluded, still living in harsh environs.[1] Land has been one of the sources to secure their unstable livelihood in terms of legal entitlements and property but an onslaught by governmental agencies along with other factors has pushed the indigenous into the pit of poverty and deep economic vulnerability. The present paper "Land Alienation of Tribals in Andhra Pradesh" will delineate the fundamental causes of pervasive alienation of land from tribals in Andhra Pradesh and ensuing displacement of tribals under the garb of development by State authorities. The legal framework and constitutional protections guaranteed will be discussed and a viable solution as suggestions will be incorporated towards the end of the paper.

Understanding the Theme

To fully understand the problems with respect to land alienation of tribals in Andhra Pradesh we have to first evolve an analytical step by step approach. The socio-cultural aspects will be subsequently made clear on our better comprehension towards the concepts of alienation, outlining as to qualify as tribals and the geographical regions of the State involved in maximum land alienation. All these questions might seem of trivial importance at the first glance but it is to be mentioned that all the root causes of tribal underdevelopment vis-à-vis land alienation emanate out of these vital areas.

Concept of Alienation

The concept of alienation is a problem which strikes discord with the existing socio-economic order of the tribal society and this concept is based on the central idea that land is the greatest asset belonging to the tribals without it their survival in the state of nature is not only difficult but excruciating. Alienation is inherent in exploitative relations of production and its nature varies with that of exploitation.[2] Therefore the inference drawn is that causes of alienation vary in different systems and the problems of land alienation may be different from another in a different state. Land has always been a major source of living for people from all walks of life in the pre-historic era however in the modern economy-oriented society the model of private property has resulted in huge tracts of natural land being acquired by few. This land holding pattern violates equality on all counts and has become a major source of exploitation through creation of fake paucity of land. As John Locke had stated "The measure of property nature has well set by the extent of men's labour and the conveniences of life: no man's labour could subdue, or appropriate all; nor could his enjoyment consume more than a small part; so that it was impossible for any man, this way, to entrench upon the right of another, or acquire to himself a property, to the prejudice of his neighbour, who would still have room for as good, and as large a possession (after the other had taken out his) as before it was appropriated."[3] Land inequalities has occasioned a grave structuralist problem depriving equal right to land to all especially tribals and power to procure lands in hands of few who are powered through monetary, political and muscular means. The indigenous people have been vulnerable victim of these influential agencies and as a consequence, alienation of their land which qualifies as their dwellings have been forcibly occupied or put into industrial use.

Alienation was defined by Hegel and was used by Marx to describe and criticise a social condition in which man far from being the active initiation of the social world seemed more a passive object of determinate external processes.[4] Alienation's manifestations also differ among societies based on slavery, serfdom and capitalism etc.[5] The process of land alienation has revealed itself mainly in large-scale migration of tribal communities from fertile plain areas to the neighbouring forests.[6] Developments of only a certain section of society has resulted the tribals to forcibly live in places unsuitable for comfortable living. Some examples of this kind of development can be extensive construction of railways and roadways, sale and purchase of fertile land, expansion of cities and towns on account of huge capital influx, indiscriminate land holding patterns etc., and as a consequence of this kind of development peasant struggles in various states has also been witnessed. Land alienation is not only caused due to the above said factors but certain sociological issues such as poverty, indebtedness, illiteracy also result in alienation of tribal land. The history of alienation of tribal land is a result of forced evacuation of tribals in the wake of industrial growth in the 17th and 18th century.[7] There has been declining land holdings and increasing landless labourers for the scheduled tribes in nearly all parts of the country. The Agricultural Census, 1980-81, 1985-86 and 1990-91 has clearly delineated that the large holdings of both SC's and ST's has been on a consistent downfall from 1980-81 to 1990-91 i.e., from 0.9 per cent to 0.6 per cent and 3.4 per cent to 2.1 per cent respectively and the condition is even worse off for those possessing marginal size holdings which have increased from 39.8 per cent to 43.4 per cent for ST's and 68.9 per cent to 72.2 per cent for the SC's.[8] The clear inference which can be drawn from this data is that the majority population of tribal areas possess marginal size holdings which has continually collapsed by the wake of this millennium and it is a bitter truth that this has also led to another deeper problem that the rate of ST agricultural labourers has also been on the rise than that of non ST's implying that the landlessness among them has increased. Apart from the above causes other reasons such as incessant acts of atrocities against the tribals, migration of non-tribal community in search of alternative lands in light of an artificial co-existence of industries in their original inhabitation has also been a major factor of land alienation.

Who are Tribals?

Article 1(1) (b) of the ILO Convention No. 107 defined 'indigenous' as: "members of tribal or semi-tribal populations in independent countries which are regarded as indigenous on account of their descent from the populations which inhabited the country, or a geographical region to which the country belongs, at the time of conquest or colonisation and which, irrespective of their legal status, live more in conformity with the social, economic and cultural institutions of that time than with the institutions of the nation to which they belong." Tribals have always been the first inhabitants of any modern civilisation and over the passage of time they have been neglected in the developmental process by the state as well as by the society. It is to be observed that India's population includes nearly one hundred million tribal populations.[9] These Adivasis are mostly found in North Eastern regions of India, Orissa, Madhya Pradesh, Chhattisgarh, Rajasthan, Gujarat, Maharashtra, Andhra Pradesh, Bihar, Jharkhand, West Bengal, Mizoram and parts of Andaman and Nicobar islands.[10] Tribe has been defined as a social group of a simple kind, the members of which speaks a common dialect, have a single government and act together for achieving common purposes such as warfare.[11] However, any concrete definition of tribals has not been laid down in the Constitution of India. The essential characteristics of these communities that are considered while making such enlistments are:[12]

1. Primitive Traits,
2. Geographical isolation,
3. Distinct culture,
4. Shy of contact with community at large, and
5. Economically backward.

Profiling the Tribal Community in Andhra Pradesh

The total population of Andhra Pradesh is 76210007 out of which the tribal population reaches up to 5024104 therefore per cent of STs in the State to Total State Population amounting up to 6.60 per cent.[13] Twelve tribes, namely, Bodo Gadaba, Gutob Gadaba, Bondo Poraja, Khond Poroja, Parangiperja, Chenchu, Dongaria Khonds, Kuttiya Khonds, Kolam, Kondareddis, Konda Savaras and Thoti have been recognised as Primitive Tribal Groups (PTGs).[14] These tribes are mostly found in adjoining tracts that have been designated as Scheduled Areas overseen by the Integrated Tribal Development Agencies (ITDAs). In conformity with the national Tribal Sub-Plan (TSP) strategy, Andhra Pradesh tribal population is divided into four categories: (i) those living in tribal concentration areas in the scheduled villages and adjoining areas, i.e., the TSP areas administered by ITDAs. (ii) Primitive Tribal Groups (PTGs), i.e., communities who live in near isolation in inaccessible habitats in and outside the Scheduled Areas who are at the pre-agricultural stage of the economy; (iii) those living in small pockets outside the scheduled areas, i.e., Modified Area Development Agency (MADA) areas and tribal clusters; and (iv) Dispersed Tribal Groups, i.e., those dispersed throughout the state.[15]

Table 25.1: List of Scheduled Tribes of Andhra Pradesh[16]

Sl. No.	Schedule Tribe
1.	Andh, Sadhu Andh
2.	Bagata
3.	Bhil
4.	Chenchu
5.	Gadabas, Bodo Gadaba, Gutob Gadabad, Kallayi Gadaba, Parangi Gadaba, Kathera Gadaba, Kapu Gadaba
6.	Gond, Naikpod, Rajgond, Koitur
7.	Goude (in the agency tracts)
8.	Hill Reddis
9.	Jatapus
10.	Kammara
11.	Kattunayakan
12.	Kolam, Kolawar
13.	Konda Doras, Kubi
14.	Konda Kapus
15.	Konda Reddis
16.	Kondhs, Kodi, Kodhu, Desaya Kondhs, Dongria Kondhs, Kuttiya Kondhs, Tikiria Kondhs, Yenity Kondhs, Kuvinga
17.	Kotia, Bentho Oriya, Bartika, Dulia, Holva, Sanrona, Sidhopaiko
18.	Koya, Doli Koya, Gutta Koya, Kammara Koya, Musara Koya, Oddi Koya, Pattidi Koya, Rajah, Rasha Koya, Lingadhari Koya (Ordinary), Kottu Koya, Bhine Koya, Raj Koya
19.	Kulia
20.	Malis (excluding Adilabad, Hyderabad, Karimnagar, Khammam, Mahabubnagar, Medak, Nalgonda, Nizamabad and Warangal districts)
21.	Manna Dhora
22.	Mukha Dhora, Nooka Dhora
23.	Nayaks (in the agency tracts)
24.	Pardhan
25.	Porja, Parangiperja
26.	Reddi Dhoras
27.	Rona, Rena
28.	Savaras, Kapu Savaras, Maliya Savaras, Khutto Savaras
29.	Sugalis, Lambadis, Banjara
30.	Thoti (in Adilabad, Hyderabad, Karimnagar, Khammam, Mahabubnagar, Medak, Nalgonda, Nizamabad and Warangal districts)
31.	Valmiki (in the Scheduled Areas of Visakhapatnam, Srikakulam, Vizianagaram, East Godavari and West Godavari districts)
32.	Yenadis, Chella Yenadi, Kappala Yenadi, Manchi Yenadi, Reddi Yenadi
33.	Yerukulas, Koracha, Dabba Yerukula, Kunchapuri Yerukula, Uppu Yerukula
34.	Nakkala, Kurvikaran
35.	Dhulia, Paiko, Putiya (in the districts of Visakhapatnam and Vizianagaram)
36.	Porja, Parangiperja

Table 25.2: Basic Information about Scheduled Tribes in the State[17]

Andhra Pradesh population (2001 Census)	762 lakh
ST population	50.24 lakh (6.59 per cent); Male - 25.48 lakh, Female - 24.76 lakh
ST population in tribal areas	30.47 lakh
ST population in plain areas	19.77 lakh
Tribal groups	35 tribal groups
Primitive Tribal Groups (PTGs)	8
Integrated Tribal Development Agencies (ITDA)	10 --- Seethampeta, Parvathipuram, Paderu, R.C.Varam, K.R.Puram, Bhadrachalam, Eturunagaram, Utnoor, Srisailam and Nellore
ITDA area	31, 485, 34sq.kms.
Modified Area Development Approach (MADA) pockets	41
Clusters	17
Scheduled villages	5938
Non-scheduled villages	809
No. of habitations in ITDA areas	11855
Total No. of SHGs in tribal areas	495646
Total No. of ST members enrolled	1046371

Chronological List of Tribal Laws Implemented in Andhra Pradesh.[18]

1. Ganjam and Vizagapatnam Act, 1939 (Act No. XXIV) of 1839.
2. Scheduled Districts Act 1874 (Act XIV of 1874).
3. Agency Tracts Interest and Land Transfer Act, 1917.
4. The Andhra Pradesh Agency Rules, 1924.
5. Government of India Act, 1935 – Excluded and Partially Excluded Areas.
6. Andhra Pradesh (Andhra Scheduled Areas) Village Courts Regulation, 1940.
7. Andhra Pradesh (Andhra Scheduled Areas) (Estates Land Repealing) Regulation, 1943.
8. The Andhra Pradesh Scheduled Areas Land Transfer Regulation, 1959.
9. AP Scheduled area Land Transfer Regulation (APSALT) Rules.
10. Andhra Pradesh (Andhra Scheduled Areas) Estates (Abolition and Conversion into Ryotwari) Regulation, 1951.
11. Andhra Pradesh Mahals (Abolition and Conversation into Ryotwari) Regulation, 1969.
12. Andhra Pradesh Schedule Areas Ryotwari Settlement Regulation, 1969.
13. Andhra Pradesh Scheduled Area Land Transfer (Amendment) Regulation, 1970.
14. Madras Scheduled Areas Estates (Abolition and Conversion into Ryotwari) Andhra Pradesh Amendment Regulation, 1960.

15. The Andhra Pradesh Scheduled Areas Laws (Extension and Amendment) Regulation, 1963.

16. Nugur and Bhadrachalam Scheduled Areas (Validation of Transfer to Khammam District) Regulation, 1963.

17. Andhra Pradesh (Scheduled Areas Ryotwari Settlement) Regulation, 1970.

18. Andhra Pradesh Scheduled Area Land Transfer (Amendment) Regulation, 1971.

19. Money lending regulation for the relief of the tribals from indebtedness:
    (a) Andhra Pradesh (Scheduled Area) Money Lender Regulation, 1960
    (b) Andhra Pradesh (Scheduled Area) Money Lender Rules
    (c) Andhra Pradesh (Scheduled Tribes) Debt Relief Regulation, 1960
    (d) Andhra Pradesh (Scheduled Tribes) Debt Relief Rules, 1960
    (e) Andhra Pradesh (Scheduled Tribes) Debt Relief Regulation, 1970

20. The Andhra (Telangana Tribal Areas) Regulation, 1359-F.

21. The Hyderabad Tribal Areas Regulation, (Regulation No. III of 1359F).

22. Notified Tribal Areas Rules, 1359-F.

What are Scheduled Areas?

To understand the problem of land alienation, we have to deal with the laws pertaining to administration of scheduled areas. The indigenous people of any community are found in a particular area and these along with adjoining contiguous areas form the basis of their natural habitat. These areas are termed as "scheduled areas" but howsoever, no rigid definition is found in the constitution.

During the pre-independence era, the British enacted several land laws which alienated the tribal people from their rightly owned lands. After independence, all these scheduled areas which were identified by the government were brought under the fifth schedule of the constitution of India and special laws as enunciated in the constitution remained in force in these areas. Part C of the Fifth Schedule of the Constitution, under Article 244 (1), defines Scheduled Areas as such areas as the President may by order declare to be Scheduled Areas. The President has a power to declare any area as scheduled areas through power granted to it under this schedule vide a Presidential Order subject to clauses (a), (b) and (c) of Article 244 (2). The rationale behind implementation of Article 244(1) and 244(2) is to enable the government to enact a separate set of laws with respect to these scheduled areas for better administration and governance.

The executive power of the Union can give instructions to the state for better administration of the areas which are defined as "Scheduled Areas", more over the governor shall submit a report to the president with reference to the administration of these areas and this is provided for in Part A Para 2 and Para 3 of the Fifth Schedule respectively. Establishment of a Tribes Advisory

Council has been provided for in Part B of the Fifth Schedule which is another significant feature for welfare and advancement of tribals. Paragraph five of the Fifth Schedule of the Constitution lays down the laws applicable to these Scheduled Areas. It is given that the governor can exempt these areas or may make regulations necessary for peace and good governance in scheduled areas. Paragraph six of the Fifth Schedule of the Constitution prescribes following route for scheduling, rescindment and alteration of Scheduled Areas.

The scheduled areas in Andhra Pradesh include Visakhapatnam, East Godavari, West Godavari, Adilabad, Srikakulam, Vizianagaram, Mahboobnagar, Prakasam (only some mandals are scheduled mandals).[19]

Tribal Land Alienation: Causes and Ramifications

Land has always been the major source of livelihood for tribals and the reasons for land alienation are many. Howsoever, this has resulted into lack of tribal development and social exclusion of this particular ethnic group. Land alienation in a predominantly agrarian economy characterised by highly skewed distribution of land and adverse land-man ratio aggravates the inequalities in terms of income and wealth.[20] Tribal lands are rich in hydrologic, mineral, oil, gas, forest, and other resources, and this easily makes them the most attractive sites to locate development projects of various kinds.[21] Thus, many development projects in India are located in areas that are densely inhabited by tribal people.[22] The development projects by the state in Andhra Pradesh reflect that massive industrialisation and privatisation has led to incursion of non-tribals into tribal territories. The economic advancement of the country is the argument forwarded by the governmental authorities which cannot be justified on any grounds. Due to poor economic conditions and illiteracy the tribes have not been able to understand the vicious circle thrown by their non-tribal exploiters.[23] This has resulted into tribals turning into landless labourers and long term impoverishment as a consequence. In a tribal economy land comprised the major source of income for the indigenous people. Any deprivation of tribals from their rightly owned land does not only hamper the inclusion of tribals into mainstream society but also alienates them from availing any further legal recourse as the authorities favour the government. In a number of areas new industrial and mining complexes, many major irrigation projects were located in the tribal areas resulting in the submergence of extensive lands belonging to the tribals.[24] This flawed idea of development amounts to a systematic violation of the land laws placed in the state by the state being an accomplice in such a crime. Various studies have pointed out that the lack of political and administrative will continues to be the cause for perpetuation of the problem of land alienation amongst the tribals as reflected in the reluctance to amend legal provisions and plug the existing loopholes and swift administrative action to identify alienated land, and restoring it to the tribals with delivery of possession.[25] Displacement takes place mainly on account of development projects, which include – large irrigation dams, hydro-electric projects, open-cast and underground coal mines, super-thermal power plants and mineral-based industrial units.[26] The trauma of resettlement is exacerbated for tribal people because of their close spiritual ties to their home-land and their apprehension that once they move, their way of life will be lost forever.[27] In large mining projects, tribals lose their land not only to the project authorities, but even to non-tribal outsiders who converge into these areas and corner both land and the new economic opportunities in commerce and petty industry.[28] The solution, as provided by the State, of such land alienation on account of displacement is inadequate compensation through rehabilitation processes. Often the tribals are cornered into barren lands rendering majority of tribal income deficient. Moreover, the impoverishment that tribal people encounter soon after displacement mainly arises from delayed payment of compensation and the exclusion from compensation calculations of the common property resources on which they largely subsist.[29]

Another major cause of land alienation particularly in areas of Srikakulam, Vishakhapatnam, and East and West Godavari districts is lending meager amounts of money to tribals with the ulterior motive of land grabbing. Usually the tribals are unable to re-pay the debt resulting in the landlessness.The rates of interests charged on such sums of money were exorbitant and ridiculous ranging between 25-50 per cent, and sometimes the interest charged on the sums advanced were a whopping 100 per cent.[30] The sahukars of landlords cultivate their lands through Benami transfers and whenever a question arises, the poor tribals are made to state that the lands are in their possession and they are only cultivating their lands.[31] Any form of legal recourse is also a distant dream because these land owners threaten them with dire consequences thereby illegally depriving them of their lands. The reasons for resorting to such money lenders can be narrowed down to inadequate institutional rural credit among the tribal population as one of the important reasons for this state of exploitation coupled with lack of education.[32] The literacy rate of the tribals in Andhra Pradesh is just eight per cent as against the state average of 30 per cent.[33] The condition of the tribals in the state is pathetic and they are being continuously exploited and neglected by the non-tribals and the government.[34] However, the legal measures to curb the activities of money-lenders and traders have failed to have much impact on the severity of the problem due to the ineffective enforcement machinery and lack of alternative sources of credit for meeting the tribals' consumption and productive needs.[35]

Apart from the above, there are various incidental reasons such as a non-tribal marrying a tribal woman and thereby procuring tribal land through such marital relations. The tribal women are kept as concubines or second wives and even there offsprings are treated as tribals furthering non-tribal intrusion into indigenous lands. This gives leeway to non-tribals to prevent legal hurdles and occupy more and more land subsequently. Land alienation through polygamy has been found in Visakhapatnam (Koyyuru Panchayat Area), East Godavari and West Godavari districts.[36]

In Srikakulam and Vizianagaram, tribal areas have preserved a bond of friendship called NESTAM and it has different names in different regions. The tribal groups enter into specific relations with each other by means of exchanging gifts. The aim of this bond is to provide for welfare of each other in times of hardship but the shrewd non-tribals have used this as a means of exploitation for procuring lands from tribals in the garb of affability thereby resulting in landlessness. Another means employed by non-tribal communities to occupy tribal land was to procure false scheduled tribe certificates.[37] Such cases included Plain Kapus being regarded as Konda Kapus, Plain Kammaras as Konda Kammaras, and Plain Reddys as Konda Reddys.[38] The problems of the densely populated plains and urban areas are potentially a much greater threat to the continuing control of the ruling class than those of the peripheral, politically less vocal tribal areas.[39] Therefore the most expedient course of action for any government - state or national - is not to use scarce resources developing the tribal peoples, but rather to exploit the tribal areas for timber, minerals and cheap labour and to invest the surplus created in the potentially explosive non-tribal plains and urban areas.[40]

Judicial Decision Supporting Tribal Rights

In *Samatha vs. State of Andhra Pradesh* the apex court held the mining activity in tribal areas can go on as long as it is undertaken by the government, or instrumentality of state or a cooperative society in favour of the tribals.[41,42] It was also stated that all lands leased by the government or its agencies to private mining companies apart from its instrumentalities in the scheduled areas are null and void. In addition it also held that transfer of land to the government or its instrumentalities is entrustment of public property as the aim of public corporations is in public interest and hence such transfers stand upheld. Transfer of land in Scheduled Area by way of lease to non-tribals, corporation aggregate, etc. stands prohibited to prevent their exploitation in any form.[43] Transfer of mining lease to non-tribals, company, corporation aggregate or partnership firm, etc. is unconstitutional, void and inoperative.[44] State instrumentalities were held to be under the exception and institutions such as APMDC were included in it.

Constitutional Safeguards for Tribals

The Indian constitution has afforded protection to tribals through implementation of both directive principles of state policies and fundamental rights. Tribals possess a unique and different set of culture which is typical to them but including them in the mainstream society cannot be overlooked by the government as it is an obligation under the constitution to promote welfare of all the citizens on an equal basis. For the betterment of these downtrodden societies the framers of the constitution had incorporated various provisions. Article 46 epitomising this policy calls upon the state (Central and State government) to promote with special care the educational and economic interests of Scheduled Castes and Scheduled Tribes and protect them from social injustice and all forms of exploitation.[45] A brief overview of the relevant provisions is made on account of in the following:

Administration: Article 244(1) the administration and control of all the scheduled areas are subject to the fifth schedule.

Tribal Development: Article 275(1) provides for Grant-in-Aid from the consolidated fund of India for a state to meet with the expenses involved in implementation of welfare activities for Schedule Tribes.

Political Safeguards: Reservation of seats for Scheduled Caste and Schedules Tribe communities has been provided for on the basis of population in the House of the People as per Article 330 and in the LegislativeAssemblies of the states as per Article 332 for a certain length of time in the hope that in course of that time its need would disappear.[46]

Employment: Article 16(4) of the constitution expressly empowers the state to promulgate "any provision for the reservation of appointments or posts in favour of any backward class of citizens (including STs) if not represented adequately in the services under the state".

Promotion of Education: Article 15(4) along with subsequent amendments empowers the state to make any special provision for the advancement of any socially and educationally backward classes including STs and also enables the state to reserve seats for them in educational institutions.[47]

Policy Regulations

It is already observed that the Andhra Pradesh government had passed many laws to regulate the administration of tribal lands. We will discuss a selected few legislations which deeply pervaded the rights of the tribals and this will be comprehended thoroughly only after we understand as to the rationale behind enforcing separate laws. It is evident in the contemporary society that the tribals have been excluded and lived in geographical isolation from the non-tribals. The tribals are proven to be culturally backward and that their social and other customs are different from the rest of India.[48] The common trait which is visible in every tribal group is that they are self-contained and homogenous; any intermingling from the outside world is virtually absent. Because of their extreme ostracisation from the non-tribals an inevitable gap has pervaded between the two which is visible. The conventional, and largely accepted, solution is to balance the dichotomy between assimilation of tribal peoples and their independent identity, and delineate the contours of a national policy that would allow them to preserve their way of life without compromising development.[49] The tribals have been a victim of incessant migration of non-tribals into their lands on account of expansion of cities and gestating industrial developmental activities. Apart, from this their ethnic identity is in grave danger owing to pervasion caused by the non-tribals into their daily affairs. Post-independence, the question asked was whether the tribals are competent enough to regulate their administrations on their own? The answer was in the negative on account of excessive disparity between the tribals and non-tribals in parameters of social justice, economic viability and political recourse. This made it imperative on the State to enforce laws which can be read along the lines of tribal improvement and understand their position.

Two Major Protective Regulations

The Agency Tracts Interest and Land Transfer Act, 1917

This was the first ever comprehensive protective legislation that was brought out to check and regulate the rates of interest and also the transfer of land in the Agency Tracts of Ganjam, Vishakhapatnam and Godavari districts.[50] It was enacted primarily to safeguard the interest of the hill tribes in the area over which it extended and to protect them from exploitation by non-tribals and moneylenders.[51] It permitted transfer of land only among tribals and lay down that the interest accrued over the debts borrowed by the tribals shall not exceed the principal amount.[52]

The Andhra Pradesh Scheduled Areas Land Transfer Regulation, 1959

It extends the provisions of the Agency Tracts Interest and Land Transfer Act, 1917. Land has been the major source of livelihood for the tribals taking advantage of ignorance of the latter however; many non-tribal immigrants in the Scheduled Areas have fraudulently alienated large areas of fertile land of tribals.[53] This Regulation was enacted to regulate the transfers of land in the Scheduled Areas in the Districts of East Godavari, West Godavari, Visakhapatnam, Srikakulam, Adilabad, Warangal, Khammam and Mehaboobnagar in Andhra Pradesh. According to Section 3(1) A of the Regulation, "any transfer of immovable property situated in the Agency Tracts by a person, whether or not such person is a member of Scheduled Tribe, shall be absolutely null and void, unless such transfer is made in favour of person, who is a member of ST or a society registered or deemed to be registered under the AP Cooperative Societies Act 1964 which is composed solely of members of Scheduled Tribes." The term "Transfer" as defined in sub-section G of Section two of Regulation 1959 means a Mortgage with or without possession, lease, sale, gift, exchange or any other dealing with immovable property, not being a testamentary disposition and includes a charge on such property or a contract relating to such property in respect of such; Mortgage lease, sale, gift exchange or other dealing. Further as per sub-section (4) of Section 3 of the A.P.S.A.L.T.R, the expression transfer includes a sale in execution of Decree and also a Transfer made by a member of a ST in favour of any other members of ST, Benami for the benefit of a person who is not a member of ST: but does not include a partition or a devolution by succession.[54] Hence even Benami transfers are prohibited under the Regulation. This legislation has prospective effect.

Other Landmark Legislations

(I) The Andhra Pradesh (Andhra Scheduled Areas) Estate (Abolition and Conversion into Ryotwari) Act 1948.

(II) The Andhra Pradesh Mahals (Abolition and Conversion into Ryotwari) Regulation, 1969.

(III) The Andhra Pradesh Mutta (Abolition and Conversion into Ryotwari) Regulation, 1969.

These are revolutionary laws which facilitated state proprietorship of private lands in the Scheduled Areas and made the path clear for tribal sovereignty. Prior to these enactments, private ownership largely regulated the day to day affairs of tribal lands. Mahals were private estates in certain parts of the present Khammam District. These mahals were leased out for cultivation to private estates thereby depriving right of ownership over their inherited land. In the Scheduled Areas of Visakhapatnam and East Godavari districts, the then rulers allowed "Muttarights" to individuals who rendered assistance for revenue duties. Since these were basically grants, the tribals did not have absolute rights over these properties. Through abolition of Estates, Mahals and Muttarights and their conversion into Ryotwari Pattas the issues were settled in favour of the tribals who tilled these lands.

Conclusions and Suggestions

Today the tribal is under severe pressure and their life is being seriously threatened by the massive in roads made into their territories, the rape of their lands by companies and the mining mafia, the decimation of their forests by the forest and land mafia.[55] Along with this is the fact that no real 'development' has been implemented and the last factor to complete their hopelessness and despair is the fact that they have never received any hearing or any form of redressed of their problems.[56] It is observed through the above academic discourse that tribal lands have been alienated to a great extent and this is on the rise because of various factors such as legal loopholes, non-retrospective land regulations, powerful outsiders and a continuing lack of political commitment to protecting tribal rights.[57] The non-tribals have invaded into the private sphere of tribals which has resulted in forced migration of tribals into unchartered territories. Oppression faced by the tribals because of massive corruption and political intervention has also acted as reinforcement into tribal land alienation. Divisive tactics such as establishing friendship and subsequent usurpation of land has resulted in the tribal landlessness. Land alienation due to displacement of tribals for various development projects, and encroachment/possession of tribals' lands by the non-tribals has rendered a considerable number of tribal families landless and this has further added to their poverty.[58]

In Andhra Pradesh, the tribal areas are used to attract private capital for exploiting mineral resources; the tribals are forced to pay a far higher price in the case of irrigation projects as the lion's share of expected benefits would accrue to non-tribals.[59] According to 2001 Census, the percentage of literate persons (those who can read and write with understanding), aged seven years and above, among ST population of Andhra Pradesh is 37 per cent, which is lower than 60.5 per cent reported for state population as a whole. This clearly points to the fact that the tribal population in the state is unaware of its legal rights and therefore the existence of safeguards in the constitution and state laws do not yield any positive results. Hence, there is an imminent need to provide for legal literacy within the tribal populations which might reduce the rampant land alienation. The illusion of development in the garb of land usurpation is violative of fundamental rights of the tribal who are equal citizens in the eyes of law. Development should positively benefit the tribals and this can be achieved only when tribals are rehabilitated in consonance with sociological factors concurrent to their culture. Such dubious development plans by government are to be detested by the state authorities and only after greater consideration of the harmless indigenous people any project is to be approved.

Active participation by the tribals along with co-operation of the forest officials should be the objective to resist deprivation of property rights of tribals. Granting of arbitrary powers to local authorities has been the root cause of land alienation throughout the country. This coupled with forced eviction will lead not only to economic loss but also loss of a great multitude of tribal life and consequent extinction of tribal culture from the state. Special incentive and training should be provided to forest officers so that they may stick to their duty as guar.

References

1. M. Gopinath Reddy and K. Anil Kumar, Political Economy of Tribal Development: A Case Study of Andhra Pradesh, Working Paper No. 85, February (2010), p. 6.

2. Ramdas Rupavath, Tribal Land Alienation and Political Movements: Socio-economic Patterns from South India, Cambridge Scholars Publishing, (2009), p. 14.

3. John Locke, two treatises on government, Section 36, (1690).

4. Shyama Prasad Rout, Land Alienation and Tribal People's Rights: A Case Study of Mayurbhanj District in Orissa, 1990.

5. *Ibid.*

6. *Supra* Note

7. Samantha Benerjee, In the wake of Naxalbari, Sourna Rekha Publications, Calcutta, 1980, pp. 32-33.

8. Chapter 7 of report of National Commission on Backward Areas of Development available at http://lawmin.nic.in/ncrwc/finalreport/v2b1-2ch9.htm#_ftn9.

9. Hari Priya, Tribal Laws in Andhra Pradesh, available at: http://works.bepress.com/hari_priya/3.

10. *Ibid.,* p. 5.

11. *Anjan Kumar* v. *Union of India,* 2006 AIR 1177.

12. "Basic Statistics on Schedule Tribes of Andhra Pradesh", Tribal Cultural Research and Training Institute, Tribal Welfare Department, Government of Andhra Pradesh, Hyderabad, January 2008 p. 11.

13. Census of India 2001.

14. *Supra* Note 1 p. 9.

15. *Ibid.*

16. Annual Report - 2006-07, Ministry of Tribal Affairs, Government of India available at http://goo.gl/ylbc2.

17. *Supra* Note 1.

18. *Supra* Note 9 p. 45.

19. Issues of Social Justice: Scheduled Castes, Scheduled Tribes and Other Backward Classes–An Unfinished National Agenda, National Commission to Review the Working of the Constitution, p. 11.

20. T. Prabhakar Reddy, Tribal Land Alienation in Andhra Pradesh, Economic and Political Weekly, Vol. 24, No. 28 (July 15, 1989), pp. 1571-1573 available at http://www.jstor.org/stable/4395073.

21. Priya Pillai, Vinuta Gopal, Kanchi Kohli(Greenpeace), Singrauli: A Coal Curse: A Fact Finding Report On The Impact Of Coal Mining, available at http://goo.gl/00DRj.

22. *Ibid.*

23. *Supra* Note 4.

24. Report: National Commission on Backward-Areas Development (1980).

25. Schedule Tribes, Tenth Five Year Plan by Planning Commission, available at http://goo.gl/ZehOR.

26. *Ibid.*

27. Hari Mohan Mathur, *Tribal Land Issues in India: Communal Management, Rights, and Displacement,* Asian Development Bank, 2009.

28. *Ibid.*

29. *Ibid.* p. 182.

30. G.B. Reddy, Land Laws in Andhra Pradesh, Gogia Law Agency, p. 157.

31. BN Bordoloi, Alienation of Tribal Land and Indebtedness, (1986).

32. *Supra* Note 20.

33. *Ibid.*

34. *Ibid.*

35. *Supra* Note 25 p. 17

36. *Supra* Note 31 p. 14.

37. *Supra* Note 9 p. 85.

38. *Ibid.*

39. Steve Jones, Tribal Underdevelopment in India, Development and Change ISAGE, London and Beverly Hills), Vol. 9 (1978) 1, 41-70.

40. *Ibid.*

41. 8 SCC 191 (1997).

42. Issues of India available at http://socialissuesindia.wordpress.com/2012/09/06/the-samatha-judgment-and-the-fifth-schedule-of-the-constitution/.

43. The Fifth Schedule of the Constitution and the Samatha Judgment Available At http://goo.gl/8xzVY.

44. *Ibid.*

45. Dr R.P. Rai, Constitutional Safeguards For Tribals In India And Tribal Administration: Behavioural Aspects, Central India Law Quarterly available at http://indiankanoon.org/doc/1163757/.

46. *Ibid.*

47. *Supra* Note 1.

48. Constitutional Assembly Debates (CAD), Vol. VII. Apps. C and D, p. 157.

49. Shubhankar Dam, Legal Systems As Cultural Rights: A Rights Based Approach To Traditional Legal Systems Under The Indian Constitution, Ind. Intl & Comp. L., Rev. 295, (2006).

50. *Supra* Note 9 , p. 47.

51. *Supra* Note 1, p. 37.

52. *Ibid.*

53. Tribal Welfare Department Departmental Manual available at http://www.aptribes.gov.in/.

54. *Supra* Note 9, p. 51.

55. Shachi Chakrabarty, Rights of the Indigenous People over Forest in India: Rhetorics and Reality, Indigenous People and Human Rights: the Quest for Justice, Kolkata : R. Cambray & Co., (2009).

56. Srilatha Swaminatahan, Tribes and Human Rights, Speech given at Seminar of International Institute of Human Rights Society on 28th August, 2007 at New Delhi.

57. *Supra* Note 9, p. 51.

58. *Ibid.*

59. *Ibid.*

26

Contesting Inclusive Development: Exclusion and Marginality among Scheduled Tribes in North Coastal Andhra Pradesh

KR Rama Mohan

Scheduled Tribes in Visakhapatnam district are experiencing social exclusion and rendered vulnerabilities to various forms of exploitations. The paper explores the different dimensions of power relations which constitute the marginalisation process. The political limitations and social experience of marginality are mainly focussed in the context of their undeclared scheduled areas in the Ravitamakam Mandal in Visakhapatnam district of Andhra Pradesh. The paper contest the notion of 'Inclusive Development' in the light of plights suffering by the scheduled tribes as their villages are denied the status 'Scheduled Areas' according the Fifth Schedule of Indian Constitution. The paper further explains about resource politics and the role of NGO towards fighting for their rights and privileges of the scheduled tribes in this region. Few suggestions are made towards making these scheduled tribes as partners in the 'Inclusive Development' process.

Introduction

Until recently, the concept of 'Social Exclusion' has become a contested concept. The plethora of definitions on social exclusion ranges on different categories, various social, economic, political, religious processes experienced at both individual and collective level reflects the nature and magnitude of the issues that confronts especially the marginalised sections of the society. The inadequacy of a single definition that can be applied to all the socially excluded categories across time is noted to be both an obstacle and a benefit to its meaningful application. (deHaan, 1998, Silver,1994)

In its original conception, idea of social exclusion sought to replace many labels, categories, and issues such as social problems, debates on poverty, caste discrimination, alienation of religious minorities, and any other aspect which affects individuals well being. However, in the case of Scheduled Tribes of Visakhapatnam and Scheduled Tribes of other districts elsewhere, whose villages are not included and undeclared as scheduled areas are caught in a disadvantaged position due to historical and political process.

Madanipour, *et al.*, (2000) takes on the relational view of social exclusion, emphasises structural or social process affecting society in such a way that some groups experience social boundaries as barriers preventing their full participation in the economic, political and cultural life of the society within which they live, is clearly manifested in the villages of whose habitats come under non-scheduled (plain) areas, thus PESA is not applicable for these scheduled tribes.

The paper is an empirical study to call into question the popular and largely uncontested ideas of inclusive development, to unravel the social realities of the scheduled tribes non-inclusion of scheduled areas by the Government of India in many parts of Andhra Pradesh.

Taking a processual approach as its base, the paper seeks to understand how the scheduled tribes are being marginalised in the context of modern politics. The hegemonic and minority dominant non-scheduled caste communities operate and exploit the vulnerable tribal communities are becoming victims in everyday life. Attempt is made to record the social experiences and social responses to the predicament of marginality of these scheduled tribes. Few suggestions are given for the policy-makers to alleviate the suffering and marginality of the scheduled tribes of Ravitavakam mandal of Visakhapatnam district.

What are the Scheduled Areas

'Scheduled Areas' has been defined in the Indian Constitution as "such areas as the President may order /declare to be Scheduled Areas". Paragraph six of the Fifth Schedule of the Constitution prescribes following procedure for scheduling, descheduling and alteration of Scheduled Areas.

The criteria followed for declaring an area as Scheduled Area are preponderance of tribal population; compactness and reasonable size of the area; under-developed nature of the area; and marked disparity in economic standard of the people.

These criteria are not spelt out in the Constitution of India but have become well established. They embody principles followed in declaring "Excluded" and 'Partially-Excluded Areas' under the Government of India Act 1935, Schedule 'B' of recommendations of the Excluded and Partially Excluded Areas

Sub Committee of Constituent Assembly and the Scheduled Areas and Scheduled Tribes Commission 1961.

At the time of devising and adopting the strategy of Tribal Sub Plan (TSP) for socio-economic development of Scheduled Tribes during Fifth Five Year Plan (1974-79), certain areas besides Scheduled Areas, were also found having preponderance of tribal population.

A review of protective measures available to the tribals of these newly identified areas vis-a-vis Scheduled Areas was made and it was observed that a systematic use of protective measures and other powers available to the executive under Fifth Schedule will help in effective implementation of the development programmes in Sub-Plan Areas.

Therefore, in August 1976 it was decided to make the boundaries of the Scheduled Areas co-terminus with the Tribal Sub-Plan areas. Accordingly, Clause (2) of the paragraph 6 of the Fifth Schedule was amended vide the Constitution (Amendment) Act, 1976 to empower the President to increase the area of any Scheduled Areas in any State.

Andhra Pradesh Scenario

- The 1950 'Scheduled Area Order' by the President of India, declared nine districts in Andhra Pradesh.
- Adilabad, Mahaboobnagar, Khammam, Warangal, East Godavari, West Godavari, Visakhapatnam, Vizianagaram and Srikakulam.
- A total of 5,400 Tribal villages were declared as 'Scheduled Areas' in the Fifth Schedule.
- In 1976, the GOI has given consent to modify the 1950 Scheduled Area Act.
- Madhya Pradesh, Bihar, Orissa, Rajasthan, Gujarat, Maharashtra, Himachal Pradesh, Tribal Villages were identified and added to the list.
- During that time, the GOI has requested to send the list of villages with Tribal population.
- The A.P. State Govt. has identified 753 villages with predominant tribal population.

In 1980, the AP Govt has sent the list to GOI

In 1980, the Government of Andhra Pradesh enumerated 805 Girijana (adivasi) villages to incorporate into the 5th Schedule of the Constitution.

Tribal villages of Maharashtra, Rajasthan, and Bihar, who submitted lists at the same time, have been incorporated in the 5th Schedule.

Yet, Tribes of the 805 villages in AP have been waiting for the government to implement this measure!

The State of Andhra Pradesh, where the Tribal sub-plan areas are not coterminous with Scheduled Areas, has also furnished a proposal to this effect which is under examination.

• Andhra Pradesh Govt has identified the following villages as 'Villages with Tribal Population'

• Srikakulam District : 240 villages
• Vizianagaram District : 170
• Visakhapatnam : 55
• East Godavari District : 40
• West Godavari District : 1
• Khammam : 3
• Warangal : 77
• Adilabad : 164
• Mahaboobnagar : 3
• Total : 805 Villages

* *Source:* Tribal Welfare Department Andhra Pradesh Government.

Andhra Pradesh State Government Initiatives

• 1976 Andhra Pradesh State Cabinct Resolution
• Ordered a Fresh Cabinet Resolution to declare the Scheduled Areas
• Koneru Ranga Rao Committee : To study the agricultural Land issues
• 50 per cent or more tribes can be declared as Scheduled Area
• State Government Agreed, could not implement – Central Government consent is required
• 1/70 act : Tribal Areas lands need to be protected from Non–Tribes
• (This is not applicable to Non- Scheduled Areas) though lands belong to Tribes
• East and West Godavari Districts Villages of Andhra Pradesh: Do not register Tribes lands to Non-tribes (Pending)
• The ITDA Project Officer has written a letter to MRO of Ravitakam Mandal MRO soliciting Population List of Tribes/ Non-Tribes, Land particulars - What for ?

Ravitamakam Mandal Scenario:

Cheemalapadu Panchayat

The sixteen habitations: 1. Cheemalapadu 2. Mulakalapalli 3. Kalyanpulova 4. Bangarubanda 5. Kadapeda 6. Jogumpeta 7. Gangampeta 8. Rochupakalu 9.Thatiparti 10. Dokulampadu 11. Kunjarti 12. Valasapalem 13. Ajaypuram 14. Venkatapuram 15.Tamakampeta 16. Jogaripeta Valmiki, Konda Dora and Manne Dora Tribe certificates are issued by the RDO, while Bagata, Khond and Gadaba Tribe certificates are issued by the MRO.

All the scheduled tribes practice settled cultivation, along with minor forest produce collection from the surrounding denuded forests. While there are some economic disparities between Bagata Valmiki, Konda Dora, Manne Dora and the most vulnerable tribes Khond and Gadaba. These two tribal communities are the victims to the non-tribal population compared to the other tribal groups, due to illiteracy and low negotiation skills.

Loss of Autonomy and Non-political Representation

Though there is 90 per cent of tribal population in all the habitations and more than thirteen habitations are 100 per cent tribal population, there is no political representation from the tribes. Few non-tribes are representing the whole Cheemalapadu panchayat of Ravitavakam mandal

PESA is not implemented in these tribal hamlets, as MPTC and ZPTC elected members are from the Non-Tribal members, due to the fact that these villages come under Non Scheduled Areas. In the context of the present Panchayat Raj elections, tribes have no control of governance and are being represented by the Non Tribal members.

Agricultural Land, Land Transfers and Unused Government Lands in Cheemalapdu Panchayat.

The agricultural and non-agricultural lands (houses) can be purchased by the non-tribals in these villages, which is against to the 1/70 Act.

Even a thumb impression of the tribal who own the land is enough to purchase.

All the land disputes are settled in Civil Court Jurisdiction, against Revenue Courts in the Scheduled Areas.

Due to open land deals and any one can purchase lands belonging to Tribals, there is growing number of Touts in these villages who negotiate tribal lands for a cheaper price.

In Scheduled Areas, any government unused land can be given to the tribes either for housing purposes or any commercial development. Videh (2003) reports that despite the categorical legal imperative, land alienation of the tribes in scheduled areas persist, and in large areas of the country it is now endemic. Behura (2006) points out that the Article 19(5) of Indian Constitution safeguards tribal interest in property. While the rights of free movement and residence throughout the territory of India and of acquisition and disposition of property are guaranteed to every citizen, special restrictions may be imposed by the state for protection of the interests of the members of the scheduled tribes under Article 19(5). Unfortunately this constitutional provision is not practiced in these villages.

Non-locals from Z. Bennavaram (8 Kms to Cheemalapadu) encroaching land in Cheemalapadu area by influencing the local non-tribals. There is no mechanism to stop these encroachments.

Position of Jobs in Government Organisations

Government of Andhra Pradesh has a Special Order: In Scheduled Areas, in every Department, some jobs must be given to the Scheduled Tribes.

Educated Youth are denied Jobs in neighbouring scheduled areas.

Unemployment- Frustration – Vulnerability towards joining with extremist groups.

Loan Facilities: Institutional and Non-institutional

In Scheduled Tribal areas, Non-institutional loan arrangements by the private money lenders are guarded from high interest rates and grabbing the agricultural/houses if there is no repayment. Additionally, all the money lenders must register with the MRO.

This is not happening in these Non Scheduled tribal areas, thus tribes who have taken loans from the money lenders are paying high interest rates and are vulnerable to give away their lands.

Loss of Tribal Identity

Due to the presence of non-tribal population and are being influenced by the caste Hindus, tribal customs, norms, mores are being eroded and are being replaced by the mainstream Hindu cultural ethos.

Changes are manifested in marriage system as the Bride Price is replaced by Dowry, Construction of Rama Temple and Unnecessary spending on family functions which are not part of Tribal culture of these tribes.

Additional Issues

These Tribes could not get the jobs assigned to them in the eleven Mandals of Visakhapatnam.

Education facilities are less compared to those of the Scheduled Areas: Tribal Ashram Schools, MPP schools, Government Elementary Schools, Tribal Girls Ashram Schools.

Marriage Alliances are not taking place due to demarcation of Scheduled Areas and Non Scheduled Areas.

Livelihoods are also problem in these areas.

'Rajiv Yuva Kiranalu' jobs in the private sector are given, could not cope with the skills and demands of the private organisations, lag behind and dropped out.

The continuance of the issues in these villages is a grim reminder of the fact that the government functionaries spell out only the symptoms of the issue, but not the underlying socio-political aspects that has crippled the development in these villages.

Alternatives for Inclusive Development of the Scheduled Tribes

Guidelines must be framed to stop land purchase and land grabbing from the non-tribes in these villages with immediate effect.

A separate Cell should be formed within the ITDA to look after the welfare of these tribes in the non scheduled areas.

Ten per cent of fund should be allocated to the tribes of these non scheduled areas within the total budget sanctioned to the ITDA.

Tribal Welfare administration must not only confine to the scheduled tribes in the scheduled areas, they must ensure welfare to the tribes in the non scheduled areas.

Administrative changes are necessary to see the welfare of the scheduled tribes in the non scheduled areas.

Government functionaries must be sensitised about tribal culture, needs and aspirations of the scheduled tribes.

A Committee should look into the various land related issues of the tribes in these villages.

Separate Tribal Girls Hostel should be initiated to encourage tribal girls' education in these villages.

Employability training should be given to the needy youth for these tribes.

Initiatives to curb Malaria and provide adequate healthcare facilities to the scheduled tribes in these villages.

References

Behura, N.K. and Nilakantha Panigrahi (eds) 2006, Tribals and the Indian Constitution, Rawat Publications, Jaipur.

deHaan (1998), 'Social Exclusion' An Alternative Concept for the study Deprivation? IDS Bulletin, 29(1), 10-19.

Madanipour, A., Cars, G., and Allen, J. (Eds.). (2000), Social exclusion in European cities: Processes, experiences, and responses. London: The Stationery Office.

Ministry of Tribal Welfare, Government of India, Report on Scheduled Tribes.

Silver, H. (1994), Social exclusion and social solidarity: Three paradigms. International sLabour Review, 133(5-6), 531-578.

Struggle of Non-Scheduled Adivasis, Association of India's Development, 2013. Retrieved on 28-5-13.

Upadhyay, Videh (2003), Their Lands and Our Laws, India Together Org. Retrieved on 30-5-13.

www.aptribes.gov.in retrieved on 29-5-13.

27

Trends in the Cropping Pattern and It's Impact on the Tribal Households in the Scheduled Areas: A Case Study of Three Scheduled Area Villages from West Godavari District of AP

B Nageswara Rao

Introduction

The inventions of non-tribal population into the tribal areas, the non-tribal lifestyle, production methods, and marketing mechanisms have influenced significantly and the self-sufficient based socio-economic conditions of tribal people have transformed into surplus and market oriented characters, and influenced the cropping pattern in the tribal areas. (Catalyst Management Services Pvt Ltd, 2000; pp.).[1] It leads to more deprivation of the communities and more dependence on non-tribal communities and the State. The changes in the cropping pattern lead to the land alienation in the tribal economy. The dis-economies created due to the changes in the cropping pattern are concerned with more technical which could not understand by the innocent tribal people.

The temporal changes (per cent) in the area share of main crops and crop groups at all India level during 1966-67 to 1996-97 shows that there is tremendous changes in the cropping pattern. The area under cereals (coarse cereals and milets) or under dry cultivation has drastically replaced by the Rice cultivation or wet cultivation (C.R. Hazra, 2000).[2] These trends show that there is continuous surge of diversification in agriculture in terms crops, primarily on economic considerations during post Green Revolution period in India. The changes in the cropping pattern are the outcome of the interactive effect of many factors.

Resource related factors like irrigation, rainfall, soil fertility; technology related factors like seed, fertilizer and water, marketing, storage and processing; household related factors like fodder, self-sufficiency requirements and investment capabilities; price related factors like input and output prices and institutional and infrastructural related factors like farm size, nature and arrangement of tenancy and Government policies etc. (C.R. Hazra, 2000).

But there is another serious problem of food in-security and un-employment has raised in the tribal areas due to chronic declining rate of area under the cultivation of Coarse Cereals, and diversification of Dry cultivation into Wet cultivation, using new technology and HYV seeds became problem in the tribal economy without proper knowledge, training, inputs and infrastructural facilities among tribal farmers in the tribal villages (Mruthyumjaya and Praduman Kumar, 1989 and M.V. Nadakarni, 1986).[3,4] Hence, this study examines the problems and consequences of the changes in the cropping pattern in the tribal economy. This study focuses the changes in terms number of working days, wages and food security among the tribal households of the selected villages. It is a historical study of three villages of Scheduled Area from West Godavari district of Andhra Pradesh.

Three villages are selected for this study from the Scheduled area of West Godavari District of AP. 1. Reddy Ganapavaram from Buttayagudem Mandal (Plain Village), 2. Darbhagudem from Jeelugumilli Mandal (Forest based village) and Reddy Nagampalem (Hill based village) for this study. The sample households are selected randomly through Stratified Sampling method. From Ganapavaram village 78 (16.74 per cent) landholding households are selected out of 466, from Darbhagudem village 34 (25.19 per cent) landholding households are selected out of 135, from Nagampalem 25 (20.16 per cent) landholding households are selected out of 124 randomly in 2005. Total 137 (18.89 per cent) landholding households have selected out of 725 in the three villages. In the West Godavari district Jeelugumilli, Buttayagudem and Polavaram are scheduled mandals. Jeelugumilli and Butyagudem mandals come under excluded area and Polavaram mandal comes under partially excluded area (Tribal Welfare Department, 2002).[5] The situation and existed major occupations among the tribal households in the selected villages in 1932-33.

The changes in the cropping pattern of an economy determine by the nature of the soil and access to water and the nature, attitudes of the economic agents, production methods, and instruments uses by the farming community within the economy. The trends in the cropping pattern in the tribal economy are different from the non-tribal economy. The tribal households collect forest produce for their daily life and material needed for their home and infrastructure. The methods of collection of forest produce and cultivation of food items are traditional and casual but scientific. They are very much attached with the forest and environment. They are self-sufficient but not surplus and market orientated. They maintain barter and share the work, but not wage paid and monetised.

Reddyganapavaram is a semi-forest and plain village, cultivation is the main occupation among the tribal households. They get food grains from cultivation and performing agricultural works provide by the non-tribal farmers in the village. The remaining food and material for shelter collect from the nearby forests. In the case of agricultural labour households the dependency was more on non-tribal farmers for work and they depend on forest for edible roots and fire wood. In the case of Darbhagudem, the situation and nature of the economy is different. Majority of the households were depended on forest resource and they were interested to perform their traditional occupations. They have collected forest produce like Gumkondagogu, Myrabolans, Nuxvomica, Tamarind fruits, Tamarind leaves, Tamarind seed, Pungum seed, Cleaning nuts, Rock bee honey, Marking nuts, Wild brooms, and Amla and other items. They have collected fruits like Jack fruit, Mango, Banana, Papaya, Pine-apple, Water melon, Custard-apple from the forests. Hunting was one of the major occupations among them. Majority of them have collected food and other material and they have used for the self-consumption. Major share of the collected bamboo and fuel wood they used for self-consumption and with reaming bamboo they make baskets, and other agricultural implements to store the produce, to carry seeds, other inputs which uses for agricultural operations. Majority of the forest produce collecting households are depended on basket making and its marketing. Majority of the tribal households they use to take sweet toddy as a main food item in the summer which is un-season for cultivation. They usually practices to collect the forest produce during the months from July to February months. From March to June they depend on sweet toddy and hunting birds and small wild animals of the forest. 95.00 per cent of the households have bamboo baskets which uses to collect the forest produce even today. It shows the level dependency of tribal households on forest produce. 30.00 per cent of the households have arrows which uses for hunting, it shows that hunting is the second occupation among them. Land holding households were less among them.

In the case of Reddynagampalem, the entire structure of the economy is different from other two villages. Ganapavaram and Darbhagudems are revenue villages, whereas Reddynagampalem was a Zamindari village under the control of Hukumpet Zamindar during the pre-independence period. Kondareddi and Koya communities were living together in the village. Among these two communities Kondareddis feel as Kings and superior to other tribal communities. They also feel as superior to Hindu castes people. Basically they prefer hunting, collect forest produce and cultivation. Majority of the households were landholders and but not efficient farmers. They don't prefer to work as labourers in the other non-tribal fields like Koya tribes, and they use the non-tribal labourers in their own fields for cultivation. All the landless households have been practiced hunting Goats, Sheep, Wild boar, Birds, Deers and some of them have practiced fishing. Hunting is two types: 1. Individual hunting and

2. Community or group hunting. Any one or more than one members of the family may perform the activity in the individual hunting which they make for family needs and they hunt birds and small wild animals from the forest. They can claim individual right on such kind of collected or hunted food items. But in the case of community needs like festivals, rituals and traditions, they have to be needed to collect more amount of food and they are needed hunt big animals by a group of experts with the arrows, nets and other materials and they distribute among them equally. Sometimes the share of food also given to the absentee's member of the team or group. They don't claim individual rights for such kind of collected item of food. Majority of the households have been maintaining the arrows and nets which uses for hunting till today in Darbhagudem and Nagampalem. They preferred hunting, fishing and they have used non-tribal labourers for cultivation and household works in Nagampalem. They participate in the non-tribal markets for household's material like cloth, chapels, ornaments, pots, other and agricultural implements.

The Methods of Cultivation among Tribal Farmers in the Selected Villages during Pre-1930s

In Darbhagudem village panchayat hold three Koya tribal gudems namely, Panduvarigudem, Cheemalavarigudem and Thapasivarigudem. Majority of tribal households live in Panduvarigudem. In the Ganapavaram the non-tribal lands are situated very close to the tribal cultivating lands and tribal houses also situated very close to the non-tribal houses in the village. In the Nagampalem, the tribal cultivating lands are situated around the Hill foot and far from the non-tribal lands. In the three villages, the tribal households have cultivated only small millets like Cholam or Korram, Bajra, Ragulu, Varugulu. Mixed crop system they have practiced in Ganapavaram, whereas in Darbhagudem and Nagampalem, they have practiced mono-crop system. In the three villages, they have practiced dry cultivation during pre-1930s. The animal grazing has existed predominantly in Ganapavaram and Nagampalem compared to Darbhagudem. Podu cultivation is two types 1. Individual and 2. Community. In ganapavaram the individual or family type of podu cultivation has practiced by the tribal households, whereas in the Darbhagudem and Nagampalem, the community *podu* cultivation has practiced. In the family or individual cultivation, generally the family members participate in the cultivation and individual or rights may claim for such kind of land and produce which comes from that. It is prevailed in the Ganapavaram where the tribes are very close to non-tribes and they depended on non-tribes.

In the Community or group 'Podu cultivation', a group of people generally male they clean the bushes and trees and they burn the dead trees and plants after falling and cleaning. They till the land with the help of wood tiller and buffalos or axes. The female sow the seeds before when the rain comes, the level of growing germ or sprout depends on the rainfall. The heavy or insufficient rains losses the seeds. They lower level of rainfall helps to fertile the soil and growing the plants healthy in the primitive stage. After 25 to 30 days from the day of seed sowing, the both male and female labourers weed-out once and provide the water to the plants. The ash which comes from the burning of the trees and plants used as best pesticide to protect the growing plants. They use animal dung as best fertiliser to the crop. Generally they cultivate each plot of land or area for 15 to 20 years. After 20 years they go for cleaning another plot for cultivation either it may be individual plot or community plot.

The average size of the holding under Podu cultivation was noted higher in Hill based and forest based villages like Nagampalem and Darbhagudem, whereas it was lower in Ganapavaram where they have practiced mono-crop system. The extent of area under podu cultivation is noted as low in the plain village like Ganapavaram, where they practiced individual podu cultivation with mixed crop system during pre-1930s. The duration of shifting gap from one plot to another is also varying by cropping pattern and access to irrigation. The duration between old plot and new plot was more as 20 years in the case of mixed crop system, whereas it was less as 10-15 years in the case of mono-crop system. Due to this, the extent of area under podu cultivation has noticed more in the forest based and Hill based villages compared to plain villages during pre-1930s. After many years, they may come back to the old plot which has cultivated before. This process continued to the generations. The gap duration between one plot to another has been declining from 15 years to 10 years during 1930 to 1950. As a result of this, the extent of area under Podu cultivation is noted more in 1950. And this type of cultivation has declined in 1970.

The Status of Food Security and Livelihoods

The status of food security is determined on the basis of access to food or food material and drinking water. The status of food security was very low among tribal households during pre-1930s due to heavy dependency on forest resources. They could not collect food material (fruits and vegetables) from the forest during the time of floods and heavy rains but only small animals, fruits and roots. They have been facing problems from the forest department officials. Both the Revenue officials and Forest officials' collects assessment or taxes and fines from the tribal households who collect the forest produce. The economic advantages were low due to migrating nature and Podu-cultivation among the tribal households.

Development of Irrigation Facilities and Change in Cropping Pattern in Reddyganavaram during 1930-50

The tribal farmers have practiced mono-crop system with the help of Sivudu Cheruvu which was based on the rain-fed but whereas the non-tribes have practiced mixed crop and rotation crop system. In the tribal farming, cereals crop has occupied the extent of 26.20 per cent 43.20 acres (26.20 per cent). Small millets like Cholam, Ragi, Samai, Varugu, Bajra and others were the major among the cereals. Pulses crop was occupied in the extent 25.60 acres (15.50 per cent), Condiments and Spices were occupied in the extent of 26.70 acres (16.20 per cent), Topes were in the extent of 25.80 acres (15.60 per cent), Drugs and Narcotics were in the extent of 30.00 acres (18.20 per cent) and Industrial crops were in the extent of 6.60 acres (4.00 per cent). Cereals, Drugs and Narcotics, Topes, Condiments and Spices were the major crops cultivated by the tribal farmers in 1933. Redgram and Horsegram were the major crops among pulses. Only castor is noted among industrial crops. Plantains were major among vegetables, only fruit trees are noted among Topes, Tobacco is noted among Drugs and Narcotics. Leafy crops are also noted among vegetable in Ganapavaram in1933 (R.S.R., 1933).[6] The cultivation of Black Paddy was very difficult to the tribal famers. This crop has introduced by the non-tribal farmers in the village. The demand for Cholam has declined in the non-tribal market due introduction of the new crop in the village. The tribal famers have also habituated to cultivate the Black Paddy; but the productivity among tribal farmers was low compared to non-tribal farmers, because they are not efficient in cultivation of wet crop. Some of the tribal farmers have preferred to leased-out their land to non-tribes instead of cultivating black paddy. Some of them are leased-out to non-tribal farmers. And the dependency on non-tribal farmers and non-tribal market has increased among the tribal farmers to learn the methods of cultivation and marketing their produce in the village market.

During 1930-50, the demand for tribal land has increased due to increase in the irrigation facilities (widening Jilleti Canal) and the conversion of tribal dry crop cultivation land into wet crop cultivation. The extent of cereals cultivation area has increased from 26.20 per cent in 1933 to 40.90 per cent in 1950 among tribal farmers in Reddyganapavaram. One more trend has noticed that some of the non-tribal holdings were situated around the Sivudu Cheruvu and major share of their holdings were situated at a little more distance from the Sivudu Cheruvu. The non-tribal lands get water after the tribal lands were using only, this situation was very difficult to the non-tribal farmers. The demand for tribal lands has increased by having easy access to water. The non-tribal farmers have purchased the major share of the land during 1930 to 1950.

Change in Cropping Pattern in Darbhagudem during 1930-1950

The number of tribal landholding households is noted as 18 in Darbhagudem village. They owned 20 land holdings with the extent of 170.70 acres in 1933. If observe the cropping pattern among the tribal farmers, Cereals has occupied the extent of area 38.60 per cent (59.20 acres), Topes 15.70 per cent (24.00 acres), Condiments and spices 12.40 per cent (22.30 acres) and Drugs and Narcotics 11.90 per cent (18.20 acres) as major crops to the total operational area (RSR-1933).[7]

Tribal gudems are situated besides the Aswarao peta vagu (canal. Tribes have stated that small canals have dig by their fore-fathers. But most of the non-tribal lands are situated around the canal and Pond in 1933. In the rainy season the Pond gets full of water and would be sufficient for a single crop to the extent of nearly 200.00 acres to the surrounding area. But the tribal farmers are not able to get water. Under these conditions the tribal farmers were cultivating rain-fed crops like Cholam, Ragi for food, Tamarind, Fruits and Castor. But the Aswararo pets Vagu has widen during 1933-50 by the Government, the extent of irrigated area has increased among both tribes and non-tribal farmers in the village. The percentage of area occupied by Cholam, Ragi, Varugu crops have declined and that has replaced by Black Paddy among Cereals in Darbhagudem during 1933-50. But the trend was reverse to what happened in Ganapavaram. The tribal households in Darbhagudem did not attracted towards wet cultivation due to increasing irrigation facilities but they have continued dry cultivation and bended towards collection of MFP again during 1950-70. When the tribal households had alternative opportunities in the form of forest resources, they have diverted to easy crops or dry crops again and they have avoided dependency on non-tribal farmers in Darbhagudem. But some of the tribal farmers, they have leased-out their land to non-tribal farmers. The demand for tribal land has increased due to increasing irrigation and the neighbour non-tribal farmers have purchased and occupied the tribal land during the same period. The tribal famers have been alienated 25.30 acres of land to non-tribals during the same period.

Change in Cropping Pattern in Reddynagampalem during 1930-1950

Among the selected landholding households, they had 11 holdings with the extent of 84.70 acres in 1920. But they have operated 69.90 acres and remaining 23.50 acres were leased-out to the non-tribal farmers (Survey -2005).[8] The percentage of cereals cultivated area is noted as 41.80 per cent (28.90 acres), Condiments and Spices is noted as 27.50 per cent (19.00 acres) and Topes is noted as 19.20 per cent (13.30 acres) to the total operated area in Nagampalem in 1920. Among Cereals, Cholam, Ragi and Varugu have been cultivated and Cholam was the main food crop. Among Condiments and Spices, Turmeric and Tamarind are noted and Tamarind was the major crop. Only fruit trees are noted as major crop among Topes in 1920. Only one Panta Kaluva (Government canal) was situated in the fields of the village and most of the tribal lands are situated at the bank of the canal, which comes from the hills. Among cereals, the cholam and ragi cultivated areas were occupied as major shares, among Condiments and spices tamarind and castor, among topes, tamarind and other fruit trees except mango have drastically decreased and that was replaced by food crops like cholam and ragi have replaced. The extent of ownership land declined from 84.70 acres to the extent of tribal land has alienated 52.40 acres during 1920 to 1950. The operating land also declined from 69.20 acres to 32.80 acres during the same period. The Black Paddy has not introduced in the Nagampalem.

The Kondareddi community used the non-tribal labour force; among them SCs used for agriculture, other OBC communities used for both agricultural labour and household labour services. The Kondareddi landholders did not pay either money or kind as remuneration for their services, but a piece of land as annual payment to all the catgories of non-tribal labourers. Kondareddi tribal landholders have paid in-terms of land of 1.40 acres as annual payment to Barber and Washer man during 1933-50. This was a different situation taken place in Nagampalem. But in the same village the Koya community did not used the services of non-tribal labour for household activities. But they also took the help of SCs for agricultural works. This was the one of the main reason to alienate major share of land, and changes in the cropping pattern by non-tribal farmers in the tribal areas was the second reason.

Changes in the State of Food Security during 1933-50

The tribal households have been performing their traditional occupations like collection of NTFM, Hunting, fishery, animal husbandry, Animal grazing but Podu cultivation also significantly increased during 1930-50. Due to the declaration of productive forests as reserved forests by the British Government of India, the dependency of land and cultivation has increased. The state of food security has improved during the same period. The access to food grains (cholam, ragi and varugulu) has improved and substituted in the place of roots and other forest food. The state of livelihood also improved in terms of no. of working days, collecting and producing of food and others. But the extent of land alienation also increased by the more involvement non-tribal into the affairs of tribal economy. The dependency on non-tribes has also increased particularly in Ganapavaram where the tribes are very closely situated with the non-tribes. The economic advantages were low but better compared to the previous conditions. But state of food security was un-certain due to land alienation during the same period.

Changes in Cropping Pattern in Ganapavaram during 1950-51 to 1970-71

The extent of operated area has declined from 101.30 to 75.30 acres during 1950-70 in Ganapavaram. They have cultivated two crops in a year, cereals have cultivated in kharif season and dry crops like pulses, condiments and Spice, Industrial crops, and Topes have cultivated in rabi season in 1970 among tribal farmers in the village. The percentage of extent of cereals cultivated area has increased from 40.90 per cent (41.45 acres) in 1950 to 74.80 per cent (56.30 acres) in 1970, the percentage of extent of area of remaining all other have declined significantly. Because, the population pressure, non-access to forest produce are one side, the land alienation is another side, they created food insecurity among tribal households, they gave more priority to food crops like cereals. The extents of cultivating area of ragi, varugu have declined significantly, cholam area also declined and replaced by white paddy during the same period. The percentage of pulses cultivated area also decreased from 8.21 per cent (20.81 acres) to 9.70 per cent (7.31 acres) during the same period. The extent of topes, condiments and spices cultivated area declined significantly due to dry land conversion into wet land by increasing irrigation facilities during the same period.

The tribal farmers have borrowed money for cultivation of wet crop like black paddy at higher rate of interest. The cost of cultivation has increased due to habituating using more inputs and instruments and labour, but the returns were noted as low compared to non-tribal farmers. They also borrowed money for purchasing animals like sheep, goats, buffaloes and cows from non-tribes during the same period. In this practice, the ideas of non-tribal farmers have played major role because, the tribal farmers are very close to non-tribes in not only economic activities but also in performing social and religious events and activities in Ganapavaram. With the result of this, they could not repay the debt and lost their land to repay the debt and it has been lead to large scale of land alienation in the village.

Changes Cropping Pattern in Darbhgudem during 1950-51 to 1970-71

Two small canals were constructed. One is from Jeelugummilli and another one from Chinthalapudi mandal during this period. These two canals are rain fed canals and can facilitate the irrigation for 250 acres in rainy season. Aswaraopet vagu and Dirisinam Varikunta are the other irrigational sources. The surrounding tribal lands of Vagu and Kunta have been alienated during 1950-70. Then small canals have become main source for tribes. On the other hand the non-tribes have started using bore-well or motor pump-sets for irrigation for second crop, whereas tribes could not have bore-wells or motor pump-sets. The percentage of extent of Cereals cultivating area has increased from 60.67 per cent to 62.62 per cent during 1950-70 in Darbhagudem. Among cereals, cholam, ragi, varugu and samai crops have declined and replaced by black paddy during 1950-70. The percentage of area under Black Paddy has increased from Zero per cent to 7.79 per cent (2.05 acres) during the same period.

They exchange Tamarind with money or other agricultural implements which are needed for "Podu cultivation". The Podu cultivation was started to transform into settled cultivation among tribes by the interference of and interactions with non-tribes. It is connected with the nature of land rights. The village community property right has transformed into individual property right. The changing cropping pattern was one of the reasons to change the ownership pattern of land among tribes during 1950-51 to 1970-71.

Changes Cropping Pattern in Nagampalem during 1950-51 to 1970-71

The irrigation facilities were same during 1950-70 in Nagampalem. The extent of operating area has declined from 35.60 acres to 28.10 acres during 1950-70. The percentage of cereals cultivating area was almost same, but the percentage of area under pulses has declined from 22.47 per cent to 14.59 per cent, the percentage of area under condiments and Spices has also declined from 11.24 per cent to 7.12 per cent during the same period. But the area under industrial crops has increased from 5.62 per cent to 10.68 per cent. The area under topes also has increased from Zero to 7.12 per cent to the total Operating area during 1950-70 in Nagampalem.

Among cereals, the percentage of extent of area under cholam has declined from 70.23 per cent to 62.35 per cent; the area under varugu has declined from 17.59 per cent to 8.65 per cent to the total cereals cultivating area. But the area under ragi crop has increased slightly. The population has increased in one hand, the land alienation has continued on the other and the average size of the per-capita land has declined.

Changes in the Methods of Cultivation during 1950-51 to 1970-71

During this period many major changes have taken place, the shifting cultivation has transformed into settled cultivation is one of the major event. The identification of land right was very much difficult to the local administrators during the previous period, when the tribal farmers have practiced shifting cultivation, but it was easy during 1950-70. And the imposition of land assessment also became clear on whom to impose by the administrator. The individual rights (family right) on a particular piece of land which is cultivated by a tribal family under Podu cultivation could be recognised by the tribal community but it is difficult to the outside community or non-tribal administrator or outside individuals of the tribal community. These difficulties have been overcome by the habituating settled cultivation among tribal farmers during 1950-70.

One more change has noted the practice of traditional methods of cultivation which were used in the cultivation of millets (cholam, ragi and sajjalu) is adapted to the cultivation of black paddy as well as White Paddy during 1950-70. The practice of eco-friendly methods of pest-control and fertilizers has continued in the cultivation of paddy also. But on the other non-tribal farmers have started using new technology (bio-chemical and mechanical) in the cultivation of paddy.

Changes in the State of Food Security during 1950-51 to 1970-71

The state of food security was moderate during 1950-51 and 1970-71. There was recognition of right of land ownership and improvement of alternative occupations like animal husbandry helped in satisfying the needs of agriculture and as well as household. The practice of grazing animals at will is transformed into occupation and became essential to the tribal community for assistance in terms of work and money, when the bartered economy has transformed into semi-money economy. It is easy to transform the surplus (savings) into non-movable permanent assets in the money economy. And increasing land assets provide food security. The dependency on non-tribal farmers also has increased among tribal farmers. These changes have helped the tribal communities to improve the relations with other communities, but at the same time it has made the hurdles, insecure, exploitation and land alienation in the tribal economy. The range of negative effects was more in the Ganapavaram, where the tribes are very closely situated to non-tribes compared to other villages where the tribal households are situated isolated during 1950-70. The external and internal economies have declined due to transformation of economic landholdings into non-economic holdings due to hereditary transfers and land transfers. The state of food security was better in isolated villages like Nagampalem and Darbhgudem and which has forest base compared to semi-plain village like Ganapavaram.

Changes in the Cropping Pattern in Ganapavaram during 1970-71 to 1990-1991

The extent of ownership land has declined from 80.10 acres in 1970-71 to 72.50 acres in 1990-91; the extent of operating area also has declined from 75.30 acres to 70.60 acres during the same period. The percentage share of cereals cultivating area has increased from 74.80 per cent in 1970-71 to 76.50 per cent to the total operating area. Among cereals, the percentages of extent area under black paddy, cholam and ragi have declined but the percentage or extent of area under white paddy has increased significantly from 4.44 per cent in 1970-71 to 62.43 per cent in 1990-91 to the total operating area under cereals in Ganapavaram. Varugu and Samai crops have disappeared during the same period. Among the food grains, White paddy and blackgram have become major crops in the tribal economy, cholam. varugu, ragi and black paddy have disappeared during 1970-71 and 1990-91 in Ganapavaram.

Changes in the Cropping Pattern in Darbhagudem during 1970-71 to 1990-1991

The extent of owned area has declined from 75.30 acres in 1970-71 to 60.10 acres in 1990-91, but the extent of operating area has increased from 42.00 acres to 45.00 acres during the same period. It shows that the extent of leased-out land has decreased in Darbhagudem. If see the trends in the cropping pattern, the percentage of extent of area under cereals has increased from 62.60 per cent to 69.10 per cent; the area under pulses has increased from 12.40 per cent to 34.40 per cent (rabi season); the area under Industrial crops has also increased from 7.6 per cent to 21.60 per cent in rabi season and 16.00 per cent in rabi season during the same period. But the percentage of area under condiments and spice and topes has declined significantly during the same period.

Among the cereals, the percentage of area under cholam has declined from 68.14 per cent in 1970-71 to 6.82 per cent in 1990-91, the area under ragi has increased from 8.89 per cent to 11.09 per cent, the area under varugu has disappeared and replaced by the new crop Maize with the percentage area of 4.60 to the total area under Cereals during the same period in the Darbhagudem. Among the industrial crops, the percentage of area under castor had disappeared and replaced by Sugarcane 45.83 per cent, and other 54.17 per cent to the total area under Industrial crops during 1970-71 to 1990-91 in Darbhagudem.

Changes in the Cropping Pattern in Nagampalem during 1970-71 to 1990-91

The total ownership land has declined from 35.10 acres in 1970-71 to 24.30 acres in 1990-91. The extent of operating area has declined from 29.20 acres to 23.10 acres during the same period. The ownership land has declined due to land alienation and the operated land has declined due to leased-out the land to non-tribal farmers in the Nagamapalem village in 1990-91. The percentage area under cereals has declined from 60.50 per cent to 59.30 per cent the percentage of land under condiments and Spices also has declined from 7.10 per cent to 4.30 per cent, but the percentage of area under pulses has increased from 22.50 per cent to 23.80 per cent, the area under industrial crops has increased from 10.70 per cent to 21.60 per cent, the area under topes also has increased from 7.10 per cent to 10.40 per cent to the total Operating area during 1970-71 to 1990-91 in Nagampalem. Somewhat a new trend has noted in Nagamapalem that is the area under Topes and Industrial crops has increased, whereas in Ganapavaram and Darbhagudem it has declined. The area under Cereals has declined in Nagampalem but in the other two villages it has increased during 1970-71 to 1990-91. Because, the Nagampalem is Hill based village, and less irrigated compared to other two villages. The tribal farmers could not transform themselves as completely wet cultivable and still they have been performing their traditional occupations like hunting and fishing.

Among cereals, the percentage of area under cholam has declined from 62.35 per cent to 15.47 per cent, it has replaced by White Paddy from Zero per cent to 49.64 per cent; the percentage of area under ragi has increased from 13.76 to 24.45 per cent; the varugu crop has disappeared and it is replaced by maize by 10.44 per cent to the total cultivating area under cereals among the tribal farmers during 1970-71 to 1990-91 in Nagampalem. The tribal farmers have been continuing their traditional eco-friendly methods of cultivation during 1970-71 to 1990-91, but the neighbour non-tribal farmers have started using technology and machinery, HYV seeds, chemical fertilizers and pesticides during the same period. The power of chemical pesticides and fertilisers are generally high compared to traditional objects. If a neighbour non-tribal farmer applies the chemical objects for pest-control, the pests shift from that particular holding to neighbour holding which did not have or apply the chemical pesticide. Generally majority of the non-tribal famers are habituated to apply the chemical fertilisers and pesticides within a week or two weeks, the pest automatically shifts to the tribal holdings, which have applied traditional methods of pest-control and fertilisers. It leads to loss of crops among tribal farmers. By this kind of practice, the resistance power of pests has improved and could not control by the traditional objects. The tribal farmers also need to be using the same chemical pesticides and fertilisers. These conditions made the tribe to use chemicals which are new to them and don't know about the name, Brand and function of the Pesticide. It has lead to depend on non-tribal pesticide and fertiliser shopholders and sellers. The tribal farmers also cheated by shop holders through selling duplicate brands and chemicals. This is one of the reasons to increase the cost of cultivation among the tribal farmers in 1990-91 in Ganapavaram and Darbhagudem. This impact was low in Nagampalem.

Changes in the Food Security among Tribal Households during 1970-71 to 1990-91

The state of food security is noted as low, it has declined from state moderate in 1970-71 to state low in 1990-91 in the three villages. It is determined on the basis of access to food grains, access to work for food and other related parameters have taken to compare the state of food security during a period of time. During 1970-71 to 1990-91, the state of food security has come down or worst among tribal households, because the average size of holding has declined from 3.64 acres to 0.55 acre in Ganapavaram, from 3.58 acres to 1.77 acres in Darbhagudem and from 0.92 acre to 0.45 acre in Nagampalem during the same period. Most of the economic holdings have transformed into non-economic holdings by both hereditary transfers and land alienation. The marginal cost of cultivation has increased to highest level among the tribal farmers due to adaptation of technology (bio-chemical). Among the agricultural labour households, some of the labourers have transformed into farm servants (un-secure and lowest wage), and majority of agricultural labourers shifted from usual status to usual subsidiary status during the same period. The per capita production of food grains also noted very low in 1990-91 compared to 1970-71. The per capita household's debt, cost of cultivation and incidence of poverty also increased during the same period. These are the main reasons to decline the state of food security during 1970-71 to 1990-91 in the three villages, the condition was more severe in Nagampalem (lack of land) and Ganapavaram (non-tribal exploitation on tribes). The conditions of tribal households were worsen during this period due to lack of access to forest resources (due to expansion of reserve forests) in one hand and cultivating land on the other (due to land alienation). But by the strong democratic tribal movements during 1990-91 to 2005, the tribal households could be able to restore some of the alienated land and socio-economic conditions have changed positively at significant level.

The Changes in the Cropping Pattern in Ganapavaram during 1990-91 to 2005

The extent of ownership land has increased from 72.50 acres in 1990-91 to 148.20 acres in 2005, and the extent of operating area is noted as same, because they did not leased-out their land to the non-tribal farmers in Ganapavaram during 1990-91 to 2005. The percentage of extent of area under Cereals has declined but the extent of area has increased from 54.00 acres in 1990-91 to 101.50 acres in 2005. The percentage of extent area under pulses has increased from 6.40 per cent to 30.50 per cent; the percentage of extent of area under condiments and Spices increased from 6.40 per cent to 10.50 per cent; the percentage of area under Industrial crops also increased from 13.60 per cent to 15.90 per cent during the same period. The area under major categories of crops has increased during this period due to restoration of alienated land.

Among Cereals, the percentage of area under millets like cholam, ragi, varugu and cereals like black paddy has disappeared, and it is replaced by white paddy during 1990-91 to 2005. The percentage of area under white paddy has increased from 62.43 per cent to 83.98 per cent; Maize area has increased from 2.65 per cent to 10.33 in Kharif and 14.90 per cent to the total area under cereals in rabi seasons during the same period. Among pulses, the percentage of area under blackgram has increased from 4.50 per cent to 25.65 per cent (Rabi); the area under redgram has increased from 3.30 per cent to 10.36 per cent. And area other pulses also increased from 4.50 per cent to 9.19 per cent during the same period in Ganapavaram. Among Industrial crops, the percentage area under cotton and sugarcane has increased significantly, and new crop groundnut has introduced during the same period. But the growth rate of area under Cereals and Pulses is noted more compared to Industrial and other crops area during 1990-91 to 2005 in Ganapavaram.

The Changes in the Cropping Pattern in Darbhagudem during 1990-91 to 2005

The ownership land has increased from 60.10 acres to 210.60 acres and the extent of operating area also has increased at the same extent during 1990-91 to 2005 in Darbhagudem. Here, also tribal landholder did not leased-out to non-tribal farmers during the same period. The percentage of area under cereals has declined from 69.10 per cent to 58.70 per cent; the percentage area under pulses and industrial crops also declined, but the percentage of area under Topes has increased from 5.10 per cent to 19.10 per cent during the same period in Darbhagudem. The extent area under cereals and pulses also significantly increased, but it shows low in percentage in 2005 due to higher base in the base year 1990-91.

Among cereals, the percentage of area under cholam, ragi and varugu has disappeared and it is replaced by white paddy. The area under white paddy has increased from 77.49 per cent in 1990-91 to 86.84 per cent in 2005. The area under maize has increased from 4.60 per cent to 8.90 per cent to the total area under cereals in Darbhagudem. Among Pulses, the extent of are under blackgram, redgram and other pulses also has increased during the same period. But the percentage of area is shows as lower in 2005 due to higher base value of the base year 1990-91. Among Industrial crops, the percentage of area under sugarcane, cotton has declined and extent of area under the same crops could not get much change except the area under other pulses in Darbhagudem during 1990-91 to 2005. Here, a new trend that is the importance to the food crops has increased compared to Industrial crops during this period. The profits and revenue from cultivation of Industrial crops became uncertain, noted heavy cost of cultivation and led to increased debt among tribal farmers due more borrowings at higher rate of interests from the non-institutional sources. The price fluctuations are more for the production of Industrial crops compared to food crops. And the average cost of cultivation is also noted low for food crops during the same period.

The Changes in the Cropping Pattern in Nagampalem during 1990-91 to 2005

The extent of ownership land has increased from 24.30 acres in 1990-91 to 50.00 acres in 2005. The operating area also has increased from 23.10 acres to 50.00 acres during the same period in Nagampalem. The percentage of area under cereals has increased from 59.30 to 78.40; the area under Industrial crops also increased from 15.20 per cent to 30.20 per cent in Rabi season; the percentage of area under Condiments and Spices also increased during the same period. But the percentage of area under Pulses and Topes has declined during the same period.

Among Cereals, Black Paddy, Ragi, Varugu and Cholam crops have moved out and White Paddy is replaced. The percentage of area cultivated under White Paddy has increased from 49.64 per cent to 68.72 per cent to the total area under Cereals during the same period. Among Pulses, the percentage of area under Blackgram has declined from 56.36 per cent to 44.78 per cent to the total area under Pulses; but the percentage of area under Redgram and other pulses has increased during same period. Among the industrial crops, the percentage of area under Sugarcane and other industrial crops has declined, but it is replaced by Groundnut. The percentage of area under Groundnut is noticed as 56.52 per cent to the total area under Industrial crops.

Changes in the Methods of Cultivation in the Selected Villages during 1990-91 to 2005

The alienated land has restored successfully in the Darbhagudem and some of the land in Ganapavaram and Nagampalem during 1990-91 to 2005.

The average size of the operational holding among the tribal farmers. The average size of the operational holding has increased a little due to restoration of alienated land. The average size of the household has increased from 0.60 acre to 0.95 acre in Ganapavaram; from 0.85 acre to 3.10 acres in Dabhagudem; and from 0.49 acre to 0.81 acre in Nagampalem during 1990-91 to 2005. The single crop system has changed into double crops both Kharif and Rabi in a agricultural year. Majority of food crops are cultivated in Kharif season and majority of Industrial crops are cultivated in Rabi season in 2005.

The most important change among all, the cost of cultivation has increased significantly by adopting new technology and using chemical fertlisers and pesticides. The demand for chemicals and machinery instruments has increased in the tribal economy. Tribal farmers are habituated both wet crops and as well as dry crops, even though, they are not efficient in wet cultivation.

Changes in the State of Food Security during 1990-91 to 2005

The state of food security has improved from lower stage to moderate stage during 1990-91 to 2005 in the selected villages. They could be able to restored alienated land through movements and the average size of the holding has improved a little. The extent of cereals and pulses cultivated area has increased more than double in the three villages. The white paddy cultivating area also has increased significantly with the constant returns. Majority of the landless agricultural labourers are access to agricultural works and get minimum earning for the existence of life. They did not leased-out their lands to non-tribes and completely cultivating by themselves. The permanent and annual farm servants have transformed into daily wage labourers, majority of usual subsidiary labourers have transformed into usual daily wage labourers due increase in average number of working days among tribal agricultural labour households in the three villages. It is noted more in Darbhagudem due to restoration of highest extent of alienated land during 1990-91 to 2005. Actually, the state of food security has to be highest among tribal households during the post-restoration period, but it is noted as moderate due to lowest net incomes, highest cost of cultivation, highest debt among tribal farmers and still the Industrial crops are occupied significant extent of area and the growth rate of extent of area is noted highest for Industrial crops during 1990-91 to 2005 in the three villages. Particularly, the majority share of the land is not suitable for wet crop in Darbhagudem and Nagampalem which has restored to tribal farmers. But some of the holdings have bore facility.

Main Findings

- An increase in the irrigation and transport facilities in the scheduled areas led to the increase in demand for tribal lands in the non-tribal land market and it has led to massive land alienation.

• An increase in the irrigation facilities influenced the cropping pattern; the small millets and course cereals have been changed into rice, wheat and other pulses which are unknown to the tribal people.

• The tribal farmers felt uncomfort and difficult in the cultivation of rice and commercial crops and it led increase in the leased-out status among the tribal farmers. Major share of the land has leased-out to non-tribal farmers.

• The status of food security among the tribal households has come down due to changes in the cropping pattern from core cereals to rice and other commercial crops.

• The majority of the tribal farmers borrowed money at higher rate of interest from the non-tribal traders and landlords and it has led to fallen in debt trap and increasing poverty among tribal households.

• Most of the tribal farmers have transformed into farm servants and agricultural labourers in their own field in the process of clearing the debts.

• The tribal economy has forcibly transformed from barter to monetary; self-sufficient to surplus by the pressures of the non-tribal farmers, traders and administrators in the tribal areas or Scheduled areas.

Suggestions

• The tribal villages which are included in or merged with the non-tribal villages and Gram Panchayats in the Scheduled areas should be excluded from them and must be reorganised as tribal gram panchayats.

• The tribal villages should be recognised as gram panchayats to habituate institutional system of governance and leadership among the tribal people.

• The Government should take action against violation of LTR Acts 1959 and 1970. The alienated land should be restored in the tribal villages.

• The government officials should prepare the precautions and guidelines to the local authority to restrict the violation of tribal rights, controlling money lending, exploitation of tribal labourers and exclusion of tribal farmers from the availing service of the government.

• The government should provide training to the tribal people on survey, availing baking, educational and other government services.

• The government officials should give priority in providing their services in the Scheduled area or tribal areas.

• The government also should educate the non-tribals to understand the rights of the tribal people and importance of their participation for the development of society as a whole.

Notes

1. Catalyst Management Services Pvt. Ltd, (2000). Impact Assessment of Agriculture Interventions in Tribal areas in MP–Final report.
2. C.R. Hazra (2000), "Crop Diversification in India, Agriculture Commissioner.

3. Mruthyumjaya and Praduman Kumar (1989), "Economics of cropping pattern," Economic and Political Weekly, Vol. 24, No. 51/52 (Dec. 23-30), pp. A159-A161 and A169-A166.

4. Nadakarni, M.V. (1986), "Backward crops in Indian Agriculture: Economy of Coarse Cereals and Pulses, Economic and Political Weekly, Vol. 21, No. 38/39 (Sep. 20-27), pp. A113-A115 and A117-A118.

5. Tribal Welfare Department (1997-98), Annual Report of the Governor on the Administration of Scheduled Areas in AP.

6. R.S.R. (1932-33), Reddyganapavaram village, Government press, Madras Presidency, Madras.

7. R.S.R. (1933), Darbhagudem Village, Government press, Madras Presidency, Madras.

8. Household data (2005), Land registration details, sub-registrar, Kovvur Taluk and MRO, Polavaram.

References

1. C.R. Hazra (2000), Crop diversification in India, Agriculture Commissioner, Department of Agriculture and Co-operation, Ministry of Agriculture, Krishi Bhavan, New Delhi.

2. Catalyst Management Services Pvt. Ltd., (2000). Impact Assessment of Agriculture Interventions in Tribal areas in MP-Final report.

3. Mruthyumjaya and Praduman Kumar (1989), Economics of cropping pattern.

4. Nadakarni, M.V. (1986), Backward crops in Indian Agriculture: Economy of Coarse Cereals and pulses.

5. Tribal Welfare Department (1997-98), Annual Report of the Governor on the Administration of Scheduled Areas in AP.

Table- 27.1: Trends in the Cropping Pattern in Reddyganapavaram during 1933 and 2005

Name of Crop	2005		1990		1970		1950	1933
	Kharif	*Rabi*	*Kharif*	*Rabi*	*Kharif*	*Rabi*	*Kharif*	*Kharif*
Cereals	101.5	21.3	54		56.3		41.45	43.2
Pulses	11.6	45.2	3.3	4.5	14.7	7.31	20.81	25.6
Condiments and spices	15.1	15.6	3.7	4.5		2	17.38	26.7
Industrial	14.2	23.5	9.6	9.67	4.3	0	8.21	6.6
Vegetables		12.3						7.2
Topes		11.2		3.6		2	13.45	25.8
Drugs and Narcotics	5.8							30
All	148.2	129.1	70.6	22.27	75.3	11.31	101.3	165.1
	Percentage to the total operated area respectively (priod-wise)							
Cereals	68.5	16.5	76.5	0.0	74.8	0.0	40.9	26.2
Pulses	7.8	35.0	4.7	20.2	19.5	64.6	20.5	15.5
Condiments and spices	10.2	12.1	5.2	20.2	0.0	17.7	17.2	16.2
Industrial	9.6	18.2	13.6	43.4	5.7	0.0	8.1	4.0
Vegetables	0.0	9.5	0.0	0.0	0.0	0.0	0.0	4.4
Topes	7.6	8.7	5.1	16.2	0.0	17.7	13.3	15.6
Drugs and Narcotics	3.9	0.0	0.0	0.0	0.0	0.0	0.0	18.2
All	100.0	100.0	100.0	100.0	100.0	100.0	100.0	100.0

Table 27.2: Changes in the Percapita Food Grains (in kgs) in Ganapavaram

	2005	*1990*	*1970*	*1950*	*1933*
Population	486	434.5	255	94.5	42
Black Paddy	0.0	11.4	27.2	9.7	0.0
White Paddy	338.1	112.5	8.8	0.0	0.0
Cholam	0.0	24.8	96.4	160.9	330.3
Ragi	0.0	8.9	15.6	43.9	110.7
Samai	0.0	0.0	10.7	16.3	40.8
Varugu	0.0	0.0	9.4	12.3	44.4
Maize	76.2	3.1	8.2	10.3	31.2
Others	29.6	0.0	7.5	8.1	0.0
Millets	109.7	35.4	143.2	252.6	565.7
All	439.0	137.3	180.8	270.1	565.7

Table 27.3: Trends in the Cropping Pattern in Darbhagudem during 1933

	2005		*1990*		*1970*		*1950*	*1933*
Name of Crop	*Kharif*	*Rabi*	*Kharif*	*Rabi*	*Kharif*	*Rabi*	*Kharif*	*Kharif*
Cereals	123.6		31.1		26.3		45.9	59.2
Pulses		51.3		15.5	5.2	3	10.2	19
Condiments and spices	16	22.45	2		4		4.2	22.3
Industrial	26	30.1	9.6	7.2	3.2	2		6.5
Vegetables		5						4
Topes	40	5.5	2.3		3.3	2	13.4	24
Drugs and Narcotics	5						5.2	18.2
All	210.6	114.35	45	22.7	42	7	78.9	153.2
Percentage to the total operated area respectively (period-wise)								
Cereals	58.7	0.0	69.1	0.0	62.6	0.0	58.2	38.6
Pulses	0.0	24.4	0.0	34.4	12.4	7.1	12.9	12.4
Condiments and spices	7.6	10.7	4.4	0.0	9.5	0.0	5.3	14.6
Industrial	12.3	14.3	21.3	16.0	7.6	4.8	0.0	4.2
Vegetables	0.0	2.4	0.0	0.0	0.0	0.0	0.0	2.6
Topes	19.0	2.6	5.1	0.0	7.9	4.8	17.0	15.7
Drugs and Narcotics	2.4	0.0	0.0	0.0	0.0	0.0	6.6	11.9
All	100.0	54.3	100.0	50.4	100.0	16.7	100.0	100.0

Table 27.4: Changes in the Percapita Food Grains (in kgs) in Darbhagudem

	2005	*1990*	*1970*	*1950*	*1933*
Popua	306	265	182	95	49
Black Paddy	0.0	0.0	6.8	0.0	0.0
White Paddy	408.6	80.4	0.0	0.0	0.0
Cholam	0.0	5.1	59.7	202.1	369.5
Ragi	0.0	6.7	6.9	43.9	183.3
Samai	0.0	0.0	0.0	19.1	42.4
Varugu	0.0	0.0	4.2	14.0	69.9
Maize	36.5	3.1	0.0	0.0	0.0
Others	21.1	0.0	7.5	8.1	79.4
Millets	58.0	15.2	75.1	282.7	758.3
All	598.1	93.3	96.1	343.4	910.0

Table 27.5: Trends in the Cropping Pattern in Reddynagampalem during 1920 and 2005

Name of Crop	*2005*		*1990*		*1970*	*1950*	*1933*
	Kharif	*Rabi*	*Kharif*	*Rabi*	*Kharif*	*Kharif*	*Kharif*
Cereals	39.2		13.7		17	21.6	28.9
Pulses		9.2	1	5.5	4.1	8	4
Condiments and spices		7	1		2	4	19
Industrial	4.6	15.4	5	3.5	3	2	4
Vegetables							
Topes	4.2		2.4		2		13.3
Drugs and Narcotics	2						
All	50	31.6	23.1	9	28.1	35.6	69.2
	Percentage to the total operated area repectively (priod-wise)						
Cereals	78.4	0.0	59.3	0.0	60.5	60.7	41.8
Pulses	0.0	18.4	4.3	23.8	14.6	22.5	5.8
Condiments and spices	0.0	14.0	4.3	0.0	7.1	11.2	27.5
Industrial	9.2	30.8	21.6	15.2	10.7	5.6	5.8
Vegetables	0.0	0.0	0.0	0.0	0.0	0.0	0.0
Topes	8.4	0.0	10.4	0.0	7.1	0.0	19.2
Drugs and Narcotics	4.0	0.0	0.0	0.0	0.0	0.0	0.0
All	100.0	63.2	100.0	39.0	100.0	100.0	100.0

Table 27.6: Changes in the Percapita Food Grains (in kgs) in Nagampalem

	2005	*1990*	*1970*	*1950*	*1933*
Popua	486	434.5	255	94.5	42
Black Paddy	0.0	0.0	0.0	0.0	0.0
White Paddy	102.5	22.7	0.0	0.0	0.0
Cholam	0.0	5.1	35.3	96.3	238.6
Ragi	0.0	6.6	6.9	15.3	64.3
Samai	0.0	0.0	0.0	0.0	0.0
Varugu	0.0	0.0	4.3	21.3	59.1
Maize	0.0	3.0	0.0	0.0	0.0
Others	44.9	0.0	7.6	0.0	0.0
Millets	22.5	14.8	41.3	128.0	348.6
All	121.5	40.8	51.7	128.0	348.6

Table 27.7: The Impact of Changes in the Cropping Pattern on Food Security, Land Alienation, Livelihood and Dependency among Tribal Communities during 1930 to 2005

S.No.	Period	Changes in Cropping Pattern	Food Security	Land Alienation	Dependency on State and Non-tribes	Livelihood	Economies/ Advantages	Non-tribal exploitation	Forest dept. exploitation
1.	pre-1933s	Collecting NTFP, hunting, fishery, animal grazing and others	very low	less	very low	very low	very low	very low	low
2.	1933-1950	shifting cultivation of small millets, NTFP, hunting, animal husbandry, fishery and other	low	moderate	low	low	low	moderate	moderate
3.	1950-70	Settled cultivation of cereals, pulses, condiments and spices, industrial, vegetables, topes, drugs and narcotics, fishery, hunting, animal husbandry	moderate	high	moderate	moderate	low	high	high
4.	1970-90	Cereals, industrial, vegetables, fishery and animal husbandry	low	low	high	moderate	moderate	moderate	moderate
5.	1990-05	Cereal, industrial, vegetables and animal husbandry and others	moderate	very low	moderate	high	moderate	low	low

Source: Field survey and study documents of SAKTI (NGO).

28

Rural Employment Act and Tribal Women in North East

Kapil Sikka and ***Vijender Singh Beniwal***

Abstract

The National Rural Employment Guarantee Act, 2005 (NREGA) notified on 7th September 2005 and came into effect on February 2, 2006 in 200 of India's most backward districts. However, from April 1, 2008 the Act covers all of rural India. Vide an amendment in the NREG Act, on 2nd October, 2009, the name of the act has been changed to Mahatma Gandhi National Rural Employment Guarantee Act.

MGNREGA is a unique employment opportunity for rural women who really get a chance to earn through their own income.[1] Women earn same as men on MGNERGA, in a survey it is mentioned that majority of women workers collect their own wages (79 per cent) and also keep them (68 per cent).[2] MGNREGA has significant achievements with regard to mobilisation of women wage workers, gender parity of wages and increased control over women's earnings from MGNREGA. There has been acceptability from large sections of society that MGNREGA has provided better working conditions, exploitation free work culture and of course better wages for women. Though not conceived on the gender lines, it incidentally impacted the empowerment of women at the rural level as it certainly provided the mobility to women at village level, which is one of the essential factors of empowerment. The statistics from the 2006 to the year 2010 show that the participation of the women at national level had increased from 42 per cent to 48.8 per cent which is clearly determining how the scheme has roped in the women at the village and made them the catalyst of rural growth.[3]

Schedule II of the paragraph six of the acts emphasis on the word, priority, which is itself evident of gender mainstreaming, as the text denotes that "*Priority*" should be given to women in the allocation of work in such a way that "*at least one-third of the beneficiaries shall be women*".[4]

This paper will focus upon how the national rural employment scheme is contributing in the development of the rural women, which in turn are contributing to the development of North East. The increase in per capita income of women is directly influencing the indicators of growth like education for rural children, medical services for elder women, repayment of debts. Over to all, the national level migration rate has come down to 59 per cent, which in turn is a sign of developed society and hence MGNREGA is doing a lot in terms of development of North East.[5]

MGNREGA: The Legislation

The National Rural Employment Guarantee Act, 2005 (NREGA) notified on 7th September 2005 and came into effect on February 2, 2006 in 200 of India's most backward districts. However, from April 1, 2008 the Act covers all of rural India. Vide an amendment in the NREG Act, on 2nd October 2009, the name of the Act has been changed to Mahatma Gandhi National Rural Employment Guarantee Act.

The preface of the Act clearly mentions the reason behind the implementation "An Act to provide for the enhancement of livelihood security of the households in rural areas of the country by providing at least one hundred days of guaranteed wage employment in every financial year to every household whose adult members volunteer to do unskilled manual work and for matters connected therewith or incidental thereto."[6]

MGNREGA is a unique employment opportunity for rural population who really get a chance to earn their livelihood within their own villages. Moreover it is a right based programme, the rights of MGNREGA workers include employment on demand, minimum wages, payment within 15 days and basic worksite facilities, among others.[7] MGNREGA have been a lifeline for rural poor as it had lowered the rural migration level (59 per cent); moreover it had economically benefitted the rural poor by giving an employment guarantee which ensures that they have basic education for their wards, money to get treated for illness, measure for repayment of debts and the non-hazardous quality of work.[8]

Salient Features of Act

1. The Act made supplementary livelihood in rural areas through unskilled manual work a legal right.
2. The Act permits certain categories of work like water conservation, drought proofing, irrigation, land development, rejuvenation of traditional water bodies, flood control and drainage work, rural connectivity and work on the

land of SC/ST/BPL/IAY beneficiaries/land reform beneficiaries/ individual small and marginal farmers to be taken up for providing employment to the job seeking rural households.

3. Crèche, drinking water, first aid at worksites.
4. Grievance redressal mechanisms for workers.

The Act had become an important towards realisation of right to work and right of dignified work. It had been an influential in "arresting out-migration of rural households in search of employment simultaneously enhancing people's livelihood on a sustained basis, by developing the economic and social infrastructure in rural areas." The works under the Act seeks to address. MNREGA works are capable of addressing the causes of chronic poverty such as drought, deforestation and soil erosion. If effectively implemented, the employment guaranteed under the Act has the potential of transforming the geography of poverty.[9]

MGNREGA is a response to sudden economic crises and manmade disasters. The author focuses on the term "livelihood security" enshrined in the preamble of the Act. The rural unemployment remains the genesis of the birth of this Act.[10] The Act had the minimum wage rate for the casual workers which had impacted the wages of the workers in the open market as well. The author tagged the scheme as "bottom up, demand driven". This paper further examines the performance of MNREGA in various states through NSSO data 2009-10. The various stake holders like SC's, ST's and women were also studied to analyse the demand for work vis-à-vis unemployment. Moreover, a comparison had been drawn among the various states based on the "Demand Effect" of poverty.[11]

Gender Status in Informal Labour Markets

Gender equality is both a core concern and an essential part of human development. All too often, women are discriminated against in health, education and the labour market, which restricts their freedoms.[12] The extent of discrimination can be measured through the Gender Inequality Index (GII), which captures the loss of achievement due to gender inequality in three dimensions: reproductive health, empowerment and labour market participation, the higher the GII value, the greater the discrimination, based on 2012 data for 148 countries, India ranks 132.[13]

Women's employment in the informal sector had risen due to various reasons. With the adoption of the structural adjustment programme women tend to loose ground in the formal sectors of the economy. The growth of ancillarisation and industrial employment through sub-contracting appears to be gaining importance. Stagnating and falling incomes of households due to poor performance of the economy also leads to increased entry of women into the labour market. The process of globalisation, export-oriented industrialisation and relocation of industries from the developed to the developing countries also lead to the increase in the employment in the informal sector. Women's employment is often favoured in many of these industries.[14] It has been argued that the growing flexibility in the labour market, or increasing informalisation, had led to feminisation of the labour force (Standing, 1999). Feminisation implies that more women find themselves in jobs traditionally taken by men. Or certain jobs could have changed to have characteristics associated with traditional women's work. Such as informal contracts, lower remuneration, less security provided and lower skills. This process was actually leading to a convergence of male and female patterns of labour force participation. However, it has been argued that this process of narrowing of gender differentials in paid work should in fact be described as "masculinisation" (Elson, 1999). It is part of a process where a large part of women's work becomes directly subject to market force, as was the characteristics of men's work. International evidence has shown a tendency for the female share of non-agricultural employment to rise (Standing, 1999), though the share remains small, in most countries in Africa, Latin America and Asia.[15] Much of women's work remains unrecognised and unvalued. This has an impact on the status of women in society, their opportunities in public life and the gender-blindness of development policy.

Engendering MGNREGA

The preface of the act clearly mentions the reason behind the implementation "An Act to provide for the enhancement of livelihood security of the households in rural areas of the country by providing at least one hundred days of guaranteed wage employment in every financial year to every household whose adult members volunteer to do unskilled manual work and for matters connected therewith or incidental thereto".[16]

The statistics from the 2006 to the year 2010 show that the participation of the women at national level had increased from 42 per cent to 48.8 per cent which is clearly determining how the scheme has roped in the women at the village and made them the catalyst of rural growth.[17] Schedule II of the paragraph six of the acts emphasis on the word, priority, which is itself evident of gender mainstreaming, as the text denotes that *"Priority"* should be given to women in the allocation of work in such a way that *"at least one-third of the beneficiaries shall be women"*.[18] The famous slogan "*Har Haath Ko Kaam Do, Kaam Ko Poora Daam Do*" determines the equality concept amongst the NREGA workers. NREGA provides women an opportunity to earn a minimum wage, and lessens their largely unrecognised role in providing for and sustaining their families. The recognition of the problems they face in accessing the Employment Guarantee and some creative thinking about how to deal with these would go a long way in extending the benefits of the Act to this fundamental section of society.[19]

The NSSO 66th Round indicates that MGNREGA has reduced the traditional wage discrimination in public works. As per the data, average wage for labour in MGNREGA was Rs 90.9 per day for men, and for women it was Rs 87 per day. The difference was larger for labour in other public works; Rs 98.3 per day for men and Rs 86.1 per day for women. Other studies also suggest an upward movement of unskilled wages for women post-MGNREGA. For instance, in Kerala, the wages for women in agriculture and forest work rose from Rs 70–80 in 2007 to Rs 110–25 in 2009. In fact, real wages increased more rapidly for female workers than for male workers. In a survey of 75 villages across four states—Bihar, Gujarat, Kerala and Rajasthan—it was found that the ratio of male-female wage rates, on an average, declined from 1.40 in 2007–08 to 1.30 in 2009–10.[20]

Review of Literature

There is large number of studies related with the impact of MGNREGA on women's participation which generally shows positive impact; some of them are as follows:

1. Jandu (2008) carried out a research in four states namely, Chhattisgarh, Madhya Pradesh, Orissa and Tamil Naidu Survey data shown that women workers are more confident about their roles as contributors to family expenditure and their work decisions and it gives them space in public sphere. Most of the respondent felt that the act is very important for them. The study found positive impact of the MGNREGA on migration patterns.

2. Hazarika (2009) examined the impact of MGNREGA on gender empowerment in Morigaon and Bongaigaon district of Assam. This study showed that almost 70 to 80 per cent of sample workers had meaningful income other than unpaid family work during the pre-NREGA. Majority of the worker felt that they are now in better position to fulfill their own requirement without looking at others. Nearly 65 to 70 per cent women workers attended gram sabha meeting held in connection with NREGA. In Bongaigaon District, a large number of job card holders were found who have become Panchayat representatives.

3. Ramesh and Kumar (2009) in their study also found that MGNREGA hold the powerful prospect of bringing major changes in the lives of women. MGNREGA is playing a substantial role in empowering women economically and laying the basis for greater independence and self-esteem. It has become a beacon of light in the empowerment of the rural women, and contributed substantially for the increased living and economic conditions by creating equal wages to male and female workers and increasing the minimum wages. Their study was conducted in 2009-10 by selecting 500 women beneficiaries. Out of the 670 workers, 74.62 per cent are women and the rest are men. The beneficiaries expressed that this programme helped in easing out the debt burden to some extent.

4. Khera and Nayak (2009), through their sample survey in six Hindi speaking states of North India focuses on impact of NREGA in the lives of women

workers. This study reveals that there is significant benefits reported by women include increased food security and better ability to avoid hazardous work. They pointed out that as per survey data, NREGA works increases average wage rate comparing to private labour market. Besides this in NREGA, the working hours are limited to 7-8 hours in a day and therefore it is helpful to prevent harassment of women workers. By using random sampling they found that NREGA work has allowed women to spend money on their own needs, while earlier they might not have been at the liberty to do so. Some women reported that work with private landlords and contractors are often replete with an underlying threat of possibility of sexual abuse and exploitation. NREGA has brought mental satisfaction.

5. Panda, B. Dutta, A.K. (2009), through their study found that this Act empowered rural tribal women in Sikkim and Meghalaya by enhancing their confidence level and by ensuring some degree of financial independence. They mentioned that in the traditional institution like Durbars women are not allowed to have political representation. But mandatory involvement of women in PRI institution has given boon to women empowerment in the state. Around 94 per cent of women workers in Sikkim and 38 per cent in Meghalaya felt that they have been able to access health facilities better after working in NREGA.

6. Sudarshan (2009) reviews the place of MGNREGA within the border of social protection and gender concern. As examined by him, social protection was applicable mostly in organised sector until 1990s. Since the early 1990 public policy and public works in India tried to include women as a percentage of beneficiaries and have not paid much attention to gender sensitive design. But MGNREGA in its design has attempted some gender sensitivity. In Kerala there has been some shift out of agriculture into MGNREGA, mainly with respect to female workers. The minimum wages paid under the MGNREGA is far greater than agriculture wages. The good performance of MGNREGA in Kerala is possible because of state government commitment and the managerial role of the Kudumbashree and area development supervisors. This study reveals that MGNREGA not only stimulate local development but also overcome the women's weak position in labour market.

7. Pankaj and Tankha (2010) examines the empowerment effects of MGNREGA through field survey in Bihar, Jharkhand, Rajasthan and Himachal Pradesh. The study shown that a women worker's earning from MGNREGA constituted 14 per cent of the total annual income of the household on average across the four sample districts in 2008-09. Majority of women workers collect and retain their wages. Before NREGA 44 per cent women said that they were able to meet their personal needs through their own earning where after NREGA it is 71 per cent. This study shows an increased participation of women in gram sabha meetings. Besides this 73 per cent of women which had attended the gram sabha spoke in the meeting.

Gender Inclusion in North East

National Rural Employment Guarantee Act (NREGA) was originally implemented in 16 districts of eight North-Eastern States, namely Arunachal Pradesh, Assam, Manipur, Meghalaya, Mizoram, Nagaland, and Tripura, but from April 1, 2008, it was extended to all seven states.

Measuring the inclusion of women in MGNREGA in the seven states of North East in past three years gives a very contradicting scenario, as we can see vide Table 28.1, that Meghalaya and Tripura had registered more than 33 per cent women participation in NREGA work in all three years, whereas Arunachal Pradesh had registered a sudden dip in women participation in the year 2012-13. On the other hand, Assam, Mizoram and Nagaland are still to benefit women in essence, as it can be noticed, that in all three financial years, the average rate of participation had remained around 25 per cent. Whereas Manipur, except in the financial year 2010-11, had achieved the 33 per cent benchmark of women reservation.

Table 28.1: Participation Rate of Women in North-eastern States in India

State	*Women's participation Rate (Per cent) 2010-11*	*Women's participation Rate (Per cent) 2011-12*	*Women's participation Rate (Per cent) 2012-13*
Assam	21.22	24.91	25.71
Manipur	29.87	33.58	35.82
Meghalaya	36.54	41.59	41.94
Mizoram	20.45	23.61	23.52
Nagaland	25.12	27.05	25.16
Tripura	37.67	38.64	41.09
Arunachal Pradesh	35.44	40.33	29.39
INDIA	**46.41**	**48.81**	**52.44**

Source: www.nrega.nic.in

Table 28.2: Notified Wages (2012-13)

State	*Wages in Rs*
Assam	136
Manipur	144
Meghalaya	128
Mizoram	136
Nagaland	126
Tripura	124
Arunachal Pradesh	124

Source: www.nrega.nic.in

Participation of Women under MGNREGA in North East:

There have been many positive aspects of the Rural Employment Act in North East:

Increase in average wage

Statistics had shown that average wage in post MGNREGA period had increased many folds. The economic empowerment of female had led to the enhancement in decision making in household matters.

Household Income

- Moreover females now have alternate employment opportunities, which has enhanced women's contribution in household income.

Income-earning Opportunity

- MGNREGA creates opportunity for women to be economically independent. It allows them to fulfill their needs without depending on others. It can be witnessed from the above mentioned statistics that women participation under MGNREGA is very moderate, ranging from lowest in Assam to highest in Tripura and Meghalaya.

Areas of Concern:

Non-availability Crèche Facilities

- According to the act when there are more than five children under the age of six, a female worker is to be appointed to take care of them. Due to non-availability of crèche facilities women either leave the toddlers at home or prefer not to work under this scheme.

Nature of Work under MGNREGA

- As majority of work under this is the unskilled one which requires rigorous labour, which remains another factor of women skipping it.

Inadequate Facilities at Worksite

- Moreover lack of facilities such as drinking water, first aid, shade at worksite etc is a problem for the workers. Because of non-availability of shade for resting, pregnant and aged-women find difficulties to participate in MGNREGA.

Delay in Payments of Wages

- Delay in payment of wages in another area of concern as it is a harassment for women workers to inquire for wages on daily basis.

Conclusion

Nevertheless, the NREGA had been an effective wage earning opportunity for the poor women who use to migrate to nearby villages and towns in search of wage employment along with their children. NREGA has also proved to be a boon for SHGs as many were not able to repay back loans borrowed from the bank because few members use to default as they didn't had much earning opportunities. The act has also brought in improvement in the health status of the women workers. It has further ensured a strong social safety net for the vulnerable rural women, women empowerment happens to be the most visible impact during NREGA. The provision of equal wages for men and women in the Act, the opportunity to share information during the course of work in NREGA work site the opportunity and necessity of interacting with the bank/ post office/government officials have all in a fundamental way empowered the rural tribal women by enhancing their confidence level and by ensuring some degree of financial independence.[21]

References

1. Mahatma Gandhi National Rural Employment Guarantee Act, 2005.
2. Khera, Ritika (2011), The Battle for Employment Guarantee, p. 54, Oxford University Press.
3. Mahatma Gandhi NREGA National Reports 2006-10, MoRD (http://nrega.nic.in/netnrega/home.aspx).
4. Mahatma Gandhi NREGA, Schedule II, Section 6.
5. Dreze, Jean, Ritika Khera (2011),The Battle for Employment Guarantee, p. 51, Oxford University Press.
6. Preface, NREGA, 2005.
7. Dreze, Jean, Ritika Khera (2011), *The Battle for Employment Guarantee*, p. 49, Oxford University Press.
8. Dreze, Jean, Ritika Khera (2011), *The Battle for Employment Guarantee*, p. 51, Oxford University Press.
9. All-India Report on Evaluation of NREGA: A Survey of Twenty Districts (2008). Institute of Manpower Research, Narela.
10. Krishnamurthy, J., 2006. Employment Guarantee and Crisis Response. *Economic and Political Weekly*, Vol. 41(9), pp. 789-790.
11. Dutta, Pooja, Murgai, Rinku and Others, 2012. *Does India's Employment Guarantee Scheme Guarantee Employment?* Policy Research Working Paper, The World Bank.[Online]Availableat:http://www.wds.worldbank.org/servlet/WDSContentServer/WDSP/IB/2012/03/21/000158349_20120321082953/Rendered/PDF/WPS6003.pdf[Accessed 12 November, 2012].
12. Human Development Report (1995), UNDP.
13. Human Development Report (2013), UNDP.
14. Unni, Jeemol, Rani Uma (2000). *Women In Informal Employment In India{Private }* Available at [http://previous.wiego.org/papers/unnirani.pdf].
15. *Ibid.*
16. Preface, NREGA, 2005.
17. Mahatma Gandhi NREGA National Reports 2006-10 , MoRD (http://nrega.nic.in/netnrega/home.aspx).
18. Mahatma Gandhi NREGA, Schedule II, Section 6.
19. Raja, Annie, 2007. Ensuring the Right to Work for Women: A Review of the NREGA from the Gender Perspective. *Gender and Governance – A Review of the*

Women's Agenda in the National Common Minimum Programme, Wada Na Todo Abhiyan, New Delhi-16.[Online] Available at http://www.wadanatodo.net/images/160407/GenderNCMP_Eng.pdf [Accessed 15 November 2012].

20. Ministry of Rural Development, Government of India, *MGNREGA Sameeksha, An Anthology of Research Studies on the Mahatma Gandhi National Rural Employment Guarantee Act, 2005, 2006–2012*, edited and compiled by Mihir Shah, Neelakshi Mann and Varad Pande, New Delhi: Orient Black Swan, 2012.

21. IIM Shillong, 2009; *Appraisal of NREGA in the states of Meghalaya and Sikkim*, A Project report by B. Panda, A.K. Dutta and S. Prusty.

29

Livelihood Security through Land Distribution: An Empirical Study on Chenchus of Andhra Pradesh

L Reddeppa

Abstract

The fulfillment of the country's development objectives depends on the improvement of income and livelihood of the people living under poverty. The stark reality is that the proportion of such people is relatively high in the case of SCs and STs than that of the other social groups in the country. This is more so in the case of Primitive Tribal Groups (PTGs). There is one such PTG, Chenchu a food gather tribe living in Andhra Pradesh. Their livelihood is under threat after the declaration of their areas as tiger reserve forest and the inroads of modern development. To compensate their loss meted out due to policies and the dwindling natural resources in their areas for livelihood, several welfare schemes have been implemented, particularly after establishment of Integrated Tribal Development Agency (ITDA) in the late eighties. Market based Land distribution is the most prominent scheme that the financial assistance under the scheme is higher than that of other schemes for the exclusive benefit of individual landless households. Apart from the land, provisions were also made for promotion of agriculture in order to improve their livelihood. In this context, several questions are raised for greater understanding of their livelihood security. How far the land and other support measures contributing to the family income? What are the other livelihood options available to generate threshold income for crossing poverty line? The study is an attempt to understand the livelihood security from land achieved and suggest appropriate policy. It is observed from the study that the LPS is made effective in improvement of livelihood and crossing poverty line for about 10 per cent of the families and an additional income for about another 20 per cent of the families. However, a large majority of them could not translate their land into income due to various socio-economic and cultural barriers. Half of them not even cultivated their land due to purchase of land with poor quality from private party for lack of adequate budget; pending partisan land to individual beneficiaries; delay or pending energisation bore wells, and lack of small investment and plough bullocks for cultivation. Thus, the ITDA has to provide better land of at least two acres with irrigation facility and timely supply of all inputs needed on subsidy including access to institutional credit for each family, particularly first generation cultivators.

Introduction

The fulfillment of the country's development objectives depends on the well being of the poorest of the poor 'or' the people living under poverty. They have a right to benefit from the growth and development efforts of the Government. But, the high level of poverty that persists in some sections of the people reflects the denial of such right. The stark reality is that the proportion of such people is relatively high in the case of SCs and STs than that of the other social groups in the country. This is more so in the case of Primitive Tribal Groups (PTGs). There is one such PTG, Chenchu a food gather tribe living in Andhra Pradesh. However, after the declaration of their areas as tiger reserve forest, drain of natural resources in their areas, and the inroads modern development with public private partnership, their livelihood is under threat. For them, the Government has distributed lands under Land Purchase Scheme (LPS) and implemented other schemes for promotion of agriculture and allied activities in order to improve their livelihood. Thus, the intension of the Government for intervention is to improve their livelihood and income through settled cultivation.

The sustainable agriculture in the context of individual farmers depends on access to economical size of land holding with irrigation facility. The First Five Year Plan itself suggested the concept of an economically viable land holding size, which was about two acres of irrigated land for self-cultivation. The Maharashtra law defined the economically viable holding as four permanently irrigated acres. However, majority of the states have not defined the economically viable land holding size due to variation in the quality of the soil and irrigation facility, seasonal and climate conditions that are required for the cropping pattern. In recent years, many states have concentrated more on distribution of vacant lands after exhausting the land distribution under land ceiling Laws due to disposal of such land is with the Government. This has significant contribution in Andhra Pradesh. A disquieting feature of land use has been a declined pastures and grazing lands in the country due to distribution of such lands to the landless particularly to the weaker sections of the society. But, the lands are not producing any surplus to the families for their sustenance.

A study carried out by the NSSO (2003) reveals that nearly 40 per cent of the farmer households disliked farming and wanted to give up the profession due to its unprofitable nature.

A significant proportion of the rural poor are living in backward areas that are challenged by difficult agro-climatic conditions, and inadequate infrastructure and support services. At the household level. It is likely to be harder to escape poverty, if the household lives in persistently poor district; is a member of scheduled tribe; relies on casual labour for a significant portion of its livelihood, possibly involving migration from a remote, especially forest area, and is illiterate and lacks kinship and other networks, and is large". Thus, majority of Chenchus are manifested with several such factors and are vulnerable to poverty. In this context, several questions are raised for greater understanding of their livelihood security. How far the land and other support measures helpful in improvement of livelihood in terms of income? What are the other livelihood options available to generate threshold income for crossing poverty line? The present study is an attempt to understand the livelihood security achieved from land in terms of income to suggest appropriate policy.

The study is mainly based on the primary data collected from 322 sample families (proposed one third, but it is 35 per cent) out of 928 families received lands and other inputs for the promotion of agriculture during the period 2000 – 2005. The data was collected from all the villages where the LPS implemented. One third households were chosen from each study village on simple random sampling method. The land use pattern, household data and income has been collected for the cross-section year 2006-07. Apart from this, secondary data had also been collected from the Integrated Tribal Development Agency (ITDA) with regard to the expenditure on various schemes implemented for development of Chenchus, and village wise data on LPS. The study is broadly divided into five sections after brief introduction to the study – (1) Approaches and Schemes implemented for Livelihood improvement of Chenchus; (2) Distribution of Land under LPS and its utilisation; (3) Contribution of Livelihood from land and other Options; (4) Level of poverty and shifting of families from below to above; and (5) Conclusions.

1. Approaches and Schemes for Livelihood Improvement of Chenchus

The Chenchu tribe was declared as a Primitive Tribal Group (PTG) in the year 1975. A separate ITDA was established in the late eighties to look into the all-round development of the Chenchus. The total population of the Chenchus is 41,787 as per the records of ITDA Srisailam. The profile of Chenchus indicates that they are living in 338 gudems (villages) which are close to and within the forest boundaries. They live in 36 mandals all over the six districts. Their population in Prakasam District is substantially high at 13,321; followed by Mahabubnagar (10,406), Kurnool (7,915), Guntur (6,376), Ranga Reddy (2,700), and Nalgonda (1,069) districts. On the whole, their population is more than

3,001 in five mandals; 1001 to 3000 in nine mandals; 501 to 1000 in four mandals; 301 to 500 in six mandals and less than 300 in the remaining 12 mandals. The size of the family among the Chenchus is very small and mostly three to four members. The total population of the 322 sample families consists of 1,121 members, of which 537 are male and 574 are female.

The livelihood patterns of the Chenchus have interwoven with forest resources for centuries.

They consume the fruits, roots and tubers, etc, besides animal meat available in the forests, and also engage in the collection of minor forest products. "The Chenchus do not care much for money or material wealth. They have hardly developed any technique for preserving food. Their care for the future is marginal as they are used to living on a day-to-day basis. Though the tribal work as forest labour at times, they mostly prefer to fall back on their native skills to hunt and gather food". After the inroads of modern development, allotment of vast stretches of tribal lands for mining activity, construction of irrigation projects and declaration of their area as a tiger reserve, imposition of Wild Life Protection Act, the tribals have lost their self-reliance.

Agriculture has been the secondary source of livelihood for them even after many years of Independence. It is observed that the proportion of Chenchu families depending on own cultivation are only 12 per cent, which is far below the level of people in general (27.74 per cent) and STs as a whole (41.19 per cent) in Andhra Pradesh, according to the 1991 Census. The tribals living in forest areas in general are better accessed to the land than that of other social groups. But, it is entirely different in the case of Chenchu tribe that large majority are landless. They are sparsely populated in a separate village with close proximity to forests and also to the non-tribals. But they depend on others only on wage employment from agriculture, which is seasonal for a few days. The situation has changed in recent years as the forest resources are dwindling in their areas. The time has now come to find some alternative sources of income on a sustainable basis. Otherwise, their life would be under threat.

Of late, realising their backwardness, a separate Integrated Tribal Development Agency (ITDA) was established in the late eighties to look into the overall development of them. The welfare schemes implemented for the development of the Chenchus can be broadly classified into four categories – (a) educational programmes, (b) creation of basic infrastructure facilities like drinking water, health, housing, road and bus facility, etc., (c) Economic Support Schemes (ESS) (d) other development schemes like supply of daily requirements through Public Distribution System (PDS).These schemes have been implementing with the funds made available to them under the Special Central Assistance, special budget for PTG development, State Tribal sub-plan and mobilisation of institutional finance.

In the case of ESS, the more important schemes are the land based schemes like land purchase, land development, irrigation, supply of plough bullocks, provision of modern agriculture implements and inputs supplies on free/ subsidised rates, promotion of dairy, sheep rearing, etc., besides youth development through self employment in the lines of industry, service and business (ISB) sectors. The ITDA, Srisailam had spent an amount of Rs 100.32 crores in a period of 17 years, i.e., from the year 1990-91 to 2006-07 for the benefit of total population (41787 people) or about 12,000 households. The amount spent on each family on an average is Rs 83,630 over a period of 17 years. In spite of all the schemes, the problem of poverty is more predominant and persistent among them. Realising this, all Chenchu families were issued Antyodaya Anna Yojana (AAY) ration cards. They get 35 kgs of rice per family per month. Apart from these, they also get red gram, cooking oil, kerosene on subsidy and other essentials on whole sale prices from the Daily Requirement Depots DRDs. This would create physical access at least larger extent of their cereals requirement and over and above are to be managed to get economic access. Apart from this, the ITDA has implemented Land Purchase and allied schemes for promotion of agriculture as permanent solution to their food security and livelihood improvement. But how far these objectives are fulfilled under LPS is discussed in the following sections.

2. Land Purchase Scheme Implemented by ITDA, Srisailam

The traditionally held view is that ownership of agriculture land in rural areas has a bearing on the family in various socio-economic spheres of rural setting—the land ownership ensures family with income, food and livelihood security, social status in the village, community and society at large and credit worthiness. In the modern context, it also facilitates to avail other benefit of the Government for creation of irrigation facility and take up other activities like horticulture, animal husbandry and dairy. Thus, Land Purchase Scheme is being implemented by the ITDA, Srisailam, since 2000. About 1,850 acres of land was purchased for the benefit of 1,149 families in the districts of Kurnool, Prakasam, Mahabubnagar, and Guntur during 2000-2007. The total expenditure incurred during the period was 475.766 lakhs. This shows that the beneficiaries have received, on an average, about 1.61 acres each with an average cost of Rs 25,692 per acre. In the process, the Government has spent an amount of Rs 41407 per beneficiary. However, there were no year-wise targets as such for the scheme. It was observed that land was not purchased during 2003-04 and 2004-05. This may be either due to lack of budget for the scheme or non-availability of lands for sale from land owners.

It was also observed from the data that a major portion of the land was purchased by the ITDA, Srisailam under the Andhra Pradesh Participatory Tribal Development Project (APPTDP) programme during 1999-2003. More specifically, half of the total expenditure on the scheme was incurred in one financial year, i.e., 2002-2003. This could be due to the availability of funds for the ITDA in the closing year (2003) of the project APPTDP. For details, see Table 29.1.

Table 29.1: Expenditure and Extent of Land Purchased from 2000-01 to 2006-07

Year	*Beneficiaries*	*Extent of Area in Acres*	*Expenditure (in Rs)*	*Per Acre Land Cost (in Rs)*
2000-01	117	140.63	3743800	26621
2001-02	95	124.53	3309249	26574
2002-03	556	1052.95	23841887	22643
2005-06	251	322.07	9189800	28533
2006-07	130	211.59	7491890	35407
Total	**1149**	**1851.77**	**47576620**	**25692**

Source: ITDA Office, Srisailam.

The data on land prices indicate that the per-acre price of the land was Rs 26621 during 2000-01; this continued more or less even in the next year. However, during 2002-03, it steeply fell to Rs 22643. This could be due to the three-year drought period that ended in 2003. Subsequently, the prices of the lands increased more steeply to Rs 28533 during 2005-06 and to Rs 35407 during 2006-07 due to better monsoon conditions and introduction of new irrigation projects.

Extent of Farming Activity among the Beneficiaries of the Land

The land was distributed mostly in the name of women and their families were mostly (97 per cent) landless prior to distribution of land under LPS. How far the land distribution programme has helped to bring them in fold of self cultivating category is the moot point? It is observed that about 127 beneficiaries out of the 322 (about 39.4 per cent) have taken up own cultivation; about 46.9 per cent have not cultivate; and 13.7 per cent have leased out their land. The utilisation of land is relatively better in Kurnool district where the number of beneficiaries not cultivated is only 9.4 per cent and remaining are at least leased out their land, if not take up own cultivation. The beneficiaries not take up own cultivation quite high (about 60 per cent) in other district. For district wise details, see Table 29.2.

Table 29.2: Number of Beneficiaries Who Have Taken up Own Cultivation

S.No.	*District*	*No. of beneficiaries*			
		Own cultivation	*Not cultivated*	*Leased out*	*Total Sample*
1.	Kurnool	48(56.5)	8(9.4)	29(34.1)	85(100)
2.	Guntur	16(31.4)	32(62.7)	3(5.9)	51(100)
3.	Prakasam	25(28.7)	62(60.9)	9(10.3)	87(100)
4.	Mahabubnagar	38(38.4)	58(58.6)	3(3.0)	99(1000
	Total	127(39.4)	151(46.9)	44(13.7)	322(100)

Source: Field Data.

The quality of the lands distributed to them is more crucial for analysis before the assessment of lands utilised. It was observed from the field as well as discussions with the beneficiaries on the quality of lands distributed under LPS indicate that 21 per cent of the land was not cultivable, of which eight per cent of the land was not even fit for land development. It means the lands are occupied with big boulders, rocks, and contiguous rock structures. Of the remaining, 13 per cent is cultivable, if taken up land development in terms shrimp clearance and take up soil conservation work, which need more investment. Again, the soil is not sure of good quality.

There are instances that the ITDA had provided alternative land after their rejection due to poor quality of soil or not fit for cultivation. Why the ITDA had purchased the land not fit for cultivation without the approval of the farmers? It is observed that the sellers have disposed their lands by adopted lobbying methods with the ITDA officials. Generally, the beneficiaries would expect a good quality of the land with irrigation facility from the ITDA. Such lands could not come up for sale from the land owners. Even if they come for sale, the offered price for the land from the land owners would be high which is beyond the eligibile limit of the ITDA under LPS as expressed by the ITDA officials. Thus, proper utilisation of land can be expected from the Chenchus, if the soils are good, availability of irrigation, access to crop loans from formal financial institutions and supply of other inputs on subsidised prices. Otherwise, it would be difficult to achieve good results by the Chenchus from the lands.

Utilisation of Lands and Cropping Pattern

It is clearly observed that own cultivation is observed mainly in villages where the soil is good and land has some irrigation facility, and also the farmers

Table 29.3 : District-wise Area and Yield Distribution under Different Crops

S.No.	*Type of crop grown*	*Area*		*Yield (in quintals)*	
		In Acres	*Per cent*	*Total*	*per acre*
1.	Red gram	129.46	44.62	229.00	1.77
2.	Maize	41.00	14.13	151.00	3.68
3.	Sunflower	33.45	11.53	107.00	3.20
4.	Paddy	27.50	9.48	158.00	5.75
5.	Jowar	21.20	7.31	62.00	2.92
6.	Castor	15.00	5.17	31.00	2.07
7.	Cotton	7.00	2.41	15.00	2.14
8.	Mirchi	3.00	1.03	12.00	4.00
9.	Turmeric	1.50	0.52	20.00	13.33
10.	Others	11.00	3.79	12.00	1.09
	Total	**290.11**	**100.00**	**79.70**	**2.75**

Source: Field Data.

have past experience as agriculture labour in their vicinity. The extent of area irrigated out of the total land purchased was 5.4 per cent. It shows that most of the area purchased was not irrigated. Subsequently, the ITDA has drilled the bore wells who ever asked to provide irrigation depending on ground water feasibility. But more than 60 per cent of the lands yet to receive either bore wells or other sources of irrigation. It is interesting to note that the bore wells drilled were also not energised. Majority of them are waiting for power supply for more than three years even after installation of sub-mergible pump-sets. On the whole, the extent of area cultivated by the sample beneficiaries including land leased out is 290.11 acres out of the total land of 582.68 acres, which constitutes about 49.77 per cent of the area purchased to them. For details of area and yield per-acre, see Table 29.3.

The crops grown by the beneficiaries were paddy, maize, turmeric, mirchi, groundnut, cotton, etc., under the source of bore well and tank irrigation. The other crops grown were red gram, jowar, sun flower, castor, horse gram, green gram, etc. as rain-fed crops. The area under each crop indicate that red gram was the predominant crop grown by them in 129.46 acres, followed by maize (41 acres), sunflower (33.95 acres), paddy (29.50 acres), jowar (22.2 acres), castor (15 acres), cotton (7 acres). The remaining area under each crops like mirchi, ragi, groundnut, bajra, green gram, horse gram, turmeric, korra, black gram, etc were cultivated in less than three acres. The average yield per acre is much less in most of the beneficiaries for lack of adequate experience of crop cultivation. Despite this, about ten beneficiaries have been practicing modern methods of cultivation and their yield levels are also relatively better. It is important to note that the beneficiaries who studied up to the upper-primary and high school level are utilising the land relatively better than the illiterate. For instance, in the Mittameedapalle of Guntur District, the leader of the group studied up to high school; she is utilising the land more productively, cultivating commercial crops like *mirchi*. She produced about 10 to 15 quintals of *mirchi* per acre of land. Though the land was neither distributed to the individual beneficiaries nor provided irrigation facility by the ITDA, the beneficiaries informally shared the land among themselves, purchased water from the landlords and cultivated their lands. This is a classic example that education has made them utilise the land more productively, and proves that education, especially of the younger generation, is important for bringing about a change in living patterns and lifestyles.

It is observed that value of the lands greatly increased in recent years in most of the villages, due to the newly planned irrigation projects and canals in their vicinity and various other reasons. In fact, the land prices were doubled in some of the villages, while they increased by up to 75 per cent in many villages, and many times more in a few places. For example lands purchased for up to Rs 20000 per acre increased to Rs 15 lakhs per acre in Amangal Mandal of Mahabubnagar District due to the land is close to *Outer Ring Road* and real estate market boom in Hyderabad. At present, one of the beneficiaries is using the land for brick manufacturing.

Reasons for Non-cultivation and Leasing Practice

It is observed that about 60 per cent of the beneficiaries are not take up own cultivation. The main reasons for non-cultivation of land as expressed by the beneficiaries of the LPS are: Land was not partitioned to the individual beneficiaries after registration; no irrigation facility to the land; no plough bullocks; crop loss in the previous year; no credit facilities; chronic health problems for one of the family members; and dispute among the co-beneficiaries after partisan the land. In most cases, the beneficiaries have expressed multiple reasons for non-cultivation of their land. The reasons for leasing out land are also similar to those of non-cultivation other than the reasons like non-partisan of land to individual beneficiaries and the land is not fit for cultivation. Land can be leased out if there is good demand. Leasing out land to others for cultivation is always better option than leaving the land fallow, provided good tenants are available in their areas. The beneficiary would get some income in the process, even if it is less. The leasing income for land ranged from Rs 400 to Rs 1000 per acre in case of dry lands, which can be used for the cultivation of rain fed crops, where the scope for irrigation is nil. There is other category that land can also be cultivated with irrigated crops depending on the availability of irrigation in their vicinity, if water is provided for a price. Such cases were seen in the case of a few beneficiaries in two to three villages where the annual lease income vary from Rs 2000 to Rs 4000 per acre.

The land was leased out mostly to non-tribals. The tenants mostly utilised the land to cultivate irrigated crops such as paddy, maize, sunflower and groundnut. After observing the benefits their tenants derive through cultivation, the beneficiaries take over the land for own cultivation in few cases. The crops like paddy, turmeric and mirchi cultivation have also been practiced by Chenchus mainly due to demonstration effect, though it is meager area by very few. This shows that they are under transition to take up own cultivation in the near future. Hence it is observed that the tenant builds the capacity of the beneficiaries or owners of the land, and the owner of the land gains experience through the investment of tenant by working as wage labour under him. More importantly, the beneficiaries personally oversee the type of crops grown, extent of yield extracted from the land and the cost involved for each crop. There is no scope for land alienation or selling land to the tenant as the beneficiaries of LPS have no legal right to sell the land to others. Moreover, as the land is registered in the name of the women beneficiaries, who are more concerned about their family, the scope for alienation of land is considerably less.

3. Livelihood from Land and Other Options

The yield from the crop was nil or less than the value of the cost of cultivation in case of 19.0 per cent of the beneficiaries out of the total land cultivated by them. It shows that they have lost their hard earned money due to the cultivation of the crops, which excludes the loss of their own labour. The total loss in terms of the paid-out cost was varied from Rs 500 to Rs 3,000 per beneficiary. The loss incurred to them mainly due to lack of adequate rains and continuation of long dry spell in the rainy season. In some of the cases, the seed was also not germinated and in some cases, the tender crop was withered away. The loss incurred to the few have a negative effect on cultivation of crops in the subsequent years, particularly rainfed crops. They are not affordable to take such risks. They are not aware of the crop insurance schemes. Even if they have awareness, it is difficult to get claims due to cumbersome procedures, which is even difficult for developed and educated farmers. The farmer's suicides can be minimised, if the insurance policy is consumer friendly. The poor Chenchus not ventured into own cultivation based on the previous experiences. Non-cultivation of land by majority of the beneficiaries (56 per cent) itself reflects the risks involved in cultivation of crops. Despite this, 44 per cent of the beneficiaries have generated a little income either from own cultivation or leasing out their land. The farmers with little income from own cultivation are about 32 per cent, they are mostly covering the opportunity cost of their labour and a little surplus from land. The income generated anything more than Rs 5000 is really achievement for them. This would cover at least opportunity cost their labour. Such families constitute about 10 per cent out of the total families cultivated their land. About 11 per cent are generating between Rs 3001 and Rs 5000. The remaining not even generating opportunity cost of their labour.

Other Livelihood Options

The livelihood options prior to Land available for food security and income were agriculture labour, collection of Minor Forest Produce (MFP), non-agriculture labour, own cultivation, migration, firewood selling, coal preparation and selling, cattle rearing, etc. All these activities are continuing by them even after receiving land depending on the need and survival strategy of the family. Prior to land distribution, the extent of average income generated from own agriculture was Rs 4333 per year for three families, while it was Rs 4008 for 103 families and another 44 families have income from lease of land. It shows that while own agriculture was one of the livelihood activities for just one per cent of the families previously, it increased to 46 per cent after the land distribution; the remaining (54 per cent) did not have any income from agriculture.

MFP collection is also one of the important livelihoods for generation of income to 66 per cent of the families. Mostly, they engage on collection of minor forest produce like gum, honey, tendu leaves, mohua flower, soap nuts, tamarind, etc., and sold these items either to the Girijan Cooperative Corporation Limited or in the private market. Similarly, non-agricultural labour is one of the activities for 45 per cent of the families prior to the land increased to 49 per cent of the families after land. It shows that majority of them are depending on multiple activities for their livelihood. Among all the activities, minor forest produce is the main source of income for them that each family was generated on an average income of Rs 6,953 prior to the land, which was declined to Rs 6,773 after the land. It is also important to note that MFP collection is not available for about half of the households.

The income from agriculture labour is next in the order of highest average income generated to them. The extent of average annual income was at Rs 5,302 per family for 89 per cent of the families prior to the land, which was Rs 5,022 per family for 92 per cent of the families after the land. It shows that agriculture labour and MFP collection are the most important sources of income. For details of average income generated by a family under different source, see Table 29.4.

Table 29.4 : Generation of Income from Different Occupations

Sl. No.	*Occupation*	*Before Land*			*After Land*		
		Total income in lakhs	*Per cent*	*Average income in Rs*	*Total income in lakhs*	*Per cent*	*Average income in Rs*
1.	Own agriculture	0.13	0.33	4333	5.17	11.4	4008
2.	Minor Forest Produce	14.88	38.10	6953	14.41	31.9	6773
3.	Agriculture Labour	14.85	38.00	5302	14.92	33.0	5022
4.	Non-agri. Labour	6.04	15.45	4194	6.67	14.76	4245
5.	Parents	0.08	0.20	2666	0.09	0.20	3000
6.	Other sources	3.12	8.00	5026	3.91	8.66	3994
	Total	**39.08**	**100.0**	**12138**	**45.17**	**100.0**	**14028**

Source: Field Data.

It is important to note that the distribution of land has created seriousness and confidence among them to improve their livelihood depending on multiple activities. This can be observed that the families depending on agriculture labour, MFP collection and other activities have increased even after land.

Improvement of Total Family Income after Land

It would be appropriate to analyse the income levels of the beneficiary families before and after land based on the classification of the families into different size of income. The income generated before and after land are comparable, because majority of the beneficiaries were received lands in the year 2003-2004. The change in the prices of food items and living patterns within a period of two to three years is much less. The ITDA has also been implementing various welfare schemes including supply of food items under public distribution system. The income before land was less than Rs 12,000 per year in 55.6 per cent of the families declined to 36 per cent after land.

On the other hand, the annual income was above Rs 12,000 per family in 44.4 per cent of the families before land increased to 64 per cent of the families after land. It shows that 20 per cent of the families improved their level of income from below to above Rs 12,000 per year. It shows that there was no much improvement in the level of income in the case of the other 80 per cent of the families even after land. This may be perhaps due to non-cultivation of land by a majority and the income generated by a few was very limited. For details, see Table 29.5.

Table 29.5 : Improvement of Family Annual Income before and after Land

Level of Family Income (Rs.)	*Before Land*		*After Land*	
	Nos.	*Per cent*	*Nos.*	*Per cent*
Up to 6,000	14	4.3	2	0.6
6001 – 9000	58	18.0	38	11.8
9001 – 12000	107	33.2	76	23.6
12001 – 15000	79	24.5	103	32.0
15001 – 18000	46	14.3	72	22.4
18001 +	18	5.6	31	9.6
Total	**322**	**100.0**	**322**	**100.0**

Source: Field Data.

4. Families Crossed the Poverty Line

The poverty line was defined in the country that a person need an intake of food which is required to generate 2400 calories of energy in rural areas and 2100 calories in urban areas. Apart from the food needs, every family expects a minimum income to meet other basic needs like cloth, shelter, health, education to their children, etc., besides the cost of transport and recreation. If a family is not able to generate income sufficient to meet these basic needs, then the family can be treated as living Below Poverty Line (BPL). The requirement of such income varies from place to place, and family to family depending on their socio-economic background, educational level and living patterns. Expenditure is appropriate method for assessment poverty that families can meet the expenditure from reserves and assets without participation in any income generating activity. The Planning Commission has been defining poverty line periodically for the population in rural and urban areas separately for both the country based on monthly per capita expenditure data collected by National Sample Survey Organisation (NSSO). Similar estimates are prepared for the states based on the subsidies available for food and for other basic needs, cost of living, etc. According to this, a person needs a per capita monthly expenditure of Rs 356 in rural and Rs 538.6 in urban areas in the country for the year 2004-05. Such figures for the state of Andhra Pradesh are Rs 292.95 in rural and Rs 542.89 in urban areas for the year 2004-2005. Thus, if anybody in the family either individually or collectively not able to generate such income according to their number in the family expenditure can be treated as living under absolute poverty. It shows that the required income to cross the poverty line is much less in the state of Andhra Pradesh compared to the country as a whole.

According to this, a family needs a per capita income of Rs 3,515 per year to cross poverty line in the rural areas, which is applicable for tribal areas. If the family is not generated such income can be treated as living under below poverty. It is observed from the study that the per capita income of the family was up to Rs 3,515 in the case of 47.5 per cent of the families before land declined to 36 per cent after land. It shows that 47.5 per cent of the families were lived below poverty line before land declined to 36 per cent after land. It shows that 11.5 per cent of the families crossed poverty line after land and the other 36 per cent of the families are still living under poverty even after land. The remaining families are living above poverty both before and after the land (Table 29.6).

Table 29.6: Families Crossed the Poverty Line after Land

Per capita family income (Rs.)	*Before Land*		*After Land*	
	Nos.	*Per cent*	*Nos.*	*Per cent*
Up to 2,000	30	9.3	11	3.4
2001 – 3515	123	38.2	105	32.6
Sub Total	**153**	**47.5**	**116**	**36.0**
3516 - 4000	53	16.5	54	16.8
4001 - 5000	55	17.1	64	19.9
5001 +	61	18.9	88	27.3
Sub Total	**169**	**52.5**	**206**	**64.0**
Grand Total	**322**	**100.0**	**322**	**100.0**

Source: Computed based on field data.

Type of Families Improved from Below to Above Poverty Line

It is important to analyse the families' movement of income from below to above poverty or above to below poverty or living in the same income status. It was observed from the data that the level of annual per capita income was less than Rs 2,000 in 30 families before land, of which 30 per cent of families were remain in the same income level. Of the remaining, 54 per cent were shifted to the next level of income from 2001 to 3515 and 16 per cent were crossed the poverty line after land. Similarly, 123 families were lived in an income level of 2001 to 3515. Among them, 70 per cent were remaining in the same level of income without any change, 29 per cent were crossed the poverty lines and one family or one per cent declined their income level prior to the land level. The other 169 families were above poverty line prior to the land also. Among them, 53 families were in the per capita income of Rs 3516 to 4000, of which

62 per cent were remain in the same income level, 34 per cent improved their income level and the other three per cent fallen back into the poverty. Similarly, 55 families were in the income range of Rs 4001 to 5000, of which 69 per cent were in the same income level without any change, 27 per cent improved their income to next level and the other four per cent again fallen back into the poverty. The remaining 61 families were in the income level of above 5001 without any change (Table 29.7).

Table 29.7: Shift of Percapita Income Before and After Land among the Families

Per capita income before land	*Per capita income after land (Rs)*					
	Up to 2000	*2001 - 3515*	*3516 - 4000*	*4001 – 5000*	*5001 +*	*Total*
Up to 2000	9(30)	16(54)	1 (3)	3(10)	1 (3)	30(100)
2001 - 3515	1 (1)	86(70)	20(16)	7 (6)	9 (7)	123(100)
3516 – 4000	1 (1)	1 (2)	33(62)	16(30)	2 (4)	53(100)
4001 – 5000	-	2 (4)	-	38(69)	15 (27)	55(100)
5000 +	-	-	-	-	61 (100)	61(100)
Total	**11 (3)**	**105(32)**	**54(17)**	**64(20)**	**88 (27)**	**322(100)**

Source: Computed-based on field data.

On the whole 116 families or 35 per cent of the families are still living under poverty even after land. The remaining (65 per cent) were above poverty line prior to land distribution. Of which, seven per cent slipped to below poverty line due to crop loss. About 31 families or 10 per cent of the families actually crossed the poverty line after land and made them to improve their income in 61 families (20 per cent) out of the total.

Poverty Assessment Based on the Family Consumption

The family expenditure data has been collected from the sample households and per capita family expenditure is computed for purpose to assess the level poverty among the Chenchus. According to this, the per capita annual expenditure of the family was below Rs 3515 in 27 per cent of the families. Thus, the poverty level according to expenditure method is 12 percentage points lower than the income method. It shows that they may be mobilising loans for meeting their basic needs of the family or may be reported an under estimate of the family income. Whatever may be the reason, 27 per cent of the families are still living under absolute poverty even after distribution of the land as per the family expenditure method. The per capita monthly expenditure requirement to cross the poverty line according to the revised estimate of poverty for rural areas (Tendulkar Committee) is Rs 694 and it is Rs 8328 per annum for the year 2009-10. The per capita expenditure is collected for the year 2006-07. Based on the revised estimate, the sample families living PBL are more than 50 per cent at any rate, if it is revised according to the price index for the year 2006-07.

Their proportion in the total population varies from region to region depending on the livelihood options available to them. It is important to note that large majority of the Chenchus are landless. Thus, the Government is providing wage employment under MNREGP for each family at the rate of Rs 2000 per month to protect them from the poverty. Thus, there is need to build assets under MNREGP works for sustainable livelihood.

Conclusions

Majority of the Chenchus are landless though they are living close to forest areas where the demand for land is relatively less. Land Purchase Scheme (LPS) is an alternative to become owners of the land. The results show that LPS is made effective in improvement of livelihood and crossing poverty line for about 10 per cent of the families and an additional income for about another 20 per cent of the families. However, the land has not brought about any significant changes in food, income and livelihood security for majority of the Chenchus that they have not utilised land properly due to their socio-cultural barriers, lack of small investments for land development and irrigation facility. Apart from these, the LPS beset with problems, such as purchase of poor quality land from private party for lack of adequate budget, delay and dispute in partisan to the individual beneficiaries. Energisation is pending for most of the beneficiaries for the bore wells drilled and installed submersible pump sets for more than three years ago. However, there is no alternative other than the land for livelihood improvement of the PTGs due to their living in remote and backward areas with mass illiteracy, thinly spread population with no or little infrastructure and also no or little network of formal financial institutions where the scope for promotion of non-farm sector growth is limited. It is observed from the study that the land is capital asset and its value is increasing even in tribal areas, and it has potential for improvement of livelihood, if provided with a minimum size of two acres and allocation of higher budget. Thus, distribution of good quality land with viable size, irrigation facility and supply other inputs on subsidy is most essential to achieve productive results, particularly to the PTGs and first generation cultivators.

Index

D

E